VINCENT DE PAUL

the Trailblazer

VINCENT DE PAUL

the Trailblazer

BERNARD PUJO

Translated by Gertrud Graubart Champe

University of Notre Dame Press
Notre Dame, Indiana

English Language Edition Copyright © 2003 by University of Notre Dame
Notre Dame, Indiana 46556
www.undpress.nd.edu
All Rights Reserved

Manufactured in the United States of America

Translated by Gertrud Graubart Champe from *Vincent de Paul, le précurseur,*
by Bernard Pujo, published by Albin Michel, Paris, France.

© Éditions Albin Michel S. A., 1998

The publisher is grateful to THE FRENCH MINISTRY OF CULTURE—
CENTRE NATIONAL DE LIVRE for support of the costs of translation.

Library of Congress Cataloging-in-Publication Data
Pujo, Bernard.
[Vincent de Paul, le précurseur. English]
Vincent de Paul, the trailblazer / Bernard Pujo ; translated by
Gertrud Graubart Champe.
p.   cm.
Includes index.
ISBN 0-268-04361-2 (cloth : alk. paper)
1. Vincent de Paul, Saint, 1581–1660.   2. Christian saints—
France—Biography.   I. Title.
BX4700.V6 P7413   2003
271'.7702—dc21

2003012368

∞ *This book is printed on acid-free paper.*

Contents

Translator's Note

Vincent de Paul le précurseur by Bernard Pujo opens a bright window into the turbulent world of a great saint in a great century. Unlike preceding biographies of Vincent, this one presents politics, war, and one man's personality as essential elements in the construction of a vast and lasting network of charitable works. There is very little of the usual hagiographic style in this account. Instead, the reader is invited to see in action the heroic virtue that makes a saint, and see it in the midst of life. To insert the details into his portrait, Pujo uses rich and varied language, often quoted directly in the French of the seventeenth century, tantalizing in its slight difference. Terms from farming, law, finance, medicine, the life of the court, and always, the life of the Church lead the translator a merry chase. Indeed, the very difficulty encountered in finding English words for some of these concepts underlines the distance at which we now live from Vincent's world; probably the reader will recognize the tension of some of these problems immediately. Titles of government offices and branches of government are given as they appear in English-language histories of the period. Ecclesiastical terms are based on the Catholic Encyclopedia of 1912. The names of most individuals are spelled in their respective languages of origin. As for weights, measures, and sums of money, the translation uses the author's information: distances originally given in leagues are converted to kilometers at the rate of four kilometers to a league. The arpent, a measure of area which varied from province to province, is calculated as one-half hectare, or five thousand square meters. Ancient units for the measure of large volumes, such as amounts of grain, are elusive because dictionaries generally define them in terms of other ancient measures and these also vary from province to province; Mr. Pujo has nothing to say about them. Finally, there is the matter of money. The units which appear in the translation are the livre and the écu, which is equal to three livres. An estimate made in 1990 by the historian Pierre Goubert puts the livre at around 200 contemporary French francs.

Two works have been particularly helpful in making this translation: *Vincent de Paul and Louise de Marillac: Rules, Conferences, and Writings,* edited by Frances Ryan, D. C., and John E. Rybolt, C.M. (New York and Mahwah: Paulist Press, 1995), and Pierre Coste, C.M., *The Life and Works of Saint Vincent de Paul,* translated by Joseph Leonard, C.M. (New York: New City Press, 1987).

Bernard Pujo's book leaves no avoidable large gap in the account of Vincent's life but it cannot be all-encompassing. Fortunately, the author provides the interested reader with many signposts for further study of the saint's life and his times. He provides excellent documentation of his work with the Archives of the Congregation of the Mission, and the generous biographical notes are as attractive as clues in a treasure hunt.

The present translation has profited significantly from the work of its first reader, Paula von Haimberger Arno. Her eagle eye for accuracy and fine ear for language have made her an ideal and valued collaborator.

Prologue

On August 26, 1660, King Louis XIV and his young wife, Marie Thérèse, made their ceremonial entry into the stately city of Paris. The exceptional pomp of the occasion celebrated a high moment in the history of France; a war which had lasted a quarter-century had ended the year before with the signing of the Peace of the Pyrenees. It seemed the beginning of an era of peace for Europe and an age of prosperity for a France ruled by a young king, admired all over the world for his imposing bearing and personal strength.

This emblematic entry into the capital city marked the beginning of the new time. Early in the morning, the royal couple was received at a square outside the city walls, near Saint Antoine.[1] On a stand surmounted by a dais draped in blue taffeta dotted with fleurs-de-lis, Louis XIV seated himself on a throne covered with gold brocade. His clothing was of silver and of crimson silk, and the bouquet of plumes in his hat was held in place with a diamond brooch. At his side was the queen, robed in a gown streaming with gold, silver, pearls, and gems.

Before them paraded the delegations of the courts and the civil bureaucracy, the clergy of the capital's thirty-nine parishes with their banners and crosses, the university's faculties of medicine, theology, and canon law, gowns adorned with ermine, then the six bodies of merchants, the corporations, and the syndics with their insignia. They were followed by the members of the four sovereign courts, the court of the mint, the court of taxes, the treasury and the tribunals. . . . A flight of doves was released and the royal retinue began its majestic progress, not to reach the Louvre until several hours later. At the head of the cortège came the seventy-two mules, in opulent harness, of His Eminence, Cardinal Mazarin. They were followed by his sedan chair and his carriage. Then came the equerries of Monsieur, of the queen, and of the king. Behind them paraded the light horse cavalry, the hundred Swiss who made up the royal guard, the heralds at arms, the musketeers of His Eminence, and those of the king.

Finally Louis XIV appeared, shining with youth and grace. He was only twenty-one years old. He rode a prancing bay, with a saddle cloth embroidered with silver and harness studded with gems. His brother, Monsieur, and the princes of the royal family formed his escort. Among them, there stood out an elegant horseman with an eagle's profile, wavy tresses falling to his shoulders—the Grand Condé. After years of rebellion, he had submitted and resumed his place as the first prince of the blood. The queen, ensconced in a carriage drawn by six splendid horses, was surrounded by a cavalcade of princes and young lords who almost outshone her in elegance.[2]

The cortège made its way through the faubourg Saint-Antoine. From the balcony of the Hôtel de Beauvais, two people gazed down upon the procession. There was Anne of Austria, majestic and still beautiful, no longer regent now, but Queen Mother. She had passionately desired the Spanish marriage for her son, whom she had guided step by step to this day. Now he rode alone, impatient to rule in his own right.

Beside Anne stood the man who had been her counselor for seventeen years, her strength, and her chief minister, Jules Mazarin. Exhausted by the disease that was devouring him, the cardinal had not been able to take part in this triumph, which was largely his own. The two watchers, high up on their balcony, observed the celebration with satisfaction and with nostalgia. It was indeed their reward, but it marked the beginning of their eclipse.

The cries and acclamation of the crowd, solidly massed along the route of the procession, the tolling of all the bells of the capital city, the canons of the Bastille—all these sounds were carried on the wind to the priory of Saint Lazare, not so far from the parade as the crow flies. In a little bare-walled room with uneven floor boards and scanty furnishings, a feeble old priest heard the echoes of the people's joy. It was not hard for him to imagine what it all looked like or to conjure up the principals. He had been in the presence of all of them, and most of them, he had known.

On visits to the royal palace of the Château St. Germain, he had seen the young king clutching his mother's skirts; now he reveled in triumphal entry into his capital. And he remembered the young monarch's father, the pious King Louis XIII, whose long, painful death he had witnessed. As for Mazarin, he had confronted him many a time at sessions of the Council for Religious Affairs, until the cardinal banned him from these proceedings so that he could act with a freer hand. Dressed in his modest black cassock, he had rubbed shoulders with the princes and military leaders who formed the procession, covered with jewelry and lace, whenever he went about his business at the court.

But the old priest knew all about the other side of the coin. In contrast to this flaunted luxury, these riches on display, this festival splendor, there was the misery of the people, this very people now joyfully hailing the return of its king. He had seen all too much, from the provinces to the very gates of the capital, of the ravages wrought by the campaigning armies: the famine, the sinister advance of the plague, fire, pillage, murder, rape. Against the advancing wave of physical and spiritual misery, he had tried to raise a fragile barricade with a tiny band of missionaries. He took the Daughters of Charity, with their unflagging devotion, and also laymen of good will, and sent them out along the roads of the kingdom giving them this charge: "Let us love God, my brothers, let us love God, but let it be with the work of our hands and the sweat of our brows."[3] Now he had reached the end of his own strength. In his eightieth year, he knew that he had but a few days to live. What a road Vincent had traveled since his days as a young shepherd in the Landes, tending his father's sheep!

VINCENT DE PAUL

the Trailblazer

PART ONE

In Search of a Substantial Benefice

A Little Shepherd of the Landes
1581–1596

Early every morning, Vincent dressed in his ragged old clothes. They were patched, patched again, and re-sewn by his mother because before Vincent, they had served his two older brothers. Ripped by thorns, stained with the mud of paths and swamps though they might be, there was still some wear in them. Over these clothes, he added a long cape when the weather cooled down or the sea wind warned of rain. The downpours which come without warning to drop torrents of water on the Landes soak the sandy, yet impermeable soil and disappear as suddenly as they come. Woe to the careless fellow taken by surprise out in the fields without a tree for protection if he cannot wrap himself in a heavy cape and shelter under a wide-brimmed hat.

Then Vincent would sling over his shoulder the strap of an ancient leather pouch, hard with age but still solid, into which his mother, Bertrande, slipped a bite to eat—a hunk of bread and maybe a piece of bacon. Proudly he would take up the long staff which was the sign of the shepherd's charge. He used it expertly along the way to test the resistance of the spongy ground or he managed the flock with it, moving the slow animals along

3

or bringing the frisky ones back into line. Perhaps, in the way of some shepherds, he also had a horn slung around his neck to round up strays or scare away the occasional wild animal or roaming dog with an eye on his beasts.

Equipped and armed, Vincent led his flock. Depending on the season and the circumstances, it might consist of cows, sheep, or sows with their piglets. Later, he would write, "I am the son of a plowman; I have herded swine and cows." Vincent was indeed born the son of a peasant, Jean de Paul, on March 28, 1581.[1] But his father was not a simple hired hand working for the benefit of a master. He owned a little property with its own dwelling called Ranquines. In the dialect of the Landes, the name means "gimpy"; in fact, Jean Paul limped, whether the result of an accident or of an illness we do not know. Ranquines stood in the parish of Pouy, a village lying about four kilometers north of Dax.

There had long been a de Paul family in this area of the Landes on the banks of the Adour river. Documents dating from the end of the fifteenth and beginning of the sixteenth centuries already attest to this patronymic in the Dax region. It might originate in the Latin *palus*, swamp, which is also found in the Spanish *pául*, pronounced "paoul." In fact, in a document executed in 1615 when he became canon of Écouis, Vincent's surname was spelled de Paoul.[2]

As spellings were not yet standardized in the seventeenth century, one finds the name spelled indiscriminately as "de Paul" and "Depaul." The particle added to the patronymic does not necessarily denote nobility.[3] More often, it indicates residence in a particular place or dwelling. Now, there is a brook near the village of Pouy called the Paul,[4] and in the village of Buglose, a little over four kilometers from Pouy, there is a house called the house of Paul. Thus, nothing permits us to say that Vincent's father was anything more than a man farming his own land, well thought of in his parish, but with no claim to a title of nobility. Vincent himself always signed his name "Vincent Depaul."

On the other hand, his mother, Bertrande de Moras, belonged to a family of the bourgeoisie or maybe even of the local petty nobility. According to tradition, since there are no documents, she was born in the village of Pouy itself, in a house on the country estate of a family belonging to the nobility of the robe. [These are the nobles who achieved their rank by service in the government and the courts—*Trans.*] Living in Dax, she spent her summer vacations in the country there. Bertrande's brother, Jean de Moras, was a lawyer at the superior court of Dax.

He married a certain Jeanne de Saint-Martin, related to a Monsieur de Comet.[5] This man soon became young Vincent's patron.

Depending on the weather and the season, the young shepherd led his flock to different grazing spots his older brothers probably showed him. The best one was a long, wide strip of land called Les Barthes (the Basins), along the Adour, which flooded when the water was high but gave good pasturage the rest of the year. The village of Pouy, clustered around its church and its cemetery, stands on a slight rise of land, safe from floods. Because of its relative elevation some thirty or forty feet higher than the Barthes, its name could come from the Latin word *podium*. The de Paul family's house, Ranquines, a bit outside the village, stood in the midst of a grove of trees — a sure sign that it was old.[6] Beyond the house, there are the moors, marshy in spots, where the grazing is good.

The village of Pouy included an old, cultivated oak forest. Access and use were strictly controlled for it is a long, hard project to grow trees on the moors. The soil is sandy with an impermeable clay stratum called alios running from two to six feet under the ground. This kind of terrain favors the formation of swamps while preventing trees from sending their roots down toward nourishment. Under these conditions, a forest is a treasure that merits jealous protection by the community.

Village communes like Pouy enjoyed a certain degree of independence. They were organized around their own hierarchy based on a class of small landowners called *capcazaliers*. Vincent's father was of this class, one of whose privileges was the use of the forest. The *capcazaliers* were allowed to gather fallen wood there and, with special permission, to fell trees for firewood. Wood could also be taken for house repairs and, every fifteen years, for the repair of the boats which were essential for crossing the Adour.

Finally, and this affected the young shepherd in particular, every *capcazalier* maintaining a kettle and a hearth had the right to raise up to thirty swine and to take them to the forest between September and Christmas to feed on acorns. Suckling pigs could be in the forest as early as July.[7] Vincent, charged with herding the pigs, must have spent many long days in these woods, deep and dark to a child's eyes.

When Vincent came home in the evening, after stabling the animals, he would find his family gathered in the common room of Ranquines. This space was in the center of the building with the parents' room on the south side and two more rooms, one for the girls and the other for the boys. On the north side was a stable for two oxen, with the grandparents' room on one side and a workshop on the other. An opening in the wall of the common room was used to feed the animals and keep watch over them. Like all the Landais houses of the time, this one had half-timbered walls filled in with rye straw overlaid with clay. The floors were of beaten earth, but there was a ceiling below the thatched roof, which showed that this was a master's house and not a laborer's. The windows were covered by wooden shutters at night or against the cold. The hearth in the common room served both to heat the house and to cook the food.

The head of the family presided at the large table and the children took their places around it. There were four boys—Jean, Bernard, Vincent, the third son, and Dominique, nicknamed Gayon—and two girls. One was the Marie who was to marry Jean de Paillole; the other, also Marie, was to marry Grégoire de Lartigue. The mother was busy at the fire. The great, steaming bowls she brought to the table were eagerly scraped clean to feed hearty young appetites. In later years, Vincent remembered these family meals: "Where I come from, people live on a small grain called millet, served boiled in a pot. When it is time to eat, it is poured into a bowl and the household gathers around to make a meal."[8]

On this poor soil, the principal crops were indeed rye and millet. The basic food was millet gruel, made savory with vegetables, celeriac, cabbage, beans, and peas. The bread dipped into the soup in thick chunks was chiefly made of rye, which kept better than bread made of wheat. The drink was water from the well, sweetened for the grown-ups with a little wine or cider. Later, Vincent would suggest this to one of his priests on a mission to Dax: "Cider is fairly common in those parts; it might do you better than wine."[9] Did he remember the wine of his country as not very good?

Vincent never said whether the millet gruel was eaten from bowls of wood or of clay. The spoons could have been made of wood as well. Forks were not found on country tables. As for the chicken in the pot, dear to good King Henry, that was only for feast days, days when work clothes were set aside, replaced by Sunday clothes fit for mass at the parish church or to carry the newborn to the baptistry.

At the de Paul house, there was no lingering at the table because work always called. Vincent painted this little scene of country life, and particularly the girls' life. "They would come back to the house from their work to eat a bite, bone weary and splashed with mud. Hardly had they gotten there when, if the weather was good enough to work, or if their mother and father told them to, they would go back, with no mind for the mud or their tiredness."[10]

Sometimes a diversion entered this hard-working, monotonous life. Vincent would visit his mother's family at Orthevielle, a village twenty-four kilometers to the south of Dax. Just across the Adour begins the region called Chalosse, where the land is no longer flat like the Landes, and the sedimentary soil bears a rich cover of vegetation. The road runs south through forested valleys to Peyrehorade at the confluence of two streams, the Gave de Pau and the Gave d'Oloron. In the leafy forests, oaks grow together with beech and chestnut; rich meadows nestle in the little valleys. At Peyrehorade, a noble castle with four tall corner turrets looks down on the flowing streams. Vincent must have stared wide-eyed at this exuberant landscape, so different from home. The horse farm at Peyroux,[11] home of the Moras family at Orthevielle, was a large stone building by the side of the road, about two kilometers outside the village, in the midst of farm land. It belonged to Jacques de Moras, either a brother or a cousin of Bertrande. According to tradition, Vincent's grandmother lived there and it was she whom Vincent came to visit. He made himself useful by taking animals to pasture, sheep or goats or cows. At Orthevielle, on a little hill overlooking the flood basins of the streams at the confluence, stands a fortified church and a fort grandiosely called the Castle of Montgaillard. In those days, it was flanked by four towers. From this height, Vincent gazed over a panorama which, on clear days, stretches as far as the foothills of the Pyrenees.

Many years later, when the bishop of Saint-Pons, Persin de Mont-gaillard, spoke with great satisfaction about his family castle, Vincent shot back with a wicked twinkle, "I know it well. In my youth, I was a shepherd, and that's where I led my beasts."[12] In fact, the bishop's castle was a different Montgaillard, near Montauban.

Visits to Peyroux were rare. But a stretch that Vincent probably knew well, a good hour's walk from home, was the road to the priory of Poymartet (or Pouymartet). The prior there, called Étienne de Paul, was a close relative, maybe even a brother or cousin, of Vincent's father. The priory stood on one of the routes to Compostella. The days of the great pilgrimages were over, but some pilgrims still came from all the countries of Europe, passing through Vézelay, Le Puy, or Arles. They made for Saint-Jean-Pied-de-Port to cross the Pyrenees at the pass of Roncevaux. Poymartet was one in the chain of hostels and inns established to shelter the pilgrims.

The priory had been devastated and put to the torch in 1569 by the Huguenot bands of the count of Montgomery,[13] who was moving toward the Béarn. Traces of this dark period were doubtless still to be seen on the buildings. For young Vincent, it was a first contact with the realities of a cruel and blood-stained world. At the same time, the pilgrims showed him that human beings could be moved by a faith strong enough to make them face the risks and trials of a long road dotted with hardship and suffering.

For his part, Vincent's father lost no opportunity of comparing his life as a farmer struggling from morning to night to carve out a decent, modest existence for his family to the life that Étienne de Paul was leading. The prior was able to live at his ease, thanks to the income attached to the priory,[14] and could even come to the aid of his family. The need for aid arose because the fields of Ranquines would never suffice to support all four sons once they were grown. Thus, it seemed wise to encourage some of them to look in other directions. Since of the four, Vincent seemed the most talented, it would surely be this boy whom they would encourage to undertake studies that would qualify him for the priesthood.

Doubtless the prior encouraged his relative in this decision, since he too recognized Vincent's abilities. Monsieur de Comet was in agreement with this step as well. His position as judge at Dax gave him many opportunities to visit an estate he owned near Pouy, at Préchacq. From there, he visited the de Pauls, where Vincent's lively mind made its impression on him. It was decided to have the boy study and aim for a career in the Church. At first, this course of action would require financial sacrifice, but it was considered a good investment. Once in possession of the right kind of benefice, which Monsieur de Comet's connections would surely obtain for him, Vincent would become, like the prior of Poymartet, a support for his family. It is quite conceivable that the thoughts of Vincent's family ran in this direction.

In any event, to reach the ecclesiastical state in life, Vincent would have to attend a preparatory school and, before that, to acquire some basic learning and a little Latin. We do not know whether his parents were literate, and he never talked about his own primary education. No doubt he had had lessons with the pastor at Pouy or the prior at

Poymartet. He would have to be quick to learn what he needed in order to enter school.

Vincent never gave a precise date for his departure from Pouy. In a talk he gave some fifty years later, he had this to say: "As the son of a poor farmer, and having lived in the country until I was fifteen . . ."[15] If we take him at his word, he would have left the village in 1596. We know with certainty that he entered the University of Toulouse in 1597; his diploma for the degree of bachelor of theology, granted in 1604, states that the required studies were completed in seven years. Even if we take it that when he gave his age, Vincent meant to say "in my fifteenth year," and not "when I had turned fifteen," which was customary, he would have spent only two short years in school at Dax. This seems rather unlikely. Rather, one might speculate that Vincent, calling to mind his "country life up to the age of fifteen," was including in that phrase his stay at Dax, close to the village where he was born. His reference point would have been the departure for Toulouse, the big city. This is the date that really marks the end of his youth and life with his family.

According to this hypothesis, Vincent would have been sent to Dax at the age of eleven or twelve and would have spent four years at school there. Perhaps this is what he was alluding to when he humbly excused himself for his ignorance, saying that he was nothing more than a "fourth-year pupil."[16] Whatever the length of his stay in Dax, two or more probably four years, one thing is certain—he worked well and achieved brilliant results. Upon hearing of his performance as a student, Monsieur de Comet invited the youth to come live in his house as tutor to his own children, while continuing his work at school. Of course the de Paul family was pleased to accept Monsieur de Comet's offer, since the cost of keeping Vincent at Dax was a heavy financial burden. His room and board with the Franciscans (*Cordeliers*),[17] whose house shared a party wall with the school, had cost about 60 livres during his first year at school.

We can imagine young Vincent's delight when he crossed the bridge over the Adour and discovered the walled town of Dax and admired the traces of the Roman days—the grand pool where a warm spring never stops running, the gothic cathedral with its storied portal, the liveliness of the streets, the shopkeepers' displays. For the little shepherd accustomed to long solitude out on the empty moor, it was a world of marvels. He must have felt important in his own right just walking down the street, and probably his father walking beside him in a farmer's smock embarrassed him. Later, he would remember, "When I was a little boy and my father took me to town with him, I was ashamed to walk with him and acknowledge him as my father, because he was poorly dressed and limped a little."[18]

Soon he was ready to deny his peasant origins, eager to melt into the urban surroundings which were home to most of his fellow students and to enter the bourgeois society of the Comet family. And so, when his father came to Dax to take care of some business and called at the school to see his son, Vincent refused to go and greet him: "I remember that once, at the school where I was studying, they came to tell me that my father, who was a poor peasant, was asking for me. I refused to go and speak to him, and that was a great sin."[19]

These are the only two memories that Vincent spoke of, toward the end of his life. They must have tormented his heart with piercing remorse toward a father who had given up so much so that his son could succeed.

Vincent was a brilliant student and his agreeable demeanor in a leading family of Dax convinced church authorities to confer minor orders upon him late in 1596. He was only fifteen and a half years old.[20]

The ceremony in which he received the first four orders could not have taken place in Dax, since the episcopal throne of this diocese was empty at the time. Vincent must have gone to the collegiate church of Bidache, where Monseigneur Salvat Diharse, bishop of Tarbes, officiated. This prelate, native of the city of Bardos very close to Bidache, was commendatory abbot of the abbey of Arthous, four kilometers to the north. No doubt the Moras family, living in Orthevielle near Bidache, was acquainted with the Diharse family. Thus, Vincent did not feel out of place at this church.

On the way there, he must have admired the proud silhouette of Bidache Castle, property of the count de Gramont, prince of Bidache and viceroy of Navarre. He had no idea that one day, at court, he would meet this great man's son, himself a marshal of France.[21]

Coming out of the collegiate church and walking away a few steps, Vincent would have had a vista extending as far as the first peaks of the Pyrenees. Probably the bishop advised him to stop on his way back for a prayer at the abbey of Arthous, where he was still abbot. This monastery, founded in the twelfth century, is nestled in the hollow of a little valley.[22] Its church is in pure Romanesque style and has a remarkable apse. The place is an ideal spot for withdrawal and prayer. Did Vincent feel this? He never spoke about it, nor about his journey to Bidache. Now duly tonsured and entered into orders, Vincent was ready to begin studying for the priesthood at the University of Toulouse. The first page of his life's story had been turned.

The time of Vincent's youth is shrouded in the mists that hang over the ponds and marshes of the Landes, blurring the outlines of the landscape. His first biographer, Louis Abelly,[23] knowing that he was writing a saint's life, has illuminated these childhood years with many edifying anecdotes. Although he was able to speak to people who had known young Vincent and to members of his family, we need not take everything he wrote as historical truth. As to Vincent himself, he remained remarkably discreet on the subject of his early years, as well as about the rest of his life. Out of purposeful humility and a desire to point out his simple origins, he reported nothing about this period except his lack of charity toward his father at Dax and his role as a swineherd. But we must realize that this excessive humility caused him to alter the shape of reality; the de Paul family belonged to a relatively comfortable peasant class and counted among the notables.

How should we portray this young man from the Landes who, at an age of less than sixteen, was about to plunge into the student life of Toulouse? Raised in a large family, he had received a solid moral grounding based on the traditional virtues of work, mutual assistance, and obedience to parents. These parents were Catholics, like all French country people of the time, living their faith and seeing the hand of God in everything. This is the spirit in which they raised their children, but nothing points to the possibility that they were particularly devout. Their wish to see Vincent become a priest seems to have arisen from purely worldly motives.

Outdoor life and long marches with his animals had made Vincent hale and hearty, with a loving sense of nature and detailed knowledge of the countryside, its work and its inhabitants. His intellectual gifts and his ability to adapt were accompanied by a friendly disposition and an ease with people that made him most likable. He was a young Gascon with the sparkling wit, quick tongue, and vivid gestures this origin implies. Urged toward the priesthood, he accepted his parents' will without having a vocation. He was impatient for success, both to honor the trust and hope others had invested in his abilities and, perhaps, to satisfy his own personal ambition.

An Impatient Student
1597–1605

While Vincent was pasturing his flock in the Landes and learning the rules of grammar and Latin declensions and conjugations at the secondary school in Dax, the situation throughout the kingdom of France was lamentable. The country was still suffering the last of the calamitous thirty-year period when Catholics and Protestants had stood opposed, weapons in hand. It had begun on the first day of March 1562, with the massacre of Protestants at Vassy after the failure of talks between Queen Catherine de Medici and Chancellor Michel de l'Hospital in search of common ground for the two parties. This final attempt was brought down by the intransigence of both sides— the Catholic side with Cardinal de Tournon and Father Lainez, the General of the Jesuits, and the Calvinist side with Théodore de Bèze. After that failure, the situation had deteriorated steadily, culminating on August 24, 1572, the dark day of the St. Bartholomew massacre.[1] Hostilities had never really ceased; periods of relative calm alternated with new explosions of murderous violence. The civil war, with its procession of atrocities, split France into two irreconcilable parties and foreign interventions were growing in number.

A weak and effeminate king, Henry III, accused of favoring the Protestants, was opposed by a League of Catholic ultras led by Henry de Guise, who did not hide his ambition to mount to the throne. In an access of energy, the king, who felt threatened, had de Guise assassinated in December 1588, at the Château of Blois. Eight months later, it was the king's turn to fall, under the knife of a young monk who was a creature of the League. Since the king had died without an heir, it was a distant cousin, the king of Navarre, who succeeded him under the name of Henry IV. This choice was not one that brought peace, for Henry of Navarre was a Protestant. Before he could ascend to the throne, he had to fight the troops of the League. But this had not enabled him to enter the capital city; to win this prize, he brought himself to make a solemn abjuration of the reformed religion. On July 25, 1593, Henry IV was crowned in the cathedral of Chartres and eight months later, he was able to make his entry into Paris. He still had to pacify the provinces, force the Spaniards who had come to the aid of the League out of the kingdom, and finally, find a way for Catholics and Protestants to live together in peace. This he accomplished by promulgating the Edict of Nantes, signed in April 1598.

For the country folk, who in this period constituted eighty percent of the population of France, these domestic struggles translated into towns pillaged and put to the torch, fallow fields gone to brambles, and famine marching hand in hand with pestilence. The peasant families tried to take cover from armed bands inside city walls, but there they were at the mercy of the soldiery, whether Protestant or Catholic. Both camps, always short of funds to pay their troops, maintained extreme pressure on the regions they controlled.

The region of the Landes, although it was relatively isolated and offered only meager resources, was not spared, for the neighboring county of Béarn had become a bastion of Protestantism under the rule of Jeanne d'Albret.[2] When she joined the Calvinist party at La Rochelle in 1568, the regent, Catherine de Medici, immediately decreed the confiscation of all her estates and sent the viscount de Terride to take possession of the Béarn and reestablish the Catholic religion. Jeanne d'Albret, with the help and support of the English, put into the field an army of 3,000 men under the command of Montgomery that descended like a torrent on the Béarn, the Bigorre, and Navarre as well as on regions bordering the Landes, such as Marsan, Gabardan, and Tursan.[3] Catholic villages and towns were sacked, churches and monasteries destroyed. It was at this point that the priory of Poymartet and the abbey of Arthous were partially ruined. Terror rained down on all that region for three years. Orthez was taken by storm in August 1569 and all its population put to the sword. The chronicler reports that Catholic blood streamed in the streets and flowed into the Gave.

The reaction of the Catholics was just as brutal. Blaise de Monluc,[4] the king's lieutenant general in Gascony, was charged with restoring order. He meted out prompt justice in order to reclaim localities taken by the Protestants. His path was lined with Huguenots hanging from the trees. With Mont-de-Marsan retaken in September 1569, Monluc turned his soldiers loose to massacre the Protestants and devastate the city. But the city of Dax was saved by its walls and the vigilance of the city militia; it repelled Huguenot attacks, especially those that came in August 1570.

For young Vincent, these were more or less historical events, even though traces of these battles were still quite visible and the massacre and devastation were vivid in memory. And yet, in a family totally given to working the soil, talk about the troubles that plagued the kingdom must have been limited. When he was with Monsieur de Comet, Vincent, confined to his position of tutor to the children, had little occasion to be particularly aware of political problems. In any case, all through his life he never made allusion to this dark time; as for so many other topics, he would keep his thoughts and opinions to himself.

After 1570, the region of the Landes may have been calmer but, in contrast, the city of Toulouse where Vincent arrived early in 1597 was directly involved in the events that shook the kingdom after the assassination of Henry III. Toulouse was ardently on the side of the League, even going so far as to assassinate the president of its parliament, who was considered too favorable to the royal cause. A League army, under the command of the duke of Joyeuse,[5] held Languedoc with the help of Spanish reinforcements and refused passage to the royal troops. But the army of the League was beaten in October 1592 and Joyeuse capitulated to Henry IV, who brought him into his own party by creating him a marshal of France. [The title of marshal of France in the sixteenth century indicated that the holder was a royal functionary and second in authority to the commander in chief of the army—*Trans.*] Meanwhile, Toulouse remained sympathetic to the League; its parliament only entered the Edict of Nantes into the books after two years of discussion, in April 1600.

Thus, it was an unquiet city where young Vincent arrived to matriculate in the university. The University of Toulouse took in students from all the provinces of the kingdom and foreign countries as well. They came to attend courses in theology and law and for this purpose, joined colleges conducted by various religious orders, with the Jesuit college having the highest reputation. For less prosperous students, there were foundations that distributed scholarships, but it does not seem that Vincent was able to profit from this. Therefore, in order to defray the costs of his studies, his father made the considerable sacrifice of selling a pair of oxen (which shows, in passing, that the de Paul family was not as poor as Vincent made it seem). Provided with this nest egg, Vincent was able to manage the first registration fees and the first stage of his studies. After this, he had to find other resources for a stay that was meant to last for seven years.

At Toulouse, students grouped themselves according to their home provinces. Often these groups faced off in quarrels that degenerated into real armed combat, so that the university authorities had to intervene harshly and bring in public officers of the peace, for the violent confrontations sometimes became deadly. The students from Burgundy and Lorraine seemed to be the rowdiest and most insolent and the promulgation of the Edict of Nantes in 1598 gave rise to new student turmoil.

It is very likely that Vincent held himself aloof from these disorders; he was much too concerned to complete his studies of theology. According to Abelly, he did take the time for a stay at the University of Saragossa: "During this time, he traveled to Spain and stayed at Saragossa, to study there as well."[6] Numerous authors question this supposed time in Spain. It is true that we have nothing to document Abelly's statement, because he had access to texts that have since disappeared, but Vincent's letters and lectures contain certain allusions that may point to a stay there.[7] At this time, the Pyrenees did not constitute a cultural barrier and contacts and exchanges between the province of Aragon and the southern regions of the kingdom were more usual, so a student could pursue his university studies while moving between Toulouse and Saragossa. However, if Abelly is to be believed, Vincent did not stay at Saragossa long, because he was discouraged by the theological disputes taking place at the Spanish university.[8]

Something else may also have moved Vincent to shorten his stay: the report that his father had died toward the end of 1598. In his testament, Jean de Paul divided his goods among his children and then asked explicitly "that his son Vincent be helped and supported in his studies to the extent that the inheritance permitted."[9] At this point, not wanting to be a burden to his family, which was already hard pressed, Vincent began to look for work that would allow him to continue his studies. He took on the management of a little boarding school at Buzet-sur-Tarn, about thirty kilometers northeast of Toulouse, where well-to-do families of the region placed their children. Later, he seems to have succeeded in moving the school to Toulouse, which made it easier for him to carry on his studies while still remaining in charge of this establishment. Abelly, from whom we have this information, cites a letter Vincent wrote his mother on this subject. Unfortunately, the letter has not been preserved. His need to run a boarding school or to take a post as tutor in a local noble family, obtained through the recommendation of the Comet family, makes it clear that Vincent's situation was precarious and explains his eagerness to attain priesthood in order to acquire reliable means, which is to say, a good benefice.

Now it happened that a fine parish became vacant, the parish of Tilh in Chalosse. This is a large market town in a prosperous region, about twenty kilometers from Dax on the road to Orthez. This was an ideal situation for Vincent; he would be provided with a good benefice and live close to his family. Monsieur de Comet, who watched over Vincent and was aware of his financial problems, especially after the death of his father, did what was necessary to have the parish of Tilh awarded to him. It is true that Vincent had not yet been ordained, but at this time it was possible to award parishes to laymen. Until such time as Vincent was ordained, the parish would be administered by a curate. The only evidence concerning this matter is Abelly's text that states, "The chancellors of the diocese of d'Acqs, the episcopal see being vacant, no sooner heard that he was a priest than they awarded him the parish of Tilh, upon the appeal of Monsieur de Comet."[10]

The clause, "the episcopal see being vacant" dates the document to which Abelly refers. In fact, the episcopal see at Dax had been vacant since the death of its last incumbent, Gilles de Noailles,[11] in 1597. His successor, Jean-Jacques Dusault,[12] did not accede to the position until

October or November 1598. From this it can be deduced that Vincent received the parish before this latter date. Consequently, there is a contradiction in Abelly's statements: at this time, Vincent was not yet a priest. This confusion in chronology is perhaps neither completely accidental nor innocent, just as Vincent's birth date was changed to make him five years older. There is a tendency to erase anything in his biography which could seem shocking, such as the awarding of a parish to a young man who was not yet ordained.

Clearly, it was advisable for Vincent to become a priest as soon as possible so that he could take full possession of his benefice. At the end of his second year of theology, in September 1598, he obtained dimissorial letters for the reception of the sub-diaconate, the first of the major orders. This document, signed by Guillaume de Massiot, vicar general of Dax, confirms that the episcopal see is vacant and specifies that "our beloved Vincent De Paul" is recognized as "capable, satisfactory, of legal age and of sufficient means (*bene intitulato*)." But at this time, Vincent was only in his eighteenth year! It seems that eyes are to be shut to this bending of canon law regarding age, but in fact, the decrees of the Council of Trent[13] have not yet been received into the Church of France. As for the formula *bene intitulato*,[14] it refers to the ecclesiastical regulation that restricts orders to persons offering a financial or legal guarantee. Such a guarantee could be based on one's patrimony or on an ecclesiastical assignment already received. Since Vincent had no significant inheritance at his disposal, it must be the parish of Tilh that entitles him to receive the dimissorial letters for the sub-diaconate.

Vincent lost no time; the vicar general of Dax signed the letters on September 10. The first major order of the sub-diaconate was conferred on him on September 19 by the bishop of Tarbes, Salvat Diharse. It was normal for Vincent to approach him once more, the episcopal see of Dax still being unoccupied, when only two months later, on December 19, he was ordained a deacon in the cathedral of Tarbes.[15]

Tarbes, the capital of the Bigorre, had remained faithful to the Catholic religion despite its proximity to the Béarn, which had gone over to Protestantism. The city had been pillaged and set aflame in 1569 by the count of Montgomery. By the time Vincent was living there, traces of the violence were no doubt still visible. But the cathedral, a fine Romanesque building in the austere style characteristic of the Cistercian Rule, had been restored. It was here that Vincent received the two major orders that consecrated and definitively engaged him in the priestly estate. And yet, he would never allude to this visit in Tarbes, which represented an important moment for him.

No doubt he found it just one stepping stone. His energy and his thoughts were focused on his university work as well as on the management of his boarding school. There was no losing sight of his objective: to be elevated to the priesthood as promptly as possible. Was it Monsieur de Comet who actively looked after his interests in Dax? In any case, on September 13, 1599, only nine months after being ordained to the diaconate, he received dimissory letters for the priesthood,[16] being only in his nineteenth year.

This time, the document was signed by the vicar general of Dax, acting in the name of the new bishop, Jean-Jacques Dusault. The bishop, duly consecrated in Paris, entered into possession of his see at the beginning of the year 1600, and in June he convoked a synod. One would suppose that Vincent could be ordained in regular fashion in the cathedral of Dax. But nothing of the sort! On September 23, 1600, Vincent de Paul was ordained at Château-l'Évêque by the bishop of Périgueux.

Once in possession of his dimissorial letters for the priesthood, Vincent would normally address his bishop, Monseigneur Dusault, to request ordination. But this prelate, who had just been installed at Dax, was struggling with inextricable complications. Immediately upon his arrival, he had convoked a synod to undertake the reform of his diocese in accordance with the decrees of the Council of Trent. The assembly convened on April 18, 1600, and the decisions taken were immediately made public. They concerned the clergy in particular: priests who were not living in their parishes were obliged to return to them within the month under pain of sanction. This tends to confirm the hypothesis that the parish of Tilh was awarded to Vincent before Monseigneur Dusault was enthroned. This prelate would not have approved his nomination as long as Vincent was not ordained and was kept far from his parish by the obligations of study.

The canons of the cathedral chapter of Dax had refused to approve the decisions of the synod or to participate in liturgies celebrated by the bishop. Because of this, he was unable to officiate pontifically. One recalcitrant canon had even been arrested by the police, which had sparked an uprising in the city. A trial was held before the parliament at Bordeaux, which found in favor of the bishop. But the chapter persisted in refusing to provide him with the documents of the diocese. The matter dragged on until the beginning of 1604, when Rome imposed a compromise.

Under these circumstances, there was no question of going forward with solemn ceremonies at Dax. Thus, Vincent was obliged to turn to another prelate, something he was authorized to do according to the very terms of his dimissory letters: "so that you may receive and be competent to receive, at a time determined by canon law, the sacred priestly orders from whichever lord archbishop, bishop or ecclesiastical pontiff you may choose. . . ."

Why did Vincent not approach the bishop who had conferred upon him the orders of sub-deacon and deacon? There exists no document that could help us answer this question. We only know that His Grace, Monseigneur Salvat Diharse did not die until three years later, in 1603. Vincent could also have gone to the bishop of Toulouse, since he lived in that city, but he preferred to ask the bishop of Périgueux to ordain him to the priesthood. To explain this rather surprising choice, some have suggested that Vincent had among his students at Buzet a close relative of this prelate, who might readily have offered to ordain the zealous young teacher, of whom he had heard much good. In fact, we do not know what induced Vincent to make the long journey from Toulouse, a distance of about 200 kilometers through territory that was not very safe. A peasant revolt of the so-called Croquants had erupted not long before, brought on by excessive taxes imposed on a region already impoverished by raging armed battles. In September 1600, when Vincent ventured there, the region had still not been pacified.

The bishop of Périgueux, François de Bourdeilles,[17] was himself in an awkward situation. He had not been able to take possession of his episcopal see because the city of Périgueux had been ravaged and occupied by the Protestants. The cathedral of Saint-Étienne was half in ruins and the episcopal palace had been completely destroyed. The prelate had settled at Château-l'Évêque, twelve kilometers north of Périgueux, on the very estate where his predecessor had been taken and killed by the Huguenots. Outside the fortifications stood a chapel and it was in this sanctuary serving as a cathedral that the bishop officiated. In this place, on September 23, 1600, Vincent was elevated to the sacred order of the priesthood in a general ordination performed by the trembling hands of François de Bourdeilles. The bishop died one month after the ceremony, at the age of eighty-four.

Here was Vincent in his twentieth year, definitively committed to the priesthood. Was he equal to all its grandeur and difficulty? Fifty years later, Vincent, who was so discreet about his personal feelings, was to admit: "As for me, if I had known what it was all about when I was rash enough to enter it, as I have come to know since, I would rather have worked the soil than engage in such a fearsome state in life."[18]

A first disappointment awaited the man whom we may now call Monsieur Vincent. He learned that there was another applicant for the parish of Tilh, a certain S. Soubé,[19] who had supposedly applied for it at the Roman court, and who had been named to the position in his place. Vincent's candidacy had only local support from some notables at Dax, so he did not measure up to his competitor who had a more powerful protector. Presenting an application in Rome doubtless took some time, which explains why the decision only became known two years later.

Did Vincent give in willingly or, inflamed with the ardor of youth, did he decide to go and press his case in Rome? There are no traces of any action he might have undertaken at the pontifical court; all we know is that he set out for the Eternal City, probably in October 1600, before the resumption of classes at Toulouse. This jubilee year was being celebrated in Rome, with many pilgrims traveling to obtain the indulgences attached to this event. Doubtless, Vincent joined forces with them, no matter what his real reason was for making the journey.

Vincent's emotion on his first visit to Rome is expressed in this letter addressed thirty years later to one of his priests going there on a mission: "O Father, how fortunate you are to walk on soil trodden by so many great and holy people! That thought touched me so much when I was in Rome thirty years ago, that although I was weighted down with sins, I could not help but be repeatedly moved to tears, as I remember it."[20]

Tradition has it that while he was in Rome, Vincent visited the brothers who maintained the Hospital of the Holy Spirit, dedicating themselves to the care of the poor and the dying. They were members of the order founded by Camillus de Lellis,[21] who declared his mission in these words: "The poor are our lords and masters" and "prayer which hinders charity is good for nothing." It is tempting to declare a relationship between these thoughts and those that Vincent de Paul was to express later when he had advanced along the way of charity and service to the poor, but there is nothing to show any contact whatsoever between this young pilgrim during his first stay in Rome and the disciples of Camillus de Lellis. On the other hand, he had the opportunity to see the pope, Clement VIII, in the course of various ceremonies. He was deeply impressed by this pontiff, about whom he would later say, "he was a very holy man, so holy that even the heretics called Pope Clement a saint."[22]

The stay in Rome must have been fairly short. Vincent had to continue his studies at Toulouse in order to obtain a university degree, which would allow him to aspire to a more prestigious and more remunerative position than a simple country parish. Once more he took up his theology courses, taught by the Dominicans, whose beautiful church stood at the very center of the university. On October 12, 1604, after seven years of study, he received the baccalaureate degree in theology. His diploma is duly signed by Father Esprit Jarran, Master of Theology at the University of Toulouse. It specifies that this degree gives him the right to explicate and teach publicly "Book Two of the *Sentences* of Peter Lombard."[23]

Would Vincent de Paul, ordained priest and bachelor of theology, place himself at the disposal of the bishop of Dax, his canonical superior? At this time, he was only twenty-three years old, but entitled to hope for something better than a modest parish in the country. His ambition pushed him to look farther afield. Vincent's diploma allowed him to apply for a position as a "sententiary bachelor," assistant to a master, who commented freely before students on this famous second book of the *Sentences*. Without doubt he accepted such a position and took up his duties around November 1604.[24] When he later called himself ignorant, "a poor secondary-school student," he did not boast of his two university degrees and a start toward a professorate, moved by the "holy ploy of humility," in the pious report of his biographer Abelly.

In spite of his qualifications, Vincent was beset with financial difficulties. Had he contracted loans to create and build up his boarding school, or for some completely different reason? He never offered any further details other than to mention in a letter written at this time that he was in debt: "The need I had for money to take care of debts which I had incurred."[25] At that point, there seemed to be an opportunity for him to get that good benefice he had been hoping for ever since setting out on the path toward the priesthood. Toward the middle of June he embarked on a mysterious trip to Bordeaux, saying that he was "on the track of a project my foolhardiness forbids me to mention."

Once more we are reduced to hypothesizing. The most likely supposition on the basis of data collected by Abelly is that he went to present himself to the duke of Épernon,[26] at his residence in Cadillac, a few kilometers from Bordeaux. This personage had enjoyed a dazzling career, thanks to the good graces of Henry III, one of whose favorites he was. Vincent might have been recommended to this duke, since he had had one of his nephews as a student in his school at Toulouse. Did he hope that this might lead to the offer of a good abbey or a rich parish? It seems that all these illusions went up in smoke and that Vincent returned from his costly mission, his hands empty and his purse flat after the expenses of the long journey.

It was at this moment that a marvelous gift seemed to fall at his feet from a clear blue sky. Upon his return from the unfortunate escapade in Bordeaux, he learned that a good old woman of Toulouse had made a will in his favor. Would this be the end of his money troubles? Far from it; it was to be the beginning of a roguish adventure.

Odyssey on the Barbary Coast 1605–1607

Vincent was now twenty-four years old. Gone was the little shepherd watching his animals in the Landes, the secondary student just beginning to discover the world and his own gifts, the theology student at university, impatient for ordination. Monsieur Vincent, bachelor of theology, responsible for courses at the university, director of a respected boarding school, could well be satisfied with his situation, at least on the level of worldly success. In fact, this is what he wrote in 1607 to Monsieur de Comet, who had been watching over him attentively since childhood. "Two years ago, judging by the apparently favorable progress of my affairs, one would have thought that fortune, without my deserving it, had no goal but to make me more envied than imitated."[1]

Nevertheless, Vincent was struggling with financial difficulties and foresaw that he would even have to incur new expenses if he were to pursue the mysterious project which began with a journey to Bordeaux. In other words, Vincent was not satisfied with what he had already achieved. He aspired to a more lucrative position, one that could provide a stable, substantial income without taking him far away from his family. At this time, there was no lack of priories, abbeys, and canonries to be generously distributed to those who knew how to please or flatter the powerful. Still, one needed to make oneself known, be seen in places where the great ones gathered, present oneself in a favorable light. For this, a well-filled purse was essential. And here came this good old woman of Toulouse who named him in her will. Who was she? Vincent did not think it necessary to name her. It could have been, for instance, his landlady, who must have liked this amiable, studious young priest. Here we already see Vincent's gift of awakening friendly feelings in those around him, especially the honorable friendship of the female sex, in this case, a good old woman. But to enter into possession of this providential legacy, which turned out to have been embezzled by some rascally character, Vincent had to go to Castres. He did not hesitate for a moment to make this trip of about sixty kilometers, which could be covered in five or six hours with a good horse. He thought he would have the matter settled in two days. Instead, he disappeared without a word for two years!

The mystery of those two years of silent absence would later be cleared up by letters that Vincent wrote from Avignon in July 1607. They were addressed, respectively, to a notary in Dax, Monsieur Arnaudin, to his mother at Pouy, and to Monsieur de Comet. The last, a long missive, has been saved, thanks to a remarkable concatenation of circumstances.[2] This letter has been duly authenticated as coming from the hand of Vincent. What did it say?

Vincent tells how, returning from Bordeaux, he learned of the inheritance from his benefactress and what it comprised—"some furniture and some tracts of land," estimated by the bipartisan chamber of magistrates of Castres[3] to be worth 300 or 400 écus. He was informed that these goods had been embezzled by a merchant of shady repute, and that he ought to go to Castres to get to the bottom of the matter. And that is what he did, only to discover that the fine gentleman had left the region to hide out in Marseilles where he was going about his business with ample means at his disposal. The prosecutor in charge of the case advised Vincent to go to Marseilles, where he could force the scoundrel to disgorge his ill-gotten gains.

From the very beginning, the plot thickened. The journey changed from a simple outing on a horse to a long and costly voyage with a trial before the tribunals of Marseilles, with all the dangers this entailed. But that did not deter Vincent, who was young and enterprising. He felt that he was in the right and determined to defend himself. He needed money to travel about 300 kilometers as well as money to live on in Marseilles and to pay for the costs of a trial. He had no cash, but never mind— he would sell his rented horse, with the intention of reimbursing the owner as soon as he returned. But with this transaction, he made himself guilty of a crime which, in those days, was severely punished with imprisonment or even forced labor in the galleys.

Once he arrived in Marseilles, he would have to lay hands on his quarry and have him put under lock and key. This did not trouble Vincent, for he was sure of his rights, thanks to the advice of the prosecutor at Castres. "So I took this advice, caught my man at Marseilles, had him put in prison, and settled for 300 écus that he forked over in cash." The matter was briskly settled and Vincent was able to rejoice: the gold coins ringing in his purse made up a considerable sum, more than enough to repay his debts with plenty left over to provide a good nest egg for future projects.[4]

So ended the first act of his odyssey, which can hardly be called exemplary. For Vincent, the end had justified the means, and he was not too remorseful about it. At most, he regretted the fact that his misfortune kept him from repaying the livery stable as soon as he would have liked, as he wrote to Monsieur de Comet. He wrote that he would never have failed to do this "if God had granted me as happy an outcome to the affair as the matter promised."

The second act of Vincent's odyssey was played out at sea. Having shared his room at an inn at Marseilles with an apparently respectable man, he let himself be persuaded to embark on a ship leaving for Narbonne, since this was more economical and more comfortable than traveling overland. He would then have only a short coach trip back to Toulouse. The season was fine for sailing along the coast, "the wind was favorable for us to arrive in Narbonne by daylight, a trip of 200 kilometers." At this point, everything fell into ruin. In those days, there was a great fair at Beaucaire, beginning on July 22. The Turkish corsairs knew this and "they coasted along the Gulf of the Lion to seize vessels hailing from Beaucaire." Three Turkish brigantines waylaid Vincent's ship. The captain, wishing to defend himself, ordered the crew to fire on the aggressors. Enraged by their losses, the Turks "attacked so forcefully that two or three of our men were killed and all the rest wounded. Even I received an arrow wound that will serve me as a reminder for the rest of my life. We had no choice but to surrender to these felons worse than tigers, who in their first burst of rage hacked our captain into a hundred thousand pieces."

After being hastily bandaged, Vincent was chained up at the bottom of the hold. The corsairs held their course for seven or eight days, "perpetrating a thousand larcenies" before reaching their home port of Tunis, a "lair and a den of thieves." Brought to land together with his companions in misfortune, Vincent was sold into slavery. It was "testified that we had been captured from a Spanish ship because without this perjury, we would have been freed by the consul whom the king maintains abroad to ensure free commerce to the French." In fact, a treaty to this effect had been signed between Henry IV and the Grand Sultan at Constantinople, but local rulers at Tunis and Algiers did not honor it. As Vincent rightly reported, they acted "without the consent of the Grand Turk."[5]

Now began the third act of the Barbary adventure. Vincent's captivity lasted for about two years, during which he passed successively into the hands of four different masters. His description of the slave market is sharply precise and vivid: "After they had stripped us quite naked, they tossed each one of us a pair of breeches, a linen tunic, and a bonnet, then marched us through the city of Tunis. . . . After they had led us around the city five or six times with chains around our necks, they brought us back to the ships so the merchants could come to see who was a good eater and who wasn't, and that our wounds were not fatal. Then they took us back to the square, where the merchants came to check us over, as though they were buying a horse or a cow. They made us open our mouths to show our teeth, poked our ribs, and probed our wounds. They had us walk, trot, and run, lift heavy loads, and fight each other to check our strength. These things and a thousand other brutal tests they visited upon us."

First Vincent was sold to a fisherman who got rid of him after only a month or two because he was a useless slave who found nothing so impossible to bear as the sea. No doubt, Vincent suffered from seasickness.

His second master was a very curious person, "an old spagiric[6] physician, sovereign extractor of quintessences." This scholar had labored long to find the philosopher's stone. Not having found it, he practiced transmutations of metals, producing alloys of gold and silver while working with quicksilver in order to fix it as fine silver. He charged Vincent with tending the fire in ten or twelve furnaces "in which, God be thanked, I did not have more pain than pleasure." This master was, in fact, very humane and accommodating.

"He loved me well," affirmed Vincent, "and took great pleasure in lecturing me on alchemy and its laws, to which he tried with all his might to attract me, promising me abundant wealth and all his knowledge." Their conversations were particularly about medicine. This is how Vincent learned a way to treat stones. He would have liked to give the benefit of this knowledge to the brother of Monsieur de Comet, who died from complications of this disturbance.[7]

Vincent implied that he was not unhappy with his benevolent master. The man hoped that in this curious and open-minded young slave, he had found a disciple. Of course, Vincent would have had to accept Islam. Did he have to fight the temptation to yield to the intense persuasion of this master whose learning he admired, for whose goodness he was thankful? He states that never, throughout his whole captivity, did he suffer from despair or discouragement. "God always kept alive in me the belief that I would be delivered through the fervent prayers I offered Him."

For eleven months, Vincent remained in the possession of this master, from September 1605 to August 1606. But the renown of the scholar-alchemist was such that the Grand Sultan, Ahmed I, ordered him to be brought to Constantinople. With a heavy heart, the old man set out on this long trip and "he died of regret on the way."

Then began a new period in Vincent's captivity. He was left to the nephew of the spagiric physician. In the meantime, a mission dispatched by the king of France had arrived in Tunis: Monsieur de Brêves,[8] the king's ambassador to Turkey, was carrying letters patent from the Grand Turk, permitting him to reclaim Christian slaves. Vincent must have rejoiced that freedom had come, but when his new master learned of this, he acted quickly: he re-sold his slave to a farmer in a distant region where there was no hope the ambassador could find him.

This fourth master was a renegade from Nice in Savoy. He had obtained a property which he managed as a tenant farmer of the Grand Turk. In his letter, Vincent described this property as a 'temat', really known as a 'timar',[9] that is, a concession made by the sultan in favor of a soldier who has served well, on condition that this soldier hold himself ready to be recalled in time of need. The land was situated "in the mountains, where the countryside is extremely hot and arid." This seems to correspond to the little mountain chain of Cap Bon, northeast of Tunis.

The renegade lived peaceably in the Muslim fashion with his three wives. The arrival of Vincent at his temat set off a chain of reactions. He was assigned to work in the fields under a burning sun. There he was visited by two of his master's wives who were curious to catch a glimpse of this young slave who sang while he dug ditches. They began to speak to each other, and this is how Vincent learned that one of the renegade's wives was Greek-Christian but schismatic.

He recounted that she "had some cultivation, and a liking for me." But it was the other wife who played the decisive role. Although she was a natural Turk, she was greatly interested in Vincent and urged him to speak about his country and his religion. "To satisfy her curiosity about our way of life, she came every day to visit me in the fields where I was digging." She asked him to sing and Vincent, who had a warm Gascon voice, probably mimed expressively as he sang his hymns. The Muslim woman fell under his charms. This reminded Vincent of the psalm *Super flumina Babylonis,* the plaint of the children of Israel captive in Babylon, *Quomodo cantabimus in terra aliena* (How shall we sing in a strange land?).[10] The emotion called forth by this association, he reports, "brought tears to my eyes."

If Vincent is to be believed, the woman was so captivated that she went to her husband and said that he had been wrong to abandon his religion, telling him of the marvels she had glimpsed while listening to the slave sing of the glory of his God. The renegade, shaken in his turn by her vivid testimony, or perhaps suddenly touched by divine grace, called his slave before him the next day to announce his decision: "It wants but for the right moment and soon we will make a run for France." In the event, preparations for the escape were long and this soon became a matter of ten months.

Given the fact that Vincent was bought by the renegade in August 1606, and that the little company finally fled at the end of June 1607, it seems that the Turkish woman acted quite swiftly to influence her husband. The effect of Vincent's words and songs must have been immediate and stunning. As for the delay of ten months, it was required not only by the detailed but discreet preparations, but also by a wait for favorable weather to sail on the Mediterranean in a little skiff. Without a doubt, during these months which seemed so long to him, Vincent was very well treated, both by the women whom he had charmed and by his master, who had become an accomplice in his escape.

The fourth and last act of this Barbary odyssey is retold all too briefly in Vincent's letter: "We escaped in a little skiff and arrived, on June 28, at Aigues-Mortes." Did the two men set out on this adventure alone? Were there other passengers and pilots? What happened to the renegade's wives? Vincent did not find it useful to share these details. The crossing from Cap Bon to Aigues-Mortes, with favorable wind and weather, must have taken a good two weeks, though. Did Vincent languish for all those days in the bottom of the boat, wracked by seasickness? We do not know, for his account is brief indeed. By the time he wrote, he was on dry land and free, and that is what interested him.

The tale of Vincent de Paul's captivity seems to have presented no difficulties for Vincent's first biographers. For instance Abelly, the first among them, was more interested in highlighting Vincent's virtue than in writing with historical rigor. So he did not hesitate to censor certain passages of this letter, particularly those dealing with alchemy, a practice held in low esteem by the Church of his day.

It was Pierre Grandchamp, in a study published in 1928,[11] who first cast doubt on that famous letter. His position was adopted and elaborated by the writer Antoine Redier in his book *La vraie vie de St. Vincent de Paul* (The true life of St. Vincent de Paul). More recently, André Dodin, official historian of the Congregation of the Mission, did not hesitate to write that "numerous difficulties prevent even the least prejudiced minds from taking the captivity in Tunis as a historic fact."[12]

The questions raised by Grandchamps and taken up again by Dodin do not seem insurmountable. Without long examination of what Vincent might have meant by one word or another, one must concede that certain points remain obscure. This is particularly true of passages dealing with the conversion of the renegade and the flight of the master with his slave. Was it Vincent's religious songs alone that moved the Muslim woman so deeply that, in her turn, she easily convinced her lord and master to change his life? Writing about this, Coste does not hesitate to say: "Vincent de Paul was twenty-six years old. He enjoyed the double charms of youth and intelligence. Two of his master's wives felt irresistibly attracted to him."[13] He goes no further, but he implies that one might wander down this trail. Many stories told by former captives or by travelers recount idylls with Muslim women, without going as far as the novels of Cervantes. But might we not also think that the renegade was firmly convinced by his conversations with Vincent, who surely did not hide the fact that he was a priest? Vincent disposes of this dangerous escape in a single short sentence, whereas he took the time for intensely evocative descriptions of other incidents in his captivity. Perhaps he wished to obscure this episode so that he would not have to explain any help or collusion which made his escape possible, such as the bribe his master may have paid so that they could stow away on a ship that had put into a Tunisian port.

Shadow veils this period; as long as he lived, Vincent remained wordless about his captivity in Barbary. This strange silence about such an important passage in his life is an endless, intriguing mystery. To try to understand it, we must consider it in the light of the deep transformation his personality underwent in the course of the years. This is a matter to which we will return,[14] but we can already stress the fact that after this time, Vincent always refrained from talking about himself and that it was very rare for him to reminisce.

In spite of unclear moments, much evidence can be advanced for the truthfulness of Vincent's narrative. He not only wrote this letter to Monsieur de Comet, he sent numerous letters to his family—from Avignon in 1607, from Rome in 1608, and from Paris in 1610—in which he alluded to his captivity.[15] So the hypothesis of a purely imagined story, invented to camouflage a long adventure, hardly rings true. In addition, there are few indeed who have hazarded a credible guess as to what else Vincent might have been doing during the two years he was missing.[16]

The story itself is full of details which Vincent could neither have invented nor picked up in the dives of Marseilles, where some people claim he squandered the precious coins left to him by the "good old woman." In particular, how could he have learned the exact date of Monsieur de Brêve's mission to Tunisia, which corresponds exactly to the time when he was passed from his second master to his third?

When all the contradictory arguments are added up, one may well claim to be confused. It remains likely that Vincent was captured by corsairs, sold into slavery, and held in captivity for two years. Did those two years unfold in exactly the way he described? If some doubts remain, it is not so much because of what he said as because of what he omitted. To illuminate the shadowy corners, some new document would be required, and finding such a thing grows less and less likely with the passing of the years.

Throughout this odyssey, Vincent appears as an enterprising young man unburdened by scruples. In his misfortune, his lucky star delivered him into the hands of benevolent masters, and being in their good graces made his captivity much more bearable. Already then, he had the gift of winning other people's good will, and he would keep this gift all his life. His charm, no doubt, was a subtle mix—a mischievous glance, sparkling wit, the good cheer of a Gascon, and a wellspring of optimism that survived even the hardest luck. His faith sustained him, he wrote in a letter: "God always enkindled in me a belief in deliverance, through the ceaseless prayers I raised to him and the Holy Virgin Mary, by whose sole intercession I firmly believe I was rescued."

A Roman Sojourn
1607–1608

When they were unable to board a ship at Aigues-Mortes on June 28, 1607, Vincent and his companion in flight soon set out by road to Avignon. We know this from the letter which Vincent wrote in this city on July 24. The renegade had taken a little Barbary ape with him, which he turned to his former slave's profit. This made it possible for them to rent a mount or a horse-drawn barge; their weakened state after a difficult crossing would have made it impossible for them to cover the distance of a good sixty kilometers on foot.

Once arrived in the pontifical city, they attempted to present themselves at the palace of the vice-legate, His Excellency, Bishop Montorio.[1] To convince this great prelate to receive two fugitives lacking both official documents and recommendations, probably dressed in less than splendid style, Vincent once more had to call on his finesse and eloquence. Before he could even be admitted to the presence of this high dignitary of the Church, he probably obtained the help of some priest or monk met in the town to persuade the guards all the way from the door of the palace through a series of chamberlains charged with escorting away importunate visitors. We see from his letter that Vincent succeeded in breaching all barriers and convincing Monseigneur

Montorio himself: "the vice-legate received the renegade publicly with tears in his eyes and a sob in his throat, in the Church of St. Peter."

Unfortunately, this solemn ceremony of abjuration is not recorded in the archives at Avignon; at least, it cannot be found in what remains of them. But it is inconceivable that Vincent's story could be a fabrication. Bishop Montorio was a well-known person of some importance; a public ceremony over which he presided could not pass unnoticed. So at the time, it would have been easy enough to verify Vincent's declarations. Vincent adds that the vice-legate promised "the penitent to obtain entry for him to the austere convent of the *Fate ben fratelli*, where he vowed [to go]." Did the renegade really enter this convent in Rome, maintained by the brothers of St. John of God, or did he vanish along the road to make his way to his native Savoy? There is nothing in writing to answer this question and Vincent never spoke about it again.

As for Vincent, in a few weeks he had won the favor of the prelate. The latter, who was ending a three-year mission to Avignon, was only awaiting the arrival of his successor before leaving for Rome. He suggested that Vincent should come along with him and even proposed to have him supplied with some advantageous benefice. Why this sudden infatuation with young Vincent, who had arrived at the palace in tatters and told such an extraordinary tale? No doubt Monseigneur Montorio was delighted to crown the end of his mission with the ceremonious recantation of a renegade, even though such events were relatively frequent.[2] The reason for his enthusiasm was quite different, and Vincent confessed it ingenuously: "He does me the honor of being exceedingly fond of me and catering to me for the sake of an alchemical secret I have taught him."

Vincent continued to be favored by unbelievable luck. After succeeding in his remarkable flight, instead of ending his days in slavery, here he met a prelate who, by happy chance, was much taken by alchemy.[3] The secrets confided to Vincent by the old spagiric physician were of more importance to Montorio than "*se io li avesse datto un monte di oro,* for he has been working on this all the days of his life, and there is no other contentment for him." Playful, humorous Vincent could not help but act like a true Gascon and play with words, drawing a parallel between the name of his new benefactor, Montorio, and "*monte di oro*": "if I had given him a mountain of gold."

He already saw himself in possession of the benefice that this powerful prince of the Church would obtain for him without fail. But to support his claim of who he was, Vincent had to produce his letter of ordination and his bachelor's diploma in theology. He asked Monsieur de Comet to send him these documents directly to Rome, where he would soon be heading. As a sign of his gratitude and perhaps as proof of the truthfulness of his tale, Vincent enclosed with his letter one "of the two stones of Turkey which nature has carved into the shape of a diamond." Of course, this is not irrefutable proof of his time in Barbary.

He ended his long letter by expressing regret for the scandal he had caused by leaving without settling his debts. He would now be able to satisfy them, thanks to the money he had received from the renegade, but he did not think it wise to strip himself of these funds before he returned from Rome. In a lovely flight of optimism, he concluded: "I imagine that all this scandal will turn out to be for the best."

Reading this letter which tells us so much, one is struck by its spirited joy and optimism. At first, one may be tempted to call Vincent's story unlikely, but a more attentive re-reading gradually overcomes the reflex of incredulity elicited by a chain of episodes from which the hero emerges, miraculously free and almost entirely unscathed. Eventually, the account comes to seem quite factual. If the author of this letter had invented the whole thing, he would have to be considered an extraordinarily gifted storyteller, with an imagination that was never at a loss.

In fact, the story continues in another letter, again addressed to Monsieur de Comet and dated from Rome on February 28, 1608.[4] Vincent stayed in the palace of the vice-legate at Avignon for three months. In October of the same year, the new vice-legate, Monseigneur Joseph Ferreri, archbishop of Urbino, arrived and Montorio left for the Eternal City by carriage, taking along his young protégé as promised. Vincent reports that "it is in this city of Rome that I continue my studies, supported by Monseigneur the vice-legate."

The prelate's infatuation continues as Vincent is still showing him "very wonderful things, curiosities which I learned during my servitude with that old Turk . . . among which is the beginning, but not the total perfection of the mirror of Archimedes, an artificial device to make a skull speak . . . and a thousand other geometrical things that I learned from him, of which my lord is so jealous that he does not even want me to speak with anyone, for fear that I might instruct him. For he desires to be renowned as the only one who knows these things."

It should be noted that in this letter, Vincent no longer uses the term "alchemy." Is it Rome that has made him more prudent, since he saw that the topic had a bad reputation there? Rather, he speaks of magical tricks, like the mirror of Archimedes, which ignites objects at a distance or of the skull the old man manipulated, making a credulous audience believe that this was Mohammed's form of expression.

A curious prelate indeed, this Monseigneur Montorio, who would use such artifices to shine at the pontifical court, showing them from time to time to His Holiness and the cardinals, and holding Vincent under strict surveillance so that he would not reveal his secrets to anyone else. But Vincent did not chafe at the whims of his protector; he was too pleased with the renewed assurances concerning his future: "This earnest affection and benevolence causes him to promise me the means of obtaining a comfortable haven, providing me for this purpose with some substantial benefice in France."

After all his trials and adventures, Vincent had not budged from the goal he had been pursuing since entering the priesthood: to obtain a benefice of substance, which would shelter him from want and allow him to contribute to his family. There were still well-defined steps to be carried out; the Roman administration was punctilious and formalistic. The letters of ordination requested from Monsieur de Comet did in fact arrive in Rome, but they were judged to be invalid for they were not marked with the seal of the bishop of Dax. Vincent asked for the documents to be sent to him again, duly certified, as well as a recommendation stating that "I was always known for living as an honorable man, together with all the other necessary little rituals."

At the end of this letter, Vincent alludes discreetly to his debts, for he certainly intended to satisfy "what I owe at Toulouse, for I am resolved to clear my accounts, since it has pleased God to provide me with sufficient means to do so." He entrusted this missive to a venerable old priest, who was on the point of leaving for the Béarn. For this reason, he hastened to conclude it in spontaneous fashion: "in haste I end this carelessly scribbled letter," and promised to come back as soon as possible.

This second letter of Vincent's, like the first, has been preserved by fortunate circumstance. This one completes and confirms what Vincent had written six months earlier from Avignon, and yet, it does not agree completely with the first one. Not only are the references to alchemy obscured, but his judgment of the spagirist physician has clearly developed. In the first letter, Vincent presented him as quite humane and accommodating. He sold mercury, which he transmuted to give to the poor. But in the second letter, this same man is called miserable, one who tried to seduce the people into believing that he knew the will of his god Mohammed by revelation. How can we explain this change of tone, except by concluding that Vincent, sensitive to the atmosphere of Rome, had learned to guard his pen.

Vincent was to spend a whole year in Rome, waiting for the documents that he had requested from Dax, validated with all the necessary attestations and signatures. When they arrived, Monseigneur Montorio would have to be willing, armed with these extracts from the register of ecclesiastical documents[5] that proved that Vincent had indeed been ordained, to take the steps necessary for obtaining that much-desired benefice. In the meantime, the vice-legate was steadfast in his paternal care for his protégé. Vincent confirms it in his second letter: "I continue my studies, supported by Monsieur the vice-legate . . . who does me the honor of giving me his friendship and desiring my advancement."

No details are given about his studies; it is likely that they involved theology and that he was polishing his command of Italian. What is more, Vincent probably took this occasion to discover the remnants of ancient Rome, the sacred places of Christianity, as well as the monuments of more recent times. The Basilica of St. Peter had not yet been completed, after a century of construction under a parade of different architects, but Michelangelo's admirable dome was already partly there. We can imagine this young priest in his modest cassock down to the ground, threading his way through the mazes of the pope's city, his eyes alert and his ears attentive. He encounters cardinals coming from their palaces surrounded by their watchful courtiers, members of the pontifical household, chamberlains of the cape and sword, noble guards or militiamen in their shimmering uniforms.

In this year of 1608, several religious orders were convening their chapters general. Halls and chapels were filled with Capuchins and Minorites in their homespun habits, Dominicans in their white robes and black cloaks. Among the latter was Father Coeffeteau,[6] who held an important position in the chapter of his order. He was soon to return to Paris, where he was superior of the convent of Saint-Jacques and chaplain to Queen Marguerite of Valois. No doubt Vincent seized the opportunity to greet this important person and make himself known.

Above all, Vincent was learning to know the usage and customs of the Holy See and the motivating forces behind its administration. He studied the calculated languors and subtleties of the Romans, and this understanding would be of great use to him later. Of course, he attended the great ceremonies, probably glimpsing from far away Pope Paul V[7] as he blessed the crowd and officiated at ceremonies with pomp and solemnity. Probably too, during this second stay in Rome, he visited the hospital maintained by the Congregation of the Servants of the Poor Sick (Camillians) for later, his work would show the mark of their methods and spirit.

Nor did he neglect to pay his respects at the embassy of the king of France. In particular, he became acquainted with Étienne Gueffier, a secretary who, by 1632, would be chargé d'affaires and with whom he stayed in contact.[8] Above all, he learned in July that a new ambassador had just arrived in Rome, François Savary, lord de Brêves, the same man who had attempted to free French slaves in Tunisia. Surely Vincent made every effort to be presented to him, so that he could tell the tale of his Barbary adventure.

During the autumn of 1608, Vincent left Rome. He did not head for Dax, his home diocese, nor even to Pouy to greet his family from whom he had been absent so long. He chose the road to Paris. This change of destination is yet another puzzle and there is not a single document to shed light on it. We can only make surmises.

Vincent's protector in Rome, Monseigneur Montorio, having delivered a report of his mission as vice-legate should normally have returned to his episcopal see at Nicastro. It is likely that after he gave his protégé some letters of recommendation to help him obtain the promised benefice, he suggested it was time for the young man to return to France.

Tradition has it that Vincent was charged with carrying a confidential message of the highest importance to Henry IV. Unfortunately, Abelly, who seems to have originated this legend, says that it was the Cardinal d'Ossat who entrusted the mission to Vincent, but this cardinal had already been dead for several years. Someone else could have given Vincent a message that could not be committed to paper, for the king or someone near to him. In any case, a search in the diplomatic archives for the traces of such a mission has been fruitless. It remains possible that the ambassador, Monsieur de Brêves, charged Vincent with carrying an envelope to Paris and that over the course of years, this matter has accumulated importance, finally becoming a secret mission to the king. In any case, bearing a message he was to deliver, Vincent arrived in the capital city during the last days of 1608.

Shaped by Bérulle
1609–1613

Vincent arrived in Paris at the end of 1608. Eager to fulfill the mysterious mission with which he seems to have been charged, he had not stopped in the Landes of his birth. Or perhaps he did not want to come home before having achieved the benefice for which he had been working for so long, the phantom that had led him into so many adventures. His first years in the capital city are shadowy, for we have no documents on which to base a chronology; the events of those times sometimes appear to overlap and contradict each other.

We find Vincent neither at court nor in a princely dwelling, but modestly settled in a room he shares with a compatriot passing through the capital, Bertrand Dulou,[1] a judge from the city of Sore. The rented room was located in the faubourg Saint-Germain, where all the Gascons gathered. This might indicate that the letters of recommendation that Vincent supposedly received before leaving the pontifical city had not had much effect so far.

Not far from where he lived, Vincent could see the barges on the Seine, and on the other bank, the Louvre and the palace of the Tuileries. Walking toward the river brought him to the Quai Malaquais, bordering on the estate of Queen Marguerite de Valois,[2] where the gardens sloped down to the water.

In the same neighborhood stood the Hôpital de la Charité, established by Maria de Medici. The management of this hospital had been entrusted to the Brothers of St. John of God, who also conducted a charity hospital in Rome.[3] Vincent might have met some brothers there whom he had known while he was in Rome; pious tradition has it that he volunteered there to care for the poor and sick and to comfort them. This would have taught him useful lessons for the development of his own charitable works.

In the first months of his time in Paris, Vincent had a very disagreeable experience. Stricken by fever, he was immobilized in the room he was still sharing with his compatriot, the judge from Sore. The apothecary's clerk who was bringing some medicine took advantage of the fact that the feverish Vincent was huddled in his bed and rummaged in his cupboard under the pretext of looking for a cup. There he found a purse holding 400 shiny écus, which he was quick to put in his breeches. When the judge returned, he saw that he had been robbed. Stormily he accused Vincent of the theft in public and even had an ecclesiastical bulletin, a *monitoire,* published about the crime.[4] Rather than defending himself and throwing suspicion on the clerk, Vincent chose to be silent and bear the unjust accusation without flinching. A few months later, the thief was discovered in the act of stealing again and admitted to making off with the judge's purse. When the judge had returned to his home, he wrote to Vincent to ask his forgiveness for having vilified him. So goes the story told by Vincent[5] without identifying a hero, but everything points to the fact that he was the victim, wrongly accused, who bore this humiliation without complaint. If the story is true, this would be the first hint of a new behavior, this willingness to practice the Gospel's counsel that one should bear injustice without a murmur.

Naturally, Vincent had to move because of this affair. Did he stay briefly with Jean Duvergier of Hauranne,[6] another compatriot, or did he settle in immediately at the Sign of St. Nicholas at the corner of rue de Seine and rue Mazarine? This is the address he would give for all his official documents between 1610 and 1612.

Vincent actively sought work, unwilling to be like the many young Gascons who came to Paris to find their fortunes and gallivant around, hoping to attract the attention of some aristocrat or profit from the gullibility of a burgher. What is more, his nest egg—a gift from his former owner, the renegade, and travel money from the vice-legate to make up for not getting Vincent a benefice—was surely dwindling fast. But Vincent had an innate gift for striking up relationships that usually turned into friendships. That is how he made the acquaintance of Charles du Fresne,[7] secretary to Queen Marguerite of Valois, who brought him into the ranks of the queen's chaplains. Very probably, Vincent also made use of the recommendation of Father Coeffeteau, whom he had met in Rome, and above all, the recommendation of his bishop in Dax. In fact, Jean-Jacques Dusault was not only on good terms with Henry of Navarre, who had become King Henry IV, but he was first chaplain of Queen Marguerite of Valois. This prelate was well acquainted with Vincent's situation. In fact, the year before, he had signed the document forwarded to Rome certifying and authenticating the letters of ordination of "Master Vincent de Paul, priest of our diocese."[8] Thus, after several difficult months, Vincent was supplied with employment and a title: counselor and chaplain of Queen Marguerite.

An astonishing personality, this dispossessed queen was now no longer the scandalous princess who loved ostentatious luxury. Suffering and the years had marked her face and her figure, but she retained her haughty air, conscious of her rank as daughter of France and heiress of Valois. In 1609, she was fifty-six years old. Without relinquishing the pleasures of the flesh—she still displayed her titled lover—she was moving toward piety and devotion as she grew older. She went to mass every day and regularly had alms dispensed to the poor. For this task, she had ten chaplains at her disposal; we have a roster of their names for the period from 1608 to 1611.[9] Together with Father Coeffeteau, there are Monseigneur Cospéan, bishop of Aire, and Father Suarez, a Cordelier who would become bishop of Séez. Vincent is not listed in this document, but in all official documents published in May 1610 and October 1611, he is listed as "counselor and chaplain of Queen Margaret, duchess of Valois."[10] Thus it is possible that while functioning as almoner, which is to say a distributor of alms, he also played the role of counselor and was listed under this office on another list. Indeed we know very little of how Vincent served Queen Marguerite and how long he remained in her service. Nor do we have a portrait of him from this period.

Weaving together the words of his contemporaries, one can try to sketch the appearance of this twenty-eight-year-old priest. Of average height and sturdy build, he carries a strong head on solid shoulders, nose long, ears large, and the wide open nostrils of a man accustomed to breathing in the smells of nature. His chin is prominent and willful; behind luxuriant eyebrows, his eyes sparkle, alert and mischievous; his face gives the impression of a cheerful nature, immediately likable. He probably speaks with a Gascon accent, rolling the consonants as the Adour rolls the pebbles in its stream. Broad gestures underscore his points.

And so the young Gascon walked through Paris, eagerly discovering its noise and energy. No doubt, he was attracted by the Sorbonne, and maybe he attended courses there. It would only be known later, when his diploma was found in his room, that he was licensed in civil and canon law.[11] The distribution of alms left him sufficient time to pursue this kind of study, since he learned quickly, motivated by the will to advance. He also had enough time to visit the countless churches, chapels, and religious establishments that dot all the neighborhoods of the capital city. He made his way to the newly opened Place Royale, he admired the gardens of the Tuileries, designed in the Italian fashion, luxuriant and full of perfumes. He observed the great gallery under construction between the Palace of the Tuileries and the Louvre. After two years of slavery and hardship, how he must have savored his new-found liberty in a world that opened itself to his insatiable curiosity!

But he did not lose sight of his true ambition, to obtain a good benefice and return to his native region. That is what he wrote to his mother on February 10, 1610: "I regret that I still have to remain in this city in order to reclaim the possibility of advancement, which my disasters snatched away from me, for I would rather come and carry out my duties to you. But I have so much hope that God will graciously bless my efforts and that he will give me the means of fashioning a haven where I can spend the rest of my days near you."

This letter makes no mention of apostolic service or renunciation of the goods of this world. Vincent is preoccupied with the state of the family's affairs and, in spite of his own misfortunes, he encourages one of his nephews to follow his example: "I would also like it if my brother sent one of my nephews to study. My troubles, and the small contribution I have been able to make so far, take away his taste for that. But let him keep in mind that present misfortune means future good fortune."[12]

At the moment when Vincent wrote this letter to his mother, he was entering discussions with a great prelate, the archbishop of Aix, Paul Hurault de l'Hôpital, who was of a mind to cede him the abbey of Saint-Léonard-de-Chaume.[13] This Cistercian house was a commendatory abbey. By royal letters patent, it had been made over to an alderman of La Rochelle, Gabriel de Lamet, a Protestant. The archbishop of Aix had only acquired it the year before, in 1609. Soon he realized that he had struck a poor bargain and so he was eager to sell it again.

Vincent, for his part, no doubt believed that he was being offered the much-desired benefice with an honorific title that could rescue him from obscurity. In fact, he was entering a complex operation from which he would derive, as the months and years went by, little but disquiet and disillusion. We do not know how he was put in touch with this archbishop, perhaps through Jean de la Tanne, Master of the Mint of the city of Paris, or perhaps thanks to another connection, a certain Arnault Doziet, a merchant living on the rue Seine, near Vincent. Both of them are mentioned in official documents dated May 14 and May 17, 1610.[14]

In the first document, the archbishop has leased to Arnault Doziet "all the temporal revenue of the aforementioned abbey [Saint-Léonard-de-Chaume], its lands and buildings, right of overlordship, high justice, middle and low justice, taxes, rents, and profits of the land," in return for a sum of 3,600 livres a year. Vincent was listed as guarantor and security, as though he were the principal lessee.

Three days later, the archbishop relinquished his abbey in favor of Vincent, thus granting to him all the fruits, rights, and revenue of the aforementioned abbey in return for a pension of 1,200 livres per year. This second document provides that Vincent is considered to hold the lease of the temporal revenue made to Arnault Doziet. In spite of this rather complex procedure, the matter seems to have been well settled. Vincent, a commendatory abbot, was to receive the amount of the lease negotiated by the archbishop simply in exchange for an annuity. But what was to follow would not be quite so simple.

The deed of transfer was signed on May 17 and the royal letters patent granting the abbey to Vincent was signed on June 10, not by King Henry but by Louis! For while Vincent had been busy with this amazing negotiation, a drama had shaken the kingdom of France. On May 14, 1610, Henry IV was assassinated by a madman, Ravaillac. The king had been preparing to leave at the head of his army for yet another war in the Spanish Netherlands on the pretext of the badly jumbled succession to the duchy of Clèves. Add to that the torments of a last passion Henry suffered for the beautiful Charlotte de Montmorency. The king had married her to his nephew, Henry de Bourbon, prince de Condé, who enraged his uncle by taking his young wife away to Brussels to protect her from the advances of her royal admirer. As a matter of precaution, Henry had his wife, Maria de Medici, crowned on May 13 in the basilica of St. Denis before he went on campaign. The whole court was present, even Queen Marguerite of Valois. She was escorted by some gentlemen of her household but it is not likely that Vincent was part of this company as his position was still too humble. Surely he was present at the ceremony in some obscure spot and saw the nine-year-old Dauphin Louis in the procession with his mother. Vincent could not have suspected that thirty years later, he would be at the deathbed of this little dauphin, who became Louis XIII.

For the moment, Vincent was full of joy at possessing his abbey, but he would have to wait until his nomination as abbot of Saint-Léonard-de-Chaume was confirmed in Rome by a papal bull. This document was signed in September by Pope Paul V and immediately transmitted to the interested party by the bishop of Dax, Jean-Jacques Dusault. Now Vincent was able to take official possession of his benefice. He knew that the convent had been uninhabited for some time but he could not have imagined the desolation which greeted him on Saturday, October 16. The document which records the taking of possession of the abbey by the "respectable and sober person, Messire Vincent de Paul" speaks volumes in its bureaucratic terseness: "After opening the doors, inspection tour among the spaces and ruins of the church . . . where there is not a single altar and only a few scraps of walls, inspection tour among the ruins of the buildings and cloisters that used to be there . . . inspection tour of the ruined buildings surrounding the aforementioned ruined and fallen church, with only fragments of foundation and a few remnants of walls."[15]

Not only were the buildings in this deplorable state, but some of the lands of the abbey, which were meant to provide its revenues, had been embezzled. The archbishop of Aix had in fact alluded in his document of resignation to the various lawsuits then in progress concerning Saint-Léonard-de-Chaume, but Vincent had not realized how debt-ridden the domain really was. He began to understand that he had been duped. Yet, confident in his star, he must have hoped that he could improve his situation. On October 28, before a notary, he signed a proxy empowering a certain Pierre Gaigneur to conduct the affairs of the abbey during his absence,[16] and returned to the capital.

During this same year of 1610, Vincent met a person who would have a decisive influence on the further course of his life. This was Pierre de Bérulle.[17] He was a man of aristocratic birth who, from his earliest youth, had been destined for the priesthood. Ordained in 1599, he was named chaplain to the king. Very soon, he distinguished himself by his knowledge of theology and his talent for debate, achieving much talked-about conversions of great persons of the court. Cardinal du Perron,[18] himself renowned for eloquence, said, "If it's a matter of convicting heretics, bring them to me; if they are to be converted, present them before Monsieur de Sales; but if they are to be both convicted and converted, they must be brought to Monsieur de Bérulle."

Pierre de Bérulle was associated with his cousin, Madame Acarie,[19] in establishing the reformed Carmelites in France. To advance this purpose, he organized a mission to Spain, to the court of King Philip III, who in 1604 authorized six Spanish nuns to found a house in Paris. On his own initiative, he made himself Perpetual Visitor of the Carmels in France, which led to quarrels with Madame Acarie and the Carmelites, for under his suave exterior, Bérulle was an authoritarian, as one can judge from events. He was unshakable in his opinions, with a clear-cut will to rule. But it must be said that he was inspired by an elevated vision of the mission of a priest, obligated to live by Christ's example.

Vincent was intensely affected by this man who was not his senior by much but who exercised decisive power over him. On the surface, they had nothing in common: on the one hand, an aristocratic intellectual of serious and stern demeanor; on the other, a pragmatic peasant, a mischievous, cheerful Gascon. This was not a friendship that was formed; Vincent was not attracted, but subjugated. Bérulle dictated and Vincent conformed. Speaking of Bérulle later, he stressed his learning and saintliness: "He attained a holiness and a learnedness so firm as to be hardly equaled."[20]

Thanks to Bérulle, Vincent was brought into the circle of mystics and reformers among whom shone minds like the learned Father Duval,[21] doctor of the Sorbonne and royal professor of theology, or the Jesuit Father Coton,[22] the king's confessor.

In this young priest so eager for titles and benefices, Bérulle was able to detect an exceptional nature and a vocation to sainthood. He was to help him discover himself. Vincent, who up to that time had been centered on himself, seeking material success within the framework of his priestly estate, discovered in Bérulle's company a completely different vision of the Church and a conception of the priesthood as a high calling. In one leap, Vincent's gaze was raised from the contemplation of temporal goods to consideration of spiritual things, as though a gust of wind had torn a window through the fog. But it is not so easy to slip the moorings of the temporal; for years, Vincent would still be caught between his desire for comfort and his aspiration to the spiritual life. To this struggle was added an interior crisis that shook him grievously.

Among the courtiers of Queen Marguerite of Valois, Vincent made the acquaintance of a celebrated doctor who had become renowned as a theologian in the battle against heretics. The queen had attached him to herself for his piety and learning. Was it the lack of useful occupation or some harmful atmosphere that pervaded the court of this princess? The learned doctor was shaken with violent temptations against faith. He revealed his trouble to Vincent, who reported,[23] as a witness, the terrible struggle this unfortunate man underwent before being delivered from his pitiable state shortly before he died, at peace and reconciled with God. What Vincent did not recount but is recorded in the biography by Abelly, who transcribed the testimony of a person most worthy of belief, is the manner in which the theologian was delivered from his temptations and despair. Vincent, who witnessed with great distress the physical and mental illness of this man tortured by the evil spirit, was inspired to pray that God would deliver the sufferer and impose upon him, Vincent, the poor man's pain. The theologian departed this life in peace but Vincent, in his turn, experienced the horrors of doubt and temptation. From that time on, he was to walk through a long period of darkness, which would not leave him for many years.

The many problems which had to be resolved in order to restore the abbey of Saint-Léonard-de-Chaume and its dependencies brought Vincent to the region of La Rochelle repeatedly. He alluded to these journeys indirectly in his Conversations.[24] The chief reason for his numerous trips was the many lawsuits concerning the abbey. In the year 1611 alone, there were no fewer than five verdicts pronounced by the courts of the city and government of La Rochelle.[25]

Most of these suits were brought by Brother André de la Serre, who held the title of prior of the abbey of Saint-Léonard-de-Chaume against "Messire Vincent de Paul of the said abbey." But Vincent, for his part, counterattacked and haled the so-called prior before the court. All these suits arose from the interpretation of the original lease signed in May 1610 with Vincent as guarantor. Specifically, this document stipulates that the renter, the holder of the lease, commits to establishing in the abbey two religious of the Cistercian Order, who will be named by the abbot of the place and confirmed by the abbot of Cîteaux, one of which brothers will be the prior of the cloister. Who had named this André de la Serre, whom Vincent seems to reject? Does this prior have any rightful claim to one third of the abbey's revenues, an amount mentioned in the verdict pronounced on March 17, 1611? We are lacking the information which could clarify the matter. One thing is certain— Vincent had walked into a wasps' nest and would have the greatest difficulty escaping.[26] In May 1611, Vincent was even pursued by Monseigneur Hurault de l'Hôpital who, not satisfied with having transferred this questionable business to him, now demanded, through notaries, the arrears of his pension.[27]

We must try to understand the spirit of the times. Although this abbey turned out to create more annoyance than revenue, it nevertheless gave Vincent considerable status in his society. Vincent was no longer the modest priest who had arrived in the capital sixteen months before with a skimpy little bundle of possessions: he had a fine title and this made him a person of esteem. Thus, when Jean de la Tanne, the Master of the Mint and friend of Vincent, wanted to make a discreet transfer of 15,000 livres to the hospital of La Charité, he chose as intermediary "Messire Vincent de Paul, commendatory abbot of the abbey of Saint-Léonard."[28]

In the course of the year 1611, while engaged with these troubles, Vincent was an increasingly frequent member of the group surrounding Pierre de Bérulle. This man believed that the necessary renewal of the Church required not only reform but a much holier clergy. This point of view caused him to dream of founding a congregation that would restore and elevate the very idea of the priesthood: "The priestly estate requires two things of itself. First is a great perfection and even holiness, and second, a personal connection to Jesus Christ."[29]

At this time, Bérulle was even in the process of forming the first nucleus of what was to become the Congregation of the Oratory. In November 1611, he gathered a little team of five priests whom he settled in a house in the rue Saint-Jacques (where the Val-de-Grâce now stands). He did not invite Vincent to join them, thinking that he was meant for a different vocation, but among his first companions was François de Bourgoing, pastor of the parish at Clichy-la-Garenne at the gates of the capital. Bérulle asked him to resign his position there in favor of Vincent. It is conceivable that Vincent, without giving up his function as a chaplain to Queen Marguerite of Valois, spent a few months at this newly founded oratory in order to prepare himself for his new responsibilities. The document establishing him in the office of pastor of Clichy-la-Garenne is dated May 2, 1612.[30]

So here was Vincent de Paul, at the age of thirty-one, placed at the head of a parish. At that time, Clichy-la-Garenne had about 600 inhabitants, peasants and market gardeners, people of humble circumstance who somehow reminded Vincent of his native village. They sold their poultry, dairy products, and vegetables at the markets of Paris, just as the farmers of Pouy brought their produce to the fairs held at Dax. The parish lay spread out beneath the walls of the capital, with the Seine as its northern boundary, the parish of St. Ouen to the east, of Villiers to the west, and of Madeleine and Saint Roch to the south.[31]

At first, Vincent was uneasy conducting the liturgies and intoning the chants. In the more than ten years since he had been ordained, how often had he had occasion to celebrate in public? Later, he would recall these first ceremonies: "To my own embarrassment, I will say that once I found myself in my own parish, I had no idea of how to proceed; I heard these country folk intoning the psalms and I admired them, for they did not spoil a single note. At that moment, I said to myself, 'You, their spiritual father, don't even know how to do that.' It gave me great pain."[32] But very soon he overcame his first shyness and found himself making contact with these good people. He zealously fulfilled a pastor's duties, preaching, teaching the catechism, hearing confessions, and visiting his parishioners. He occupied himself with the sick and the poor and tried to bring peace to family quarrels.

The little church of Clichy, dedicated to Saints Sauveur and Médard, was not in very good condition, with aged baptismal fonts, pews, and vestments. Vincent, together with his curate, Égide Beaufils, went straight to work to restore the sanctuary and its furniture. But the day-to-day resources of the parish were meager and so Vincent had to press not only his richest parishioners but also his connections in Paris for contributions.

The lord of Clichy, who owned a country house there, was Alexandre Hennequin. Vincent was of an age with him and rapidly began an acquaintance that soon became a friendship.[33] The lord of Clichy had not only honorific rights there, attached to his title, such as a choir stall, burial, and liturgical honors, but also duties, like the maintenance or restoration of that same choir. There is no doubt that Vincent reminded him of this.

Alexandre Hennequin did much more than provide financial aid; he brought Vincent together with a family that was to play an important role in his life. The young lord had been orphaned early and was brought up by his uncle and tutor, Michel de Marillac. It was in this family circle that Vincent might have made the acquaintance of Louise de Marillac, who with her cousin, Isabelle du Fay, would become a tireless benefactress of Vincent's charitable works.

This young and enterprising parish priest, who was not afraid to work hard, either in the church or in the rectory's kitchen garden, attracted the young people of the parish. Beyond catechism classes, he started a sketch of a school. One of his first students was a young man called Antoine Portail who in a few years was to become a very close collaborator.

After so many adventures, wish-dreams, and bitter disappointments, could it be that Vincent had finally arrived at a peaceful harbor? It seems believable when one hears him declare: "I was a parish priest out in the fields. My people were so good and so obedient to my requests that when I told them they ought to come to confession on the first Sunday of the month, that is what they did. They came and they made their confession, and I saw these souls prosper, day by day. I found this so comforting that I said to myself: My God, you are fortunate to have such good people! And I added 'I think that not even the pope is as fortunate as a parish priest in the midst of a congregation of such good heart.'"[34]

Vincent painted this idyllic picture forty years after the fact. Did some memory make his recollections more beautiful or was he really perfectly happy and fulfilled as a country priest? But if he was, then why, after little more than a year, did he accept a new task that would keep him far away from his parish in Clichy-la-Garenne?

Tutor in the House of Gondi
1613–1616

"I believe that not even the pope is as fortunate as a priest in the midst of a congregation of good heart," said Vincent. And yet, after only sixteen months of ministry, while still retaining title to the parish of Clichy, he entered the great household of the Gondis. There is no document to reveal the motive for this move, only the statement of Abelly that "It was about the year 1613 when Reverend Father de Bérulle convinced Vincent to accept the position of tutor to the children of Messire Emmanuel de Gondi."[1]

At first sight, it seems surprising that Bérulle should have encouraged this move. Was it not he who had drawn Vincent away from the court of Queen Marguerite of Valois?[2] Had he not been the one who chose to place Vincent in a parish, to make him recognize his true vocation? It is not surprising that Bérulle, very much an insider with the high aristocracy, knew that the Gondis were seeking a teacher for their children; perhaps he had even been charged with finding one. But there is a big difference between this and deciding to remove Vincent from a parish he had just taken on. One can imagine that

49

Bérulle might have alluded to this position in Vincent's presence in order to test the firmness of his resolve to lead the life of a shepherd of souls when he had a free choice.

Thanks to Bérulle, Vincent had certainly come to recognize the nobility of his priestly estate and been filled with enthusiasm at the prospect this revealed to him—to model his life in the image of Christ. But there is a long road from becoming aware to becoming converted. At this moment, Vincent was perhaps not yet ready to change his life so profoundly.

He had been sincerely happy to bear the responsibility of a parish; it answered his need for action. But it probably did not take him long to become very familiar with every facet of this work. Vincent was not without ambition. If he already felt called upon to accomplish great things, the horizon of Clichy could have seemed very confining, and he must have felt capable, as he would all his life, of attending to more than one task at a time.

Vincent had a particular gift for making connections with people. He was already good at it as a child, then in Dax, in Toulouse, and Avignon, and Rome. Wherever he went, he acquired friends. He certainly managed to be appreciated in Paris by the rich and powerful who were to be seen in the palace of Queen Marguerite of Valois and by the intellectual elite that included Bérulle. Even in the country parish of Clichy-la-Garenne, he managed to become close to people of consequence. Later, Vincent would place this exceptional gift at the service of Charity but for the moment—why hide it?—he used his gifts for his own advancement.

It may very well be that it was he who suggested himself for the position in the Gondi household: in any case, wasn't he particularly well suited to carry out the function of tutor, having exercised it successfully at Dax and Toulouse, with his university degrees and good reputation? In any case, whether by the wish of Bérulle or by Vincent's initiative, the decision was made and he was chosen. There was already a curate in place at the parish in Clichy, but Vincent retained the title of pastor, visiting and participating as much as possible in the religious life of the community.

The Gondis belonged to an old Florentine family which had experienced varied fortunes. An Antoine de Gondi had emigrated to Lyon at the beginning of the sixteenth century, where he directed a bank. His wife, Marie-Christine de Pierre-Vive, had given him ten children. She had been singled out by Catherine de Medici when she was traveling to Lyon in 1530 to marry the dauphin, the future Henry II. Catherine took the Gondi household with her and she made their fortune.

Antoine de Gondi was named master of the palace to the dauphin and his wife was made governess to the Children of France. Their own children later received highest offices in the State and the Church. Their firstborn son, Albert, favorite of Charles IX, acquired titles and wealth: marquis de Belle-Isle, marshal of France, General of the Galleys, governor of Provence and, by his marriage, duke de Retz. Later, he linked his fortune to Henry IV, who appreciated his wit and courage in any difficulty. Aside from these qualities, Albert de Gondi had not one scruple and no moral sense. His model was Machiavelli. Certain of his character traits reappeared later in his grandson, the future Cardinal de Retz, conspirator and memoirist.

Antoine de Gondi's second son, Pierre, was destined for the Church. He was bishop of Langres, then bishop of Paris, before being elevated to the cardinalate. Pierre was an excellent prelate who tried to put his bishopric in order and played an important part in improving the relations of Henry IV with the Holy See.[3] He resigned his episcopal function in 1596 in favor of his nephew, Henri de Gondi. Thus the bishopric of Paris was occupied by four Gondis of three generations in uninterrupted succession. The office had become a veritable family prerogative, like the office of General of the Galleys, which was held successively by four members of the family.

Albert de Gondi, like his father, had ten children. His firstborn, Charles, inherited the supervision of the galleys, the titles of marquis de Belle Isle and duke de Retz. His second son, Henri, who succeeded his uncle as bishop of Paris, devoted his energies to maintaining discipline in his diocese and favored the foundation or strengthening of religious institutions. When he received the cardinal's hat, he took the title of Cardinal de Retz. At his death in 1622, his younger brother, Jean François, doffed the habit of a Capuchin friar to succeed him in the bishopric, which had been transformed into the archbishopric of Paris.

Between these two brothers came Philippe-Emmanuel de Gondi, whose household Vincent entered in 1613 as tutor. At this time, Philippe-Emmanuel was thirty-one years old; in the words of his son, he was "the handsomest, most skillful, and most valorous man in the kingdom." In those days, he was taken up with the pleasures and intrigues of the court. Upon the death of his older brother, Charles, he acceded very early to the position of General of the Galleys and lieutenant general of the king (on the Eastern Seas). He distinguished himself at the head of a fleet of galleys, winning a victory against the pirates of the Barbary coast. In 1604, he married Françoise-Marguerite de Silly, a sweet and virtuous young woman who gave him two sons. When Vincent became their tutor, one was seven and the other was two years old. A third son was born on September 20, 1613. He was baptized Jean-François Paul and would become the famous churchman and writer, the Cardinal de Retz.

When Vincent first took up his duties, he had only one pupil, Pierre de Gondi. This boy had inherited from his grandfather a difficult and unbending character. Early on, he would prove his rare bravery when he distinguished himself at the siege of La Rochelle. He was also destined to plot, first against Richelieu and then against Mazarin in the days of the Fronde. In accordance with the family tradition, Philippe-Emmanuel's second son was destined for the Church. Unfortunately, this young Henri died at the age of eleven, after a horseback riding accident. So it was the third son who was groomed for the Church, even though, by his own admission, he had "perhaps the least ecclesiastically minded spirit in the universe."[4] This would not prevent him from becoming a cardinal, but it would happen through intrigue rather than through piety.

Vincent's assignment was to teach the children the first elements of classical studies before they entered secondary school at around twelve years of age and the basic lessons of Christian doctrine, which was of even greater importance to their pious mother. Thus Pierre de Gondi, the oldest son, was only under Vincent's influence for a few years, after which he went off to school. Subsequently he entered the Royal Academy, where young noblemen under the direction of Antoine de Pluvinel, the famous riding master, were trained for a military career. His behavior when he reached young manhood was hardly edifying; Pierre's morals did no honor to his former teacher. We cannot judge of Vincent's effect on the second son, Henri, who died so long before his time. It is the third son who remained under Vincent's influence the longest, before entering the Collège de Clermont at the age of twelve. At this school, he made himself famous with his flashes of rage and his lack of discipline. His tutor had not succeeded in reining in his impetuous temperament. The excesses of his former student, well after he had received holy orders, no doubt caused some regret to Vincent, who always kept a certain doting fondness for the young man. In his memoirs, Cardinal de Retz only alluded to Vincent in a single passage, where he tells of a retreat he made at Saint-Lazare before ordination: "Monsieur Vincent, who applied this passage of the Gospel to me: that I was lacking in piety, but that I was not too far removed from the kingdom of God."[5]

In addition to his function as tutor, Vincent was charged with the religious instruction of all the domestics of the household. Later, he would add another function, when he accompanied the family to their estates. Although we have very little information about Vincent's life with the Gondis, it stands to reason that as he began his work for them, his role was quite humble and his demeanor modest and discrete. During this period, he was still immersed in the black moods which had begun when he was trying to bring comfort to the theologian at the court of Queen Marguerite of Valois. Perhaps he found a certain serenity during his time at Clichy-la-Garenne, through the active life which was so necessary for him. But now, he had to struggle with the mood once more, and with the extremes of his disposition. Abelly writes of his bilious and melancholic temperament, of which he caught a glimpse in private and which was supposedly even remarked upon by Madame de Gondi. Vincent is supposed to have said at the time: "I used to address myself to God, and beg Him to transform this dry and unwelcoming disposition and give me a mild and benign spirit, and by the grace of Our Lord, with the little bit of care I gave to repressing the turbulence of my nature, I lost a bit of my black mood."[6]

Later, in a conference to his missionaries, Vincent spoke about the work of a chaplain in a great family. Surely it was his experience in the household of the Gondis that inspired these reflections. He said that in order to fulfill this office well, one must be "a man of prayer" and that great piety was worth more than great knowledge. He told a story which revealed that, once, he managed to break through his reserve enough to speak to his lord and master quite firmly: "There was once a chaplain who knew on good authority that his master was planning to fight a duel. After celebrating holy mass, when everyone had left, he threw himself before his master, who was kneeling there and said to him: 'Sir, permit me in all humility to address a word to you. I know that you intend to fight a duel and I say to you, in the service of my God, whom I have just shown to you and whom you have just now adored, that if you do not abandon this evil plan, he will impose his judgment upon you and your posterity.' Having said this, the chaplain withdrew."[7]

The context of this is, as Abelly tells us, that the General of the Galleys, Philippe-Emmanuel, wanted to avenge one of his close relatives killed by a gentleman of the court. Shaken by Vincent's admonition, he abandoned his plan to duel and retired to one of his estates in great displeasure. A little later, he learned that the murderer had been exiled by the king, and this appeased him.

Was it perhaps in consequence of this episode that Vincent's status seems to have changed somewhat? To his limited role of tutor and chaplain to the domestic staff, he now added the office of personal chaplain to the Gondis. At the same time the General of the Galleys expressed his esteem and gratitude to Vincent by causing the parish of Gamaches[8] to be assigned to him as a prebend in February 1614. This was a supplement to his salary as tutor.

Philippe-Emmanuel's wife, in her turn, observed Vincent's work with her children and was well disposed toward this discreet and attentive priest. Françoise-Marguerite de Silly was a scrupulous and anxious soul. She asked Vincent to become her spiritual director, and when he hesitated to accept this office, which would plainly be difficult, she asked Pierre de Bérulle to intervene on her behalf. Vincent had to yield, while still trying to preserve some distance from his penitent who soon proved to be quite demanding. She wanted to have him in her presence at all times, so that she could speak to him of her problems of conscience and ask for his advice. Vincent tried discreetly to suggest that she might visit the sick and help the poverty-stricken people who lived on her estates and she turned to this work with ardent enthusiasm, drawing Vincent along in her wake.

In Paris, the Gondis first lived in one mansion in the rue des Petits Champs, and then moved to another in the rue Pavée. They lived in great style, even if it meant going into debt[9] or asking for the financial help of their oldest brother, the cardinal, who enjoyed a very comfortable income. When not in Paris, the Gondis would often spend time in one of their châteaux in the provinces—at Montmirail, Folleville, Villepreux, or Joigny.

Philippe-Emmanuel de Gondi, in addition to his title of marquis of the Îles-d'Or (Îles d'Hyères) and his position of General of the Galleys of France, was baron of Plessis-Écouis in Normandy. What is more, he owned large estates in Champagne, as baron de Montmirail and Dampierre, and in the Île-de-France, where he was baron of Villepreux, west of Versailles. From his uncle, Cardinal Pierre de Gondi, he had received the county of Joigny. As for his wife, Françoise-Marguerite de Silly, she had inherited from her mother estates in Picardy, which made her lady of Folleville, Paillart, Sérévilliers, and Cannes, south of Amiens. Through her father, she was lady of Commercy and sovereign of Enville in Lorraine.

As Vincent accompanied Madame de Gondi on her charitable visits around the estates, he became aware of the deep misery reigning in these countrysides. In addition to being afflicted by poverty, families were badly lacking in religious care because the local clergy were not equal to their task. With the agreement, and sometimes even at the request of Philippe-Emmanuel and his wife, Vincent tried to supplement the insufficient work of the village clergy, catechizing, hearing confessions, and preaching.

In a homily on the subject of the catechism, the text of which has been preserved, he opened with these words: "I do not stand up in the pulpit to preach to you in the usual way . . . but because the count has requested it, since he knows that the Lord has not established the aristocrat only to collect rents from his subjects but also to administer justice to his people, uphold religion, and show them how to love, serve, and honor God."[10] In his pastoral work, Vincent found new balance, and in the years 1614 and 1615, he emerged from his somber period of doubt and darkness. The Gondis showed him their satisfaction and esteem in various ways. In particular, on May 27, 1615, Philippe Emmanuel assigned to him the office of treasurer and canon of the collegiate church of Écouis, of which he was the collator.[11]

This nomination elicited some agitation, for Vincent had only been at Écouis once, in September 1615, to pronounce the oath of fidelity before the general chapter and to invite the company to dine on the next day. No doubt he took the time to admire the lofty nave of the church and the handsome disposition of the square, with a dozen little canon's houses planted in their little gardens. After this, Vincent went away and never again set foot in Écouis. A co-patron of the church, Pierre de Roucherolles, assembled the chapter a few months later to remark on the absence of several members, including the treasurer, and to summon them for an explanation. In the absence of the General of the Galleys, his wife had to muster her eloquence in a letter declaring that Monsieur Vincent de Paul was obliged, by the duties of his position, to remain with her. We have no indication of how long Vincent retained the prebend after this incident.

Having tried for so long to obtain a substantial benefice, Vincent could now count himself satisfied. By the age of thirty-five, he had accumulated a good number of titles, with the accompanying income. He kept the parish of Clichy-la-Garenne at the same time as the parish of Gamaches. He was still commendatory abbot of Saint-Léonard-de-Chaume and he enjoyed the position of treasurer and canon of the collegiate church of Écouis. Moreover, he held an honorable and no doubt well-paid position in a household of some stature.

After so many travels and shifts, with his goal finally attained, Vincent began to realize the emptiness of everything that he had wished so ardently to grasp: material ease, important titles, the company of the powerful. It was his work with the rural poor that brought him a sense of his own accomplishment. After a long passage through a tunnel, he caught sight of a glow that promised light and certainty.

In February 1616, after the death of Cardinal Pierre de Gondi, Philippe-Emmanuel took full possession of the title of count of Joigny. Accompanied by Vincent, his family spent most of that year there. Joigny is remarkably situated on an eminence overlooking the valley of the Yonne. The walled city was built around the peak on which a fortress had been erected in the tenth century. A modern dwelling was begun on these foundations around the year 1570, but Cardinal de Gondi had not had time to complete the work. Only one pavilion with a beautiful Renaissance façade was inhabitable. Facing this, on the site of a former monastery, rose a church which had been built in the sixteenth century. Its interior architecture was particularly fine, with nave vaulting decorated with coffers of exceptional richness. Floods of light poured through the windows. A frieze of mythical beasts decorated the transition between the gothic portion of the church and the portion in Renaissance style.

If tradition is to be believed, Vincent lived in a house below the château. He came up to celebrate the office in this beautiful Church of Saint-Jean before going to spend time with his pupils or to advise the new chatelaine. She was truly in need of his counsel for her husband was kept in Provence by his duties as General of the Galleys. It was she who must contend with the problems of administering the county of Joigny, construction work on the château, and the conduct of numerous court trials. These trials dealt mainly with seigniorial rights attached to lands in the neighboring village of Villecien. The lord of Villecien was none other than Alexandre Hennequin, whom Vincent had known well at Clichy. One can well imagine that the official reconciliation signed in September 1617 between the count of Joigny and the lord of Villecien owed much to the intervention of Monsieur Vincent.[12]

All this time Vincent, in collaboration with the local clergy of the county, was going from village to village to preach and hear confessions. Parishioners were more willing to speak with him than with their own pastors and as a result, he was forced to ask the vicar general of the diocese of Sens, which included the county of Joigny, for authorization to receive general confessions.[13]

But he himself was not secure from temptation, in particular, those of the flesh. It was probably during this stay at Joigny that he made a retreat at the Carthusian monastery of Valprofonde, near the city of the same name. He alluded to this discreetly in a letter written later to one of his missionaries. The monk who directed his retreat called to mind the case "of a holy bishop, suffering from these [temptations] when baptizing women" and the way in which he succeeded in resisting. Vincent would add in this letter that "this example destroyed a similar temptation which I suffered in carrying out the work of my vocation."[14]

Toward the end of the year 1616, on October 29 to be exact, Vincent made an important decision: he signed an instrument of resignation from the abbey of Saint-Léonard-de-Chaume.[15] Truly it seems that this abbey had brought him more financial and legal troubles than financial gain. In making this resignation, did he understand that now, with his debts paid, he could divest himself of a responsibility that had little to do with his other work and duties? Or was it not rather the first sign of a profound change of course that Vincent had chosen to impose on his whole life?

7

A Decisive Year
1617

When Henry IV died, his son Louis was only nine years old and would not be declared of age until October 1614, another four years. Consequently, by decision of the parlement of Paris, the regency of the kingdom was conferred on his widow, Maria de Medici. The regent, influenced by her court, particularly her foster sister Leonora Dori, called la Galigaï, and Leonora's husband, the Florentine gentleman Concino Concini, immediately dismissed the ministers of the dead king, including the faithful Sully. The royal treasury was devastated by this Italian group, led by Concini, who had himself named marquis d'Ancre and marshal of France.

The powerful of the kingdom did not delay in rebelling under the leadership of the prince de Condé,[1] the de Guise family, and the de Bouillon family. To appease them, the regent called a session of the Estates General, which seemed a simple expedient to her. This assembly would permit the young bishop of the little diocese of Luçon to make himself known and noticed. He would soon become Cardinal de Richelieu. The coming of age of the king a few days before the opening of the

Estates General did not change the form of government, which was still in the hands of the regent's favorites. A new rebellion of the aristocracy forced Maria de Medici to retreat and in 1616, she named one of them, the prince de Condé, chief of the Council. Then, a few months later, she had him arrested and imprisoned, and Concini once more took the reins of power.

At this point, a conspiracy was formed to assure that the young king could truly occupy his throne. On April 24, 1617, Concini was assassinated as he was entering the Louvre. The affairs of state were entrusted to Charles d'Albert,[2] the organizer of the coup and friend and counselor of the king. Maria de Medici was exiled and sent to live in the château of Blois. All in all, the year 1617 was a period of trouble and change for the kingdom of France.

In the first days of the same year, the family of the General of the Galleys was in residence at the château of Folleville[3] in Picardy. One day, word came to Monsieur Vincent that a man was dying in the village of Gannes, twelve kilometers from the château, on an estate belonging to Madame de Gondi. He was a peasant, generally believed to be a good man, asking for the help of a priest so that he could unburden his conscience of serious faults he had never dared confess to the village priest. Vincent went to the man immediately and heard his confession. The dying man was greatly comforted and appeased. To Madame de Gondi, who came to visit him, he declared that he would have been damned if he had not been able to make this general confession and even admitted his past faults to her publicly.

Madame de Gondi, sincerely moved, said to Vincent: "Ah, Monsieur, what is this? What have we just heard? Very probably the same story is true for most of these poor people. If this man, who was generally supposed to be a good man, was in a state of mortal sin, how will it be for others, who lead much worse lives?" And so she asked Vincent to preach on January 25 in the church at Folleville, to exhort the inhabitants to make a general confession. This was done, and the results were staggering: "These good people were so touched by God that they all came to make their general confession."

The preacher was overcome by his own success: "The crush of people was so great that I could not manage it, even with another priest helping me. Therefore, Madame was so kind as to send to the reverend Jesuit fathers of Amiens to come and help. She wrote about the need to the Reverend Father Rector and he came himself. However, he could not find the time to stay long and so he sent as replacement for himself Reverend Father Fourché, of his company, who helped us to hear confessions, preach, and catechize." It was not sufficient for the priests to sit in the confessional; they had to assemble the parishioners and prepare them to receive the sacrament of the Eucharist. Telling this story to his missionaries years later, Vincent ended by saying, "So here was the first sermon of the Mission and the success that God granted it."[4]

Vincent had already had numerous opportunities to preach, either at the request of Philippe-Emmanuel de Gondi on his own estates or at the request of his wife on hers. But these earlier sermons had not had the same kind of success. As far as we can judge from surviving texts, a sermon on communion and another on catechesis,[5] these were rather classic homilies with biblical references and Latin quotations, which were in danger of passing over the heads of his hearers. Probably he tried to give his sermons life by using concrete examples, but they remained speeches which the villagers would listen to in resigned silence.

The innovative element in the Folleville sermon came from the fact that Vincent was freed from the seal of the confessional because Madame de Gondi had heard the avowals of the peasant, the admissions of a reputedly good man. Mounting to the pulpit at the request of his lady, Vincent spoke with an open heart, evoking this example of a man known to all in order to urge his audience to unburden their hearts of the weight of past faults. Still profoundly moved himself, he spoke to these countrymen like a man of the country; son of a peasant, he spoke to them in their language. The effect was extraordinary! On this occasion, Vincent experienced the feeling of working as a team with the priests sent from Amiens as reinforcements. This cooperation became a principle of action for him that he never gave up.

On the crest of this first success, he went with the other priests to preach in surrounding villages belonging to Madame, with similar happy results. Everywhere he went he found signs of the mediocrity, not to say the ignorance, of the rural clergy. In fact, Madame de Gondi had already told him that very often, in the parishes lying in her domains, the priests to whom she made her confession did not know the sacramental formula for absolution and contented themselves with mumbling a few unintelligible words. She had taken to writing the words of this sacrament on a piece of paper which she handed to the celebrant.

If the truth be told, the villagers hardly offered any consideration to their priests, who for their part proved incapable of instructing them and who sometimes were even the subject of scandal because of their own behavior, surrendering to drink or living in concubinage. The people were unwilling to make their confession to these men, and so remained in a permanent state of sin. From that time on, Vincent was tormented by the idea of so many souls who were risking their eternal salvation all for the lack of good pastors to guide their way.

It was during these weeks of preaching on the lands of Madame de Gondi that everything he had dimly discovered and felt over the past years came together. Vincent realized that his vocation was to bring a knowledge of God to unfortunate rural folk and that he had a powerful instrument—an extraordinary gift of words.

It was painful for Vincent, after these intensely experienced weeks, to return to the Paris mansion of the Gondis. The magnificent surroundings of a house devoted to show, worldliness, and parties were stifling for Vincent now. No doubt he carried out his teaching duties conscientiously, but they were too bland to satisfy his need for action. He supervised the studies of two children, aged six and four. Pierre, the older, was probably already enrolled in a school in preparation for entrance into the Royal Academy, where he would receive a military education with the other young noblemen of his generation.

Vincent's only other role was to act as spiritual director to Madame de Gondi, and here he succeeded only too well; she could no longer do without him. He was required to be with her at all hours, to reassure her anxious soul and to give some direction to her piety which tended strongly toward mysticism. After the intense and striking events they had experienced together at Gannes and Folleville, Madame de Gondi was more attached than ever to Vincent, who seemed the only one who could guide her vulnerable soul to salvation.

The General of the Galleys, when he was not at court, was often away from home, detained by duties that kept him in Provence for long periods. This left Vincent alone with Madame de Gondi, Françoise-Marguerite, a beautiful woman as young as he was. We know how strongly he attracted women, and for his part, he was not blind to their charms. It is possible that his retreat at Valprofonde was not enough to deliver him altogether from the torments of the flesh? Or was Vincent totally worn down by the endless pangs of conscience brought to him by his penitent, a woman torn by excessive scruples?

No doubt Vincent discussed this situation with Pierre de Bérulle. His adviser, superior of the Oratory, did not suggest that Vincent should join his congregation, for this was clearly not his vocation. But Bérulle had recently been approached by the archbishop of Lyon who was asking for an Oratorian priest to become pastor at Châtillon-les-Dombes in the Bresse region. He suggested this post to Vincent who accepted it immediately. On the pretext of a little trip, he left Paris at the end of July and was officially installed as pastor of Châtillon on August 1, 1617.[6]

This was strange behavior indeed, both for Pierre de Bérulle and for Vincent de Paul. Here Bérulle had recommended Vincent to the Gondis and now he was helping the young priest to escape his duty to the family without even asking their advice or even warning them. As for Vincent, who would later say "[my] rule of conduct was to see Monsieur le Général in God and God in him, and so to obey him, just as [I] obeyed his late lady wife as I would obey the Virgin,"[7] he fled their house without a word of explanation or excuse, deceiving them even about the reason for his absence. What is more, he was still in charge of the parish of Clichy-la-Garenne, where he was regularly attending to his duties. He could have contented himself with returning to his parish, with a request that his teaching duties be reassigned, but he probably feared that he would still be too close to the Gondis, and that they might insist he return. He had a need to mark a voluntary and final break with his former masters by removing himself to the outermost region of the kingdom. Vincent never explained the true cause of this surprising decision.

All of this was taking place at the very moment when the peace of the capital city was troubled by a palace revolution. The regent's favorite, Concini, had been assassinated on April 24. His wife, la Galigaï, was tried and executed on July 8. To what extent were the Gondis, Florentines like Maria de Medici, affected by all the disquiet brought about by this coup d'état? It seems they were clever enough to weather all the resulting tumults and upsets which affected the courtiers. They kept their places and their offices whether ecclesiastical, in the diocese of Paris, or governmental, like the position of General of the Galleys. Since Philippe-Emmanuel de Gondi was in Provence at this time, there is no need to think that the impetus for Vincent's sudden and unexplained departure came from him. We will see what outbursts his disappearance caused.

From the post chaise which took him through Beaune and Mâcon, across the Bresse to his new parish, Vincent discovered the region of Dombes with its ponds, reminiscent of his native Landes. Then he entered a small city, nestled in the hollow of a charming valley, on whose slopes lay forests and fields and vineyards. On a rise stood a fortress, Castellum-Dunbarum, the château of the Dombes. The city was enclosed within ramparts dating to the time when it marked the boundary between Savoy and Burgundy. In the meantime, the county of Bresse had been ceded by the duke of Savoy[8] to the king of France in 1602. The region continued to be under Protestant influence since the marshal de Lesdiguières,[9] one of the chiefs of the Huguenot party, possessed the domain of Pont-de-Veysle, less than sixteen kilometers from Châtillon-les-Dombes, still a center of the reformed religion.

The town of Châtillon had about 2,000 inhabitants, a high proportion of whom had been won over to Protestantism. As for the parish, it had belonged for the last forty years to beneficiaries, the canons of the Church of Saint-Jean at Lyon, who only came there to draw their annual revenue, amounting to 500 livres. The titular pastor of Châtillon, Jean Lourdelot, had resigned his function in April.[10] The instrument of nomination, executed by the archbishop of Lyon, Denis de Marquemont, in favor of "Vincent de Paul, priest, bachelor of theology, of the diocese of d'Ascqs" is dated July 29.[11] In virtue of this, Vincent took "possession and enjoyment of the churches of Saint-Martin of Buenens and of Saint-André, of the above named town of Châtillon." On August 1, Vincent, following the traditional rites, "after opening the great door of the Church of Buenens, sprinkling it with holy water and ringing thrice on its bell, made his prayer at the high altar." He then took part in the same ceremony in the Church of Saint-André.[12]

This ceremony took place in the presence of two curates attached to the parish, Monsieur Souvageon and Monsieur Hugues Rey. Vincent did not find a decadent local clergy here or a desolate parish with an abandoned sanctuary, as most of his biographers have claimed.[13] A report of the pastoral visit of Monseigneur de Marquemont in 1614 bears witness to the healthy condition of the Church of Saint-André in which he distributed communion to 900 communicants and celebrated the sacrament of Confirmation for about three hours. The next year, in 1615, two new chapels were added to this church[14] and a mission preached by an Oratorian father was a robust success.

The rectory, which was reported in good condition in the documentation of the bishop's visit, must have been in the course of rehabilitation, for Vincent was lodging with a leading citizen of the area, Sieur Beynier, whose house stood near the church. Shortly after Vincent's installation in the parish, the curate Souvageon retired and was replaced by a local priest, Louis Girard, doctor of theology, well known for his learning and virtue.[15]

Vincent, supported by his two curates and a few associated priests living at Châtillon, went to work at once. As a team[16] and forming a little family, they gave the example of an ordered life, rising early, regularly attending the Divine Office, visiting the poor and the sick. They spent many an hour in the confessional and their parishioners, attracted by their good reputation, came in growing numbers.

Since the reformed religion was dominant in those parts, Vincent did not seek to attack it in theological controversies. He was satisfied to live by the teaching of the Gospel and the example that shone forth from him soon bore fruit. Among the conversions he achieved, one was heard of throughout the region, namely that of the count of Rougemont, a Savoyard nobleman who had withdrawn to Bugey when the Bresse was ceded to France. Curious about the new pastor of Châtillon, of whom he had heard much talk, he paid him a visit. From the first conversation, he was shaken and soon decided to make Vincent his spiritual director. But the count was to find it most difficult to renounce the practice of dueling. Later, Vincent would tell the story of how his penitent finally decided to fight no more:

I knew a gentleman of Bresse who had been a mercenary soldier. . . . It is hard to believe his tale of how many people he fought, wounded, and killed. Finally, God touched him to such effect that he looked into his own soul and realized how miserable his state was. He resolved to amend his life. One day, on a journey, he asked himself whether he had remained attached to anything in spite of the fact that he thought he had renounced everything. He went over his business affairs, his possessions, his alliances, his reputation. . . . Around and around went his thoughts, until they fell upon his sword. Why are you carrying this, he asked himself. But how can I live without it? What? Do without this cherished sword which has served me well in so many encounters and, next to God, saved me from so many dangers? If I were ever attacked again, I would be lost without it. But I have it. I could fall into some quarrel and not be strong enough to leave it in its scabbard. And what an offense to God that would be. Just then, he found himself near a great boulder. He got down from his horse, took this precious sword and beat with it on the rock, striking this way and that and this! and that! Finally he managed to break it into pieces and went on his way.[17]

This story, naive and unpolished, but lively and colorful, is a good example of the style Vincent would use when speaking to his missionaries or his Daughters of Charity.

The outstanding event of Vincent de Paul's brief stay at Châtillon-les-Dombes was the foundation of the first Confraternity of Charity. This is how he described the order of events thirty years later: "One Sunday, as I was vesting for mass, a messenger came to tell me that in an isolated house about a kilometer from there, everyone was sick, leaving no one strong enough to care for the others, and that all of them were in indescribable need. This touched me deeply."

At the announcements after the sermon, Vincent put out an appeal for help for this family in such vivid terms that the parishioners were also greatly moved. When he came back there in the afternoon, he met many people who were also on the way to that family or who were already coming back from there. "As it was summertime the heat was great, and these good ladies were stopping along the wayside to rest and refresh themselves. Finally . . . there were so many that it looked like a procession." After he had comforted the family himself and brought them communion, he gathered a few people of good will to explore ways to continue offering this kind of help. "I suggested to all these good people whom charity had inspired to visit the sick family that they could tax themselves one day each, to put something into the stew pot, not only for the one family but for those who would follow."[18]

No sooner said than done. On August 23, less than a month after his arrival, Vincent assembled the first eight ladies and presented a draft charter to them. The members of the group would obligate themselves to helping the needy, each on her own day, both in body and in spirit and to cultivating humility, simplicity, and charity in themselves, with great attention. After a three-month trial, Vincent drew up a more detailed rule for this confraternity, whose members would be "servants of the poor or of charity."[19] On December 8, he solemnly placed this rule in the chapel of the old hospice of Châtillon. The document would serve as model for all the charitable groups which soon sprang up throughout the kingdom of France. Thus, Vincent's first foundation was based on the efforts of the laity, women in particular, working co-operatively with the clergy in a task that was both material and spiritual.

Vincent had left Paris without telling anyone but Pierre de Bérulle. Once arrived in Châtillon, he wrote to the General of the Galleys, who was then on a mission in Provence, to excuse himself for having abandoned his post. His pretext was "that he had none of the qualities required of a tutor to a family of such high nobility."[20] But he had been doing this work for four years without suffering from such scruples.

Immediately, the general informed his wife, who was shattered by the news. She sent Vincent a letter expressing her profound disturbance: "The anguish I feel about this is unbearable." She declared that she could not manage without his help and that her husband's need was as great. "Do not reject the good you can do for our spiritual welfare, for one day, it will allow us to work for the salvation of many others." She ended her letter by appealing to his pity: "Remember the anxiety you saw in me in my recent illness, when we were in a village; I am about to fall into a worse state and the very fear of this causes me so much pain that I do not know whether, without the great help I had before, I will survive."[21]

Vincent was not deaf to this heartbreaking appeal but he resisted, sending Madame de Gondi words of encouragement and an "invitation to submit to God's pleasure."[22] At this point, the Gondis called on everyone who might be able to influence Vincent—the bishop of Paris and Charles du Fresne, his close friend. They even had the children write letters. Philippe-Emmanuel de Gondi, in a voice more measured than his wife's, also appealed to him: "I beg you only to consider that it seems as though God wanted the father and the sons to become good people through your intervention."[23] And so Vincent agreed to come to Paris in December to reconsider the situation. Back in the capital on December 23, he met Pierre de Bérulle, who convinced him to re-enter the Gondi household.

While in Châtillon the parishioners were desolate at the sudden departure of their pastor, the Gondis could not hide their satisfaction with this outcome. They did understand, however, that they could no longer confine Vincent to the role of tutor and the family's spiritual adviser. He made them understand the enormous task remaining to be accomplished among poor rural people. In consequence, Madame de Gondi gave him the opportunity to expand his ministry to all the people living on the family's lands in Picardy, Champagne, and Burgundy. All in all, there were about 8,000 souls to evangelize. Vincent accepted this proposal. He immediately submitted his official resignation from the parish of Châtillon on January 31, 1628, to be replaced by his vicar, Louis Girard, a man well prepared to continue the work they had begun together. Vincent retained the title of tutor to the children, but received help in carrying out the work. He now had complete freedom of movement to organize missions and establish charitable groups on the Gondi lands. Vincent would devote himself entirely to this work for seven long years.

The year 1617 was truly a decisive one for Vincent de Paul; a radical transformation took place within him. The ambitious young priest, looking everywhere for benefices and considerations, became a new man who had found his way, inspired by a different, higher ambition. No doubt this was not a sudden transformation but the result of long periods of seeking, groping, and dissatisfaction. But the year 1617 showed him much that brought him back to the path he had chosen. He was constantly confronted with misery, both physical and spiritual. This brought him an interior illumination, an understanding that his personal vocation was to place himself at the service of the poor and the sick where they were most abandoned, in the countryside. He was pierced with a conviction that would be the foundation of his future work—that help for the least favored of society should be both material and spiritual. Christ's message was a signpost to the road he must follow. It is true that he had a long way to go before he could cast off the old man, but now he knew where the road was.

PART TWO

To Serve the Rural Poor

The First Missions
1618–1624

Organization of a Mission
Vincent on the Highways and Byways
Meeting with Francis de Sales
Royal Chaplain of the Galleys
The Beggars of Mâcon
Return to Pouy

From the beginning of his apostolate, Vincent de Paul was a man of action, an organizer and manager. He did not throw himself into a venture in haphazard fashion. Rather, he decided on a program, defined a method, and made sure of acquiring the wherewithal for the project. Working with Madame de Gondi, he settled on the places and dates for the first missions. They decided to start with the parishes of Villepreux near Versailles, Joigny in Burgundy, and Montmirail in Champagne before moving on to villages in Picardy: Folleville, Paillart, and Sérévillers. Then he set forth his method: he would settle into a parish for several weeks, preaching, catechizing, and confessing. On the momentum of this mission, he would be able to found a Charité to give material and spiritual support to the work he had begun. As for the resources, the primary one was a team of priests who would work together during the mission. Vincent called on his connections, on those of the Gondis, and on religious of various orders who were won over by his enthusiasm and his ability to convince.

Money was indispensable for the workers could not live at the expense of the parishes where the missions would be preached. On the contrary, Vincent's workers were the ones who had to come to the aid of the worst misery and bring medicines to comfort the sick. Missions had to be repeated periodically in each parish, but so that the good effects did not die out in the meantime, like a fire made only of straw, a Charité had to be established at the end of each mission to keep the flame burning in people's hearts. Good organizer that he was, Vincent found it necessary to give these Charités a rule to ensure the permanence of the work done so far. His model was the Rule he had drafted for the Charité of Châtillon.

In his Rule, Vincent did not hesitate to go into detail such as the manner in which the servants of the poor should work with the sick. "The lady who is on duty will bring the dinner and carry it to the sick. In approaching them, she will greet them cheerfully and with kindness. She will place the tray comfortably on the bed, cover it with a napkin, set a dish to drink the soup from, a spoon, and some bread, help the patient wash his hands and say grace. She will dip the stew into a bowl and place the meat on a plate, and then she will kindly encourage the patient to eat for the love of Jesus and His holy Mother. She will do all this as though she were caring for her own son, or rather for God, who takes for Himself every good thing she does for the poor." But Vincent went further with his recommendations, specifying the order in which the sick should be served: "One must remember to serve first those who have someone with them and finish with those who are alone, so that one can spend a longer time with them." Finally, he warns that all these material attentions are not an end in themselves: "Since the purpose of this institute is not only to give material sustenance but also spiritual aid, these servants of the poor will take care to lead them by the hand to God."[1] This Rule, which Vincent wrote out in one sitting, is remarkable for its precision and for the fact that it was the fruit of long reflection. He was inspired above all by a great flow of love for the poor, following the very words of Christ: "For what you have done to the least of these, you have done to me."

At the beginning of February 1618, Vincent established himself in the large village of Villepreux with his little band consisting of a doctor of theology, Jean Coqueret, and two counselor-clerks in the parlement of Paris, Berger and Gontière. On a cart drawn by a mule or an ass, they brought some scant furnishings and their own bits and pieces—

whatever they needed to live independently in an empty house which had been placed at their disposal. At first the villagers watched them with curiosity and a little fear, these strangers the pastor had told them about without himself understanding why they had come to the parish. What they saw was the newcomers going up and down the streets, to the most out of the way places, to announce the meetings at which they would preach.

The missionaries began by teaching the children the catechism and hymns to sing at services. The villagers overcame their mistrust and crept forward timidly. Soon they were filling the church. The atmosphere warmed gradually; people moved from being spectators to being participants. At the end of the mission, three weeks later, everyone thronged to the confessionals to prepare for the closing ceremonies where they would approach the Communion table. In the afternoon of February 23, Vincent gathered in a chapel the women and girls who had declared themselves willing to constitute the Charité of Villepreux. Once more, he explained to them at length what it was they were promising to do: they were putting themselves at the service of the poor, and through the poor, at the service of Christ. In language full of images, emphasized by gestures that underlined the most important part of his talk, he captivated them and found words that moved and shook them. He radiated so much warmth and conviction that they all volunteered for this battle against misery that he was proposing.

After Villepreux, Vincent left to hold a mission at Joigny and in the surroundings of this city, especially at Villecien and Paroy-sur-Tholon.[2] With the urging of Madame de Gondi, the ladies of Joigny rallied to the number of forty under the banner of the Confraternity of Charity, which was founded on September 6.[3] To finance this Charité, Madame de Gondi, in her position as the countess of Joigny, offered the proceeds of the tolls levied on the sailors who passed under the bridge of the city on Sundays and feast days. At Villecien, Vincent found himself among acquaintances since the lord of the region was Nicolas Hennequin du Fay, whom he must have met at the house of his cousin, Alexandre Hennequin, while he was pastor of Clichy-la-Garenne. In particular, he renewed his acquaintance with Mademoiselle du Fay, who was to become one of the great benefactors of his work.

Without time for a rest, in this same year of 1618, Vincent and his team went to Montmirail in Champagne, where they immediately began a mission. A Charité was founded there on October 6. It would work not only with the poor sick but also with prisoners. At the same time that the constitution of the Confraternity of Charity was established, his financing was put on a firm footing by the bishop of Soissons, who was the diocesan for Montmirail and the neighboring parishes. He authorized "the persons of the aforementioned association to seek funds on Sundays and holidays in the parishes of Montmirail and other localities in dependency on the said lady countess."[4]

It is remarkable that in the beginning these charitable confraternities or associations were exclusively the work of women. The only authorized masculine presence was that of a procurator, whose duty it was to control financial affairs. As Vincent said, "it was not appropriate for women to have the sole disposal of these matters."[5]

Vincent was a precursor. At a time when women were restricted to the role of mistress of the house and mother, carefully kept away from any external responsibility, when they had to be satisfied with being docile companions of their men, their lords and masters, at a time when even the Church only tolerated them in strict monastic cloisters, Vincent assigned an outstanding role to them—to represent this Church, and beyond that, all of society, in the presence of the unfortunate and excluded.

It was with women that Vincent de Paul accomplished the essential aspects of his works of charity; it was largely thanks to them that he would find the financial means to succeed in his labors. His first collaborator was Madame de Gondi, who supplied the necessary funds to launch his first missions and the support for his early Charités.

At the end of 1618, Vincent de Paul experienced an encounter which would mark his character and spirituality profoundly. Without a doubt, Pierre de Bérulle had played a decisive role in the direction the young priest took when he was freshly arrived in Paris, in quest of a good position in life. In those days, Vincent needed a master who would show him the way to go and who made him aware of the nobility and the demands of the priestly calling. But Bérulle was too much an intellectual and an authoritarian figure to be Vincent's sole confidant forever. Although Bérulle was a man of action, both in the Church and in politics, his thoughts moved increasingly toward the elaboration of a theology permeated with mysticism. With Jesus Christ at the center of the universe, his spirituality revolved entirely about the Incarnation, thus becoming a "theology of contemplation."[6] At the same time Vincent, profoundly affected by his experience in Folleville and Châtillon and moved by his discovery of human misery, was turning in another direction, toward a spirituality of action.

Vincent made himself independent and found his own road, but he remained personally attached to Bérulle. For instance, it was at the home of Bérulle that he first came into the presence of that man of God, Francis de Sales.[7] This bishop of Geneva was in France in the company of the cardinal of Savoy, who had come to negotiate the marriage of the prince of Piedmont, Victor-Amadeo, to the sister of Louis XIII, Christine de France. The delegation remained in the capital for an entire year to finalize the delicate arrangements of which such a royal union is made. Francis de Sales was not only a great prelate and doctor of the Church but enjoyed a reputation as a preacher who could convert Calvinists and a writer of widely known works such as his *Introduction to the Devout Life,* published in 1608, and his *Treatise on the Love of God,* newly published in 1616. At the age of fifty-five, he was at the peak of his career; his fame and his influence drew everyone who was anyone in the capital city.

The presence in Paris of the diplomatic delegation provided a good pretext for banquets and receptions at court and in the mansions of the great. It is probable that Vincent was present at some of these festivities in the wake of the Gondis and of Bérulle. He had already read and absorbed the writings of Francis de Sales. Certainly he was eager to make his acquaintance and to be able to speak with him. But what a gulf lay between this great prince of the Church, descended from an ancient noble family of Savoy, and the little priest from a peasant family of the Landes! One can imagine the richly decorated salons with their press of high dignitaries and noble ladies, and Francis de Sales observing the crowd, catching the glance of the young priest in his simple cassock. That glance must have been so full of magnetism that the bishop was moved to ask someone who this was, and then to ask to speak with him. From their first conversation, a spark flew between these two souls so different and with so much in common.

At a time when brutality and ignorance reigned and pitiless religious wars still raged, Francis de Sales preached mercy and brotherly charity. In the Calvinist territory of Geneva, he was notable for his mildness and humility. An aura of peace and interior joy surrounded him. As for Vincent, he had already come a long way, taming the demons of doubt of his early days in Paris and mastering the temptations of the flesh. He still had to conquer the Gascon temper that carried him away or burrowed deep in his periods of black depression and mastered him completely. Francis de Sales helped him discover the secret of joy and serenity, fruits of the imitation of Christ, won by practicing goodness and humility.

Testifying ten years later at the beatification process of Francis de Sales, Vincent declared: "I was often honored by close association with him. . . . I came to see in him the man who best bodied forth for me the Son of God on earth . . . his sweetness and goodness poured out upon all those fortunate enough to be in his company, and I was one of them."[8]

At another time, Vincent recounted the lesson in humility that Francis de Sales taught him. Francis had been invited to preach in the Church of the Oratory on St. Martin's Day. The court was invited to hear this sermon and the crowd was so thick that the bishop of Geneva was obliged to climb a ladder and mount to the pulpit through a window.

"Everyone," writes Vincent, "was expecting an oration, a full display of the genius by which he regularly ravished his hearers. But with the intention of presenting himself humbly before all those illustrious figures he restricted himself to a flat recital of the life of St. Martin. And he heard someone among those present exclaim: 'Just look at this lout, this mountain man. See his coarse preaching style. We really needed him to come all this way to tell us what he's telling us and to try our patience.'"[9] We can be sure that this example of humility had a striking effect on Vincent who, ever afterward, never refused an opportunity to make himself small.

How many conversations did Vincent have with Francis de Sales, either in a small group or alone with him, while the bishop remained in the capital in the year from October 1618 to October 1619? We do not know exactly; their meetings could not have been frequent since neither man had much leisure. But it is certain that these encounters had a decisive effect on Vincent's life. He had already met many prelates cloaked in their dignity or learned theologians barricaded behind their science, but here for the first time he was face to face with the very image of what he called the Son of God on earth. He would be marked forever by the virtue of Francis de Sales, his mild nature, his goodness, and his humble demeanor, and strive with all his might to conform to this model. His life was influenced by members of the bishop's circle as well; during their meetings, Vincent had the opportunity to make the acquaintance of others admitted to the intimate company of Francis de Sales, and who would become his own close companions, such as Madame de Lamoignon, Louise de Marillac, and Jeanne de Chantal.[10]

Jeanne de Chantal was the widow of the baron de Chantal. She had chosen Francis de Sales as her spiritual director, and he had decided to found with her the Order of the Visitandines. The first house of this order was opened in 1610 at Annecy. During his visit to Paris, the bishop of Geneva invited her to found a house of her order there, which she did in April 1619. The first house was a modest one in the faubourg Saint-Jacques but later, it was moved to the right bank, in the Petit-Bourbon palace.

Francis de Sales explained to Vincent that his first intention had been to found a congregation of contemplative nuns who would, however, live in the world and visit the poor and the sick. Because of their mission, they were placed under the patronage of the Visitation.[11] The opposition of the archbishop of Lyon had forced him to modify his plan and found an order of cloistered nuns, but he remained convinced of the relevance of his first instinct, and he was sure that one day his idea would be revived. Thus Vincent was confirmed in his intention, still unarticulated, to found a congregation of Sisters of Charity, following the spirit of the Confraternity of Charity.

A superior had to be designated to supervise the new house of the Visitandines in Paris. According to their rule, the bishop of the diocese was to fulfill this function, and he was permitted to delegate the duties to one of his priests. The first priest designated was not Vincent de Paul as is so often written, but Charles de la Saussaye,[12] pastor of the Church of Saint-Jacques in Paris. He died in 1621, shortly after having been appointed. There were only too many possible successors for Francis de Sales to propose to the bishop of Paris from among distinguished clergymen or eminent religious whom he had met during his stay in Paris. With the agreement of Jeanne de Chantal, it was Vincent de Paul who was presented for the bishop's approval and confirmed in this position at the beginning of 1622. This was an irrefutable proof of the esteem in which Francis de Sales held the modest priest. He had been able to discern, behind the still rustic exterior of a peasant of the Landes, exceptional qualities of mind and heart.

While Vincent was dividing his time between missions on the estates of the Gondis and his visits to Paris, during which he conversed with

Francis de Sales, a royal edict was published which opened for him a new arena of charitable work. By a decision of the king dated February 8, 1619, he was officially given the office of royal chaplain of the galleys. "Because his lordship, count of Joigny, General of the Galleys of France, has represented to His Majesty that it is necessary for the good and comfort of the convicts who are now and will in the future be in the galleys, to designate a priest of known probity and qualification and charge him with the post of royal chaplain . . . His Majesty has awarded this office to Monsieur Vincent de Paul, priest, bachelor of theology."[13]

As a result of his position in the service of the General of the Galleys, Vincent had been able to visit the convicts. They were held in hideous prisons, particularly the Conciergerie, squatting in their chains. He was deeply shaken by the way in which these men, condemned to forced labor, were packed into cold, damp holes, without light or air, subject to the whims of jailers who treated them like cattle. The sight of them must have brought back stinging memories, which he never allowed himself to mention, of his own captivity on the Barbary Coast. The unfortunate slave laborer was chained by a ring riveted around his neck to posts fixed in the ground. He could neither sit nor stand. A priest passing among these men provoked only scatological outcries and hate-filled glares. Vincent went about among these beings, men almost naked, hunched in rotting, verminous straw, surrounded by a pestilential stench, and he gained direct knowledge of their bodily misery and moral despair. Moved by this experience, he decided to speak of the matter to the General of the Galleys, requesting the authorization to try to improve the lot of those whose health was most in danger. These were moved into a rented house near the Church of Saint-Roche, which was transformed into the Saint-Roche prison.[14] But money was needed for this work. Vincent spoke of it to Cardinal de Retz, whom he saw regularly at the Gondi palace, in the hope of interesting him in this charitable effort. In a pastoral letter dated June 1618, the cardinal enjoined his clergy to commend the lot of these pitiful creatures to their parishioners. Soon the donations began to arrive and visits were organized in which devout women came and cared for the ill. Vincent himself, with the help of his faithful Antoine Portail, brought them spiritual comfort.

Vincent's work was reported to the king; it inspired creation of the office of royal chaplain, the holder of which had authority over all the chaplains assigned to the galleys. As soon as he was confirmed in this new position, Vincent went to Marseilles, where he saw equally lamentable conditions on board the ships. He took the liberty of reproaching the guards and the officers on board for this situation. Forgetting for a moment all the exhortations to mildness he had received from Francis de Sales, he emitted what can only be called a bellow. He called for the construction of a hospital where the galley slaves could be tended, a project slow to be accomplished because of the lack of funds.[15]

The title of royal chaplain did not distract Vincent from what always remained the center of his concern, his mission to the rural poor. In September and October 1620, he was at Folleville again, then at Paillart and Sérévillers, two large neighboring villages on Gondi lands in Picardy. In those places, he founded separate Charités for men and women.[16]

In the same year, while he was conducting a mission at Montmirail, he had dealings with a so-called heretic. Later, Vincent told his missionaries about the objections this Huguenot made to attempts at converting him. "You told me that the Church of Rome is a conduit for the Holy Spirit, but that is what I cannot believe, because on the one hand, we see the Catholics in the countryside abandoned to vicious and ignorant leaders, and on the other, we see the cities full of priests and monks who are doing nothing. There are perhaps ten thousand of them in Paris while they abandon these poor people in the fields to the horrifying ignorance in which they are damned." Vincent tried to answer him, but the heretic was not convinced. Struck by his own failure, Vincent came back the next year with a team of clergy, friends of his from Paris, to preach another mission at Montmirail and neighboring villages. Out of curiosity, this same heretic came to hear the preaching and teaching. Touched by the zeal of these missionaries, he sought out Vincent to tell him that he was convinced now, and ready to allow himself to be converted, which, in fact he did.[17]

Vincent was not required to limit his charitable work to the missions preached on the Gondi domains, since in February 1621, the superior general of the Order of Friars Minim granted him letters of association in sign of his gratitude for services rendered to his order.[18]

In the course of his missionary work in the spring of 1621, Vincent returned to Joigny, where he established a Charité made up of men, women, and girls, in which the men cared for the healthy as well as the disabled and the women worked only with the sick. This was the first experiment with a mixed Charité. Vincent was careful to point out that "Our Lord is glorified no less by the ministry of women than by the ministry of men." The Rule of this Charité, published on May 8, 1621, provides for everything in detail, and in particular for finances: "The expenses of this work of mercy will be supported by 500 royal livres, which Monseigneur the duke de Joigny will provide every year, by eighty measures of wheat which Monseigneur the prior of Joigny will also provide every year, and by whatever reserve there is from the Hôtel-Dieu of that city."[19] Vincent never founded a new Charité without assuring that it would have the means to survive.

At the beginning of September, Vincent found himself near his old parish of Châtillon-les-Dombes, which he perhaps went to visit. He took this opportunity, according to his usual habit, to found Charités in neighboring villages, particularly at Trévoud on the Saône. At Mâcon, he was struck by the large number of beggars loitering in the streets and under the porches of churches. He heard that a good canon, Nicolas Chandon by name, dean of the cathedral there, had founded a charitable institution ten years earlier, l'Aumône, intended to give comfort to the poor and the sick. But this drew all the vagabonds of the region, the beggars and the penniless, who came there and harassed the passers-by.

After informing himself and talking things over with Canon Chandon, Vincent, who had been planning to stop at Mâcon for a few days in any case, offered some solutions to the problem of the beggars. The first reaction was unbelieving mockery: "When I established the Charité of Mâcon everyone laughed at me and pointed a finger," he wrote later to Louise de Marillac.[20] But Vincent was undeterred. He managed to persuade a large enough group of people so that an extraordinary meeting of the city council was called on September 16. The minutes of the meeting show that "a cleric, the priest of Monsieur the General of the Galleys, wanted to found a charitable organization to see to the comforting and feeding of the poor." On the next day, September 17, the assembly met again and gave official approval to a Christian Charité conducted according to the rules proposed by Vincent. First of all, this crowd of poor people, numbering as many as 300, had to be counted. Then an endowment had to be raised, which would make it possible to provide them with regular help. The money would come from the clergy and the well-to-do inhabitants and from the income from certain fines as well as from collections taken up every Sunday.

Then Vincent established a rule which was to be strictly maintained. Every Sunday after mass, the people would give to the poor bread and money in proportion to the extent of their misery and the number of children they had, on condition that for the rest of the week they would not beg, under pain of losing their alms. But Vincent did not want to be taken in by professional beggars and so he went on to specify that so as not to encourage laziness among the healthy poor, they would be given only the necessary supplement to their modest wage. The measure was effective; the village was cleansed of the beggars who had been harassing passers-by. When he left Mâcon, at the end of three weeks, having established a Charité composed of men and women both, he had to do so secretly, to avoid the honors prepared for him by the aldermen of the city and the acclaim of the populace.[21]

Faced with a specific problem, Vincent had immediately devised an appropriate solution in collaboration with Canon Chandon and the local authorities. Whereas at his arrival he had figured as an unknown, spoken of as the self-styled chaplain of Monsieur the General of the Galleys, he now enjoyed the support of all. This was a convincing demonstration of his charisma and his talent as an organizer.

In the years after 1617, the situation in France changed considerably. Young King Louis XIII, free of the guardianship of Concini, took as counselor his friend Charles d'Albert, and soon raised him to the rank of duke de Luynes. But the Queen Mother, Maria de Medici, in her fury at having been displaced from power, set out to whip up a rebellion of the nobles. She escaped from house arrest at Blois and mounted a campaign against the royal army. Her troops were defeated in a brief encounter at the Ponts-de-Cé. Finally, the skillful intervention of the bishop of Luçon, the future Cardinal de Richelieu, brought about a reconciliation between Louis XIII and his mother in March 1619.

But then the king was obliged to march with his army to the city of Pau to subdue the people of the Béarn, who had risen up in protest against a royal decision ordering the restitution of the property of clergy in this province, the oldest Huguenot domain.[22] The entry of the king into the capital of the Béarn and the re-establishment of Catholic worship, decreed in 1620, unleashed the Protestant party, which called a general assembly of Huguenots at La Rochelle. The religious wars were blazing again.

Louis XIII ordered the dissolution of the Assembly of La Rochelle, but the Protestants refused to obey this royal injunction. This was the beginning of a seven-year siege of the Protestant stronghold by land and by sea until its surrender in 1628. As part of the operation,

Philippe-Emmanuel de Gondi brought ten of his ships to Bordeaux in June 1622 to take part in an attack mounted by the duke de Guise, commandant of the royal fleet. In October, Gondi took part in battles in which the fleet of La Rochelle was partially destroyed. An armistice was signed that held for three years.

The galleys spent the winter at Tonnay-Charente near Rochefort and in the estuary of the Gironde, off Bordeaux, before returning to their home port at Marseilles. On this occasion, Vincent, in his role of royal chaplain, visited the galleys and preached a mission to the men, probably in the first months of 1623.[23] Since he was near the Landes, where he was born, he went to visit his family, whom he had not seen for twenty years.

During a conference he gave to his missionaries many years later, Vincent recalled this visit to his birthplace. He had hesitated to make the journey and before leaving Paris, he had asked two of his friends for advice: "Gentlemen, my work is about to take me near the place where I was born; I don't know whether it would be a good idea to stop by home." When they encouraged him, he decided to continue from Bordeaux to Pouy, where he was put up by a relative who was pastor of the village. He had a reunion with his brothers and sisters, met his nephews, and visited the scenes of his childhood with much emotion. People made much of him; his success and his titles impressed the family. No doubt, they expected to profit from them. But at the same time, these eight or ten days spent at Pouy were a trial for him, torn as he was between the joy of seeing his people and his duty to "dampen their desire to benefit from my prosperity, to the point of telling them not to expect anything and that even if I had chests full of gold and silver, I would give then nothing, because a priest, if he has anything, owes it to God and the poor." Vincent admitted that the departure was painful for him: "The day I left, I was so sad to be leaving my family that I cried the whole way."[24] This wish to sever all the ties that still bound him to his family and to material things marks a new stage in Vincent's inner journey. Until that moment, he had been collecting various offices and benefices without ever relinquishing one, it seems, except for that unfortunate abbey of Saint-Léonard-de-Chaume, which had brought him much turmoil. In addition to his duties for the Gondis and his recent appointment as royal chaplain of the galleys, he had kept the parish of Clichy-la-Garenne. Did he still hold the parish of Gamaches and the canonry of Écouis? Without documents, we cannot say. The revenues from these benefices had allowed him to help his family which was only fair, since they had made serious sacrifices so that he could maintain his studies.[25]

But in February 1624, in apparent contradiction of his resolve to distance himself from the goods of this world, Vincent accepted the benefice of the priory of Saint-Nicolas-de-Grosse-Sauve. The notarized document by which he gave authority to a certain Monsieur Pierre Mauferet to take possession "of the aforementioned priory, just as the aforementioned owner would do if he were present there in person," specifies that it was a matter of a decision of His Holiness, and that this priory, of the Order of St. Augustine, was located in the diocese of Langres.[26] Unfortunately for Vincent, Rome did not know that this priory had already been granted in June 1623 to the Congregation of the Oratory by the bishop of Langres, Monseigneur Sébastien Zamet. The situation was complicated by the fact that the decision of the bishop of Langres was in its turn contested by the canons of Saint-Mamès, who considered themselves solely empowered to collate this benefice. The matter was brought to court, and Vincent found himself indirectly involved in a trial which was to last for three years. In the end, the Oratorians, supported by Zamet, won the case. No doubt Vincent would have been happy to avoid a conflict of interests with Pierre de Bérulle, since his relations with his former confessor seemed to be crumbling. As for the loss of this benefice, it no longer seems important when we learn that one month later, on March 1, 1624, Vincent would receive responsibility for a secondary school with its buildings and grounds, the first stage in the foundation of the Congregation of the Mission.

Foundation of the Congregation of the Mission 1624–1632

The Collège des Bons-Enfants
Foundation of the Mission
Recognition of the Congregation by Rome
Louise de Marillac
The Party of the Devout

At the beginning of the year 1624, Vincent de Paul did not suspect that he was very close to achieving what he had not dared to wish for, the foundation of his own congregation. For the moment, he was engaged in careful self-questioning about what he ought to do. He was suspicious of the enthusiastic outbursts characteristic of his Gascon temperament and wanted to be sure that the path he chose obeyed the will of God. We know what the state of his soul was at the time from a letter written many years later to one of his missionaries,: "Keep in mind that you and I are subject to a thousand impulses of nature, and remember what I told you about my state of mind when I was beginning to plan the Mission. I was continually preoccupied with it, until I began to suspect that the whole thing was coming from my nature or a troublesome spirit. So I made a retreat at Soissons, in the hope that it would please God to cleanse my spirit of the pleasure and eagerness this project stirred up in me."[1]

It was becoming more and more difficult for Vincent to find priests who were willing to go to the countryside with him on his missions. On the other hand, Madame de Gondi was enthusiastic about what Vincent was achieving by preaching on her lands and wanted him to do this at regular intervals. She asked him to find a congregation which would be willing to take over the work. But the orders he approached, especially the Oratorians and the Jesuits, gave no reply. Since they were already conducting missions in their own styles, they had no desire to collaborate with Vincent. It was at this moment that the Gondis, after consulting the archbishop of Paris, suggested to Vincent that he should found his own, whose work would be to preach missions in the countryside. They were anticipating his fondest wish. In order to reach a final decision, he made a retreat at Soissons.

After the retreat, Vincent was assured that he was conforming to the divine will, and matters fell into place very quickly. Madame de Gondi, already ill and moved by her sense that she would die soon, hoped intensely that the work of foundation would be accomplished swiftly. The first need was for a house that could shelter the members of the new congregation. The Collège des Bons-Enfants[2] near the gate of Saint Victor was all but empty. It came under the authority of the archbishop of Paris, who agreed to put it at Vincent's disposal. The principal of this establishment, Louis de Guyart, a doctor of theology, willingly gave up his position in exchange for the payment of an annual rent of 200 livres. The letters naming Vincent de Paul principal of the Collège des Bons-Enfants were signed on March 1, 1624, and Antoine de Portail, Vincent's faithful helper, immediately took possession of the buildings and grounds.

The documents drawn up on this occasion specify that Vincent was not only a bachelor of theology but also licentiate in canon law.[3] When had he earned this title? Perhaps during his first years in the capital his duties as chaplain of Queen Marguerite of Valois left him time to attend courses at the university. Or perhaps he had only received it the year before, judging by the fact that he never used this title before March 1624.

One year later, on April 15, 1625, the Gondis signed the charter of foundation of the Congregation of the Mission[4] at their palace in the rue Pavée, parish of Saint-Sauveur. The provisions of this instrument make it clear that the main activity of the Mission would be to bring spiritual comfort to "the neglected, abandoned rural poor." To remedy their misery was the purpose of founding "the pious association of a few priests . . . who were willing to renounce all benefices, high offices, and dignities of the Church . . . in order to apply themselves entirely and vigorously to the salvation of the poor, at the pleasure of the bishops, each in his own diocese, going from village to village and living from their common fund, and bringing this help as well to those condemned to forced labor." To this end, the Gondis deeded the sum of 45,000 livres to Vincent de Paul, who was to choose six priests to work under his direction. The document lists details of administration of the funds, the interval and duration of the missions, and a concrete definition of what the Congregation of the Mission would be. Vincent's style is recognizable in this document, and so is his careful attention to proper organization and implementation.

Only two months after this contract was signed, on June 23, Françoise-Marguerite de Silly, wife of Philippe-Emmanuel de Gondi, departed this life. She died in peaceful satisfaction, having played her part in the foundation of the Congregation of the Mission. As he had promised, Vincent was with her until she died. But she wanted more; as one of her last wishes, she expressed the hope that Vincent would remain in her family. But this was hardly possible for the responsible superior of a community in the process of being formed. The General of the Galleys understood this and gave Vincent his freedom, so that he could take up residence at the Collège des Bons-Enfants.[5]

Philippe-Emmanuel, suffering profoundly at the loss of his wife, resigned from his duties in favor of his oldest son, Pierre de Gondi, who was already his second in commanding the galleys. The youngest son, Jean-François Paul, about twelve years old at the time, was placed in the Jesuit school at Clermont, where he was a brilliant student although prideful and dissipated in behavior. Once free of all ties, Philippe-Emmanuel decided to withdraw from the world. He asked for admission into the Congregation of the Mission, but Vincent wisely suggested the Oratory, which the widower entered in April 1627.[6]

Vincent de Paul was forty-four years old when he founded the Congregation of the Mission. We do not have a portrait of him at the time, but Abelly, who already knew him then, gives a vivid idea of his appearance. He describes Vincent as being "of medium size, well proportioned, with a broad, rather large head that was well made and proportioned to the rest of his body. His forehead was broad and majestic, his face neither too full nor too thin. His glance was mild, his vision penetrating, his hearing sensitive. His deportment was grave and his gravity was kindly." Abelly goes on to say that "his countenance was simple and naïve."[7] This adjective must be taken in its old sense, still current in the seventeenth century, to mean natural, without artifice, spontaneous. And we have reason to believe that the affable impression Vincent made was accompanied by a discreet charm, to which most women were particularly responsive.

The beginnings of the congregation were very modest. The buildings of the Collège des Bons-Enfants, which dated from the thirteenth century, were in very bad condition in spite of recent repairs. They stood near the ancient fortifications of Philippe-Auguste, next to the gate of Saint-Victor. Of the three groups of buildings arranged around a little interior courtyard, one was unoccupied because it stood on the brink of ruin. One of Vincent's first actions as principal of the college was to inform the provost of the merchants of Paris that "the buildings of the said college are as good as ruins, because of their great age" and to ask him for the help of two master masons so that they could determine which work should be done most urgently.[8]

When Vincent went out on a mission with his companions, he left the empty college in the care of neighbors: "Monsieur Portail and I took with us a good priest to whom we gave 50 écus a year. The three of us set out together to preach and conduct missions from village to village. When we left, we would give the key to one of the neighbors or we might ask them to sleep in the house overnight."[9]

On April 24, 1626, the archbishop of Paris, Jean-François de Gondi, gave official approval to the work undertaken by "our very dear brother Philippe-Emmanuel de Gondi . . . and by our dear sister, Dame Françoise-Marguerite de Silly . . . and a few priests who devote themselves to catechizing, preaching, and hearing general confessions for the poor people of the fields." These few priests only numbered four when they signed an instrument of association on September 4, in the presence of notaries and recorders of the king at the Châtelet of Paris.[10] On the same day, Vincent deeded to his family all of his earthly goods, which derived from the inheritance from his father, and he made official the gifts he had given earlier to his brothers and sisters.[11] He relinquished the parish of Clichy-la-Garenne at the same time.[12] As for his other benefices, it is probable that he no longer held them at this time, but the relevant documents have disappeared. Having cut all the ties that still held him, Vincent, freed of his last worldly attachments, was ready to dedicate himself to his work, body and soul. And this is what he would do for the thirty-four years of life that remained to him.

First, he had to wage a long battle to achieve recognition for his congregation. It was not so difficult to obtain approval for the creation of the Mission from the archbishop of Paris, who was a Gondi. The next year, in March 1627, he even received letters patent, signed by Louis XIII, approving the Congregation of the Mission and authorizing its members to live "in such places of our kingdom as they wish, where I authorize them to receive all gifts and alms."[13] Thus Vincent was able to draw up immediately an act of association between the Collège des Bons-Enfants, which he had held in his own name up to then, and the Congregation of the Mission, which now became its owner.

There remained the task of obtaining from the Holy See official recognition of the congregation, and this seemed to be a simple formality, considering the royal approbation which had already been granted. In June 1628, Louis XIII sent a letter to Pope Urban VIII, asking him to raise the Mission to the status of a congregation, so that it could grow and survive into the future. At the same time, the king wrote to his ambassador in Rome, Monsieur de Béthune, requesting him to perform "all the actions necessary to bring the matter to a satisfactory conclusion as a thing which concerns the glory and service of God and the consolation of my poor subjects."[14]

Vincent had neglected nothing which could contribute to the success of his request, which he addressed to the pope in June 1628,[15] and the Gondis had exerted all their influence in his behalf. But the decision of the Congregation for the Propagation of the Faith, which arrived two months later on August 22, was negative.

At Rome it was felt that an increase in the number of congregations would weaken the resources of the secular clergy by monopolizing benefices, and that these congregations would more or less escape the authority of the pope. Why found a new congregation whose sole purpose it was to preach missions, since this would be self-limiting: if the missions were successful, the need for this congregation would disappear of itself. Therefore, the Holy See only agreed to the formation of a society of twenty to twenty-five priests which would be neither a congregation nor a confraternity. This society would limit its missionary work to the territory of France, under the authority of diocesan bishops.[16]

Other hostile reactions to this project of Vincent de Paul would surface, some discreetly and others quite openly. Pierre de Bérulle, for instance, who had been made cardinal in 1627, did not see this undertaking of his former pupil with a favorable eye. The Oratory had added to its goals the project of preaching missions throughout the kingdom, and twenty houses of this congregation had already been founded in France. Bérulle felt that Vincent's project duplicated his own missionary work. In November, he sent a letter to his representative in Rome, Father Bertin, expressing his hostility to the plan which was still being supported in Rome in spite of the negative decision of the Congregation for the Propagation of the Faith: "The designs which you attribute to those who favor this matter of the missions seem so indirect that they must be viewed with suspicion. We will be obliged to depart from the restraint and simplicity which I consider appropriate in conducting the Lord's business, if everyone acts in this way." He asked Father Bertin to urge the ambassador of France to make this point at the Holy See.[17] However, it came to pass that the cardinal died in October 1629, and his successor, Father Bourgoing, did not pursue this campaign against the Mission.

Another source of opposition, this one quite open, appeared shortly thereafter, and this came from the spokesman of a council of priests of the capital. In the name of the priests of the city and suburbs of Paris he spoke against the letters patent by which the king had approved the Mission. This attitude was essentially motivated by considerations of material interest: "For although all such congregations are initially, and at their first foundation, very pure and based on exceptional piety, it happens that in the course of the years, ambition and greed change them entirely. Then, when there are then many of them, either in the little towns or in the villages, they will want to share the income of the parishes and they will say that since they serve at the same church, they should be compensated from its revenues."[18]

Vincent had foreseen clearly that such reactions could arise among the secular clergy. Therefore he had inserted into the contract of foundation a clause that the missionaries were to renounce all benefices and offices and that in the course of their missions, they were to accept "no recompense of any kind or manner whatever." The action of the priests of Paris had no effect on the parlement which, in its session of April 4, 1631, entered into the record the letters patent of the king, in favor of the priests of the Mission.

The opposition of the Congregation for the Propagation of the Faith did not discourage Vincent. His stay in Rome in the household of Monseigneur Montorio had acquainted him with the mysterious ways of the Holy See. He knew he had to be patient and skillful in manipulating the influence of various cardinals; sometimes, he understood, one even had to wait for a new holder of the office. In May 1631, he sent to Rome one of his first missionaries, François de Coudray, to advance the cause. In a letter, Vincent instructed him once more in the strategy to follow: "You should make it clear that the poor are going to their own damnation because they do not know the things that are necessary to salvation and because they do not make their confessions. If His Holiness knew of this great need, he would not rest until he had done everything possible to make order of this situation." Vincent added to this letter a memorandum which had been approved by Monsieur Duval, doctor of the Sorbonne, who had become his spiritual director on the death of Bérulle. Advised not to change a single word, Vincent exclaimed in his direct way: "So much for words, it is the substance that must remain unchanged."[19] Finally, thanks to the persistent work of François du Coudray, Pope Urban VIII announced official recognition of the Congregation of the Mission by signing the bull *Salvatori Nostri* on January 12, 1633.

For many years, this recognition of the Congregation by Rome had occupied the thoughts of the man whom from now on most people would call Monsieur Vincent. He nevertheless continued to preach actively and to recruit new members. In the course of the first six years, when the priests numbered only seven, they took 140 missions to the villages. By 1631, the Congregation had twenty-six members, fourteen of whom were priests.[20]

As he continued to direct many missions himself, Vincent came to understand the serious problem of insufficient preparation of the clergy. In country parishes, he often encountered priests who had received no instruction and who were incapable of exercising valid ministry, not to mention those who were leading a life unworthy of their priestly estate, living in concubinage, surrendering to drink, slumbering in laziness. It is true that the Council of Trent in the previous century had mandated the opening of seminaries, but this directive had not yet been fully carried out by the Church in France. Bérulle's Oratory had opened a seminary in Paris in 1612, and others in Rouen and elsewhere.

In 1620, Monsieur Bourdoise,[21] pastor of Saint-Nicolas-du-Chardonnet, had organized a seminary in his parish, before attempting to extend his efforts to the provinces. But attempts of this kind were still limited, and they were directed toward the formation of urban clergy. Many dioceses had opened seminaries, but without notable success. They recruited boys at the age of twelve for a course of study that led to the priesthood at the age of twenty-four, but candidates rejected this long preparation and dropped out along the way.

Vincent discussed the matter with the bishop of Beauvais, Augustin Potier,[22] himself concerned with the formation of clergy for his own diocese. They came to the idea of organizing retreats of two or three weeks for the ordinands, and Vincent found himself at Beauvais in September 1628 for the opening of the first retreat of this kind. From the tone of a letter he sent from this village to François du Coudray, at the head of the Collège des Bons-Enfants during Vincent's absence, we see how happy Vincent was now that he had found his way and walked along it full of joy: "How does the Company fare? Is everyone in good humor? Are they all of good cheer?" The letter ends on a friendly note: "Farewell, my dear young Father."[23]

When Vincent returned from preaching a retreat or working at a mission, he found a climate of inner peace in his house. Having relinquished any work in the cities by the articles of foundation, he lived a retired life in Paris with his companions. He described it in these terms in a letter: "In Paris, we live a life that is almost as solitary as the life of a Carthusian, since we do not catechize or preach or hear confessions in the city. Almost no one has any business with us, nor do we have business with anyone. This solitude makes us long for the work of the villages, and that work makes us long for solitude."[24]

The calm and solitude would not last. The archbishop of Paris, Monseigneur de Gondi, was interested in the retreats organized for ordinands in Beauvais. He declared that all those who were preparing to receive the sacrament of Holy Orders in his diocese would first have to make a retreat with Monsieur Vincent. Thus, beginning in 1632, the Collège des Bons-Enfants would receive from sixty to eighty retreatants before every ordination—a heavy responsibility for the young congregation.

Just as death was coming to Madame de Gondi—the woman who had brought Vincent so much anxiety with her everlasting worries and her ungovernable need to be reassured by her confessor, but who, on the other hand, had supported him so generously in his work of the missions—another tormented soul took her place in Vincent's life: Louise de Marillac.[25] She belonged to a great family which had supplied the State with diplomats and financiers. But her illegitimate birth— she was the natural daughter of Louis de Marillac, who had recognized her—marked her profoundly. At the death of her father, she was only thirteen years old and had been more or less rejected by the Marillac family. She would have liked to enter a convent of Capuchin nuns, an order which had just established a house in Paris, where women led an ascetic life of ardent piety, but she was advised against choosing this path, which people felt was too harsh for her weak constitution. She was guided toward a marriage of reason, and so she married a junior official of the royal court, Antoine Le Gras, a respectable member of the petty nobility. After a long illness, he left her a widow at the age of thirty-four with sparse means and a son, Michel, who would be a torment to her for the rest of her life.

Her spiritual director, Jean-Pierre Camus,[26] friend of Francis de Sales, led her with mildness and kindliness, helping her to overcome a serious attack of neurasthenia during the last illness of her husband. When he was named bishop of Belley, Camus left the capital and advised Louise to place herself in the care of Monsieur Vincent. She had already met him at the home of the Hennequin family at Clichy-la-Garenne and in the company of Bérulle. Her first reaction, when Camus spoke to her of Vincent, was not favorable. She even wrote that she felt reluctant to accept, agreeing only because she believed it was the will of God.[27] Thus, in 1625, Vincent became the spiritual director of Louise de Marillac.

She moved into modest lodgings in the quarter of Saint-Victor, near the Collège des Bons-Enfants. We see in her correspondence how Vincent led her by degrees to detach herself from extreme preoccupation with her son and to cure herself of her persistent mournfulness. He wrote to her: "Make sure to stay glad of heart, ready to want everything that God wants."

He worked to show her that she would find balance and interior peace by joining him in serving the poor. He knew the role he would assign to her: to take charge of all the confraternities created in the wake of the missions. These Charités had to be visited, invigorated, and sometimes reformed. After four years of training, he sent her out for a first inspection trip to Montmirail, where he was himself planning to preach a mission in May 1629. He encouraged her in these terms:

"Then go, Mademoiselle, go in the name of Our Lord. I pray His divine goodness will accompany you, that it will be your solace and your path, your shade against the heat of the sun, your shelter from rain and cold, a soft couch when you are tired, your strength in hard work, and that finally, it will bring you back to us in perfect health and filled with good works."[28] And so the fragile, anxious Louise, escorted by her maidservants, would set out in a coach to Montmirail, to Villepreux or to Verneuil, with a little bit of baggage and a huge cargo of linens, medicines, and little luxuries, to bring some help to the sick and the penniless. Once settled in the village inn, she would gather the members of the local Charité, ask about their problems, urge them forward, and tell them what they should do next.

Upon her return, she would give Vincent an account of her work, and he would encourage her, and console her if necessary, for she was not always well received. The local authorities, both civil and religious, sometimes wondered what this lady from Paris might be doing there or who had sent her. At those times, Vincent had to reassure her. For instance, once when she was making visits in Champagne, she was summoned by the bishop of Châlons. What was she to do? Vincent answered: "It seems to me that you would be well advised to pay him a call and to tell him quite simply and in good faith why Reverend Father de Gondi has asked you kindly to go to Champagne and what you are doing there. Offer to curtail your activities in any way the bishop pleases to request, and to give up the whole mission if that is what he wishes. This is the spirit of God."[29]

Founding the Congregation of the Mission and recruiting, conducting missions in the countryside, retreats for ordinands, spiritual direction for the Visitandine sisters—Vincent took care of all these things head on. He had hardly any leisure, and no desire to engage in political matters which were very complex at this time.

Just as Vincent de Paul was going forth prudently with measured steps toward a destiny of which he had only a cloudy view at this time, so another man of the Church, Armand du Plessis,[30] walked with decisive steps toward the goal he had chosen for himself, that of achieving power. He had been destined for a military career, but when his older brother decided to retire to a Carthusian monastery, he was called upon to take the episcopal see of Luçon. He was only twenty years old when he received the mitre. This zealous young prelate became the delegate of the clergy to the Estates General in 1614. Rewarded with distinctions by Maria de Medici, he was seated in the Council in 1616, with the title of Secretary of State. In the next year, he served the Queen Mother in her exile while working to reconcile her to her son. This effort succeeded in March 1619, at Angoulême. His skill and subtlety helped him to blaze a path to power in a particularly troubled period of French history. He received the cardinal's hat from Louis XIII in 1622 and was admitted to his council two years later. It was thought that he would defend the Queen Mother's interests there, but very soon, he chose the side of the king who named him chief of the council in August 1624. For almost twenty years, Cardinal de Richelieu, with the complete confidence of his sovereign, would play the part of an all-powerful prime minister.

But at the beginning of his ministry, he still had to manage the Queen Mother, Maria de Medici. She was surrounded by a party of Catholics, more or less the heirs of the League, who were called the Party of the Devout. They favored a policy, both internal and external, which would hew to the line of the teachings and interests of the Church as well as the recommendations of Rome. This would be expressed by fighting against the Protestant "heresy" and by seeking alliances with the Catholic powers, namely the Hapsburgs, whether in the Spanish or the Austrian line.

Among these Devout the Marillac[31] family stood out, as well as Pierre de Bérulle. The party was supported by the Jesuits and by individuals who would soon found the Company of the Blessed Sacrament. Other Catholics, who called themselves "the good Frenchmen" while still being loyal to the Holy See, were inspired by gallican theories. The interests of the State, embodied by a king who enjoyed the power of Divine Right, should be the supreme law. This moved them to take up the fight against the Hapsburg drive to dominate and if necessary, to contract alliances with Protestant powers.

In the meantime, the struggle against the Huguenots soon became a priority, for in July 1627, an English fleet led by the duke of Buckingham landed a force of 8,000 men on the Isle of Ré. They were to come to the aid of the French Protestants who were still besieged at La Rochelle. The English attack failed and the troops returned to their ships without having been able to lift the siege. On the contrary, with Richelieu taking matters in hand, La Rochelle was forced to surrender in October 1628, after a heroic resistance. There remained the task of overpowering centers of Huguenot rebellion in the south, kept alive by the duke of Rohan.

In the king's council, the two parties quarreled on this subject. The Queen Mother, upheld by the Devout, pushed for a campaign against the Protestants, whereas Richelieu wanted first to intervene in Italy, where the succession of the duchy of Mantua[32] was at stake. But in taking this position, the cardinal was acting against Spanish interests, secretly being defended by Maria de Medici. When Richelieu's position won the day in the council, Louis XIII set out with his minister for a lightning campaign in Italy.

The Queen Mother now swore that she would eliminate Richelieu and replace him with the councilor Michel de Marillac. It was on November 11, 1630, a day known as the Day of the Dupes that Maria de Medici, believing that she had convinced her son to disgrace Richelieu, found herself placed under house arrest, from which she would flee into permanent exile. Michel de Marillac was eliminated from the council and retired to his estates where he died of grief two years later. As for his younger brother, the marshal de Marillac, he was arrested in Italy where he was in command of the army. After a prejudiced trial on a charge of extortion, he was sentenced to death and beheaded in May 1632.

These blows to the Marillac clan brought sorrow to Louise. In a letter, Vincent attempted to bring some peace to her soul, inviting her to surrender her grief: "What does it matter to us how our dear ones go to the Lord, provided that they reach Heaven. And making a good death in this way is one of the most assured paths to eternal life. So let us not repine, but let us accept and adore the will of God."[33]

During this whole period, Vincent de Paul kept himself aloof from the tumultuous politics around him. He knew many eminent members of the circle of the Devout and spent time in their company, but there is nothing to show that he attended their meetings, much less took part in their efforts. His horizon was limited to his charitable works, and his energy was concentrated on establishing them firmly. Nothing was allowed to endanger this undertaking.

The Priory of Saint-Lazare
1632–1633

An Unexpected Gift
Act of Union with the Mission
The Tuesday Conferences
Beginning of the Daughters of Charity
Vincent's Recommendations for a Mission

Toward the end of the year 1630, Vincent de Paul received a visit which left him, by his own admission, most troubled and perplexed: "I was confounded, like a man surprised by the noise of a canon shot off nearby unexpectedly; he is stunned by the thunderclap."[1]

What was the cause of his astonishment? The pastor of the parish of Saint-Laurent, Guillaume de Lestocq, came to Vincent to introduce Adrien Le Bon,[2] superior of the priory of Saint-Lazare. This man proposed that he would resign his office in favor of Vincent. In other words, he was offering to install the Mission, which was beginning to be seriously cramped at the Collège des Bons-Enfants, in the vast buildings of Saint-Lazare and, what is more, to make the Congregation the beneficiary of a priory endowed with substantial revenues. After he recovered from his surprise, Vincent's first reaction was to turn away this offer, which seemed to him disproportionate to the size of the little congregation that was just coming into being. Moreover, he was aware of the problems facing the prior of Saint-Lazare, and it terrified him to think that he might become encumbered with such entanglements.

The priory of Saint-Lazare, founded in the twelfth century, originally had the mission of sheltering and caring for the lepers of the capital city. These were most often burghers or artisan bakers. In fact, it was believed in those days that bakers were more exposed than others to infection with this terrible disease. Even in the seventeenth century, the bakers of Paris kept alive a tradition of making offerings to the infirmary at Saint-Lazare. In the Middle Ages, this priory had become one of the largest ecclesiastical seigniories of the Île-de-France.[3] When they took the throne, kings came here to receive the oath of loyalty of all the orders of the city. In the same way, at their death, their coffins were carried to Saint-Lazare before being placed in the care of the monks of the abbey of Saint-Denis. At the beginning of the sixteenth century, the bishop of Paris transferred the administration of this priory of the Knights of Saint-Lazare to the canons of Saint-Victor, with the warning that it was in his power to revoke this donation.

The enclosure of Saint-Lazare,[4] situated outside the walls of Paris, was extensive, on the order of ninety-two acres. The land grew wheat, barley, and alfalfa. The buildings standing on it included lodgings for the canons, the church and its cloister, an infirmary, the prison of the seigniory, a house of detention for the mentally disturbed, and, in another part of the estate, a series of little houses meant for the lepers. In addition, there were the usual dependencies—stables, barns, cellars, and various storage buildings. The prior also owned other real estate in the capital city and neighboring parishes and had the use of revenues from the levy of various taxes, in particular from the Fair of Saint-Laurent, held near the estate. These revenues may have been sizable, but the restoration of the buildings would be a matter of great expense for upkeep of the priory had long been neglected. Very few lepers were still being brought to Saint-Lazare. As for other inmates, they were limited to three or four mental patients and a few young ne'er-do-wells, detained at the request of their families.

The monks of Saint-Victor numbered ten at this time; they were in constant conflict with their prior. For this reason, he was driven by exhaustion and discouragement to offer the priory to Vincent de Paul, who was known for his good works. In spite of the rejection he received, Adrien Le Bon remained determined and came back to speak with Vincent again, after leaving him six months to think the matter over. Once more, Vincent hesitated because of the modest size of his group and his dislike of stir and gossip. He also feared the reaction of the parish priests of Paris and of other convents of canons gathered in the Congregation of France under the energetic staff of Father Faure.[5] Adrien Le Bon then called on André Duval to intervene; he was a great friend of Vincent, who always followed his advice. This wise doctor felt that Le Bon's proposal would be beneficial for the Congregation, and Vincent finally gave in. All that remained was to establish the terms of the contract, and this was not easy. A long letter from Vincent to Guillaume de Lestocq lists the many difficulties that had to be overcome. In particular, there was the question of how the canons of Saint-Victor and the priests of the Mission would live together, given that their work and their respective ways of life differed so much. What material considerations should be offered to Adrien Le Bon and his confrères?[6]

The contract of merger between the priory of Saint-Lazare and the Congregation of the Mission was finally signed before a notary on January 7, 1632, and approved on the next day by the archbishop of Paris. This dignitary specified that he would retain jurisdiction over matters both spiritual and temporal, concerning the priory and the priests of the Mission. There were to be at least twelve of these priests, eight of whom would be permanently assigned to preaching missions without charge in the diocese of Paris and they would be required to give fifteen days a year to the preparation of clerics of the diocese for ordination.[7] Had Vincent finally reached a safe harbor after two years of difficult negotiation?

Letters patent of the king to confirm this union of two religious institutions were signed on January 22, 1632, but the parlement blocked their registration for the religious of Saint-Victor as well as the priests of the city, suburbs, and outlying districts of Paris were expressing objections. In particular, the religious of Saint-Victor presented one request after another for the annulment of the union, even though the priory of Saint-Lazare had not been a dependency of their abbey since 1625. After having hesitated for so long, and spent so much time seeking advice, Vincent suffered a moment of discouragement. He confided to a friend: "You know that the religious of Saint-Victor are contesting our possession of Saint-Lazare. You cannot imagine the expressions of submission that I have offered them, in the spirit of the Gospel, even though there was no reason to do so, according to the assurances of Monsieur Duval and everyone who knows how matters stand. It will all turn out as Our Lord wishes."[8]

Help came in the person of Vincent's compatriot, Jean Duvergier de Hauranne, abbot of Saint-Cyran. The two had met in 1609, during

Vincent's first months in the capital. They may even have shared living quarters for a while, and, as time went on, they were helpful to each other. Vincent had asked help of Madame de Gondi, sister-in-law of Monsieur de Fargis, ambassador of France to Madrid, to obtain the release of Saint-Cyran's nephew, imprisoned in Spain. Saint-Cyran had provided support for some relatives of Vincent when they were involved in an unpleasant situation. Now Saint-Cyran used some of his most important connections, particularly with the advocate general, Bignon, who was in charge of the case of Saint-Lazare. He convinced Bignon to argue vigorously in favor of the Congregation of the Mission, thus ending the case put forward by the religious of Saint-Victor.[9]

Finally, on September 7, 1632, the parlement ordered the registration of the king's letters patent. But the difficulties had not yet come to an end. In giving his approval, the archbishop of Paris had stipulated that he reserved to himself the right of visitation, in matters both spiritual and temporal. Vincent did not hesitate to request that he relinquish this requirement. "I begged him insistently to give us a dispensation from this provision. When he refused, I told him that we would rather withdraw, and we would have done so without fail if he had persisted in his demands."[10] Thus after having wavered endlessly before accepting Saint-Lazare, after having been obliged to fight to keep it, he was ready to abandon it rather than to cede even the slightest bit of his autonomy!

In signing the document of merger between Saint-Lazare and the Mission, Vincent was taking on heavy financial responsibilities. He declared himself ready to disburse annuities of 2,100 livres to the prior and 500 livres to each of the ten canons, not to mention paying for the upkeep of eight of his own priests who were to do their missionary work exclusively in the diocese of Paris. Moreover, there were urgent repairs and improvements to be undertaken in the buildings of the priory. But as would happen again so many times, Providence brought a generous donor, Nicolas Viviers, counselor of the king and master of accounts, who turned over to Vincent a sum of 10,000 livres for a foundation that would supply missions in the parliamentary domains of Toulouse, Bordeaux, and Provence.[11]

Installation of the Mission at Saint-Lazare represented a decisive step for the young congregation because it would allow expansion of all the activities developed there. The whole affair revealed much about Vincent's character. His slow progress toward any decision was part of his peasant side — to weigh the pros and the cons in deliberate fashion, to talk things over for a sense of acting correctly. His hesitation was also a reaction of modesty and humility; this gift was too handsome for his insignificant company. But once the decision was made, he was inflexible. If a trial was necessary, like it or not, he was prepared to engage. He was also immovable on the principle of authority for his congregation—he was the superior and he had no intention of ceding even a bit of his power. Vincent was willing to defend this principle before the archbishop of Paris and later, before the Holy See.

Saint-Lazare filled up rapidly. The first guests came to the retreats for ordinands of the diocese of Paris in six annual groups of about sixty each. In a letter to a friend, Vincent described the program for these retreats: "His Grace the archbishop . . . has ordered that from now on, those of his diocese who have this desire [to be ordained] will withdraw for ten days before the conferral of each order, to make a spiritual retreat with the priests of the Mission, practice meditation, which is so necessary for priests, make a general confession of all their past lives, review moral theology, particularly as it concerns the use of the sacraments, learn how to conduct liturgies well, and finally, to learn about all the other things necessary for priests."[12]

All these people were housed and fed at no charge, and this significant expense would only grow as retreats began to be offered to ordinands from the provinces and laymen. The number of visitors at Saint-Lazare at any given time was somewhere between sixty and one hundred. Vincent was able to enroll the generosity of the Ladies of Charity in this work. Thus, the wife of President de Herse[13] pledged 1,000 livres for each ordination for a period of five years. Her donation was an example for the marquise de Maignelay, sister of Jean-François de Gondi, archbishop of Paris, who would finance almost all of Vincent's undertakings.

Suitable priests had to be found to preach all these retreats. With his ability to engage people, Vincent was able to bring the city's most talented preachers to Saint-Lazare. This was the venue of the first preaching of Nicolas Pavillon, and Françoise-Étienne de Caulet,[14] both future bishops, and later of Jacques-Bénigne Bossuet, to mention only the best known.

Vincent gave thought to ways in which one could preserve for priests the good spiritual disposition which they had achieved during their ordination retreats. For this purpose, he adopted the suggestion of one of them to bring former retreatants together once a week. This was the beginning of the Tuesday Conferences,[15] attended in Vincent's lifetime by more than 250 priests from several dioceses. He found it important to preside at these meetings himself, preserving an informal atmosphere and allowing each member to express himself freely on the topic suggested the week before. The focus of these topics was the life of Jesus Christ, symbol of the priesthood, and love of the poor. For nearly thirty years, despite his many responsibilities, Vincent disciplined himself to sit quietly in the midst of this circle of priests. With his simple, image-filled speech, he meditated aloud on the vocation of the priest and on his model, Jesus Christ. Of all the good works created by Vincent, the Tuesday Conferences was perhaps the most illumined by his own personality.

The participants in these conferences soon organized themselves into an informal group for whom Vincent proposed a rule of common life that they followed while doing their own work in parishes or the diocese.[16] Word of this company of priests attracted the most distinguished churchmen—doctors of the Sorbonne, superiors of congregations, directors of seminaries. The group became a nursery for prelates: about twenty of its members became bishops or archbishops, and it must be said that Vincent, in spite of his humility, was not indifferent to these promotions as they occurred. In 1637 he wrote with open satisfaction to one of his correspondents: "The assembly of reverend priests of this diocese continues to fare better and better. Just now, three bishops have been chosen from it."[17]

Organizing retreats for ordinands and leading the Tuesday Conferences did not distract Vincent from his work of the Confraternities of Charity. These kept increasing in number as they were established in each parish where a mission was preached. Louise de Marillac made her regular visiting tours to nurture the enthusiasm of the members. In 1632, she was at Villeneuve-Saint-Georges, Launois, Herblay and the next year at Verneuil, Pont-Saint-Maxence, Gournay, Neufville-le-Roy. Vincent kept up a regular correspondence with her, now encouraging, now gently reprimanding when she gave in to her crises of scrupulosity: "I cannot help but tell you that tomorrow I will really reproach you for giving in to these vain and frivolous anxieties. Oh, prepare yourself to be well admonished!"[18] In these letters, he also kept her up to date about daily life at Saint-Lazare: "I am buried over my head in multitudes of retreatants, a bishop-elect, a first president, two doctors, a professor of theology, and

Monsieur Pavillon." Then he asks her to go to Villeneuve-sur-Yonne where the Charité is in need of some prodding. In this letter, he gives thought to the details of the journey, whether it should be in a carriage with Madame Goussault and Mademoiselle Poulaillon or on a river barge as far as Joigny. He suggests where she can get lodging, and tells her that she must visit the pastor of the place and catechize the little girls: "This will make it easier for you to win their mothers for God."[19] Now it is not the spiritual director speaking, with his occasionally demanding voice, but an attentive friend who watches affectionately over this fragile woman whom he is sending out on dangerous roads.

Vincent realized that the design of the Charités was self-limiting: good will finally tires. Married women are kept at home by the demands of the household. As for the noble ladies who could not go out and besmirch their gowns in the hovels where most of the sick and poor were housed, they delegated to their servants the task of carrying the kettle to the needy. Moreover, there was a need for persons able to provide schooling for the country girls and these were hard to find among the Ladies of Charity. As for the attempt to create Charités made up of men and women together, it had not been successful, and Vincent finally abandoned this model, coming to the conclusion that men and women working together would never agree on matters of administration.

Directly in contact with all these problems, Louise de Marillac had the idea of being helped by true servants, whom she would organize into a sort of company. Vincent, for his part, thought this over with his customary prudence and circumspection. He tempered Louise's zeal, because it had a tendency to make her act too soon: "One should not overstep the limits of Providence," he liked to say. Around that time, in 1629 or 1630, a girl of praiseworthy devoutness came to them, Marguerite Naseau. As a simple cowherd in Suresnes, she had taught herself to read and had started, all on her own, to teach the other girls in her village. She came and put herself at the disposal of Vincent, who sent her to Villepreux, where she met other girls of good will. She came back to the Charité of Saint-Nicolas-du-Chardonnet when an epidemic of the plague swept through the capital. She died in March 1633 while caring for a woman stricken with the plague, with whom she shared her bed. Marguerite Naseau provided Vincent with the very embodiment of what he had been looking for without being able to describe it. She was to be the first Daughter of Charity.[20] In November 1633, Louise de Marillac, having finally obtained Vincent's consent, welcomed four or five girls to her lodgings near Saint-Nicolas-du-Chardonnet. They would be the first core group of the Congregation of the Daughters of Charity. At first, Vincent considered them to be only helpers for the Ladies of Charity; until 1647, when he speaks of the Sisters, it is the Ladies of Charity that he means. The others were simply "the girls." Later, he would call them "my sisters," gradually recognizing their autonomy.

In the midst of his many projects, the rural missions remained for Vincent the heart and the essential center of his labors and his apostolate. He found it important to take part in the work himself as often as possible. Once, when he was on a missionary journey, his horse stumbled and fell. He was pinned under his mount, but escaped without too much injury. He made light of the incident when he recounted it to Louise de Marillac: "The horse collapsed and then fell on me. It was most dangerous, but Our Lord protected me most directly. Not a trace of the accident remains with me, except a little sprained ligament in my foot, which does not even hurt now." As was the practice of the day, doctors hastened to purge him: "I will be purged tomorrow and the next day. I'll be able to travel by carriage as far as four kilometers from here."[21]

When he did not go along on a mission because he was detained by some rather extraordinary difficulty at home, he wrote at length to the person conducting it. This happened once when Antoine Portail was at Montmirail planning to travel with his team to Joigny, a distance of about 100 kilometers as the crow flies. Vincent wanted to advise him about how the journey should be made: "If you go on foot and take only one horse, I ask for two things—make your days short, and let those who are tired take turns riding the horse." This was an important mission, with a team of ten priests. Vincent specified the assignments which should go to each one: "Monsieur Pavillon will preach, and Messieurs Renar, Roche, Grenu, and Sergis will do as follows: the first will intone the Credo; the second, God's commandments; the third, the Lord's Prayer and the Ave Maria; and the fourth will administer the sacraments; and as for the shorter catechism, Messieurs Roche and Sergis will be glad they have done it when they teach the longer catechism. As for you, Sir, you will be in charge of the company."[22] Vincent sounds like a captain giving his officers their orders for a maneuver!

In this letter, Vincent also advised Portail to see to it that the Rule was observed, the hours of rising and retiring, prayer, the Office, as well as entering and leaving the church in the proper order. He commented on his exhortation, saying: "Seldom if ever do the members of the courts fail to rise and retire, leave and return to the Palace at the same hour; most craftsmen do the same; it is only we of the clergy who are so fond of our comfort that we only act as our inclinations lead us. For the love of God, Sir, let us work to denude ourselves of this pitiful sensuality which makes us prisoners of its behest."

He then warned Portail of the difficulties inherent in this mission to a region he knew well: "Tell our priests that of all the missions we have preached, there has not been one more difficult or more important than Joigny, both because of the people who live there and because of the power the Evil One has there in some things."

Adding some specifics to his thoughts, Vincent warns his missionaries against two particular faults that were noticed during the last mission in this region, intemperance and self-involvement. With regard to intemperance, the explanation might be that Joigny is a region of vineyards, where parishioners often offered wine to the missionaries who were not very accustomed to this drink. As to exaggerated love of oneself, Vincent was alluding to the enormous vanity visible in the priests while they were preaching, the pleasure they took in beautiful flights of oratory and the sound of their own voices. Vincent often returned to this topic in letters to his missionaries, giving as a curative example the very simple manner in which Jesus preached: "Although he was the uncreated wisdom of the Eternal Father, he wanted to couch his teachings in a style that was brief, close to the people, and even more humble than that of his apostles."

At the end of this long instruction to Antoine Portail, after calling to mind the faults into which he feared the members of his company might fall, he humbly admitted his own faults: "And because, miserable that I am, I have reason to fear that I myself am the cause of all these faults, since they are all to be found in me, their teacher, and thus spread from me throughout our community, pray to God that he will forgive me." Authority and humility are the two qualities that radiate from this letter which shows Vincent just as he would be throughout his life, in his role as superior of the Congregation of the Mission.

Superior of the Mission
1633–1635

By this time, Vincent de Paul was in his fifties, an advanced age for his times. All those who had molded him and left a mark on his character were gone: his parents, Judge de Comet, the papal nuncio Montorio, Pierre de Bérulle, Francis de Sales, Madame de Gondi. He himself had changed a great deal; indeed, he was no longer the same person. How far away now the young cleric, ambitiously running after a prosperous benefice, the slave initiated into the secrets of alchemy, the tutor in the household of the Gondis casting about for his true vocation. Now he was Monsieur Vincent, superior of the Congregation of the Mission in his priory of Saint-Lazare, director of the convents of the Visitation, and royal almoner of the galleys. He had not only found his true path; he had left anonymity behind. He had become a well-known personality, in the humblest corners and the most exalted circles close to the throne. Who had not heard of this smiling, modest priest in his simple cassock, or even met him? Vincent had the reputation of doing wonders wherever he went, and in his wake he brought together people of good will, drawn into action by his example, working to comfort the miserable who suffered in body and soul.

In this first half of the seventeenth century, new religious congregations flourished and charitable institutions sprang up in great numbers. Vincent made himself a part of this general movement, this current of the Counter-Reformation that was enlivening the Catholic Church, but he held a particular place because of his personal radiance and the diversity of the efforts on which he put his mark. Departing from his initial calling of evangelizing the countryside and consoling poor people in distress, he expanded his focus to the formation of priests so that they would be worthy of their role in life. He founded Charités that would extend the beneficial effects of missions in the parishes, and this was the most characteristic of his works. At the same time, he expanded his sphere of influence. Starting on the estates and lands of the Gondis, then working in the diocese of Paris, he was soon sending his missionaries into all the provinces, before propelling them out beyond the boundaries of the kingdom. As he brought aid to the crying misery of the rural areas, he discovered more, to which he also bent his efforts: convicts sentenced to hard labor, delinquent girls, abandoned children. He did not overextend himself, but he found an appropriate response for each case. In order to be effective, he needed the right resources, and in most cases, this meant money. Vincent had a remarkable tool for raising funds — his outstanding ability to create friendships with all the great families who exercised various kinds of power in the kingdom.

From the time of his youth, Vincent had developed this innate gift of being able to arouse the sympathy of those he encountered on his way. That is how he won the protection and support of Judge de Comet and his descendants, the Saint-Martin family, with whom he remained in regular contact. In the same way, he succeeded in winning over his masters in North Africa and the papal nuncio Montorio in Avignon. As a penniless young priest with no resources but the support of his bishop at Dax, he was able to gather acquaintances who would find him a way into the household of Queen Marguerite of Valois and an introduction to Pierre de Bérulle. Named pastor of Clichy-la-Garenne, he immediately cultivated the company of the local aristocrats, the Hennequins, themselves connected to the powerful family of Marillac. Once having obtained his position in the Gondi household, he lived closely with a clan that held, from uncle to nephew, the bishopric of Paris and had entrée to the court. Presented to Francis de Sales, he soon received the office of superior of the house of the Visitation, newly established in the capital. Because of this, he would be in contact with all the noble families whose daughters were entering this convent, particularly the Fouquet family, five of whose daughters had taken the veil there. Vincent was known to Cardinal de la Rochefoucauld,[1] who entrusted him with delicate tasks such as the judgment of the guérinets.[2] The cardinal particularly wished Vincent to educate and watch over his two nephews, Louis and Claude de Chandenier.[3] They would become faithful disciples and friends of Vincent.

As for Richelieu, his relationship with Vincent seems to have been marked with a certain coldness at first. It is true that the cardinal was well aware of everything the superior of the Congregation of the Mission was doing and did not hesitate to ask him for a list of members of the Tuesday Conferences who seemed worthy to become bishops. However, because Vincent belonged to the circle of the Gondis and the Marillacs, the cardinal had a tendency to mistrust him. Later, he was to support the Mission actively, and his own niece, the marquise de Combalet, future duchess d'Aiguillon,[4] was one of Vincent's most generous and loyal benefactresses.

In this circle of acquaintances whom Vincent skillfully involved in his work, a special place must go to the Company of the Blessed Sacrament. This association was founded in 1630 by a great lord, Henri de Lévis, the duke de Ventadour,[5] who wished to bring together priests and laymen to promote the glory of God by every means possible. This company was surrounded by mystery from the time of its creation since its statutes obligated all members to secrecy. Soon the elite of the Catholic world were numbered in its membership. Among laymen, it included the count d'Argenson, the duke de Liancourt, the first president of Lamoignon, and the marshals de Schomberg and de la Meilleraye. Among the prelates were François Fouquet, bishop of Bayonne, Alain de Solminihac, bishop of Cahors, Antoine Godeau, bishop of Grasse and Vence, and Augustin Potier, bishop of Beauvais. Many friends of Vincent were members, such as Father de Condren, superior of the Oratory, Monsieur Olier, pastor of Saint-Sulpice, François de Perrochel, future bishop of Boulogne, Louis de Chandenier, abbot of Tournus, Louis Abelly, future bishop of Rodez, and Jacques-Bénigne Bossuet, to mention only the most famous.

The Company of the Blessed Sacrament wove a network which gradually covered the whole kingdom. It gave its attention to all works of charity and apostolate—visiting prisoners, aiding provinces devastated by war, evangelization of remote areas, and defending the integrity of the Catholic faith. Vincent joined the Company of the Blessed Sacrament in 1633 or 1634. His work and that of the Company were often related or connected, even though in certain cases he did not approve of the group's positions, particularly in their battle against adherents of the reformed religion. But he found in the Company men who would support him effectively in certain of his undertakings, and in many cases, the Company was a platform for the diffusion of his ideas.[6]

For a long time, Vincent de Paul had sought worldly goods, both for himself and so that he could contribute to his family. Once he became superior of the Mission, having made a vow of poverty and renounced all his possessions, he continued his incessant search for money, but now it was for the sake of his good works. He knew how to appeal to the generosity of his many acquaintances, but he was also an excellent manager. With the age-old instinct of a peasant, he gave priority to the possession of land and buildings, but like a knowing financier, he diversified the sources of his revenues, cultivating income from direct and indirect duties or from transport companies.

At the outset, the assets of the Congregation consisted of the endowment provided by the Gondis, to the amount of 45,000 livres and an annual income of 12,000 livres derived from taxes on salt. This was augmented by the donation of the Collège des Bons-Enfants. But from 1632 on, the major portion of the Congregation's wealth derived from the priory of Saint-Lazare, with all the possessions and rights attached to this seigniory. These assets included the enclosure of forty hectares at the gates of the capital, several farms in the Île-de-France, lands and numerous houses in the working-class suburbs and Paris itself. As a seigniory, Saint-Lazare held the privilege of levying various duties and taxes, including the considerable taxes on the Fair of Saint Laurent.

Some of the rents for farms were paid in currency, some in kind. For example, the farm of Gonesse was rented for 100 royal livres and in addition was expected to yield six measures of wheat a year, six capons, and a fattened pig.[7] The rental of the different houses and palaces regularly brought in around 10,000 royal livres.[8]

Vincent was not content to collect these revenues; he watched over them attentively, requiring an account of the farming operations and giving detailed instruction concerning choice of plantings or haying times. He seized every opportunity to increase the size of the domains, by purchase or exchange of parcels of land. The same degree of attention was given to following the revenues from duties and taxes. He was particularly interested in the operation of coaches and river barges, keeping track of fluctuations in income so that he could make the appropriate business decisions. All in all, he knew how to invest income in such a way that the Congregation could live on income and preserve capital.

In order to manage all this property, which increased over the course of years, Vincent often had to consult with financiers and lawyers. His signature is found at the foot of innumerable notarized documents. He took great care that everything should be done according to the law and good procedures. He knew from experience that hastily concluded contracts usually ended in a trial at law; Saint-Léonard and Grosse-Sauve had taught him a lesson. To protect the Congregation's assets, he sometimes even had to do battle against the royal power. The king was always short of money, and now and then, he wanted to sell certain domains, dependencies of Saint-Lazare, over which the Crown believed it had rights.[9] Vincent also spent time trying to make portions of the estates pay for themselves. He tried to make the many seminarians and retreatants pay for their room and board to the extent their means allowed, and he did the same with the mental patients and the prisoners housed by the priory.[10] Thanks to his careful management, Vincent was able to make his congregation live and grow, and it became possible to maintain Saint-Lazare and the Collège des Bons-Enfants, with their endless procession of missionaries, religious and lay retreatants, ordinands and seminarians. It also became possible to distribute abundant alms on a regular schedule to all the suffering people who knocked on the doors of the priory.

Vincent de Paul had enough responsibilities to prevent him from seeking others, but it was difficult for him to refuse to give advice or help. That is how the creation of the Charité of the Hôtel-Dieu came about. This hospital was administered by the canons of Notre-Dame and the Augustinian sisters cared for the sick. Ladies came to visit and bring small luxuries to supplement the ordinary fare of the hospital and to offer words of comfort. Not surprisingly, there was friction between the sisters, exhausted with their labors, and these ladies, who sometimes exceeded their role. The growing number of patients, which had required the opening of an annex in 1618, the hospital of Saint Louis, overburdened the sisters in spite of the increase in their ranks to one hundred professed members who were assisted by fifty novices (white sisters). The joint action of one sister, Geneviève Bouquet[11] and a lady visitor, Madame Goussault, bore fruit in the reform of both the Augustinian sisters and the visitors. At this point, Madame Goussault asked Vincent for the formation of a Charité of the Hôtel-Dieu. He was hesitant to become involved in the work of a hospital, which was quite different from his original vocation, assistance to rural people. But Vincent knew Geneviève Bouquet, whom he had probably met at the court of Queen Marguerite of Valois, and Madame Goussault, for her part, was persistent. She returned to the attack several times, even enlisting the intervention of the bishop of Paris in favor of her plan.

Vincent had to capitulate and at the beginning of 1634, he attended a meeting at the home of Madame Goussault, who had called together several pious ladies of the high society of Paris. This was the beginning of the Charité of the Hôtel-Dieu, which would soon have one hundred members. Its field of action would reach beyond the Hôtel-Dieu to take on the work of the Foundling Hospital and the bringing of aid to provinces devastated by war. Vincent, who had been hesitant at the beginning, was soon very happy with this foundation. In July 1634, he wrote to François du Coudray, his representative in Rome: "We established it [the Charité] in several parishes of this city, and not long ago, we established one consisting of 100 or 120 ladies of quality, who visit every day and who, in groups of four, help 800 or 900 people a day, the poor or sick people, and bring them jellies, consommés, soups, preserves, and all kinds of other delicacies, in addition to the usual nourishment which the house furnishes to them, so that these poor people may come to a state of mind in which they are ready to make a general confession of their past lives. In this way, those who are about to die leave this world in a good state and those who will be cured resolve never to offend God again."[12]

In 1630, one of the ladies of this Charité of the Hôtel-Dieu, the good Mademoiselle Poulaillon, separately founded a society for the protection of young girls in danger of being lost, in the words of Monsieur Vincent himself. Being the spiritual director of the foundress of this work, he agreed to be its superior and write a rule for it. A few years later, he was able to bring it about that these Daughters of Providence received letters patent and the approval of the archbishop of Paris, as well as the old hospital of La Santé to house their boarders.[13]

Yet another charitable institution requested the support and advice of Vincent. Their work had begun modestly in 1618 when a gentleman, Robert de Montry, and a Capuchin friar, Brother Athanasius, brother of

President Molé, undertook to help delinquent girls to change their lives and redeem themselves. The marquise de Maignelay lent her financial support, which made it possible to acquire a house in the rue des Fontaines, called La Madeleine. Girls living a disordered life were received there as students. The king endowed this establishment, which then became known as the Monastery of Sainte-Marie-Madeleine and whose boarders became known as the Madelonettes.[14]

While charitable institutions were growing in number the times also gave rise to several new religious orders. In 1632, in Avignon, the Congregation of Missionary Priests of the Most Blessed Sacrament was founded. This congregation adopted the vocation of preaching missions and opening seminaries. Its founder, Christophe d'Authier, wrote to Vincent de Paul to suggest that their two communities might unite. In a letter which Vincent wrote to François du Coudray in January 1634, we can see his hesitation about this plan. "I praise God that he has pleased to raise up in our times so many good and holy souls to help the poor. As for union, it is desirable, but such unions require oneness of faith, means, and spirit. Although we have the same purpose, there are many things that keep us apart. All the orders of the Church have the same faith, which is charity, but because they do not have the same means, they are not always in agreement. In a single order, there is the same faith, the same means, and the same spirit, but even there, there are many occasions for disorder."[15] Vincent was clear-headed and sensible. He knew from experience how difficult such a union would be. His entry into Saint-Lazare, for instance, was not without numerous tensions with the former occupants and even with the prior, Adrien Le Bon, who had been so much in favor of the move. Vincent did what he could to temper the enthusiasm of his young confrère who would try many times to change his mind, but to no avail.

Although he was more and more taken up with the many works which called for his attention, Vincent never neglected his earliest obligations. In 1622, he had been named superior of the first convent of the Visitation founded in Paris. Since then, he had presided every month over the chapter of the monastery and performed the canonical visitation once a year, in which he received all the nuns and listened to them with attention and kindness. On the occasion of various ceremonies, such as the annual renewal of vows, he delivered carefully prepared homilies.[16] The sisters of the Visitation became so numerous that soon it was necessary to increase the size of the monastery by acquiring the Cossé palace, which was connected to the first building by its gardens. Then a second house was opened in 1626 at rue du Faubourg-Saint-Jacques; Vincent was in charge of this house as well. Directing these convents was very time consuming and had little to do with his original vocation. He took the opportunity to point this out on various occasions, while insisting that he knew he was morally obligated to fulfill this duty: "It is true," he said during a conference, "that blessed Francis de Sales charged me with the direction of the house of the Visitation in this city, in spite of my unworthiness, and that blessed Mother de Chantal urged me to accept the charge."[17] He would try to be quit of this duty, but without success, and so he retained it until his death.

The relations between Jeanne de Chantal and Vincent de Paul were marked by a mixture of confidence and reserve. At the death of Francis de Sales, she asked Vincent to become her spiritual director. He was deeply impressed by his penitent and his approach to her was filled with respect. As a result, his letters took a less natural tone, very different from his usual style, as though he were trying to put himself in the place of Francis de Sales and imitate his turn of phrase: "Now, my dear Mother, would you permit me to ask you whether your unparalleled goodness will once more permit me the good fortune to enjoy the place which it has reserved for me in its dear and kind heart?"[18]

Jeanne de Chantal, for her part, told him with simplicity of her moral suffering and of the problems she experienced in directing her house. She asked him for advice, but still retained her freedom of thought and of action. Thus, when Vincent suggested to her that she should open her houses to visits from authorized priests for the purpose of maintaining a certain uniformity in her order and of avoiding possible deviations from it, she did not hesitate to express her disagreement. It was her opinion that the provision in the founders' Rule which placed each house under the authority of the local diocesan bishop was quite sufficient. She wrote to Vincent: "Our dear sister, the superior of the house in the faubourg Saint-Jacques, has informed me of the opinion that you have been pleased to give us. . . . It is good and sound, and yet, I have not been able to agree to it in my heart."[19]

Vincent remained attached to his idea of this practice of visits, which was the custom in most religious orders. Therefore, he permitted himself to repeat his suggestion a little later, but Jeanne de Chantal rejected it yet again. Vincent gave in: "I can assure you, most amiable and very dear Mother, that we did not have the least thought in the world that would be contradictory to your ideas, I repeat, not the least."[20]

What a difference in tone when Vincent addressed another of his penitents, Louise de Marillac, to whom his attachment was equally strong. In writing to her, he is simple and direct: "You think about yourself too much. You should go through life at ease and simply." He did not even hesitate to write severely and almost roughly when Louise de Marillac sighed about her son and his future: "I have never seen a woman like you, nor one who is so quick to take things as a proof of her own sinfulness. You say that the choice made by your son is a proof of the judgment of God on you. You are quite wrong to entertain thoughts like these, and even more in the wrong to speak them aloud. . . . In the name of God, Mademoiselle, correct yourself of this fault."[21]

Burdened by numerous activities, spiritual direction, and the cares of administration, Vincent de Paul nevertheless remained faithful to his essential calling of organizing missions for the rural poor. The priests of the Congregation were increasingly in demand in other dioceses. For example, in 1634 they went to labor in the diocese of Bordeaux. Vincent himself traveled to Normandy in November, to Neufchâtel-en-Braye, to found a Charité there.[22] From 1635 on, thanks to a foundation created by a disciple and benefactor, Commander de Sillery,[23] a mission was preached at Brie-Comte-Robert. Antoine Portail, who was assigned to direct the mission, wrote to Vincent that he did not feel equal to his missionary companion in the art of preaching. Vincent replied in encouraging fashion and urged him to preach in a spirit of humility and compassion: "One does not believe a man because he is learned but because he seems to be a good man and because we love him. No one will ever believe in us if we do not bear witness to love and compassion to those of whom we hope to make believers. . . . If you preach in this way, God will bless your labors. If not, you will produce fanfares and noise but bear no fruit."[24]

In August of the same year, Antoine Portail found himself in the Cévennes mountains, where he spent several months in missionary work. Vincent gave him news of the Congregation, which was burdened with requests it could not fulfill in spite of the new recruits flowing into Saint-Lazare: "Monseigneur de Mende has expressed a great deal of satisfaction with your work. Monseigneur de Viviers came to us with the same report. Only God is able to be everywhere."[25]

Once more it was necessary to find the money to pay for all these missions. Vincent insisted that each mission should have its own financing. Thus, in July 1635, he accepted from the good wife of President de Herse a donation of two farms near Étampes, Mespuits and Fréneville. This gift was in harmony with a promise to preach, in perpetuity, a mission on the estates of this lady every five years. Another team of missionaries set out in May 1635, led by Jean-Jacques Olier, to Saint-Ilpize, near Brioude in the Auvergne. After an eleven-day march, the team arrived at its destination. Vincent received an enthusiastic report from Olier: "At first, people came in numbers as great as we could wish. That is, there were as many as we could hear in the confessional. But toward the end, the people were experiencing such intense emotions and the crowd was so great that sometimes we needed twelve or thirteen priests to respond fittingly to their ardor. We saw them from dawn until the heat of noon, which was extraordinary, and all the way to the last sermon, staying there without food or drink."[26]

From letters like this, we obtain a living picture of these missions—the reserved beginning, with a little suspicion on the part of the population and the local clergy, and then the contact established through the children and their catechism lessons. This caused the adults to be less timid, and the ceremonies and preaching were a distraction for the country folk who so seldom saw anything new. Finally, souls were touched and people were moved to make their confessions. The mission ended with communion. People came from neighboring villages, there was a feast-day mood, and if it was God's will, the action of grace was felt by all.[27]

The Drum Rolls at Saint-Lazare
1636–1639

Saint-Lazare in a State of War
Vincent's Health
The Foundling Hospital
First Houses of the Mission
Growth of the Daughters of Charity

In August 1636, the news exploded in the capital like a thunderclap in a serene sky, producing general consternation and panic. The fortress of Corbie, on the Somme near Amiens, had fallen to the Spanish and the road to Paris was open to the enemy! We must place this event into context by recalling the causes of the war which had been tearing at the Holy Roman Empire since 1618. It lasted for thirty years, which gave it its name. Born of the antagonism which set Protestant princes against Catholic imperial authority, it spread all over Europe, with foreign powers intervening in a conflict which, at first, had been a purely German matter. The French policy pursued by Richelieu since 1624 consisted of opposing the ambitious Hapsburgs of Vienna and Madrid by giving secret support to the emperor's enemies. In this vein, Richelieu pushed the king of Sweden, Gustavus Adolphus, to intervene in Germany, where he landed in 1630 and won victory after victory until his death at the battle of Lützen in November 1632. The imperial forces took their revenge by defeating Sweden at Nördlingen in September 1634, thanks to the support of a strong Spanish army coming from Milan across the Alps. The victorious allied forces then advanced toward the valley of the Rhine.

At this moment, Richelieu judged that he could no longer avoid the overt engagement of France in this war. In 1632, he had ordered the occupation of the Lorraine as a preventive measure, since the duke, Charles IV, was ready to swing his support to the emperor. This was all the more likely because the duke had received on his lands the brother of Louis XIII, Gaston of Orléans, who was fleeing the kingdom after an attempted rebellion. Charles IV had even favored the secret marriage (January 1632) of his sister, Marguerite de Vaudémont to Gaston d'Orléans, a supreme outrage against French royalty.

In March 1635, the Spanish entered the Electorate of Trèves, occupying the city and imprisoning the archbishop, who had placed himself under the protection of the king of France. This had provided Richelieu with the excuse he was waiting for to declare war officially. The war would end in 1648, when France and the emperor signed the Treaty of Westphalia, but it only came to a definitive close in 1660 with the treaty of the Pyrenees signed with Spain. During more than a quarter century, at one location or another along the borders of the kingdom of France, the provinces were ravaged and populations subjected to the demands of the armed forces of the two camps who, according to one chronicler of the time, massacred friends and enemies with equal impartiality. It was in this war-torn country that Vincent de Paul would live and work for the rest of his days.

The taking of Corbie provoked a national tremor. After a moment of despair, Richelieu reacted. He had the king appeal to the people of Paris for an organized defense of the capital. At the city hall, volunteers were enrolled, horses and carriages were requisitioned, and defensive positions were built facing the plain of Saint-Denis. The priory of Saint-Lazare was requisitioned to serve as a drill field where recruits were assembled. In a letter addressed to Antoine Portail, on a mission in the Dordogne, Vincent described the dominant mood in August 1636: "Paris is waiting to be besieged by the Spanish; they have entered Picardy with a powerful army, and the vanguard is as close as forty to forty-eight kilometers from here, so that the inhabitants of the plain are fleeing to Paris, while Paris is so horrified that many are fleeing to other cities. The king is attempting to raise an army in opposition, but his armies are deployed in the far reaches of his kingdom or even outside, and the place where companies are being gathered and armed is here, where the stable, the woodsheds, the halls, and the cloister are filled with weapons and the courtyards are teeming with military men. The drum is beginning to roll, even though it is only seven o'clock in the morning, and over the past eight days, seventy-two companies have been formed here." Vincent had to take measures to protect those for whom he was responsible. He evacuated them to the provinces "so that if the siege comes, most of them will be spared the risks that go with such an event."[1]

Thereupon, at the end of August, he received instructions from Chancellor Pierre Séguier, ordering him to send twenty of his priests to Senlis, where the royal troops were assembling, to serve as chaplains to the army. If one believes Abelly, Vincent went to Senlis in person to receive the orders of the king directly. Because he did not want to leave his priests without detailed instructions as to the role they would be expected to play, he immediately composed a little rule for them:

> The priests of the Mission who are with the army will keep in mind that Our Lord has called them to this holy work:
>   1. To offer their prayers and sacrifices to God for the happy success of the king's good purposes and for the safety of his army;
>   2. To help soldiers who are in a state of sin to free themselves and to help those who are in a state of grace to maintain it. And finally, to do everything in their power to see that those who die leave this world in a state of salvation.
>   3. For this purpose, they will cultivate a particular devotion to the name that God takes in Scripture—Lord God of Hosts—and to the intention of Our Lord when he said *Non veni pacem mittere, sed gladium* (I did not come to bring peace, but the sword), and the purpose of this is to bring us the peace which is the goal of the war.[2]

Faced with a crisis, it was the man of action who emerged. Vincent, like a good patriot, hoped for the success of the king and his army, not fearing to invoke the Lord God of Hosts. When, a few days later, he wrote to Robert de Sergis, whom he had designated to serve as chaplain in a cavalry corps, we see that Vincent was possessed with a holy joy and that he was ready to ride out himself to the vanguard of the cavalry: "So go, *in nomine Domini* (in the name of the Lord), in the same spirit in which Saint Francis Xavier went to the Indies."[3]

The missionary-chaplains returned to Saint-Lazare at the end of November, after the royal army had reconquered the fortress of Corbie and
the Spaniards had withdrawn, without even mounting any great battles.
But this warlike interlude illuminates another face of Vincent de Paul,
quite different from the image of a mild pacifist that many have wished
to paint. When the drum rolled in the courtyard of Saint-Lazare, the hot
Gascon blood beat in his heart; it would not have been amazing to see
him jump on a horse to ride beside the king, *in nomine Domini*.

As often happens, the war brought epidemics with it, and the plague
flared up here and there. One case appeared at Saint-Lazare itself, but
the contagion did not spread. "All our patients are free of fever, and in
the meantime, by the grace of God, no other infection has occurred
here," Vincent wrote in 1636. He himself went on a mission toward
Orléans, visiting on the way the farm of Fréneville, which had been presented to the Congregation by Madame de Herse. On his return, exhausted from weeks of travel, he made his excuses to Louise de Marillac
for the fact that he could not visit her because of a slight indisposition.
But as his health did not improve with time, he gave in to the insistence
of people around him when they begged him to rest a little. He went to
Fréneville to stay until the end of the year: "Our people have pressed
me to go to the country because of my insignificant little fever, which
doesn't seem like much, since it passed so soon."[4]
    Vincent de Paul had a rugged constitution, which he needed con-
sidering his way of life and rhythm of work, not to mention the priva-
tion, the fasts, and the mortifications he imposed upon himself.[5] He
was frequently on the road without a rest, on foot or on horseback, to
take part in missions, visit the Charités, or inspect the holdings of the
Congregation. We can imagine what his schedule was like by reflecting
on this extract from a letter to Louise de Marillac. "I have just arrived
and am leaving now for Pontoise, to return tomorrow evening and
leave again the next day to go to the region near Dourdan, from where
I hope to return by Thursday or Friday of next week."[6]
    When he was in residence at Saint-Lazare, it was not to rest. Up at
four o'clock in the morning, he was on his knees at prayer in the church
for an hour before saying mass and then going about his tasks, various
meetings, visits to the sick or prisoners. All of this was done fasting, for
the first meal, dinner, was taken at half past ten. That was when he allowed himself an hour of relaxation with his confrères before going

to recite vespers and compline, all on his knees. Immediately after this, there were meetings, either at Saint-Lazare or on the outside, then a common reading of the breviary before the evening meal at six o'clock. After a last visit to the Blessed Sacrament, he withdrew to his room, a little chamber without a fireplace, furnished with a simple wooden table with two chairs and a bed with a coarse straw mat; there was no mattress and no tapestry to cut the cold drafts coming through the poorly jointed walls in the winter. His extensive correspondence kept him awake late, well after the bell rang nine o'clock,[7] the hour of curfew. Often, he was so tired that he fell asleep at the table, while writing a last letter by candlelight.

For some time, Vincent had been touched by the sad lot of children abandoned by their mothers before the door of a house or under the porch of some church. They were picked up by the local policeman and carried to a house in an alley going down toward the Seine, at the port of Saint-Landry. This establishment, called La Couche, received about 300 or 400 children a year. According to Vincent himself, no one had ever heard it said for fifty years that a single foundling child had lived. All of them perished, one way or another. It is no wonder, since they were already half dead when they were picked up at dawn and, because there was little money, the care they received at La Couche was quite deficient: "We were told that these poor little creatures had little help — one wet nurse for four or five children. They were given laudanum pills to make them sleep, but that's a poison." Moreover, Vincent claimed that they were sold to beggars for 8 sols each, and that these broke their arms and legs to excite pity and make the public give them alms. Then they let the babies die of hunger. What was most painful of all for Vincent was the fact that "many of these children died without having been baptized."[8]

Vincent reflected on this tormenting question for a long time, but he did not want to involve himself lightly: "I see nothing more frequently than the failure of things undertaken in haste." He first mentioned this subject in a letter to Louise de Marillac toward the end of 1637: "I thought of discussing this in detail with the Procurator General and of exploring means of helping these poor creatures at the foundling home."[9] Perhaps he even brought one of the children home himself one day, wrapped in his cape? There is a strong tradition that he did so. What is certain is that he presented the question before the assembly of the Ladies of Charity of the Hôtel-Dieu. At this meeting, it was decided to confide to Louise de Marillac the task of carrying out a first attempt, in which a few children would be taken in, to see whether they could be fed with cow's milk.

Rather than trying to attend to children from La Couche, Vincent decided with Louise de Marillac that they would open a new establishment. "The attempt which you are proposing, with a wet nurse and a few goats at your place wouldn't help much!"[10] And so instead, they made a modest beginning of the charitable institution known as the Foundling Hospital. In a second stage, the Daughters of Charity were installed together with the wet nurses in a house near the gate of Saint Victor. The number of children rescued grew rapidly. As the work succeeded, the need for finances increased. This would become a great anxiety for Vincent de Paul.

Vincent was asked with increasing frequency to establish houses of the Mission in different dioceses. He did not yet feel ready to cope with all the problems which such foundations would entail, but he did agree to make a first attempt at Toul in 1635, at the request of Bishop Charles de Gournay. This involved taking over a hospital which, until then, had been administered by two religious of the Order of the Holy Spirit, as well as preaching missions in the new diocese and conducting retreats for the priests. But the administration of the hospital took too much time from the missionaries, who were only two in number. They asked to be relieved of these duties so that they could devote themselves to the work of the missions. An agreement to this effect was arrived at with the bishop and the local civil authorities, and it was to be the source of many complaints and lawsuits, reaching as far as Rome.[11] It would require twenty years of proceedings to bring to a definitive close an affair which was essentially a matter of distributing the revenues attached to operation of the hospital. It would end, by royal decision, in a union of the Knights of the Holy Spirit at Toul with the Congregation of the Mission.[12]

This first experience convinced Vincent that before establishing any new project, he should settle all jurisdictional and financial questions beyond the slightest possibility of ambiguity so that the new house could conduct an autonomous existence. He also saw that he would have to have a sufficient number of missionaries to put effective teams into the field. But in 1636, the Congregation counted fewer than fifty priests. Vincent, always prudent, did not wish to throw himself too quickly into recruitment. Instead he prepared carefully by organizing an internal seminary in 1637, which he gave to one of his first companions, Jean de la Salle, to direct. Vincent sent him to the Jesuits for a stay of a few months so that he could observe their formation of young members. From that time on, the Congregation was to recruit an annual average of fifteen priests and several brothers coadjutors.[13]

Vincent now set about establishing a whole series of foundations: five new houses were created in three years. First at Notre-Dame-de-la-Rose, a pilgrimage site near Agen, he opened a house endowed by the duchess d'Aiguillon. In a contract signed August 18, 1637, she gave a sum of 20,000 livres for the upkeep of four priests charged with preaching missions in the villages and towns of her duchy and with celebrating daily mass for her and her family in her own chapel. The next foundation, a particularly important one, was established in the village of Richelieu, which had been raised up out of nothing by the cardinal. The latter summoned Vincent to his château of Reuil where, on June 4, 1638, he signed a contract in which the Congregation of the Mission engaged to send seven priests to the village and to increase this number to ten over the next two years. These priests were to alternate in preaching missions in his duchy and in the bishoprics of Luçon and Poitiers, while also preparing ordinands and directing spiritual exercises for the clergy of the region. Later, the cardinal took upon himself the lodging and board of this team, assigning for this purpose the revenue of the registry of documents of Loudun, steady at 4,550 livres per year. But he died before signing this contract, and it was contested by his heirs and never honored.

At the head of the team required by Richelieu, Vincent sent a confirmed missionary, Bernard Codoing, to whom he addressed a long letter filled with recommendations and instructions: "Oh, Monsieur, what spiritual need there is in that region, where there are many heretics because, as they say, they have never heard anyone speak about God at the Catholic church there. It is in that region where the heresy appeared and spread, to be most obstinately defended." After having dispensed his encouragement and his blessing, he ended his marching orders for the mission with a crystal-clear formula: "I will expect no other response than your departure."[14] This has the ring of a military command; although he devoted great effort to mastering it, Vincent had an essentially authoritarian character. In this case, he had a reason; he was familiar with Bernard Codoing's tendency to agonize and make excuses, and he plainly intended to be obeyed.

Soon it appeared advisable to relieve this house of Richelieu of double duty and to open a second one only for the diocese of Luçon. Once more, it was Bernard Codoing who was assigned to open this new house, at the end of 1638. But before this, a foundation was established at Troyes. Its benefactors were the local bishop, René de Breslay, and Commander de Sillery, who together assured it an annual income of 3,000 livres. In a contract signed on October 3, the Congregation of the Mission engaged to provide six priests and two brothers to evangelize the diocese and preach missions every five years on the lands of the Commanderie.

Already Vincent was preparing another new foundation, the house at Annecy, which was made possible by the generosity of the same Commander de Sillery, who made a gift in June 1639 of 45,000 livres for this purpose, guaranteed by support from the city of Melun. The contract called for the installation of two priests and one brother to preach missions in Savoy. This team was doubled in size in January 1640, when a complementary gift of 10,000 livres was received.

Gradually, the houses of the Congregation of the Mission were forming a network. In the course of the next twenty years it would come to extend over all the provinces of the kingdom and even beyond its frontiers. Vincent de Paul would devote a large part of his time and energy to encouraging these houses, keeping up a correspondence with their superiors, and visiting when he could.

At the same time, together with Louise de Marillac, Vincent undertook the deployment in the provinces of teams of Daughters of Charity. Their mother house had been installed in May 1636 in a small rented dwelling in the village of La Chapelle, near Saint-Lazare. Soon this was too small, and the women moved in 1641 into two houses in the rue Faubourg-Saint-Denis, facing the church of Saint-Lazare. The houses were bought by the Congregation of the Mission, as the Daughters of Charity, not yet recognized as a company, did not have the necessary official existence.[15] Louise de Marillac received postulants there. They were recruited according to criteria which Vincent later articulated in a letter to one of the superiors of the Mission, Guillaume Delville: "If you find strong, healthy girls, disposed to works of charity, of irreproachable life, and resolved to be humble, to work at cultivating virtue and to serve the poor for the love of God, you may give them hope that they can be received."[16]

The girls made their apprenticeship by visiting the poor, helping in the dispensary, and working in the class for little girls. The mother house also received women of the world who came there to make retreats under the direction of Louise de Marillac and with the counsel of Vincent. He hoped that these retreatants would make concrete resolutions: "It would be good to provide practice in this for the women who come there to make retreats with you. All the rest is nothing but a figment of the spirit which, having developed some facility and even some sweetness in considering virtue, flatters itself with the thought that it is indeed quite virtuous."[17]

The first establishment of the Daughters of Charity was installed at Saint-Germain-en-Laye, where a Charité had just been founded. Vincent had been asked to come and preach a mission there in January 1638 while the court was in residence. It was Nicolas Pavillon, member of the Tuesday Conference, recently named bishop of Alet, who directed this mission. It was a lively success; it seems that on this occasion Louis XIII and Anne of Austria had their first direct contact with Vincent.

The very success of this mission aroused the dissatisfaction of some of the nobles. In fact, the ladies of the court and the maids of honor, carried away by holy zeal, began to dress in humble garments to go and visit the poor and the sick, thus missing the worldly entertainments of the court. Complaints were brought to the king, and the argument was made that visiting the sick might bring contagious vapors into the court to infect the royal family. The queen herself came to the defense of the virtuous ladies of her household. As for Vincent, he was concerned for the virtue of his missionaries. He wrote to one of his confrères: "We had to suffer on this occasion because of the uncovered breasts." But he did not wish any insistence on this point: "In the name of God, Sir, let us be very circumspect in explaining the sixth commandment. We will have to suffer a storm for that one day!"[18]

After the establishment of the first house of the Daughters of Charity, Vincent sent a team to Richelieu. The next year, a team was sent to Angers, where eight Daughters of Charity were to work with the sick in a hospital. Louise de Marillac decided to accompany her daughters on this long voyage. From Richelieu, where he was on a visit, Vincent sent her advice for the best way to make the journey: "If you wish to take the coach to Châteaudun, you will pass through Chartres and can make your devotions there. From Châteaudun you have forty-four kilometers to Orléans and maybe less to Notre-Dame de Cléry, where the river runs by. As soon as you arrive at Orléans, you will send to the harbor to find a boat."[19] Finally, after fourteen days in a carriage and on a boat, Louise de Marillac, with her troop of girls dressed in gray serge and wearing white head dresses, arrived at Angers. The plague had broken out in the city. Without fear of this epidemic, the team of Daughters of Charity set to work at the hospital.

When Vincent received this news, he wrote immediately to Louise de Marillac: "I beg you above all to take good care of yourself among the great dangers you are encountering in Angers."[20] But a courier brought him the news that she had fallen ill. Then he, who only a few months earlier had been preaching to her in severe terms because she was too anxious about her son, expressed his worries freely and let his tender feelings for her shine through: "I beg you, Mademoiselle, to do everything in your power to recover your health, and to use all means necessary. . . . And when you return, it must be in a litter; we will try to send you one when you are well enough to travel."[21] Here, Vincent was no longer playing the part of a demanding spiritual director who managed his penitent severely. He was rather the attentive friend who is concerned for someone dear to him.

Assistance to the Lorraine
1638–1640

The Saint-Cyran Affair
Vincent at Fréneville
The Drama of the Lorraine
Assistance to Victims of Catastrophe in Lorraine

In June 1638, Richelieu received Monsieur Vincent at his château of Rueil, where the two signed a charter of foundation for a house of the Congregation of the Mission that would be located on the cardinal's lands. This demonstrated the esteem in which the cardinal held Vincent and the work of evangelization he was carrying out throughout the kingdom. But a short time after this, Richelieu summoned Monsieur Vincent again. This time, he received him coolly and submitted him to a stern interrogation about an affair which, he claimed, was threatening the tranquility of the country and the unity of the Church.

What had taken place? It seems that on May 15 of that year the abbot of Saint-Cyran had been arrested and sequestered in the château of Vincennes and accused of plotting against the cardinal and professing theories contrary to the orthodox religion. Among the documents seized at the home of the abbot was a copy of a long letter that Saint-Cyran had addressed to Vincent de Paul on November 20, 1637.

The Master of Petitions, the lord de Laubardemont,[1] charged with gathering evidence for the abbot's trial, had hoped that this letter could support his accusation of the suspect. But when Vincent was called for a deposition, he refused to speak before a layman on a matter concerned with religion. It is for this reason that he was twice summoned by the redoubtable cardinal who had tried in vain to obtain inculpatory information about Saint-Cyran. According to a witness of the last meeting, Richelieu "treated him coldly and sent him away with every sign of perplexity."[2]

Who was this abbot of Saint-Cyran and what was his relationship with Vincent de Paul? His name was Jean Duvergier de Hauranne, and he was born at Bayonne in 1581.[3] He studied theology at the University of Louvain, a Jesuit school, and there he met a young student, Cornelius Jansen,[4] known under the name of Jansenius. They became great friends and when they had completed their studies, they went together to the family estates of Jean Duvergier, near Bayonne. There, for five years, they studied biblical and patristic texts, especially the writings of Saint Augustine. Then Jansenius returned to the Netherlands where he had been ordained and where he taught theology at Louvain. There he dedicated himself to editing a monumental summa of Augustinian thought which was published after his death in 1638. This work, the *Augustinus,* became the fundamental document of Jansenism. As for Jean Duvergier, after staying in the capital for a time, he was ordained in 1618 and soon thereafter was made commendatory abbot of the abbey of Saint-Cyran near Poitiers, a substantial benefice which assured him a great degree of independence. He then settled in Paris for good and in 1622, he was named chaplain to the Queen Mother.

The abbot of Saint-Cyran made the acquaintance of Pierre de Bérulle, and no doubt it is in the circle of Bérulle that Vincent met him. The two men were similar in age and in their southern origin. Their friendship grew rapidly, and they were of service to each other. Vincent, thanks to the influence of the Gondis, managed to get a nephew of Saint-Cyran freed from imprisonment in Spain and Saint-Cyran managed a favorable outcome for a matter of interest to Vincent's family. They were so close that if we are to believe the deposition made by Saint-Cyran at his trial, they even shared expenses for a time. Saint-Cyran even offered Vincent the priory of Bonneville, which he had held before receiving his abbey, and "which he wanted only the aforementioned Sieur Vincent to have."[5]

At the beginning of their friendship, Vincent was impressed by Saint-Cyran's natural assurance and authority. Father Rapin said about him: "One of his main talents was to exercise authority over men's minds, once they listened to him, and to become their leader."[6] Saint-

Cyran, who had connections among the great men of the country, helped Vincent many times, especially to remove certain difficulties when he was installing his congregation at the Collège des Bons-Enfants and later, when he was concluding the transfer of the priory of Saint-Lazare. But eventually, their relations became less close. Saint-Cyran wanted to influence the way in which Vincent governed his congregation, a thing which the latter tolerated less and less well. Just as he had retained his freedom in relations with Bérulle, he insisted on remaining free in his dealings with Saint-Cyran. This was so important to Vincent that he soon became troubled with the ideas that his friend proposed to him, such as: "The poor Church has not existed for the last five hundred years. . . . Calvin had the right idea, but his way of expressing himself doomed his position. . . . Who will save us from the Jesuits?"[7]

Saint-Cyran's outrageous declarations, which he did not save for Vincent alone, fanned the flame of a rumor that he had secret plans and a design for conspiracy. Since the death of Bérulle in 1629, he had been seen as the leader of the Party of the Devout. In the realm of politics, he criticized the positions of Richelieu, such as the alliance with the Protestant powers against the hegemony of the Hapsburgs; on the religious front, he denounced the gallican tendencies of the cardinal, which tended to produce a progressive distancing between the Church of France and the papacy.[8]

When in October 1637 Vincent learned that Saint-Cyran was leaving for a rest in Poitou, he decided to visit him, on the pretext of saying good-bye, but with the real purpose of admonishing him about his errors. His brotherly warning had a strong effect on Saint-Cyran, who sent him a long, self-justifying letter from Dissais, where he was staying with the bishop of Poitiers. It was this letter, a copy of which was found at the time of Saint-Cyran's arrest, which caused Vincent to be summoned to the presence of the cardinal.

After his interview with Richelieu, Vincent was required to make a deposition before Jacques Lescot,[9] confessor of the cardinal. Being a prudent man, he composed this deposition carefully; it was recorded over the course of three sessions from March 31 to April 2, 1639. The document shows Vincent's skill; he managed to avoid accusing his friend without lying. Here is an example: "[I am asked] whether I did not hear the Sieur de Saint-Cyran say that God destroyed his Church five or six hundred years ago, using Solomon's phrase *tempus destruendi* (the time of destruction), and whether corruption has crept in, even into his doctrine. I reply that I heard him say these words only once. And at first this statement caused me pain, but then I thought that he was saying it in the sense (I am told) that Pope Clement VIII used it when he said that he wept because the Church was expanding to the Indies, where it would destroy itself."[10] Thus, by interjecting the authority of the pope's words, Vincent neutralized the apparent heterodoxy of Saint-Cyran's declaration.

When all was said and done, the accusation did not succeed in supporting the charges against Saint-Cyran, who was presumed guilty of having spoken against Catholic doctrine and dogmas confirmed by the Council of Trent. But on Richelieu's personal order and on purely political grounds, Saint-Cyran remained in prison. He was not released until February 1643, after the cardinal's death. Sorely tried by his captivity, he died shortly after being set free, in October, without ever seeing Vincent again.

For the first time, Vincent was involved in a political affair. Whether he liked it or not, he was now labeled as belonging to the circle of the Devout because of his relations and friendships with people like the bishop of Poitiers, Augustin Potier, and other members of the Company of the Blessed Sacrament. But in his dealings with Richelieu, he proved his skill and mastery by not allowing the cardinal to overawe him or draw him into territory outside the boundaries of pure Catholic orthodoxy. No matter the outcome of these confrontations, the very fact that anyone made the effort to obtain his testimony proves that, by this time, Monsieur Vincent had acquired fame and authority far outside his priestly and charitable sphere.

At the beginning of the Saint-Cyran affair, Vincent was staying at the farm in Fréneville to nurse his recurrent "feverlet." In the country, he rediscovered his peasant habits. It was the time for haying, and he sent word to the manager of the farm at Bourget: "Do not cut the hay while the rain lasts, even if the workers say that you should. . . . The master of the meadow opposite the Church of La Chapelle understands very well how to manage. When you hear that he is cutting his fields, you can go ahead and cut ours."[11] "Our farmer at Gonesse has the wheat field where the prior has his sainfoin planted, behind the barn, harrowed twice at once. It seems to me that the first time the harrow was turned over at one end and the second time he went across the field with the harrow in the normal position."[12]

It seems that Vincent enjoyed his farms—they reminded him of his youth—but he enjoyed them as a wise manager would. When he had to review a contract for the farm of Fréneville, he specified to a counselor of the Châtelet delegated to take care of the matter: "A price of 1,200 livres, of which we must retain an amount of 50 livres of rent at eight percent on the one hand, and of 10 livres on the other. It would be good to have them specify the number of acres of land involved, supposedly 150, a large portion of which is lying fallow."[13] He also insisted on being in control of the accounts of all the houses of the Mission: "An accident which affected the Community showed me that I must see all accounts of expenses and receipts."[14]

In his letters, Vincent moved easily from material questions to the personal problems of his correspondents. Without fail he asked them about their health and urged them to care for themselves in order to remain strong enough to follow their vocation of serving the poor: "In the name of Our Lord, Monsieur, do everything in your power to regain your health and keep it, in order to be able to serve God and the poor for a longer term."[15] It is not surprising, then, that he liked to give advice about medicines. Had he become so knowledgeable while he was working for his master, the spagiric physician, on the Barbary coast? Often, he would recommend a specific potion: "President Fouquet was cured of the dropsy by using a half glass of chervil juice, with an equal quantity of white wine, well mixed and strained through a cloth, taken on an empty stomach and with no food taken for two hours afterward. The patient should not drink more than four liters at each meal. This is a sovereign and easy remedy."[16]

As superior of the Congregation, Vincent naturally took the greatest care of the moral health of his missionaries. The virtues he hoped they would acquire are first of all mildness, simplicity, and humility. He had already given instructions to this effect at the creation of his first Charité, and he returned to it constantly in his letters: "I must only beg you to work at surrendering the high esteem in which you have held the renown and brilliance of your virtue and the vain congratulations of the world, which Our Lord rejected so firmly, and which he urges us so frequently to reject as well."[17] "Everyone says that the missionary spirit is the spirit of humility and simplicity. Hold yourselves to that. The spirit of mildness, simplicity, and humility is the spirit of Our Lord; the spirit of pride will not survive long at the Mission."[18] "One of the most important acts of charity is to support one's neighbor, and we must hold it as an irrefutable maxim that our difficulties with our neighbor lie rather with our own lack of self-control than with anything else."[19]

Vincent was very well informed of what was going on throughout the kingdom by his missionaries, who worked in every province in collaboration with the members of the Company of the Blessed Sacrament. Through them, he was receiving increasingly disquieting news about the condition of the people of Lorraine. This unfortunate duchy was subject to every trial: bad harvests due to inclement weather from 1628 to 1630, epidemics of the plague starting in 1629, and, as a crowning blow, the coming of armies, both French and foreign, who put the region to fire and the sword. The duchy of Lorraine occupied a critical position at the border between the Holy Roman Empire and the kingdom of France. Some of the possessions of the duke de Lorraine were governed by the emperor, while another portion, the Barrois, was at the orders of the king of France, who had also annexed a century earlier the three episcopal cities of Metz, Toul, and Verdun. In order to survive, Lorraine was constrained to practice a politics of strict neutrality with regard to its two powerful neighbors. But since 1626 the duke's nephew, Charles IV, had been allowing himself to be drawn into anti-French maneuvers. Moreover, he had received on his lands Gaston d'Orléans, who himself was rebelling against his brother, Louis XIII. Charles had even declared himself willing to let his sister, Marguerite de Vaudémont, marry this rebel in a secret wedding. This gave the king of France a good reason to invade Lorraine once more in 1632 and, at the end of 1633, to take possession of Nancy, its capital, while Charles IV placed himself and his army at the service of the emperor.

In May 1635, war was declared between France, the emperor, and Spain. The imperial forces and the Swedish forces under the orders of a formidable commander in chief, Jean de Werth, marched on the territories of Lorraine, while the Spanish invaded the northern reaches of the kingdom of France. From that time on, for many long years, Picardy, Bourgogne, and Lorraine would be ravaged by the movements of friendly and enemy armies. There was nothing but savagery and robbery, villages pillaged and burned, peasants tortured, survivors terrorized. Everywhere people fled to fortified castles or the deepest forest. Farming was abandoned and fields lay fallow. There are even accounts of cannibalism.

Vincent was deeply moved when he read descriptions of these horrendous scenes and heard the stories of general misery. The Company of the Blessed Sacrament started in 1636 to organize aid to the peasants around Nancy, and the missionaries at Toul did the same, but they were helpless before the vast scale of the tragedy. The missionaries asked for help. On his own initiative, Vincent decided to organize help for the suffering people of Lorraine, and on May 10, 1639, he wrote to one of the priests representing him at Rome: "With the help of Our Lord, we have undertaken to bring assistance to the poor people of Lorraine and for that purpose we have sent Messieurs Bécu and Rondet, Brothers Guillard, Aulent, Baptiste, and Bourdet, two each, to the cities of Toul, Metz, Verdun, and Nancy. I hope to supply each group with 2,000 livres a month."[20]

This was the beginning of an extraordinary enterprise of helping the population of an entire province. The work went on for ten years, during which Vincent de Paul, who had received no official charge to do this, succeeded in bringing to Lorraine help amounting to more than 1,500,000 livres and on the order of more than 33,000 meters of various fabrics.[21]

At the beginning, Vincent had absolutely no financial means to set such a project in motion. Once more, he appealed to the generosity of his Ladies of Charity, bringing them together to tell them what he had learned of the tragic situation of the people of Lorraine. In this way, he collected the first funds, but money runs out and good will is soon exhausted. At that point, he went to the highest authorities. Did he go, as in the account of Abelly, to Cardinal Richelieu to implore him to give peace to France? To this, His Eminence is said to have answered, "Alas, Monsieur Vincent, I hope for this peace as much as you do, but peace does not depend on me." No other document gives an account of this interview, but it is certain that Vincent intervened with Louis XIII on this matter, and the king entrusted a significant sum to him. Vincent announced this in a letter written in July 1640, addressed to Bernard Codoing, superior of the house of Annecy: "The king is giving 45,000 livres for this purpose, to be distributed by me according to the orders of the Minister of Justice."[22]

Vincent was not content with just collecting money; he organized payment and distribution of the funds as well. Carrying the money across regions where bands of robbers roamed as well as more or less regular and disciplined troops was not a trivial matter. The task fell to an astonishing person, Brother Mathieu Regnard.[23] In one decade, he made more than fifty journeys from Paris to Lorraine, each time carrying sums of money from 20,000 to 50,000 livres. He always succeeded in escaping all who attempted to intercept him. What is more, on the way home, he brought with him the largest number possible of people in distressed circumstances. Vincent tells of his exploits in a letter from October 1639: "He brought us one hundred last month, among whom were forty-six girls, young ladies, and others, whom he led and watched over all the way to this city."[24]

With his well-developed sense of organization and efficiency, Vincent wrote a little rule of life for the members of the Congregation whom he sent to Lorraine. In it, he insisted on the spirit of fairness which must govern the distribution of aid. This was assured by consultation with the local clergy, with whom the missionaries drew up a list of the poor in the order of their need. Finally, the missionaries were to send frequent reports about their work so that the generous benefactors could know how their money was being used and be encouraged to continue their munificence.[25]

For Vincent, charity was not a matter of impulse or improvisation. He believed that charity is only effective when it is programmed and controlled. On this subject, he wrote to François de Coudray, superior of the house at Toul, giving him precise and detailed instructions: "You must make the distributions as M. de Villarceaux orders, as for the distributions in other towns, let them follow precisely the order you have been given by the same Sieur de Villarceaux, and let the missionaries obtain receipts for all that they distribute, so that they can make an accounting of it, lest for any reason whatever the funds have been diverted or even a single penny has been applied elsewhere. And you will report to me monthly the sums you have distributed."[26]

But he never believed that this assistance should be exclusively material. Vincent intended to provide assistance for both body and soul to the poor people of the fields gathered in the towns. He developed his idea in this way: "physically, by allocating to them 500 livres for bread every month, which comes to 2,500 livres which we must find monthly, and spiritually, by teaching them all things necessary for salvation and helping them to make a general confession of all their past life."[27]

The reports rendered by the missionaries provide us with living images of the extreme misery of the people of Lorraine. Julien Guérin, priest of the Mission sent to Saint-Mihiel at the beginning of 1640, wrote to Vincent: "I find so many poor people that I don't see how I can give to all of them. There are more than 300 in the greatest need and 300 more who have reached the limit of endurance. Monsieur, I tell you truly, there are more than 100 who seem to be skeletons covered with skin and so horrifying that if Our Lord did not give me the strength, I would not dare look at them. Their skin is like tanned marble and so drawn that their teeth appear dry and uncovered, with their eyes and faces completely contorted with suffering."[28]

When the survivors arrived in Paris, alone or in groups, from the hell that was Lorraine, they immediately made for Saint-Lazare, for they knew they would find aid and comfort there. Soon it was being said in the capital that Monsieur Vincent must be from Lorraine himself, if he was doing so much good for these refugees. His actions were considered unusual because at this time, Lorraine was not France, and its inhabitants were considered foreigners. In consequence, Vincent's work was considered all the more admirable.

Among these dispossessed, there was an additional hidden misery suffered by aristocrats or other persons of some station. After having exhausted their resources and sold anything of value they had brought with them, they did not dare to go out and beg. Once he knew of this situation, Vincent appealed to a group of gentlemen whom he called together at Saint-Lazare. He understood immediately that to give help in a way that was not wounding to the recipient, he would have to use the intermediary of people who were of the same social class. On this subject, he wrote to the duchess d'Aiguillon, who had just made a gift of 15,000 livres for the people of Lorraine: "Messieurs de Liancourt, de la Ville-aux-Clercs, de Fontenay, and some other people of position assembled here yesterday to start working for the people of position who have fled to this city from Lorraine."[29]

Among these gentlemen, one in particular stood out in the performance of this charity, and this was the baron de Renty.[30] He was a member of the Company of the Blessed Sacrament. The campaign in favor of the aristocrats of Lorraine illustrates the cooperation between the Company of the Blessed Sacrament and the priests of Saint-Lazare, with the initiative coming now from one side and now from the other. Vincent, who was always ready to work as part of a team, usually acted as a catalyst for energetic people of good will. He knew how to find the funds necessary to create living and durable works, rather than flaring straw fires; this was the only way they could be effective. As part of the effort to bring help to Lorraine, he did not hesitate to make use of public opinion by having the letters of his missionaries, with their vivid descriptions of distress, copied and distributed. Many letters from the magistrates of cities in Lorraine addressed to Vincent from 1640 on express deep gratitude for the help he provided to their people and the prayer that he will continue his support.[31] This support for Lorraine is remarkable for more than the amount of aid distributed and the number of suffering people helped. It was the first attempt at organized assistance for a whole endangered region. Without having received any specific charge, Vincent de Paul assumed the role of a secretary of state for refugees and war victims. Going far beyond the responsibilities expected of him as superior of the Congregation of the Mission, he placed himself on his own initiative, in a national role.

The Rule of the Congregation 1640–1642

Faced with an emergency such as the one experienced by the people of Lorraine, Vincent de Paul proved to be a decisive man of action. He did not hesitate to throw himself into an undertaking which, at first sight, was far beyond the means of a congregation of modest size. Under such circumstances, with confidence in Providence, he relied on this formula: "Believe me, three are more than ten, when Our Lord's hand is in their work."[1] But as audacious as he was in extreme circumstances, when it came to decisions about the organization and future of his congregation, he was most circumspect.

The Congregation had already been in existence for fifteen years, and in the charter of foundation, it was clearly stated that those who are admitted to the work of charity that is the Congregation of the Mission must have the intention of serving God once they enter and of obeying the Rule on this subject. But this Rule was not yet entirely composed,[2] not to mention being approved by the relevant authorities. This was a cause of concern for Vincent, who in 1635 wrote to a friend: "I fell dangerously ill, which made me think of death. Examining my conscience to see how I might have caused some pain,

I found that there was nothing except the fact that we have not yet constituted our Rule."[3]

In the matter of composing this Rule, there was one point which troubled Vincent and upon which he questioned himself extensively, and that was the question of vows. He dearly wanted the missionaries to make those vows, but he did not want the community to become a religious order; rather, he wanted its priests to remain among the secular clergy. He explained this point of view in February 1640 to Louis Lebreton, who was representing the Mission in Rome: "I am perplexed by my doubts and have no idea how to resolve them. Either it will be enough for the priests to make a vow of stability, and in the matter of poverty and obedience, to hear a solemn threat of excommunication in the chapter once a year, or it would suffice if the members made a solemn promise once a year to observe the Rule of poverty, chastity, and obedience, and we could determine whether it is the vow of stability which constitutes membership in a religious order."[4]

In other words, Vincent was hoping to reconcile two apparently contradictory requirements: having the priests make a vow of stability to prevent members of the Congregation from leaving it to enter another, while still being sure that this vow did not make the Mission into a religious order, with the result that it would become directly subordinated to Rome.[5] He even put his problem before Richelieu, and asked for his support with the Holy See. But the cardinal was not on good terms with Pope Urban VIII[6] so he advised Vincent to wait for the election of a new sovereign pontiff to whom he could then present his request. This was communicated in veiled terms to Louis Lebreton in Rome: "The difficulty on this side has been that he who can do everything [Richelieu] did not find it a good idea to inform His Holiness and told me himself, only three days ago, that we should wait for another [pope], who would take care of our problem without urging." At that point, Vincent tended toward a simple vow of stability in the second year of seminary study with a solemn vow after eight or ten years. There remained the need to find a solution for the vows of poverty, chastity, and obedience to avoid being classified as a religious order, "although we ought to hope for the spirit of an order."[7]

While he was still thinking about how to resolve the issue of vows, Vincent was designing ways to consolidate the structure of his congregation, first of all by instituting an annual visitation of the houses by the superior general or his representative. He took the Carthusian Order as an example, pointing out that one of the means they used to keep their primary observance strong was an annual visitation. So he himself visited the house at Richelieu twice, in 1638 and 1639, and the house at Troyes in 1639. He called the first general assembly of the Congregation of the Mission in October 1642. At this meeting, the principal rules were decided upon, and a commission was created to frame the constitution in final form. In this assembly it was also decided to give the superior general some assistants, which Vincent announced in these terms: "so now I am able to die whenever it pleases God no longer to tolerate the abominations of my life."[8]

These long delays in settling upon the definitive organization of the Congregation and in finalizing the Rule are part of the Vincentian method. Vincent explained this himself in a letter addressed to the superior of the house at Annecy, Bernard Codoing, who, in order to hasten the opening of a seminary, made the mistake of taking certain initiatives without reporting to Vincent: "It would even have been useful if you had let me know the actions you wished to take in support of the seminary which you have begun to create. You will tell me that I am too slow, that you sometimes wait for six months for an answer that could have come in one, and that in the meantime, opportunities are lost and everything stands still. To this, Monsieur, I answer that indeed, I am sometimes too slow to reply and to take certain actions, but that I have never yet seen a project spoiled by such delay, where everything is done in its own good time, with all the necessary consideration and precaution. You will therefore please correct your own quickness in resolving problems and taking action, and I will work to correct my lack of speed." Continuing his analysis, Vincent revealed the basis of his thought. He only arrived at a decision after quiet reflection and frequent prayer for inspiration by the Providence of God: "As I review the most important events that have taken place in this community, it seems to me, and this is plainly demonstrable, that if they had been done before they in fact were done, they could not have turned out well. That is why I am particularly devoted to following the providence of God step by step, with adoration. And my only consolation is that seemingly it is only Our Lord who has cared for the interests of this little community unceasingly."[9]

Vincent never forgot his role as royal chaplain to the galleys. He fulfilled his duties by going to inspect the galleys at Marseilles and by organizing and preaching a mission at Bordeaux in 1623 for the galley slaves passing through the port. But at Paris, his title gave him no authority over the convicts waiting for departure. They were under the jurisdiction of the Procurator General who authorized the diocesans to bring the succor of religion to the condemned. Vincent was careful not to infringe on the prerogatives of either the secular or the religious authorities. Yet having determined that the conditions in which the poor unfortunates found themselves were deplorable, he obtained the right in 1632 to transfer the most severely ill to the tower of Saint Bernard on the Quai de la Tournelle, where the conditions of their imprisonment were more humane.

He visited the prisoners as often as his many obligations allowed. Without financial means, he could only give them words of encouragement. But a few years later, at the beginning of the year 1640, he received an inheritance, the equivalent of 6,000 livres of interest, from a former president of the Chamber of Accounts, Claude Cornuel, who specified in his testament that these funds were meant for assistance to the convicts.

Once Vincent had obtained the agreement of the Procurator General, Mathieu Molé, he devoted some of the money to stipends for the priests of the parish of Saint-Nicolas-du-Chardonnet, so that they would act as chaplains for the convicts held in the tower of Saint Bernard, and some to the upkeep of three Daughters of Charity who were charged with care of the convicts. They brought the men food, provided them with clean linen, and by their very presence and word gave them moral support. Later, Vincent asked Louise de Marillac, who was at the head of the Charité of Saint-Nicolas, to encourage the ladies to visit the convicts at the same time that the Daughters of Charity came to tend to them, and to bring them a few luxuries and concern themselves with the men's fate. But it was particularly at Marseilles, the home port of the galleys, that Vincent was able to exercise fully the function of Royal Chaplain. Soon, circumstances would permit him to do this work effectively.

Beginning in 1640, Vincent de Paul undertook a new project, the establishment of seminaries. This was a direct outgrowth of a well-established activity of the Congregation of the Mission—the retreats for ordinands. Moreover, if the benefits the missions brought to rural areas were to be lasting, it was necessary to educate good priests to take over parishes in market towns and villages. A friend of Vincent, Adrien Bourdoise, who also preached missions but only in the parishes of the capital, expressed it in this way: "To preach a mission is to give a meal to a starving population, but to create a seminary—that is to provide them with lifelong nourishment."

It is easy to understand the urgent and undeniable need for seminaries from a letter written by a bishop to Vincent. This prelate was doing his best for the good of his diocese, "but with little success, because of the inexplicably large number of ignorant and sinful priests who make up my clergy, who can be corrected neither by words nor by example. It is horrible to think that in my diocese there are almost 7,000 priests who are drunkards or unchaste, who daily mount to the altar though they have not the slightest vocation."[10]

Vincent was approached by a number of bishops: "Our lords the prelates all seem to wish they had seminaries of priests, of young men [not children]," he remarked.[11] He was not the only one to be conscious of this pressing need and to put his energy into fulfilling it. In the years from 1640 to 1642, numerous seminaries were opened throughout the kingdom—in Paris, in the parish of Saint-Nicolas with Adrien Bourdoise, in the parish of Vaugirard with Jean-Jacques Olier, and in the parish of Saint-Magloire with Father Bourgoing, superior of the Oratory, who also founded seminaries at Rouen and Toulouse, while Father Eudes did the same at Caen.[12]

Vincent, for his part, had already organized a little seminary in the Collège des Bons-Enfants, but he was not very satisfied with the results. Children who had no desire to commit themselves to the priesthood came there to take their courses in the humanities. Vincent was convinced of the need to train those who were destined to receive Holy Orders not only through the ordinands' retreats, but through one or two years of education about their duties and functions as priests. In this spirit, he had opened a novitiate in 1637, the resident seminary at Saint-Lazare, where future missionaries were formed. But for the moment, he hesitated to take the initiative in founding seminaries in the provinces.

According to Abelly, it was Cardinal de Richelieu, in the course of conversation about the situation of the Church in France, who encouraged Vincent to open seminaries, allocating to him for this purpose a sum of 1,000 écus. In 1642, with this encouragement and on the strength of the funding, Vincent inaugurated a first major seminary at the Collège des Bons-Enfants into which he received twelve candidates for the priesthood. The number of students grew rapidly and the space became too small. In order to provide more space, the students in the minor seminary were moved to another building, bearing the name of Saint Charles, on the grounds of Saint-Lazare.

In response to a request from the bishop of Geneva, Juste Guérin, the house at Annecy opened a seminary at about the same time. On this occasion, Vincent insisted on maintaining the proper mission of the seminaries, namely to take those who had already received the minor orders and prepare them for ordination to the priesthood. Their mission was not to play the role of a Catholic secondary school: "I am still of the opinion that it is not expedient to receive students who are not either priests or persons in orders, and that we should not be teaching them the various subjects, but their application, in the way that is appropriate for ordinands."[13]

Soon the bishops Nicolas Pavillon of Alet, Jacques Raoul of Saintes, and Alain de Solminihac of Cahors were asking the Congregation of the Mission to take charge of the seminaries being opened in their dioceses. The movement grew; a dozen other seminaries were founded by the Congregation in Vincent's lifetime.[14] In his correspondence and in his conversations with the priests charged with the direction of the seminaries, he insisted above all on the moral formation of the young seminarians. The directors were to: "take the trouble to educate them in the true spirit of their state in life, which consists particularly in the interior life and the practice of prayer and the virtues; the important thing was not to teach them singing, ceremonials, and a little morality. The principal thing was to form them to a firm piety and devotion."[15]

Vincent gave as an example the method of Monsieur Bourdoise at Saint-Nicolas-du-Chardonnet, where the seminarians functioned as curates while going on with their studies, since there was no better way to learn than to see how things are done. Above all, he did not want to turn the seminarians into scholars, but into humble and virtuous men: "Learning is necessary, and woe to those who do not use their time well. But let us fear, oh let us fear, my brothers, for those who have sharp wits indeed have much to fear; *scientia inflat* (learning puffs up the learned) and those who have no learning are even worse off, if they are not willing to humble themselves."[16]

The organization and direction of seminaries by priests of the Congregation of the Mission did not detract from the foundation of new houses. In 1641, at the request of the bishop of Meaux, Vincent opened a house of the Mission at Crécy-en-Brie. Of course, all these foundations could only be realized with the approval of the ecclesiastical authorities and the financial aid of members of the aristocracy and the high bourgeoisie. Vincent knew that he could always count on the support of the archbishop of Paris. This was all the more true when the archbishop chose as coadjutor in 1643 his own nephew, François-Paul de Gondi, the future Cardinal de Retz. This man had been the pupil of Vincent de Paul and always remained on excellent terms with him, despite his outbursts and his tumultuous life. We know that Vincent maintained good relations with the whole Gondi clan, which included the sister of the archbishop, the marquise de Maignelay,[17] who was a benefactress of the Congregation and of the Daughters of Charity.

Moreover, Vincent was often consulted by Cardinal de Richelieu on questions dealing with the condition of the Church. A proof of his good relations with the powerful prime minister is the fact that people did not hesitate to approach Monsieur Vincent when a favor or the good will of His Eminence was desired. In the same way, he was asked to serve as intermediary to the duchess. The duchess d'Aiguillon, niece of the cardinal, was one of the most active Ladies of Charity. Deeply dedicated to all the charitable organizations created by Vincent, she often supported them with her untiring generosity.

In return, Vincent was frequently called as an advisor or comforter by these great ladies. For example, in August 1640, he wrote to Louise de Marillac: "Yesterday I spent the day visiting Madame the duchess d'Aiguillon and Madame du Vigean about the death of the latter's son. Milady's servants came to get me."[18]

Here there is a story that wants to be told. After having presented his condolences and the assurance of his prayers to Madame du Vigean, suffering a great deal from the death of her son, a brave young officer, Vincent retired, escorted by the youngest daughter of the house. This young woman, Marthe by name and nineteen years of age, was in the full bloom of a pampered youth. She was very taken by a young prince, who was also very much in love with her. The prince was Louis de Bourbon, the duke d'Enghien, who used his sword to earn himself the title of Grand Condé. In taking his leave, Vincent said to Marthe:

"Mademoiselle, you are not made for the world."[19] She cried out that she had not the slightest intention of entering the religious life. Vincent left without replying. The next year, the duke d'Enghien, against his own wishes, made a marriage of state with a niece of Richelieu, Claire-Clémence de Maillé-Brézé. A short while later, Marthe du Vigean took the veil in a Carmelite convent and became Sister Marthe of Jesus.

Vincent de Paul's connections were not limited to the great families that revolved around the court. He was also in constant contact with members of the high administration. Thus in a letter of February 1642, addressed to Bernard Codoing, superior at Annecy, who was to travel to Rome, we see Vincent's skillful use of introductions to Cardinal Mazarin, Minister Chavigny, and the duke de Liancourt.[20] "Here is a letter from Monseigneur Cardinal Mazarini, at our recommendation, to Cardinal Antonio, nephew of His Holiness. You did well to warn me not to use His Eminence [Richelieu] for the plans involving the bishop of Geneva; otherwise, I would have written tomorrow to Monsieur de Chavigny, at Lyon, to speak to him about it." Knowing that Richelieu was not received at the court of the Holy See, he planned another intervention, through the good offices of the duke de Liancourt, whose wife was a Lady of Charity. Vincent continues: "Your presence at Rome could be very helpful in interesting the ambassador in this matter. I am having his good friend Monsieur de Liancourt write to him about it, with the best ink that he has."[21]

By this time, Vincent de Paul had acquired the stature of an authority, not only in the clerical world—many are the bishops who were formed at Saint-Lazare—but also in the salons of Paris and the circles close to the government and the court.

As though he were more sharply aware of the danger for himself and his congregation that this growing visibility represented, Vincent put more and more weight on the virtue of humility in his conversations with his missionaries and in his letters to the superiors of the houses of the Mission. Thus, in a letter addressed to Jeanne de Chantal, he made an effort to weaken the opinion that she might have of the Congregation: "I have told you many things about the good points of this little community; I beg you to take this lightly, and not to talk about it to anyone. An excessively high reputation is very harmful. Alas, Reverend Mother, if you knew our ignorance and the small degree of virtue we possess, you would have great pity on us and on the abominations of my soul."[22]

In the same spirit, he made many references to his unworthiness and his low origin: "All I am is a miserable sinner, doing nothing but ill on earth, who should hope that God will snatch him away soon."[23]

Writing to the vicar general of the diocese of Bayonne, who was asking for his advice, he declared himself unworthy to give it: "Because I am a poor digger of the soil and swineherd and what is worse, the most shocking and most contemptible of all persons on the earth, I beg of you to have no regard for what I tell you."[24]

Following the custom of his times, he closed his letters with the formula "your very humble servant" or "your very humble and obedient servant." But from the year 1640 onward, when he entered his sixtieth year, instead of signing his correspondence "Vincent de Paul, priest of the Mission," he used closings such as "unworthy priest of the Mission" or "unworthy superior of the Congregation of the Mission."

PART THREE

Responding to All the Misery
of This World

The Council of Conscience
1643–1645

In a spirit of humility and mortification, Vincent de Paul called himself an unworthy priest. This did not prevent him from being summoned, together with others, to the deathbed of the king of France in May 1643. The events had begun their course at the end of 1642. Louis XIII had marched at the head of an army toward the Roussillon to put the Spanish to flight. This campaign ended with the taking of the city of Perpignan on August 29. It was then that a plot was discovered, a plot led by a young favorite of the king, the marquis de Cinq-Mars.[1] The plan was to assassinate Richelieu, then to sign a peace with Spain. Gaston d'Orléans, the king's own brother, as well as numerous other aristocrats, were implicated in this affair, which the cardinal was able to thwart in time. This was Richelieu's last battle. He was already very ill, his body devoured by abscesses, and lying in a litter in great pain he returned from the Midi to Paris, where he died on December 4.

Louis XIII, hardly in better health than his late prime minister, took Richelieu's advice and named Cardinal Mazarin as

147

his successor in that office. During the months he had left to live, the king several times asked Vincent for advice in finding worthy candidates for bishoprics. "His Majesty has asked me through his confessor to send a list of those who seem to me worthy of this dignity," wrote Vincent in April 1643 to his representative in Rome.[2]

Soon thereafter, the king's health worsened and Queen Anne of Austria suggested to her husband that he should ask Monsieur Vincent to visit him. Vincent came to the king's bedside twice in the first two weeks of June. He told a story about one of these visits in a conference he gave to the Daughters of Charity. "What do you think they feed kings when they are sick? Eggs and bouillon, that's what they give them. God granted me the favor of being present at the death of the late king. And this is what he refused, near to his death, and he refused because he found it unappetizing and because he saw that death was approaching quickly. He did me the honor of having me called, and he said: 'Monsieur Vincent, the physician is urging me to take nourishment, and I have refused, because I have to die in any case. What do you advise?' I said to him: 'Sire, the physicians have advised you to take nourishment because it is their rule always to urge it on the sick. As long as some few breaths of life remain, they hope to find a moment at which they can bring back health. That is why, if it please Your Majesty, you would do well to take what the physician has given you.' This good king then had the grace to call the physician and had the bouillon brought to him."[3]

An astonishing private conversation with this great monarch who was mildly asking the peasant's son for advice. The shadow of death strikes down differences; these two men talked quite simply about earthly food before going on to speak of spiritual things. But given the unhappy state of the king, taking in a bowl of soup could no longer change the ineluctable course of events. On May 15, Vincent was a quiet presence, one of a large group of onlookers, as the king returned his soul to God: "As long as I have been on earth, I have never seen anyone die in a more Christian fashion," Vincent wrote soon after to Bernard Codoing.[4]

Immediately after the death of Louis XIII, Anne of Austria had herself named regent of the kingdom by the parlement. She appeared before this assembly holding her five-year-old son by the hand and thus convinced the body to break the late king's will, in which there was provision for a council of regency. With little knowledge of politics, but with a character ideally suited to authority, Anne found Mazarin to be the ideal prime minister. He relieved her completely of the hard work of government, leaving her only the privileges of power. In her youth, this beautiful Infanta of Spain had been sprightly and coquettish, and had even been willing in her scatterbrained fashion to take part in intrigues which brought her very close to treason of her adopted country. When she had not yet provided the Crown with an heir twenty years after her marriage, she found herself in a precarious situation; finally, the happy event of the birth of Louis Dieudonné, the future Louis XIV, saved her from repudiation and exile.

During her regency, Anne was haunted by a single imperative, to preserve royal authority and to protect the throne for her son until he was old enough to mount its steps himself. From her Spanish education, she had brought great piety, which was strengthened by the vicissitudes of her life. She went regularly to the Benedictines to pray in their convent at the rue Saint-Jacques, which she transformed into a handsome abbey, the Val-de-Grâce, to thank God for having granted her a descendant.

In confirming Cardinal Mazarin in his role of principal minister, she decided to retain for ecclesiastical affairs an institution created by Richelieu, the Council of Conscience. The presidency was hers, and the members she named were Mazarin, Chancellor Séguier, Bishops Potier and Cospéan, the great confessor of Paris, Jacques Charton, and Monsieur Vincent. The latter announced his election to the council in a letter of June 18, 1643 to Bernard Codoing in Rome "I have never deserved compassion more than now, nor needed prayers more than at present, in my new task. I hope it will not last long."[5] In fact, he was called upon to serve for almost ten years.

What was the function of this Council of Conscience? Its creator, Richelieu, had hoped that this organ of government "would give the king knowledge of the state and the policy of the Church."[6] Under the regency of Anne of Austria, the council concerned itself with all religious matters, the maintenance of religious discipline, repression of sacrilegious acts such as duels, which still constituted a veritable wound in the social fabric, and with resistance to the inroads of the Protestants and the surveillance of the Jansenists. In addition, the council was charged with examining all episcopal and abbatial candidates, whose nomination was the privilege of the Crown, as a result of the concordat signed in 1516.[7] The council also dealt with the collation of ecclesiastical benefices.

This last function was of capital importance, considering the sizable revenues attaching to bishoprics, abbeys, and priories. At that time, the Church was the largest landowner in the kingdom. It is common knowledge that the collation of benefices had become, after a destructive wrong turn resulting in the commendatory system, a way of rewarding a person or attaching him and his family to the Crown, without giving thought to the religious qualifications of the beneficiary. It is against this abuse that Louis XIII and Richelieu had begun to act, sometimes consulting Monsieur Vincent for the names of priests worthy of receiving the bishop's or the abbot's miter. Anne of Austria was acting in the same spirit by naming the superior general of the Congregation of the Mission to the Council of Conscience.

But Church matters were not limited to the awarding of offices and benefices. The Church of France at this time was carrying the major responsibility for hospitals, schools, and universities in the kingdom, which resulted in the diversity and multiplicity of questions submitted to the council.

At the beginning of her regency, Anne of Austria often consulted Monsieur Vincent, as we see from his correspondence or the texts of his talks. "I am obliged to go out tomorrow to see the queen at the Val-de-Grâce, after dinner,"[8] he wrote to Louise de Marillac, and to the Daughters of Charity, "I have just been to see the queen, who spoke of you."[9]

Anne of Austria was interested in the work of the Mission and showed her interest generously. She was deeply moved by an ordinands' retreat at the Collège des Bons-Enfants, and for many years she supported the retreats with donations. In 1644, she supported the work of helping the aristocrats of Lorraine who had fled to the capital. "The queen has put 2,000 livres at our disposal for the noblemen of Lorraine,"[10] Vincent reported to Antoine Portail.

At the Council of Conscience, Monsieur Vincent enjoyed unchallenged authority. Whenever the matter before the body was one of nominations to Church office, Anne of Austria regularly agreed with his choice. The secretary of state, Michel Le Tellier, described this in a letter dated July 1645: "She considers herself obligated to follow the advice of the said Vincent, and she does it with such consistency that if Milord the Cardinal were to propose a different person for a given benefice, whom this Sieur Vincent did not consider competent, she would hold absolutely to what the latter had decided and neither the recommendation of His Excellency [Mazarin] or anything else could move her from her prejudice in favor of Sieur Vincent."[11]

We find confirmation of this opinion from the pen of Mazarin himself, who wrote to the same correspondent: "As for the bishopric of Soissons, Monsieur Le Tellier has told you of it at length, and everything he told you was the truth, when he said that in this matter, Monsieur Vincent has more credit with the queen than I."[12] But the cardinal was not of a mind to tolerate such a situation. He showed himself to be very jealous of anyone who tried to come between him and Anne of Austria. In his personal notebooks, which he kept in Italian, we see his feelings about Monsieur Vincent. He suspects the priest of belonging to the Party of the Devout and of being hostile to himself. In June 1643, Mazarin wrote: "Monsieur Vincent wishes advancement for Father Gondi,"[13] and three months later, "Father Gondi has spoken to my detriment, as have Father Lambert and Monsieur Vincent." Always suspicious, he wrote a little later, "Monsieur Vincent, in with the Maignelay crowd, is the channel that brings everything to the ears of Her Majesty." In the first months of 1644, fearing that a cabal was being established against him, Mazarin noted once more: "Two persons have come to inform me that the monasteries, brothers, priests, pious men and women are taking up all the queen's time under the pretext of supporting her piety, so that she no longer has time for affairs of state and I can no longer speak with her. They hope to reach their ends by having Maignelay strike the last blow when everything is ready, together with that woman Dans, as well as the prioress of the Val-de-Grâce and Father Vincent."[14]

In such a climate, possibilities of friction between the cardinal and Vincent were never lacking. At a council in February 1644, Mazarin asked for a benefice to be attributed to a son of Monsieur de la Rochefoucauld. Vincent spoke against this and had the benefice given to Monsieur Olier, pastor of Saint-Sulpice.[15] The cardinal took his revenge by delaying the meetings of these councils. He wrote in his journal: "Don't hold the Council of Conscience for some time." Thus, the rumor soon ran that Monsieur Vincent would shortly fall into disgrace. His representative at Rome became agitated when this word made its way to the Holy See. In January 1645, Vincent reassured him: "It is true that it looked as though I would no longer be tolerated in that office, but because of my sins, I'll stay in this post and feel the enmity some other way."[16]

Contrary to what Mazarin thought and even feared, Vincent was quite decided to attend exclusively to his religious duties for the time being. In February 1644, he wrote to the superior of the house at Sedan, who was posted in the heart of Huguenot territory and had to understand the conflicting politics of both Catholic and Protestant: "It is not advantageous for us to be involved in secular matters, no matter how much they may affect spiritual matters." He applied this maxim to his own position in the Council of Conscience and continued: "In the work which it has pleased the queen to assign to me on a council concerned with ecclesiastical questions, I only intervene in matters dealing with the religious state and with the poor, no matter how pious or charitable other questions raised to me may seem."[17]

We have no archives of the Council of Conscience, but in Vincent's correspondence we find many allusions to his statements within this noble court. For instance, in February 1645, he wrote to the archbishop of Toulouse requesting information about Jean de la Valette, commendatory abbot of Beaulieu, who was insisting strongly that he should have the bishopric upon the death of his brother, the bishop of Vabres, because this office had been in his family for more than a century. Vincent wished to know "whether he is capable and pious and whether he has the qualities proper to this dignity, and especially, whether he is an ordained priest." He added, "He says that he is, but some people who have discussed the matter with me and who know him are aware of nothing of the sort."[18]

That same year in June, Vincent sent a letter in the name of the Council on Ecclesiastical Affairs to the count of Brienne, demanding that "certain scandalous behavior" being practiced on the feast of Corpus Christi at Aix-en-Provence be abolished.[19] The next month, he felt obliged to refuse the attribution of an abbey to a minor child of Monsieur de Chavigny, Secretary of State. He told this to one of his missionaries, grateful that God had given him the strength to hold firm. Then, realizing that he had perhaps been rather indiscreet, he caught himself with this endearing formula: "Let this be told to the ear of your heart. I don't know why I let myself reveal so much to you."[20]

Active participation in the Council of Conscience burdened Vincent with extra work, in particular a large flow of correspondence, and so he resigned himself to making one of the brothers, Bertrand Ducournau,[21] his secretary. This man, also born in the Landes, had some experience of business, and beautiful handwriting as well. Vincent could be very satisfied with his choice; with complete devotion, Brother Ducournau rendered great service both to his superior general and to the entire Congregation.

As though he did not already have enough work, Vincent was obliged to accept, in 1643, the vicariate general of several abbeys: Saint-Ouen in Rouen, Marmoutiers in Brittany, and Saint-Martin-des-Champs in Paris. These abbeys had been attributed to Amador de Vignerod, grand-nephew of Cardinal de Richelieu. His aunt and governess, the duchess d'Aiguillon, had asked Vincent to accept the supervision of these foundations, whose abbot, in 1643, was only eleven years old. When Amador reached his majority in 1652 and found that he had no vocation for the Church, he made the abbeys over to his younger brother, Emmanuel, so that this vicariate general remained Vincent's burden for the rest of his life.[22]

In spite of all his responsibilities, Vincent never neglected the Congregation of the Mission, which remained at the center of his thoughts. The period from 1643 to 1645 was a time of expansion for the Congregation of the Mission, both within and outside the frontiers of the kingdom. First, in 1643, a house was opened in Marseilles to care for the galley slaves, funded by the generosity of the duchess d'Aiguillon, and then a house was established at Cahors with the active support of the local bishop, Alain de Solminihac. The next year, the Congregation founded a house at Sedan, in a region of heretics, a foundation financed by the royal exchequer.[23] Another house was opened at Montmirail in Champagne, on Gondi lands, thanks to a donation made by the duke de Retz, and a third house was installed at Saintes, at the request and with the help of the local bishop, Jacques Raoul. Finally, in 1645, a house was founded at Le Mans, at the request of its bishop, Emmanuel de la Ferté, and the bishop of Saint-Malo asked Monsieur Vincent to place some of his missionaries in the abbey of Saint-Méen, in the heart of his diocese.

Although all these foundations were based on donations which permitted them to exist autonomously, without appealing either to the mother house or the parishes in which missions were preached, the large number of new foundations posed some financial problems for the Congregation, for the chief necessity was to educate priests and brothers who could be sent to the new houses while continuing to carry out existing duties, such as courses for ordinands, retreats, and seminaries, not to mention continuation of aid for Lorraine. Thus Vincent devoted a good portion of his time and energy to financial questions.

A first difficulty arose immediately after the death of Cardinal de Richelieu. This prelate had allocated to the Congregation the proceeds of the Office of Records at Loudun, and this was duly inscribed in the charter of foundation of the Congregation's house at Richelieu. But a short while before his death, the cardinal had ceded his rights over the Office of Records in order to reconvert this capital into a land fund. He had not had the time to establish the document regularizing this change to the benefit of the Congregation. Thus everything depended on the good will of his heirs, especially the duchess d'Aiguillon, who was both executrix and principal heir of her uncle's estate. But there were also other relatives who were to receive significant portions of his estate, in particular Armand de Vignerod, who was the next duke de Richelieu, and another grand-nephew, Armand de Maillé,[24] whose sister, Claire-Clémence, had married the duke d'Enghien. Since this sister had not been included in the cardinal's testament, the prince de Condé, her father-in-law, attacked the document in the courts. A long lawsuit followed that finally brought a considerable sum to the Condé family. But the Congregation, in its turn, did not suffer, thanks to the generosity of the duchess d'Aiguillon.

Another difficulty arose with the house at Crécy, which counted eight priests and two religious brothers. The house had been founded in 1641 at the request of the king, who for this purpose gave the Congregation a château and 8,000 livres of land rents, computed on the revenues of five farms and the rights of the salt depot at Lagny-sur-Marne. The charter of foundation stipulated that the Congregation was to distribute alms in the region to an amount of 4,000 livres annually, and conduct missions and courses for ordinands at the request of the bishop of Meaux. But the finances of the kingdom were at a low ebb, and the king's promises were no longer honored after 1642. Therefore, Vincent was obliged to reduce the number of missionaries at Crécy to three priests. Other sources of revenue declined at this time as well. Vincent wrote to his representative in Rome: "The king will be taking, this year and in the first quarter of next year, our land rents from Agen, those from Ponts-de-Cé, to an amount of more than 20,000 livres, and we do not know *quid futurum sit* (what will happen) in the years to come. Blessed be God!"[25]

Fortunately, the duchess d'Aiguillon continued to support the Congregation generously. This made it possible for Vincent to consider opening a house in Rome. Until then, he had had only one priest in that city, whose task it was to advance the interest of the Congregation of the Mission at the Holy See. In 1643, he was able to write to Bernard

Codoing: "I have sent you an order for the purchase of the house and for the new foundation to the amount of 5,000 livres of fees from the coaches of Rouen, executed by Madame la duchesse."[26]

Of all the foundations, the house at Marseilles had particular importance in Vincent's eyes. This city was the home port of the galleys for which, as royal chaplain, he had the moral responsibility. In 1643, a concatenation of favorable circumstances allowed him to carry out the original plans, long delayed by a lack of money and men. A new bishop, Jean-Baptiste Gault, priest of the Oratory, had been made cardinal of Marseilles. His consecration at Paris provided the opportunity for the duchess d'Aiguillon and Vincent to meet and devise a plan of action for the care of the poor convicts. The first step would be to organize a great mission to be preached in March and April on board the galleys, which were in dock at this time of year. With about 260 oarsmen in each ship, for a fleet counting at least twenty galleys, a large team of missionaries would have to be mobilized. Since Vincent could only provide five, an appeal was sent out to members of the congregation founded by Monseigneur d'Authier and to Jesuits and Oratorians. The mission would be brought to a close in May, when the galleys set out for Catalonia. It seems that this mission, strengthened by the presence of the bishop himself, had a profound effect on the galley slaves. A chronicler has written, probably with some exaggeration, "The galleys were so changed that people compared them to cloisters."

With the momentum of this success, the foundation of a house of the Mission at Marseilles was assured. The duchess d'Aiguillon signed an agreement with Vincent on July 25 that she would provide 14,000 livres for the upkeep of four priests who would devote themselves to preaching missions on the galleys. Further, the superior of the house would receive authority from Vincent, the royal chaplain, to exercise control over the chaplains assigned to each galley and to monitor the living conditions of the convicts. A royal edict of June 1644 made this delegation of authority official.

It only remained to resume the construction of a hospital at Marseilles which would care for convicts when they were sick, a project which had been begun by Philippe-Emmanuel de Gondi and Vincent in 1618 and then abandoned for lack of funds. Thanks to the action of a member of the Company of the Blessed Sacrament and a friend of Vincent, Gaspard de Simiane, and to the energy of Monseigneur Gault, the hospital was completed in two years. Once more, it was the duchess d'Aiguillon who made it possible to bring this enterprise to a successful end.

Knowing his attachment to the cause of the galley slaves, the families of these miserable men turned to Monsieur Vincent to bring them a little comfort. Thus we see, in the letters sent every week to the superior at Marseilles, notes asking that he transmit a few livres or even a few sols to a certain convict on such and such a galley, humble witness to the charitable acts of a man taken up with so many other requests and burdened with a multitude of concerns.

As an experienced manager, Vincent de Paul kept a careful eye on the flow of the various revenues of the Congregation. At the end of 1642, he noticed that the royalties for the coaches of Soissons were not coming in regularly, although they were being requested daily. Therefore, he decided to relinquish them: "We will try to sell the coaches of Soissons, which provide 2,500 livres of royalties, but they are decreasing, and the operator is asking us for a rebate because of the demands made on him by the messengers."[27] He would continue to be troubled by these coaches, for the duke de Bellegarde, having returned from exile, demanded that all the coaches be restored to him since they had been his before his disgrace. It was necessary for Vincent to ask for the queen-regent's intervention on this matter. Moreover, in February 1644, he learned that the lessor of these coaches of Soissons had just declared bankruptcy. Thereupon new taxes were created: "The king has recently created another tax on your coaches of Rouen, and we are trying to strike down your liability for them," wrote Vincent to the superior of the Mission's house in Rome, to whom the revenues from the coaches of Rouen had been allocated. A few months later, he was able to reassure Bernard Codoing: "I have been able to obtain the king's order that your coaches cannot be removed from you without appropriate reimbursement, nor surcharged without the recommendations which you have sent us."[28] One can only imagine all the steps taken, the visits made, and the requests sent out by Vincent in order to obtain this result!

The military campaigns under way against Spain and the Empire were becoming more and more costly. The royal finances were not in the most brilliant condition and every means of refilling the royal coffers was acceptable, such as discreetly selling little bits of the royal domains. Consequently, in April 1645, two leaseholds were sold, those of the mills of Gonesse and of Bourget. But these rents had been assigned to the priory of Saint-Lazare since the twelfth century for the care of lepers and now, for the work of the Mission. Vincent de Paul managed these funds as though he owned them, but in fact, they belonged to the Crown. He was obliged to address a request, executed before a notary and dated June 19, 1645, in order to express his opposition to the sale of these leases. A reading of the documents shows another diversion of royal largesse. Louis XIII had allocated an income of 4,000 livres, based on the income of seigniorial rights of the estate of Gonesse, for the benefit of the work of the Foundling Hospital and the Daughters of Charity. The instrument of allocation was dated July 1642. But in April 1643, the king placed the rights over this estate under adjudication. The buyer, the marshal d'Estrées, did not consider himself bound by the prior allocation of income from these lands. Once more, Vincent had to fight in order to win back a small proportion of this income over the course of years.[29]

In brief, the growing number of foundations and undertakings initiated by Vincent de Paul caused him endless concerns and upsets. This was exacerbated by the fact that at the level of the State itself, finances were becoming tighter and tighter; agitation and disturbances in various provinces, such as Normandy, Limousin, and Périgord, foretold a crisis. Most often, this took the form of popular revolt against excessive fiscal pressure while the country was going through a period of bad harvests. The aid expected in the countryside from the royal coffers was increasingly parsimonious and the great benefactors of the Congregation of the Mission were becoming less generous.

Yet it was during this period, 1643 to 1645, that Vincent de Paul threw himself into enterprises outside the boundaries of the kingdom. For a man inspired by a grand passion and upheld by profound faith, difficulties are not obstacles but spurs that goad him on to surpass himself.

The first of Vincent's enterprises had to do with providing aid to Christian slaves being held along the Barbary Coast. Was this Vincent's idea or that of Louis XIII, shortly before his death? The king knew about the miserable state of the prisoners, entombed in the prisons of Algiers and Tunis or bought by the Turks to work under atrocious conditions. The king had signed a treaty with the Grand Sultan to put an end to piracy in the Mediterranean, but the potentates ruling in Algiers and Tunis did not respect the promises made at Constantinople. Did

Vincent discuss this matter with the king, since he understood it better than anyone? In the testament of Louis XIII, among the bequests made in favor of the Congregation, there is a separate one for the ransom of captives in Barbary.

No doubt other religious orders were already working to ransom Christian slaves, like the Order of the Redemption or the Order of Mercy, founded in the thirteenth century, and the Order of the Mathurins, also called Trinitarians, who were founded at about the same time. But the task was so great that there was ample room for many workers. In January 1643, Vincent brought up the possibility in one of his letters that "our little community could make a kind of mission among these poor slaves from time to time, and perhaps the pretext for a first attempt could be the ransom of a small number of them."[30]

This idea came to fruition in July, the charter of foundation of the house at Marseilles stipulating that the four priests stationed there will have a double role: on the one hand, that of devoting time to the convicts by preaching missions on board the galleys or caring for those in the hospital and on the other, that of sending "when it is judged appropriate, priests of the Congregation of the Mission to the Barbary Coast to console and instruct poor, captive Christians."[31] Of course, it was necessary to find a way for the priests to gain entrance to Barbary over the objections of the Turks. To circumvent this obstacle, they made use of the clause in the treaty which specified that the king of France could be represented in Tunis and Algiers by a consul who was authorized to have a chaplain in his entourage. In this way, the first missionary, Julien Guérin, went to join the consul who had been posted to Tunis in November 1645.

Soon after this, without considering the immediate implications of her action, the duchess d'Aiguillon bought the offices of the consulates of Tunis and Algiers in order to put them into the hands of the Congregation of the Mission. This direction undertaken by the Mission in Barbary would bring Vincent de Paul and his missionaries a weighty harvest of pain and suffering.

At the same time that the project for intervention in Barbary was taking form, another possibility was opening up for Vincent de Paul: to install the mission in Babylon! The Congregation for the Propagation of the Faith suggested using his missionaries in these distant lands and giving the episcopal see of Babylon to a member of the community. In the letter he wrote to Bernard Codoing, one can sense that Vincent was originally attracted to this idea, but then he writes, "There is much to be said for and against such a plan." Wisely, he reserved his answer "while waiting till it please His divine goodness to make his will in this matter more clearly known."[32]

One year later, in August 1644, Vincent recalled this project of going to Babylon, which had not moved forward, but which was now being talked of in connection with the East Indies. He wrote to a correspondent: "Your last letter speaks of the matter of Babylon and that of the East Indies. It is, after all, difficult to get money into these countries. It goes from Lisbon to Goa and from there to Ispahan." Most of all, the incumbent of the title, the bishop of Babylon, would want a pension in return for giving up his office. Vincent was not discouraged, but he found the matter sufficiently complex to require further thought.[33] This was all the more important as at the same time, there was thought of opening a house of the Congregation so as to preach missions in Catalonia which, at that time, was under the control of France. Vincent was hesitant about this suggestion; he would not have minded letting the matter go by default as the question of means and funds for such a foundation was troubling.[34]

In addition to these possible projects, which came to nothing, two others were realized in 1645. At the request of Cardinal Durazzo, archbishop of Genoa, who had appreciated the work of Bernard Codoing and his missionaries based in Rome in various parts of his diocese, Vincent sent a mission, preparatory to the foundation of an establishment of the Congregation in Genoa.[35] In addition, the prefect of the Congregation for the Propagation of the Faith, Cardinal Barberini, wrote in February 1645 to beg Vincent to send his missionaries to Ireland: "The cardinals who are part of this Congregation have charged me with imploring you to send some of your workers to Ireland to teach the ceremonies and sacred rituals of the liturgy to the clergy, which lives in the deepest ignorance."[36] Soon some missionaries left for Ireland, where they struggled with enormous difficulties.

All of this seems very far from the initial vocation of the Congregation of the Mission, which was to evangelize the rural poor in France. Could it be that Vincent had allowed himself to be drawn beyond the frontiers of the kingdom because he did not want to ignore the cries for help of the unfortunate slaves in Barbary or of the Irish Catholics oppressed by the Protestant authorities? Or was he responding to an irresistible call because he felt that it was his congregation's vocation to confront all the material and spiritual misery of the whole world?

But Vincent continued to move forward only to the extent that the needs he saw could be supported by the means at his disposal. It seems that for a long time, he was torn between the desire to respond to every appeal of the poor, who lived without a knowledge of God, wherever they might be, and his economic prudence which kept him from throwing himself into distant ventures. He wrote to Bernard Codoing, who was always ready to undertake new projects: "The works of God are not accomplished in this way; they carry themselves out, and those works which God does not support soon die. Let us move slowly toward our ambitions."[37]

Vincent had to pray a good deal until he was sure that he was doing the will of God by engaging in the work of foreign missions. He also meditated deeply on the situation of the Catholic Church and arrived at the somber conclusion that the Church was preparing its own downfall in Europe, so that it was necessary to move it elsewhere. The analysis he made in August 1645 is significant: "I admit to you that I have much affection and even devotion to the spread of the Church into pagan countries because I fear that God is gradually doing away with it here and that one hundred years from now, there will not be much left of it because of our depravity, the new opinions growing up around us, and because of the general state of things. Over the past hundred years, because of two new heresies, the Church has lost most of the Empire and the kingdoms of Sweden, Denmark, and Norway. It has lost Scotland, England, Ireland, Bohemia, and Hungary, so that there remain only Italy, France, Spain, and Poland, with France and Poland producing many a heresy themselves. Now these losses of the Church over the last hundred years make us fear, in our present miseries, that in another hundred years, we will lose the Church in Europe entirely. In light of these fears, they are blessed who will work together to extend the Church to other regions."[38]

Firmly grounded in these thoughts, Vincent did not hesitate to send his missionaries out onto all the highroads of the earth.

Dax, where Vincent attended college. Bibliothèque Nationale, Paris. Used with permission.

Philippe-Emmanuel de Gondi
(1581–1662),
Marquis de Belle-Isle,
engraved by Claude Duflos
(1665–1727). Vincent became
tutor to Gondi's children in
1613. Bibliothèque Nationale,
Paris/Giraudon-Bridgeman
Art Library (GIR207035).
Used with permission.

Françoise-Marguerite de Silly
(1584–1626) engraved
by Claude Duflos (1665–1727).
She urged Vincent to visit
"the poor people of the
country." Bibliothèque
Nationale, Paris/Giraudon-
Bridgeman Art Library
(GIR207036).
Used with permission.

St. Vincent de Paul (1581–1660) and Cardinal Jules Mazarin (1602–61) at the Council of Conscience of Louis XIV (1638–1715), engraved by Gerard Scotin (1643–1715), ca. 1660. Bibliothèque Nationale, Paris/Giraudon-Bridgeman Art Library (GIR207037). Used with permission.

Saint Bernard's gate, Paris, engraved by Matthäus Merian (1593-1650). Annexed to the prison hospital for convicts in 1632. Bibliothèque Nationale, Paris. Used with permission.

Portrait of Louise de Marillac (1591–1660), Vincent's collaborator and the foundress of the Daughters of Charity, engraved by Gaspard Duchange (1662–1757). Bibliothèque Nationale, Paris/Giraudon-Bridgeman Art Library (GIR162664). Used with permission.

St. Vincent de Paul and the Sisters of Charity, ca. 1729 (oil on canvas), attributed to Jean André, known as Frère André (1662–1753). Musée de l'Assistance Publique, Hôpitaux de Paris/Giraudon-Bridgeman Art Library (GIR71548). Used with permission.

The hospital for convicts in Marseilles, begun by Vincent and completed in 1645, seventeenth-century engraving. Bibliothèque Nationale, Paris. Used with permission.

16

Jansenism Comes into Being
1645–1648

Once appointed to the Council of Conscience, Monsieur Vincent had become an official personage. He was summoned to the court, whether it was sitting at the Louvre or at Saint-Germain, to participate in meetings presided over by Anne of Austria or Mazarin. There he rubbed shoulders with princes, ministers of state, and great prelates, but this changed neither his attitude nor his clothes. He appeared everywhere in a simple cassock and his accustomed heavy shoes. It is reported that when Mazarin addressed a sarcastic remark to him about his clothing, he answered quite simply that his cassock might be worn, but it was neither soiled nor torn. There is also a story that one day, at the Louvre, the prince de Condé, glowing from his first victories, wanted to seat Vincent at his side. The latter refused this honor with humility, claiming that he was the son of a poor villager. Condé, first prince of the blood but also exquisitely educated, replied *"Moribus et vita nobilitatur homo"* (A man is ennobled by his character and his way of life).

Vincent's modest and reserved bearing did not prevent him from asserting his opinions and defending them vigorously; he was perfectly able to oppose a cardinal or some lord in the matter of conferring benefices or nominating bishops. The story goes that a great lady of the court applied to the queen for a bishopric for her son. The queen asked Vincent whether he would approve such a nomination. When he replied that the son in question was not worthy of the position, the queen left it to him to inform the duchess of her refusal. The duchess showered Vincent with insults and in a rage, she threw a footstool at his head and wounded him. Vincent withdrew without a word, bowing respectfully and covering his bleeding face with a handkerchief. The brother who accompanied him was indignant and wanted to intervene somehow, but Vincent calmed him down, saying, "Isn't it admirable to see the extent of a mother's love for her son!"[1]

One might think that what with his official responsibilities, the foundation of new houses of the Mission, and his plans for establishing missions in far-off countries, Vincent would have been a little less concerned with his first projects, particularly the Daughters of Charity.[2] But this was not the case. He gave strength and focus to this work by approaching the archbishop of Paris in August 1645 to request authorization to raise this company of girls and widows to the status of a confraternity. He reminded the archbishop that Confraternities of Charity had been established wherever the Congregation had preached a mission, and explained how these confraternities had given rise to the idea of founding the Daughters of Charity: "But because the ladies who make up this confraternity are, for the most part, so highly placed in society that they cannot perform lowly functions, such as carrying food around the town, bloodletting, giving baths, bandaging wounds, making beds, and sitting at deathbeds of people who are alone, they have taken from the fields a few good girls to whom God has given the desire to help the poor sick."[3]

Vincent thought in detail about their tasks. In each parish of the capital, there were two or three girls to care for the sick and instruct poor little girls. Three of these young women assisted the Ladies of Charity at the Hôtel-Dieu, ten or twelve worked with the Foundling Hospital, two or three cared for the convicts in Paris, and finally, others had been sent to the hospitals of the provinces such as those at Angers, Richelieu, or Sedan. Louise de Marillac (Mademoiselle Le Gras), who directed this confraternity, put up about thirty of the girls in her house to train them before sending them out to these different positions. Since money was needed to provide them with their necessities, the Daughters of Charity, in addition to helping the poor, worked to earn a little money to supplement the alms and donations from the queen and the duchess d'Aiguillon.

Vincent was in almost daily contact with Louise de Marillac, either in person or by letter. Thus he was very knowledgeable about problems in connection with the Daughters of Charity. He took the time to visit and speak to them regularly about their vocation, their Rule of life, or the virtues they ought to cultivate. The texts of these conversations, most of which have been collected and transcribed, reflect the mood of simplicity and good fellowship that suffused the meetings.[4] Vincent held a friendly dialogue on an equal footing with these sturdy country girls. We can see him clearly, sitting among them, chatting with them with a mischievous smile, exclaiming at their quick answers, accompanying his words with telling gestures. He might just be coming from the court, or from his desk, where he had been writing in all solemnity to some Roman prelate, and with a glee that showed through all his words, he sought out these fine girls who reminded him of his youth, his life on a small farm, his love for the poor people, and his tender care for little children.

Vincent had a particular affection for his work with the foundling children; he never failed to visit them when he had a free moment. After small beginnings, this work had developed rapidly. The number of children brought in between 1638 and 1644 rose to 1,200, with all the problems of staffing, lodging, and financing which this entailed.[5] Around 1644, the annual cost of sustaining this enterprise is estimated to have been as high as 40,000 livres, covered in part by gifts from the king and the queen, the proceeds of fund drives, and the contributions of the Ladies of Charity.[6] As for the problem of lodgings, it was temporarily solved by the construction in 1645 of thirteen little houses close to the enclosure of Saint-Lazare, which were rented to the Ladies of Charity for the Foundling Hospital.[7] But soon this proved to be insufficient. The number of children grew without ceasing, the space became too tight and funds were exhausted.

The situation became critical in the course of the year 1647, so that the Ladies of Charity who were in charge of the work began to think about abandoning the project. Vincent then came to them and implored them, in pathetic terms, to persevere in their task: "Courage, Mesdames, compassion and charity led you to adopt these little creatures as your children, you have been their mothers by grace, ever since their mothers by nature abandoned them. Now see whether you really want to abandon them as well. Stop for a moment being their mothers and take the role of their judges: their life and their death is in your hands. It is time to pronounce the verdict and to know whether you no longer wish to have mercy on them."[8]

Once more, the Foundling Hospital was saved. It was decided to move the children to the château of Bicêtre, near the capital, a large building which the queen put at the disposal of Monsieur Vincent. This solution, which had already been under consideration for some time, had been rejected by Louise de Marillac, who feared the isolation of the place and its distance from the city.[9] Her fears turned out to be justified; after many changes of fortune and adventures, it became necessary two years later to bring the children back to Paris.

All this time, Vincent de Paul was also providing for the establishment of new houses of the Congregation. Sometimes he encountered unexpected opposition. This was the case for Saint-Méen in Brittany. The bishop of Saint-Malo, Achille de Harley de Sancy, was commendatory abbot of the ancient Benedictine abbey of Saint-Méen, situated in the heart of his diocese. By this time, the buildings of the abbey sheltered only two old monks who were happy enough to accept a small pension in return for moving to a house provided for them near the abbey. The bishop then decided to open a seminary at Saint-Méen and asked Monsieur Vincent to take charge of it. A contract was signed on July 14, 1645, by which the Congregation of the Mission engaged to send five priests, three of whom would conduct the seminary while the other two would preach missions in the diocese.

As soon as they arrived in August, the missionaries began to restore the buildings, which were more or less dilapidated, using for this purpose the gift of 7,000 livres given by a pious parishioner. But the Benedictines of the province became agitated when they learned that their old abbey, the most famous one in Brittany, had been abstracted from them by the will of a bishop, a simple commendatory abbot. It was their opinion that this decision had been made in flagrant violation of the letters patent of Louis XIII who, in November 1640, had declared that no new order or company was supposed or allowed to establish itself in any location of the province without the consent of the Estates, verified and registered by the parlement. The bishop, for his part, was firmly decided to install his seminary at Saint-Méen. His initiative was approved by a diocesan synod and with the letters of renunciation of the two Benedictine monks, he traveled to Paris to have his decision ratified. He deposited the letters patent of secularization of the abbey at the parlement of Brittany to be registered there. But this assembly, jealous of its prerogatives, refused to acknowledge the royal letters and forbade the bishop to secularize the abbey of Saint-Méen, asking the Benedictines to resume their authority over it. The bishop was not impressed. He obtained new letters patent from Paris, approved by the Grand Council. On their side, the Benedictines, judging that this royal decision violated the rights of the parlement of Brittany and the laws of the Church, refused to obey. One year after their installation, the missionaries were ordered by a decision of the parlement of July 17, 1646, to leave the abbey. This was the beginning of a bitter, furious war between the forces of the Benedictines and those marshaled by the bishop in order to keep the Mission in place.

On July 20 at six o'clock in the morning, an officer of the parlement of Brittany came to the door of the abbey, escorted by ten Benedictine monks who had come to occupy the buildings. They found the door closed and barricaded. After three days of parleys, the officer managed to break in and install the monks in the premises of the convent. The missionaries with their students were forced to crowd into the abbot's quarters. For two weeks, the two camps lived under the same roof, with the young seminarians taking advantage of the disturbance to play bad tricks on the monks. The Benedictines, outnumbered, once more appealed to the parlement, which again gave the order for the Mission to leave the abbey. At the same time, the vicar general of Saint-Malo, delegated on the spot by the bishop, threatened to excommunicate the Benedictines. This moral condemnation proving insufficient, the bishop approached the king's lieutenant general in Brittany, marshal de la Meilleraye, with the news that royal authority was at an impasse and asked him to intervene. Thus, on August 20, a troop of twenty mounted soldiers arrived at Saint-Méen and forced its way, swords drawn, into the church where the monks were just singing Prime. When the sanctuary was empty, the troops withdrew. The next day, the parlement decreed that the vicar general was to be arrested and the missionaries as well. The forces sent to take them into custody found the abbey empty. The single priest who had been left behind to guard the house was seized and thrown into prison with his legs in irons. But the Benedictines had still not won the war, for the bishop, showing his great pugnacity, obtained a royal decree in his own favor on September 7. A representative of the bishop presented himself at Saint-Méen with the royal decision, enjoining the Benedictines to evacuate. He was escorted by forty soldiers who promptly showed the monks the door. The Benedictines never came back.

Vincent was naturally crushed when he heard all this. On September 1, he wrote a long letter to the unfortunate superior of the house of Saint-Méen, whose behavior had been less than heroic as he fled alone, on horseback, for fear that he might be arrested by the parlement's bullies. To tell the truth, Vincent was torn by contradictory impulses: his gratitude to the bishop, who had offered him the abbey, his reactions to the unfavorable decisions of the parlement of Brittany, the favorable decisions of the king on the other hand, and to crown all this, the teachings of the Gospel. He was forced to have recourse to all the devices of rhetoric and casuistry in trying to untangle this bundle of knots. "Saint Paul and Our Lord advised us to lose everything rather than to go to the courts. But each one of them ended up there and each one lost the trial and lost his life with it. It is true that the maxim of the Company is to accept losing everything rather than fighting for it in the courts, but that only counts when the decision is up to us."[10] As an eminent member of a council related to ecclesiastical matters, Vincent was most chagrined to have been involved against his will in a matter which set a bishop against a religious order!

Other problems confronted the superior of the Congregation of the Mission, and we can find traces of them in his correspondence. For instance, the superior of the house in Sedan, Guillaume Gallais, found it difficult to distance himself from secular affairs. It is true that he had been stationed at the very heart of a Huguenot region, which made his task difficult, to say the least. Vincent was obliged to rein in his ardor, writing to him: "It is not expedient, sir, that we should interfere in secular matters, no matter what their connection to spiritual things, because no one can serve two masters, God and the world, the spiritual and the temporal, and Our Lord has said so."

Vincent felt that the Huguenots would not be converted if the missionaries fed controversies, but only if they demonstrated living witness to the spirit of the Gospel: "Oh, Sir, what great missionaries you and I would be if we knew how to inspire souls with the spirit of the Gospel that can make them pleasing to Jesus Christ! I promise you that this is the most effective way to make Catholics holy and to convert heretics."[11]

To monitor the operation of his houses, Vincent sent his faithful collaborator, Antoine Portail, and stayed in close contact with him by letters in which he expressed himself freely. We see from them that his spirit of charity never dulled his lucidity. The evaluations he made of his missionaries were incisive: "This one is governed by black bile and always stubborn; the other one is pituitous and unpredictable."[12]

The Congregation of the Mission was developing. In 1647, it comprised about twenty houses and the number of seminaries was growing. The major seminary at the Collège des Bons-Enfants now had a student body of sixty and the minor seminary, at Saint-Charles, had about forty students. The faculty at the seminary of Cahors consisted of thirty priests; at Annecy and at Le Mans, there were eight each, and from twelve to fifteen at Saint-Méen.[13] One of the main difficulties with which Vincent de Paul had to contend was finding superiors capable of directing all these houses and seminaries. In particular, he was not able to find a competent superior for the house at Marseilles, which was very complex to govern because of the extraordinary diversity of its work—the hospital, missions to the countryside and on the galleys, matters concerning the Barbary coast, and later, the opening of a seminary. Vincent sent Antoine Portail to inspect the situation, warning him that he would find only a few workers, without a good superior, whereas this house required the leadership of an energetic personality. Vincent went over all the possible candidates for the position and sketched vivid and penetrating portraits, like this one: "We had thought of Monsieur Cuissot, who is vigilant about all the external things, but has no gift for matters of the soul, although he is completely dedicated to God." At length, Vincent urged Father Portail to leave the current superior, Jean Chrétien, in place, in spite of his weaknesses: "You will treat him as gently as is proper, so as not to discourage him."[14]

Vincent never lost sight of material questions and did not find it beneath his dignity to spend a great deal of time over minute details of management of the Congregation's holdings. For instance, in going over the accounts of the house at Le Mans with a fine-tooth comb, he found an expense he considered unacceptable and wrote: "Monsieur Aubert is wrong to ask for two pistoles for the farmer he has engaged to work in the gardens; Monsieur Gallais assures me that they have already been paid out."[15] He lodged a complaint with the magistrates of Paris because a neighbor of the estate of Saint-Lazare "extended his boundaries from the Saint-Maur Road by four rods at the top of the road, near the end, and by four rods two feet at the bottom. By this means, he has appropriated from the lands of the venerable priests of the Congregation of the Mission a piece with an area of ninety-three and one half rods."[16] Monsieur Vincent may have disliked court cases, but if he had to, he was quite ready to defend the community's estate.

At the request of the Congregation for the Propagation of the Faith, Vincent de Paul formed a team to carry a mission to Ireland. Five priests and two brothers set sail from Saint-Nazaire in the year 1646 and, after a stormy crossing, arrived in port safely. Some of the team were sent to the diocese of Limerick in the west and the others to the diocese of Cashel in the south of Ireland. The letters written in 1648 by the bishops of these two dioceses bear witness to the success of the first missions the priests undertook, but soon they were obliged to interrupt their work because of persecution. Cromwell's troops inflicted bloodthirsty reprisal on the Catholic population. Some of the missionaries returned to France and the others withdrew to the city of Limerick. This city was besieged and sacked at the end of 1651. Two missionaries were able to escape in disguise and only a single one managed to remain in the city by living in hiding. So ended the six-year attempt to implant the order in Hibernia. Vincent de Paul, not at all discouraged by this apparent check, drew the following lesson from it: "It is enough for God to know the good which has been done here. Let us place our trust in the martyrs: their blood will be the seed of new Christians!"[17]

Sending missionaries to Barbary would also be a lasting source of inextricable problems and of human dramas. A first priest, Julien Guérin, accompanied by a brother, left for Tunis in November 1645, with the official title of chaplain to the consul of France. At first, he did his work discreetly, but soon he was authorized to care for the galley slaves openly. He wrote an account of their hard lives: "We expect a large number of patients when the galleys return. These poor people suffer great misery when they are at sea, but those who remain behind are not better off. They work at sawing marble every day, exposed to the heat of the sun, which is like a fiery furnace. . . . Some others are not so badly treated, because they are confined to their owners' houses where they do whatever work is demanded, both night and day."[18] Reading these lines, Vincent must have remembered, in haunting fashion, his years as a slave in the same lands. Would he perhaps allude to those memories when he was encouraging his missionaries? As far as we know, he did not breathe a word, maintaining a silence that may seem strange.

Julien Guérin did all he could to free the slaves whose condition was particularly terrible. For instance, he ransomed a French woman who was tyrannized by her master for a sum of 300 écus, a young boy who was on the brink of renouncing his faith for a sum of 150 écus, and for 250, a young Sicilian woman whose husband "had become a Turk."[19] After the end of 1647, Father Guérin had the help of a young priest, Jean Le Vacher, sent as a reinforcement. But the plague broke out in Tunis in the next year, and Julien Guérin and the consul both died. Thus Jean Le Vacher remained alone, fulfilling the functions both of a consul and of a missionary priest.

In the meantime, on her own initiative, the duchess d'Aiguillon acquired the right to assign the consulates of Algiers and of Tunis, and offered them to the Congregation of the Mission. The purpose of doing this was to avoid conflicts between consuls and missionaries, always a possibility, and to provide resources to the missionaries, who would be able to levy duties on incoming and outgoing merchandise. By accepting this office, Vincent de Paul subjected his missionaries to unpleasant consequences they had not anticipated. Since they were representatives not only of any French citizens, but of all foreigners not represented by a consulate there, the consuls had to deal with any possible commercial disputes with the Turkish merchants. The disputes would be many and the debts to be assumed were heavy.

In 1646, to occupy the consulate in Algiers, Vincent sent a missionary, Boniface Nouelly, and Brother Jean Barreau, a former lawyer in the parlement. The latter, as consul, immediately committed an indiscretion by standing as security to the Turkish authority for a monk of the Order of Mercy, imprisoned for debts he had contracted while trying to ransom slaves. The sum involved was significant—40,000 livres; Vincent tried to raise this sum but did not fail to reprimand Jean Barreau: "I have written to the consul to tell him of our difficulty in gathering money. He will be paid once we raise money for the slaves in Paris. I beg the said Monsieur Barreau never again to promise anything, not even to act as intermediary in the ransom of a slave. Let him simply carry out the duties of his office."[20]

At this point, a new pasha was named at Algiers, and he promptly had Barreau imprisoned because he had still not been able to satisfy his debt. When he left prison in July 1647, it was to be present at the death of his colleague Nouelly and of the two missionaries who had been sent as reinforcements; an epidemic of the plague had ravaged Algiers. Jean Barreau, alone again, had to confront the hostility of Turks who did not want him there. In spite of the strict orders that Vincent de Paul had once more sent him, he went into debt again, driven, as always, by his generous impulse of pity for the unfortunate slaves. He was to suffer bad treatment and even torture many times. All Vincent could do was to preach at him in letters and do what he could to scrape together the sums that would release Barreau from the Turkish prison.

In spite of all the disappointments growing out of his hopes for Hibernia and the Barbary coast, Vincent went peaceably about his other far-flung projects. For instance, he had not abandoned the hope of the bishopric of Babylon. In March 1647, he wrote to Monseigneur Ingoli, secretary of the Propagation of the Faith, to say that he was ready to appoint one of his closest collaborators, Lambert aux Couteaux: "Truly, the loss of this man will be like tearing out one of my eyes and cutting off my own arm."[21]

Clearly, Vincent was committed to this project, and he wrote about it to his representative in Rome: "This work seems to me to be a vital act for the glory of God . . . I feel an inner drive to do it."[22] But he discovered that the superior of the Congregation of the Blessed Sacrament, Authier de Sisgau, the same man who had wanted to join his order to the Mission, wanted to be named to this office. Knowing this, Vincent de Paul withdrew. But still, he was haunted by the thought of these far-off countries remaining unevangelized. The next year, he sent a petition to the Propagation of the Faith, asking for his congregation to be chosen to preach missions in Arabia. "Since the three parts of Arabia, known as Arabia Felix (Fortunate Arabia), Arabia Petraea (Stony Arabia), and Arabia Deserta (Desert Arabia), have not yet been confided to a specific religious order or secular priest to be evangelized and brought into the Christian fold, Vincent de Paul, superior of the Congregation of the Mission, offers to send several of his priests there."[23]

He proposed to install the seat of this mission at the entrance to a port in the region of Arabia Felix where English and Dutch vessels landed. If we can believe a letter which he sent in October 1648 to one of his priests, the proposal was approved in Rome, since there he lists the different missions that had been entrusted to his Company: "Add the assignment of Barbary, Persia, and Arabia Felix, where the Propaganda is sending us, as well as that of Madagascar."[24]

But it seems that after all, this project never materialized, since Vincent does not mention it again. In contrast, the mission to Madagascar was already under way. On March 22, 1648, Vincent wrote to Charles Nacquart, just then stationed at Richelieu, to let him know that he had been chosen to direct this expedition, adding that they were to take ship in less than a month at La Rochelle.[25] In fact, the nuncio, who had designated the Congregation to go and serve God on the Island of Saint-Laurent, otherwise known as Madagascar, had written rather precipitously. He had wanted to comply with a request of the East India Company, which was asking for priests for a planned voyage to this distant island, without consulting the Holy See. He did not know that the Propaganda had already chosen the Discalced Carmelites to evangelize the island of Saint-Laurent. The situation was only clarified two years later by a new decree from the Propagation of the Faith, dated December 1650, when the missionaries had already been on the island for a long time.

Vincent de Paul, who was accustomed to weighing all sides of a project before making a decision, seems to have made up his mind in this particular case in an extraordinary rush. His decision can be explained on the basis of the nuncio's authority, but the fact remains that this enterprise was undertaken in haste and would bring much pain and require much sacrifice from Vincent and his congregation.

Vincent's ardent embrace of the foreign missions is his response to what he saw as ever-advancing heresy in Europe, with resulting compromise of the Church. Therefore, while setting his sights for Babylon, Arabia Felix, or Madagascar, he joined the fight against the new ideas which were gaining ground in France. It was not Protestantism that he was fighting against, although that was well established in many of the provinces, but Jansenism.

The struggle had begun with the appearance in 1640 of the posthumous summa of Jansenius, entitled *Augustinus*. The book aroused passionate discussions of themes such as liberty, grace, and predestination. Whereas Jansenius had intended to put forward ideas which agreed with the teaching of Saint Augustine, the Jesuits found Calvinist tendencies in his work The ensuing debates cast such confusion into the

Church that in 1642, the pope was forced to intervene and demonstrate the doctrinal errors in the *Augustinus* in his bull *In Eminenti*.

The next year saw the appearance of a work entitled *De la fréquente communion* (On the frequent reception of Holy Communion), under the name of a reputable theologian and convinced Jansenist, Antoine Arnauld.[26] This thinker's main point was a more intense interior life for Christians. Because of its high literary quality and elevated thought, the book enjoyed a lively success and wide distribution. But some readers put unbalanced weight on one of its recommendations, namely, to allow a waiting period of contrition to intervene between the confessing of sins and the granting of absolution. The consequence of this would be to prevent the faithful from approaching the communion table for a period of time, and in fact, during this period, the number of communicants in the churches decreased. Anne of Austria, who had a particular devotion to this sacrament, was especially out of charity with the Jansenists.

At first, Vincent de Paul declared himself in opposition to the new ideas. Having learned that he was being accused of a certain lukewarm attitude to the battle against the Jansenists, he wrote to Bernard Codoing in Rome, in March 1644: "I will say nothing of the accusations they are making against us on that point, except that, by the mercy of God, our company resists all the new opinions and that I am doing all I can against them, and especially those which go against the authority of the Father of all Christians."[27]

We have proof of his anti-Jansenist attitude even from Mazarin, who sent him a line to congratulate him on the "care which [he] took to cut through the intrigue of the Jansenists."[28] But Jansenism was gaining ground in France. Therefore, Vincent took the time to compose a study on an essential point at the center of the debates, the subject of grace. The Jansenists professed a narrow conception of predestination: for them, God only wished to save a small number of elect, to whom he gave effective grace. Vincent defended the traditional position: "What does this difference consist of? The age-old opinion of the Church is that God gives all men, the faithful and the unfaithful, sufficient grace for salvation. And those who hold the new opinions state that there is no sufficient grace given to all the people, that there is only effective grace, which is given only to a few people, and that those to whom it is given cannot resist it."[29] There follows a learned exposition of ten pages, written in his hand. This text proves abundantly that Vincent was not a "modest fourth-year student" as he liked to call himself in a spirit of humility.

Vincent saw that his new representative at Rome, Jean Dehorgny, was not quite immune to some of the theses developed by the Jansenists. Therefore he addressed a long letter to him on June 25, 1648, in which he took the trouble to give the reasons on which he based his outright opposition to the new ideas. In particular he was motivated by "the knowledge I have of the author's [Saint-Cyran's] intentions concerning these new ideas, of destroying the present state of the Church. He told me one day that God's plan was to ruin the existing Church and that those who were trying to save it were acting against the divine plan. When I told him that this was the standard argument of heretics like Calvin, he answered that Calvin had not been wrong in everything he tried to do, but that he had only failed to defend himself well."[30]

It must be noted that Vincent had not gone this far when he made his deposition for the trial of Saint-Cyran. Out of friendship, he had devised formulations that were less compromising for the accused. In 1639, the declarations of Saint-Cyran were made in private, whereas after his death, his opinions had entered the public arena and Arnauld had used them to stir up a polemic. At that point, Vincent felt obligated to take part in the debate officially and fight against the ideas of a man who had once been his friend. Replying to the letter of his superior, Jean Dehorgny emphasized the fact that some people had profited from reading the work of the Jansenist Arnauld on the subject of frequent communion. Vincent immediately replied, demolishing, point by point, the arguments of Arnauld, which he said led to an illogical attitude: "Only Monsieur Arnauld could do this! Here he puts the requirements for the right state of mind to receive communion so high that even Saint Paul would hesitate to approach the communion rail, and then he boasts that he celebrates mass every day."[31]

In the course of these disputes about Jansenism, Vincent revealed a hidden side of his personality: the confirmed theologian who does not hesitate to cross swords in masterly fashion on arduous topics.

The Beginnings of the Fronde
1648–1649

Birth of the Fronde
Intervention at Saint-Germain
Travel in the Provinces
Rescue at Orsigny
Stay at Saint-Méen
Return to Saint-Lazare

Vincent de Paul was well aware of the worsening political situation in the kingdom. His contacts at court and the reports from his missionaries and the Daughters of Charity kept him well informed of events in the capital and in the provinces. Therefore, he was not surprised by the events of the year 1648, which marked the beginning of a long time of troubles, a stretch of five years known as the Fronde.

The causes of the Fronde are many, and they are complex. The Party of the Devout had been experiencing a renewal of energy ever since the death of Richelieu, closely followed by the death of Louis XIII, had set political prisoners free and brought back important figures from exile. The Party of the Devout was opposed to the war declared in 1635 with Catholic kings pitted against a coalition in which France made common cause with Lutheran Sweden and Calvinist Holland. This alliance was an object of scandal for the Company of the Blessed Sacrament, which was engaged in underground activities now difficult to identify. What is more, this long drawn-out war was putting an ever heavier financial load on the people of France.

Public expenditures which had amounted to 40 million livres a year before the conflict rose to an annual average of 120 million livres.[1] Highly inequitable taxes weighed heavily on the poor and there were uprisings in the provinces whenever there were bad harvests or more new taxes. The insurgents did not blame their misfortune on the king; they directed their rage against tax collectors and customs officials of all kinds, as well as against the Ministry of Finance.

But there was one figure who drew all the dissatisfaction and vindictiveness of the people upon himself like a lightning rod, and that was the man whom Anne of Austria had chosen to succeed Richelieu as her prime minister—Cardinal Mazarin. His Italian origin, a number of awkward incidents, and especially the thwarted ambitions of all those who thought they were better qualified to govern than he was were all elements in the formation of an ill-assorted, unstable coalition of malcontents. At first, this was known as the Cabal of Important People, gathered around the flamboyant and presumptuous duke de Beaufort, illegitimate grandson of Henry IV. He had dreams of doing away with Mazarin in cold blood, but the plot was uncovered and Beaufort was imprisoned in September 1643. Next came the battle of the parlement of Paris, defending the privileges of the capital city, which was free of feudal taxation, against the schemes of the comptroller general of finance, Particelli d'Émery. At a loss for ways to fill the state coffers emptied by wars, this royal official was attempting to levy new taxes on the population of Paris. The reaction was one of growing discontent and an increasingly energetic resistance to the fiscal authorities. Delays in repayment of the bonds on the Hôtel de Ville, which were government loans secured by the municipality of Paris, affected large segments of the city's population—burghers, merchants, tradesmen, and even domestic servants. The financial troubles were exacerbated by bad harvests in the northern part of the kingdom. Starting in 1646, the price of bread in Paris doubled. The malnourished inhabitants were vulnerable to disease, and bands of vagabonds appeared on the outskirts of the city.[2]

The beginning of the conflict between the parlement and the king can be dated precisely to January 15, 1648. In the course of a solemn session of the parlement, the advocate general, Omar Talon, addressed the regent in these terms: "Madam, reflect a while, deep within your heart, upon this public misery. Add to this thought, Madame, the calamity of the provinces where hopes of peace, the honor of battles won, the glories of provinces conquered, cannot nourish those who are without bread, who cannot number palm fronds and laurels among the ordinary fruits of the earth."[3]

In the months that followed this first skirmish, a covert quarrel was taking place over the registration by the parlement of several edicts having to do with finances, such as the renewal of the "paulette."[4] Mazarin, who was unfamiliar with French parliamentary traditions, allowed matters to become acrimonious and then seemed ready to make concessions, dismissing his controller general of finances and recommending to the regent that she accept the proposals of the parlement, convened in general session. But a few weeks later, on August 26, after a *Te Deum* was sung at Notre-Dame in honor of Condé's victory over the Spaniards at Lens, Mazarin ordered the arrest of those members of the parlement who were considered leading opponents of royal power. The powder keg was ignited and without delay, barricades were thrown up in the streets of the capital. For the sake of civil order, the regent gave in and had the members set free. She then withdrew, together with her children, to the château of Rueil, a property left by Richelieu to his niece the duchess d'Aiguillon. Negotiations with representatives of the parlement were begun, and they ended with another curtailment of royal power. An observer with insight into events noted in his journal at the end of October: "The High Council lost the battle against the parlement on the day of the barricades and ever since then, the parlement commands and the High Council obeys."[5]

In this turmoil, the signing of the treaty of Westphalia,[6] a diplomatic victory for Mazarin that brought an end to the Thirty Years' War with the Empire, passed without notice. In Paris, it only meant a continuation of the war with Spain, and Mazarin was blamed for this, as it was suspected that he was interested in having it go on. But Mazarin did not consider himself beaten. Once more he persuaded the regent to leave Paris so that he could lay siege to the capital and checkmate the intransigents. In the night of January 5–6, 1649, the royal family and some courtiers quietly left the Louvre and made for Saint-Germain-en-Laye where they would pitch camp. So ended the first act of a civil war which set the royal government against the parlement, which had the support of the people of Paris.

The troops commanded by the prince de Condé and by Gaston d'Orléans under the orders of the regent now ringed the capital and blockaded it, while the militia raised by the parlement closed the city gates so that no one could leave. In spite of this, delegates of the parlement made their way to Saint-Germain to attempt negotiations, but the regent refused to receive them and they returned to Paris, enraged. On January 8, the parlement issued a decree declaring Mazarin the "author of all present disorder" and "enemy of the king and the state," and ordered him to leave the city within the week.

The struggle had begun with the parlement on one side and the court on the other, but now it took on a new dimension, for in the Fronde certain great lords ranged themselves with the parlement. This was a curious assortment of personalities with a variety of ambitions: the young prince de Conti, brother of the prince de Condé; his brother-in-law, the duke de Longueville, governor of Normandy, with his wife, the beautiful Anne-Geneviève, who brought along in her wake her lover, the prince de Marillac, future duke de la Rochefoucauld; the duke de Bouillon, older brother of Turenne, who wanted to regain his principality of Sedan; the duke de Beaufort, escaped from his prison at Vincennes; the duke d'Elbeuf, governor of Picardy, descendant of the Guise family and eternal enemy of royal power.

Another personality was to play a primary role in the Fronde, Vincent de Paul's former pupil, Jean-François Paul de Gondi, the future Cardinal de Retz. He would have liked to wear a sword and be active in politics, but his family had made him enter the Church without the slightest vocation in order to replace an older brother who had died in an accident. He said about himself that he was the least churchly soul in the world. He attacked his studies head on, earning a doctorate in theology, and led a life that was not only worldly but gallant, with numerous official mistresses. In June 1643, he was named coadjutor of his uncle, archbishop of Paris, and received Holy Orders after a short retreat at Saint-Lazare, from which he emerged with remarkable resolutions: "After days of reflection, I decided to do evil on purpose, which is incomparably the greatest evil in the sight of God, but the wisest thing in the eyes of the world. I resolved to fulfill all the duties of my profession with exactitude, and to be just as good a man for the salvation of others as I would be an evil man for myself."[7] In fact, he took pride in administering his diocese well, in presiding at all liturgies, and in preaching regularly. In this way, he gained the respect of the clergy of Paris and would not lose it, in spite of all his rages. He reported in his memoirs that Monsieur Vincent had judged him with benevolence, saying "that I was not sufficiently pious but that I was not too far distant from the Kingdom of God." Tormented by the demon of politics and by his ambition for a cardinal's hat, he took a position hostile to Mazarin and found it quite natural to join the Fronde.

The siege of the capital was organized. The royal troops camped on the outskirts began to lay waste the countryside, and the feeding of the people of Paris became increasingly difficult. At this point, Vincent de Paul decided to go to Saint-Germain to try to make the court listen to words of peace before the situation worsened yet again. This course of action seems surprising, since it is contrary to everything that Vincent had affirmed up to that point, repeating tirelessly to his missionaries that they should on no account involve themselves in worldly matters. He himself had respected this rule completely, and nothing in his correspondence indicates a single intervention on his part outside of his own religious domain, with the single exception of his approach to Richelieu to beg him to give peace to France.

But in a letter addressed to Louise de Marillac in September 1648, he made discreet allusion to the days of the August uprising in the capital, with their spirit of popular emotion. He added these prophetic lines: "For the rest, be assured that there is nothing which I felt I should say and then did not, by the grace of God; I have spoken on all subjects. The bad thing is that God did not bless my words, even though I do not believe what is being said about the person you heard me speak of."[8] Was Vincent referring to a first attempt at mediation with the regent or Mazarin, an attempt that came to nothing? Monsieur Coste, a learned analyst of Vincent's correspondence, is not sure how to read this passage. It is his hypothesis that the members of the Fronde had started the rumor that Anne of Austria was married to Mazarin and that Monsieur Vincent had blessed this union in secret. Brother Robineau had questioned his superior about this directly and the answer he got was "That's as false as the devil!"

In any case, on January 14, only a week after the court had installed itself at Saint-Germain, Vincent set out to appear there. Had he been requested by some member of the Fronde to carry a message to the queen? Did he think it his duty, as a member of the Council of Conscience, to warn the queen and Mazarin of the tragic consequences that could arise from their intransigence? Or was he so moved by the misery of the people and the risk of famine in the capital that he took the initiative, after long meditation and prayer? Monsieur Coste states, "He resolved to make use of the power he had over the heart of the queen."[9]

Thanks to the narrative of Brother Ducournau, who accompanied Vincent on this expedition, we know all the incidents of the journey, which was to last longer than expected. Vincent had not wished to report to the Parisian authorities that he was leaving, but only sent a note to President Molé[10] to keep him informed; Saint-Lazare was outside the walls of the capital and so he would not have needed a pass to travel. Having left by horseback at dawn, he wisely took the road through Clichy-la-Garenne, where he was known. The village had been pillaged the day before by marauders and guards with pikes and muskets were stationed at the crossroads. Vincent and his companion ran the risk of a bad end by being there, but one of the guards recognized his former pastor. After this first alarm, they arrived at Neuilly where they were to cross the Seine. The river was in flood and the bridge was partly inundated. They were afraid that they would be carried away with their horses by the violent current; nevertheless they set foot on the bridge, and arrived on the other side safe but drenched. Toward ten in the morning, they arrived at Saint-Germain in this sorry condition.

Vincent was brought to the queen for a long conversation, whose contents we do not know. According to the account of Brother Ducournau, he told her that it was not just to have one million innocent people die to punish twenty or thirty guilty ones, and he painted a vivid picture of the disasters which would be unleashed on her people. It seems that contrary to his habitual calm, Vincent let himself be carried away by his own discourse and that he spoke with so much force that a moment later, he was surprised and even pained at what he had done. Finally, he tried to convince the queen to separate herself for the time being from Mazarin, an action which he considered indispensable for the restoration of civil peace. Then the queen told him to go to the cardinal and tell him the same things. That is what he did, and supposedly, after he let Vincent speak, Mazarin said that he would take his advice if the Secretary of State, Michel Le Tellier, agreed.[11] This was a skillful way to elude the question, since Le Tellier could not seek the eviction of the cardinal, who was his protector and direct patron. Mazarin would never forgive Vincent de Paul for speaking against him. Not being able to make Anne of Austria forget the priest, Mazarin maneuvered to keep him as far away from the court as possible, and finally to exclude him from the Council of Conscience altogether.

Vincent announced the failure of his mission in a letter which he wrote from Villepreux a little later to Antoine Portail: "I left Paris on the 14th of this month to go to Saint-Germain, in order to be of some slight use to God there, but my sins made me unworthy to succeed."[12]

He was no longer able to return to Saint-Lazare, since his visit to the queen could have been misinterpreted by the frondeurs in the capital. He therefore decided to undertake a large-scale tour of his provincial houses, a thing he had never yet had the leisure to do. His plan was to start in the west, go to Brittany, and then travel south, all the way to Marseilles. After a stop of three days at Saint-Germain, he set out, provided with a passport and protected by an escort, for the countryside was overrun by armed bands. His first stop was at Villepreux, where he went to greet his former master, now Father de Gondi, priest of the Oratory. For Vincent, this was a kind of pilgrimage, since he had traveled to this village many times in the days when he used to accompany Madame de Gondi to her estates. One of his first confraternities had been founded here, immediately after the Charité of the Dombes.

It was not in Vincent's nature to give himself over to nostalgia. His face was turned to the future, for he still had so much to do. At this moment, he was concerned with the fate of his houses during dangerous, troubled times. He knew that he could no longer count on the revenues from the coach service or the farms. Therefore he gave precise and realistic instructions to superiors of the houses to use restraint as an effective tool for surviving this period. In the same letter to Antoine Portail, he prescribed drastic measures: "First of all, you must show no hesitation in sending away all the seminarians who are not paying enough for room and board. Secondly, tell the bishop of Marseilles what is going on, so as to motivate him to help you. And in the third place, try to find some masses to say."

In Villepreux, as he was preparing to set out for Le Mans, Vincent learned that the large farm at Orsigny, which produced the majority of the food for Saint-Lazare, was in danger of being pillaged. Immediately he sent orders to the brothers in charge of the farm to have them lead their flocks to Fréneville (near Étampes) where they could shelter in safety. He himself rode out on horseback in that direction. But it was winter, and cold weather moved in, covering the countryside with a heavy layer of snow. Vincent was snowbound at the farm in Fréneville for almost a month. He survived thanks to the devotion of two Daughters of Charity who were working in a neighboring village and who sent him gray bread and apples that the good people had given them. We can imagine him, enveloped in his heavy cape, stirring up the coals in the fireplace of the common room before taking up his pen again to encourage all his people and keep them strong amid their trials.

When he learned that the house of the generous donor of the farm, Jacques Norais, had been looted, Vincent wrote to console him, exhorting him to accept this misfortune in a spirit of submission to the divine will: "It is true that what seems to be a loss, according to the flesh, is a great advantage according to the spirit and a great reason to give thanks to God."[13] At the same time, he gave much thought to what might be going on at the Hôtel-Dieu and the Foundling Hospital. He wrote to the Ladies of Charity, who were in charge of these institutions, to encourage them to be steadfast, for the trouble of their days disquieted the soul and cooled off charity. He found vibrant words in which to address them: "Truly it seems that our own miseries excuse us from caring for the misfortunes of the people, and that we would have a good excuse, as the world counts it, for withdrawing from this service. But truly, Mesdames, I do not know how that would sound to God, who might say to us what Saint Paul said to the Corinthians in a similar situation: 'Have you resisted to the very blood? Or at least, have you sold a portion of the jewels you own?'"[14]

Then the message came that military people had passed very close to Fréneville and that they had stolen the horses from a farm. Then, in spite of the snow and the cold, Vincent decided on February 23 to lead his animals further along, to get them to safety. His purpose was to lead his flock of 240 sheep all the way to Richelieu, fifteen kilometers away. At the age of almost seventy, Vincent found himself playing shepherd, driving the bleating flock forward. In the event, the bad weather forced him to leave his sheep with a woman of his acquaintance, in a walled village near Étampes.[15] As for him, he continued to travel by way of Orléans all the way to Le Mans, where he arrived on March 4, "in spite of hardships of the weather and the road."[16] He left the horses from his two farms there in safety. For a period of ten days, he rested and visited the Daughters of Charity of Le Mans and his house there.

While on his travels, Vincent learned that the priory of Saint-Lazare had been occupied and plundered. There, 600 soldiers had bivouacked, sacking buildings, burning doors and windows, seizing the reserves of wheat, and setting stored firewood aflame. When this became known, the parlement gave the order to move these troops on and sent a squad to mount guard. But the damages were not repaired. Monsieur Lambert, in charge of the house, scrambled to do what he could to maintain some kind of care for the people who came to the doors of Saint-Lazare every day, giving them four Paris measures of wheat at the least. Vincent received the news of all these humiliations and losses with great serenity. Blessed be God, he repeated to all those who brought him bad news. But his resignation was not the same thing as passivity; he never failed to encourage his superiors to take the necessary measures to survive this agitated period in the best way possible, and at the same time, he invited them to join him in accepting the trials that heaven sent them.

Vincent continued his travels from Le Mans toward Angers. Crossing a little river, near Durtal, his horse slipped on the stony bottom and fell down in the water. Vincent was pinned under his mount. Help came promptly to free him from this disagreeable position, and he was taken, soaked from head to foot, to a nearby cottage, where everyone hastened to get him dry and warm again. He referred to this misadventure in a letter which he addressed two weeks later to Louise de Marillac, in which he confessed that his "health had worsened during the night, and that I have taken a fever, after falling into the water, with the horse on top of me, in such a way that I could never have gotten out if help hadn't come."[17]

On his arrival in Angers, around March 20, he visited the little group of Daughters of Charity working at the Hôtel-Dieu of that city. He talked at length with each of them and wrote to Louise de Marillac how exemplary their conduct was. "It fills my heart with comfort." Next he headed for Rennes, on the way to Saint-Méen in the diocese of Saint-Malo. His travels were studded with other incidents: his horse took fright crossing a narrow bridge, almost throwing him into a pond, then a gentleman he met in an inn, taking him for an adherent of Mazarin, threatened to blow his brains out with a pistol. Finally he arrived at Saint-Méen at the beginning of Easter week, safe and sound.

Vincent was most interested in seeing this old abbey that had caused him so much worry and inconvenience. Dominating the cluster of buildings was an imposing tower, decorated with four little turrets and surmounted by a graceful belfry. The twelfth-century church had a broad transept, filled with light that fell through handsome stained glass windows. Beside it was a chapter room, decorated with frescos from the thirteenth century. The buildings of the abbey were spacious and majestic; at the time of Vincent's visit, they housed the diocesan seminary. The whole establishment had such a noble appearance that it was no wonder the Benedictines were sorry to lose such a monument, a place of pilgrimage known all over Brittany.

Since Easter always attracted a great crowd of people to Saint-Méen, Vincent did not rest while he was there; besides visiting the local house of the Congregation of the Mission and the seminary, he preached and heard confessions: "My visit here is so busy that I cannot write you in my own hand," he declared to Louise de Marillac. He presided over the official installation of four Daughters of Charity, three of whom would work at the hospital and one who would be director of a school for the daughters of the poor. He also toured all the Confraternities of Charity that had been founded in the neighboring villages.[18]

Although he had only planned to spend a week at Saint-Méen, Vincent found himself marooned there by terrible weather. He wrote to Louise de Marillac: "Here, I am besieged by bad weather and flooding." A simple Breton drizzle would certainly not have been able to stop him; this must have been something like a late winter storm. But the delay allowed him to rest a little after his long journeys on horseback, and to tend to his health a little: "I took this opportunity to be purged and bled."[19]

Finally, on April 17, Vincent had to continue on his way to Nantes. There, they were waiting for him impatiently, for relations between the Daughters of Charity and the administration of the hospital where they worked were very tense. The bishop had been called upon to bring order into this conflict and had threatened to send the girls away. As soon as Vincent arrived, he looked into the matter, called upon the bishop, lectured the girls, who had not been without fault, and managed to spread peace among all concerned. In a long letter to Louise de Marillac, he suggested certain changes and asked her to send two competent, hard-working girls to reinforce the little community of Nantes.

On April 29, Vincent left for Luçon, from where he was supposed to go back north to Richelieu. This was to be the last leg of his trip, for in the meantime he had received orders from the regent to return to Paris. He regretfully reported his change of plans to Antoine Portail, who was expecting him in Marseilles. "The Lord knows how much I desire to visit the houses down there, and he knows how deep my regret is at having to obey the queen's repeated command to return to Paris. But I do not see how I could be doing the will of God by not obeying, especially when I have always taught that one must obey princes, even the evil ones, as Scripture tells us."[20]

The matter at hand was the fact that a conference had been held at Rueil in early March 1649, in which the participants were delegates of the parlement on one side and the duke de Orléans, the prince de Condé, Cardinal Mazarin, and Chancellor Pierre Séguier on the other. An accord had been concluded on March 8, submitted to the parlement for approval, and officially promulgated on April 1. This was the end of the first stage of the Fronde, and the siege of Paris was raised. Vincent de Paul had been informed of the favorable outcome of the negotiations on March 2 in a letter from the duchess d'Aiguillon, who advised him to interrupt his visitations and return to Paris. But he had turned a deaf ear and continued his travels to houses of the Congregation of the Mission.

In any case, the court had not yet returned to the capital for the Spaniards were threatening the northern frontiers of the kingdom. In order to be able to follow the operations more closely, the regent and Mazarin had traveled to Compiègne, and so Vincent had not rushed to obey the queen's command to return. Indeed, while he was still at Richelieu, he had written to ask whether he might be allowed to continue his trip, not all the way to Marseilles but only as far as Cahors, "to visit the house of Notre-Dame de la Rose and three or four other houses of the Congregation in that area."[21] But Vincent was beginning to feel the accumulated fatigue of his four months of strenuous travel. He had just begun his sixty-ninth year and at that age, recovery is not as swift, even when a person is fortunate enough to be in hearty good health. At Richelieu, he suffered again from his "feverlet" and he had to admit that he was in no condition to continue traveling on horseback.

The duchess d'Aiguillon, having received a discreet warning of Vincent's condition, sent him a brother infirmarian and the carriage that she had long been offering and he had been refusing. Once he had recovered from his fever and concluded his visits to his missionaries and the Daughters of Charity at Richelieu, he grumbled his way into the carriage and rode back to Paris. On June 13, he arrived at Saint-Lazare, after an absence of five months.

Father of the Country
1649–1651

Once back at Saint-Lazare, Vincent saw that the political climate in the capital was detestable and that the population of Paris was still deeply traumatized by the first stage of the Fronde, which had just ended. Even though distribution of food became more normal after the siege of the city was lifted, there was a sense of unease abroad. The court had not yet returned to the city. The Spanish threat still lurked in the wings and at the beginning of June, the regent and Mazarin decided to move from Compiègne to Amiens, so as to be closer to the armies campaigning in the north. Finally, believing that the danger had been averted, they decided to return, although they knew the capital was still a little feverish because of the activities of the Fronde. On August 18, 1649, the court made a triumphal entry into a city rejoicing at the return of its king.

But the calm did not last long. In January 1650 the prince de Condé, his brother Conti, and his brother-in-law Longueville were arrested and the fires of civil war blazed again. Fighting broke out first in the provinces, especially in the southwest, with the revolt of Bordeaux, incited by the young wife of the prince de Condé.[1] To put down this insurrection, the court set out again with an army, which entered the rebel city in September. This was the beginning of a second wave of the Fronde, known as the Fronde of the princes. It was to end, after many outbursts, in February 1651, with the liberation of Condé and the departure into exile of Mazarin. In the course of this extremely complex period, alliances were made and broken among three groups: the party of the princes, the party of the parlement, and the party of the court. The reactions of two individuals who played principal roles—Gaston d'Orléans, uncle of the young king, and the bishop coadjutor of Paris, the future Cardinal de Retz, were unpredictable. All this time, war with Spain continued and in their turn, the northern provinces of the kingdom, Picardy and Champagne, suffered the coming and going of armies, both of the enemy and of friends.

Vincent held himself distant from all plots and their participants. He avoided the court, knowing that his presence was not particularly wished for. Since his fruitless attempt at mediation at the outbreak of the Fronde, he knew that Mazarin was anything but fond of him. His relations with the cardinal remained unbroken, however, as we can see from a letter the cardinal wrote to Vincent on October 13, 1649, in a very courteous tone: "I am much obliged to you for your good advice and for everything you wrote me in your letter of the fourth of this month. I received your thoughts with the confidence and esteem they deserve."[2]

This façade of courtesy tells us nothing about the deep feelings Mazarin harbored for this Monsieur Vincent whom he mistrusted even more because he knew that Anne of Austria confided in him entirely. Vincent, a few months later, wrote to one of his correspondents that he hardly ever went to court anymore "where I only go if I am called, something which rarely happens."[3] Officially, he was still a member of the Council of Conscience, even though this group met only rarely now. Yet, because of this position, he was still receiving many requests concerning ecclesiastical appointments.

For instance, Alain de Solminihac, bishop of Cahors, wrote to him in May 1650: "I beg of you so to influence the queen, when the bishopric of Toul becomes vacant, that she will provide it with a worthy prelate, for it is in very poor state." In this same letter, he adds these few lines, which tell us a great deal about the behavior of certain provinces of the Church at that time: "I must tell you that my heart bleeds with sorrow at the reproaches flung at me concerning a young prelate in a neighboring see, because of the life that he leads. Recently he rented a house outside his capital city for 600 écus, so that he can keep a pack of hunting dogs and some racing dogs as well. In fact, the sum total of his activity has been the hunt, where he rides out in short garments, with a gun to his shoulder. You were absolutely right to oppose his promotion; would God that we had followed your advice."[4]

When Vincent returned in June 1649, his first task was to restore order in the priory of Saint-Lazare, that had been devastated by soldiers during the first Fronde. All the reserves had been looted, including the store of heating wood. The winters of 1649 and 1650 were ferocious; the atmosphere of the priory in those days was memorialized by the poet Chapelle,[5] incarcerated at Saint-Lazare at the request of his family. Five lines from his long poem about the austerity of his prison life, written to a friend, describe the dark and the cold:

> Smoke there is none, that I can see,
> In this dread and mortal place,
> No light of fire shines on my face
> Save from the incense burnt for Thee
> When we, O God, pray for Thy grace.

Once more, Vincent took over the management of his congregation, since all the member houses had suffered during this troubled period and their revenues had been reduced more or less drastically. He was not able to help the superiors of these houses, so he encouraged them to devise their own solutions. For instance, he wrote to Guillaume Delattre at Agen: "I think it was your ability to save that allowed you to survive. I realize that you have little coming in, that the students' fees are only a tiny help, and that with this year's high prices, you will have a hard time managing. But I also know that if you understood how impossible it is for us to come to your assistance, you would have pity on us, and it would not occur to you to ask."[6]

Writing to the superior of the house at Luçon, he advised that a certain purchase should be abandoned, reminding him that it is more important to attend first to the affairs of Jesus Christ: "I beg you to change your mind about this project, which could be more of a burden than an advantage. In the name of God, let us be more eager to spread the kingdom of Jesus Christ than to expand the inventory of our possessions. Let us be concerned for our task and He will be concerned for us."[7]

Although it was important to be prudent during this period of famine, there was a great danger of falling into the opposite vice and becoming miserly. Vincent was concerned that an excess of economy should not result in starving the family. He reproached the house at Le Mans with this kind of stinginess: "I have heard from one of our houses that the poor food provided there is harmful both to bodies and to souls" and he made it clear that it is wrong to "sell the best wine and then serve the worst stuff, or to expose the community to miserly treatment."[8]

In his role as manager, Vincent studied all the contracts involving the Congregation. For the year 1650, we have no fewer than twenty notarized documents, signed in the hand of "Vincent de Paul, superior general of the Congregation of Priests of the Mission." These are contracts for the rental of houses, tenancy fees for farms or lands, and various other agreements.[9] No file was signed without careful study. For instance, he wrote to the superior of the house at Richelieu: "I have received the copy of the rental agreement for Bois-Bouchard, and I must say that I cannot understand how it was drawn up. That house, with all its dependencies, is estimated to have a revenue of 1,000 or 1,100 livres, and you have simply set a tenant fee of 195 livres."[10]

In addition to this, he dissuaded the superior at Le Mans from engaging in a legal case in defense of the interests of his house when they were threatened: "Peace is worth more than everything they are trying to take away from you. Let us rather suffer these losses than cause scandal. God will take our case in hand, if we follow the words of Our Savior."[11]

Although Vincent devoted himself attentively to solving problems of management and finance, he was first and foremost the superior general and the spiritual director of his congregation. His chief concern was to explicate the rules of life of the Congregation in meetings and assemblies, and to see to it that they were observed. This was his motive for establishing the principle of discipline. He wrote to a superior: "You must realize that you are doing God's will when you fulfill the orders given to you, and you must convince yourself that to follow one's own will is to move away from the Divine will."[12]

He taught that this discipline was to be applied by observing the Rule, beginning with timely rising in the morning, namely at 4:00 a.m. This point appeared so important to him that he composed a letter for all superiors of the Congregation, dedicated to the question of arising in the morning. "The first advantage which comes from arising at the moment when the waking bell is sounded is that one is obeying the Rule, and thus, the will of God." Then he illustrated his point with examples from everyday life: "A merchant gets up early in the morning to get rich; thieves do the same and spend their nights lying in wait for passersby. Shall we be less diligent for the good than they are for ill?"[13]

Much as he insisted on the principles of discipline and respect of the hierarchy, both necessary to assure a well-functioning community, he moderated his statements in letters addressed to certain people: "Those who lead houses of the community should not consider anyone as an inferior, but rather as a brother. Thus, it is necessary to treat one's confrères with humility, mildness, support, and love." Humbly, he added: "It is not that I abide by all this myself, but whenever I depart from it, I count myself a sinner."[14]

Practice of the virtues of humility, mildness, and charity was the path he advocated over and over again when he wrote to his missionaries: "I pray that God will see fit to teach all the missionaries to deal mildly, humbly, and lovingly with their neighbors, in public and in private, even with sinners and the hard of heart, without ever uttering strong words, reproaches, or words of disrespect against anyone."[15]

Vincent was filled with understanding and compassion for his priests. When one of them confessed that he was locked in painful struggles with temptation, he wrote: "I am not astonished by the fact that you have been tempted, for that is the lot of those who wish to serve God. This is how it was with Our Lord Himself, so who can hope to be exempt? Courage, Monsieur, be truly faithful and His divine goodness will bring you strength."[16]

To another of his priests, who complained that he could not study, Vincent gave this advice, in the name of truthfulness. He enjoined the priest to abandon his studies because "I know that you have sufficient knowledge already and because usually, those who know the most are not those who bear the most fruit." He encouraged the man to learn in the school of Christ: "Don't worry about it. As long as you make satisfactory progress in the school of Our Lord, He will refine your knowledge far better than any book; He will give you the gift of His spirit and with His light you will enlighten the souls held in darkness by vice and ignorance."[17]

All this time, Vincent maintained his efforts against Jansenism. In June 1648 he gathered a few learned theologians at Saint-Lazare in an attempt to establish a plan of action against the "new ideas."[18] After this meeting, on July 1, 1648 one of the theologians submitted the five propositions of the *Augustinus* to the faculty of theology for critical examination, but the doctors of the Sorbonne did not wish to have anything to do with them. In May 1650, on the occasion of a general assembly of the clergy of France being held in Paris, a group of anti-Jansenist clergy including Vincent de Paul proposed the idea of presenting a petition to the pope, signed by all the bishops. It was Isaac Habert, former theology student at Paris and bishop of Vabres, who composed the text, which was distributed in all the dioceses of the country.[19] By January 1652, the signatures of forty bishops had already been collected, but this represented a scant third of the prelates.

At this point, Vincent involved himself in the campaign personally. He sent a circular letter to the bishops who had not yet signed the petition.[20] Alain de Solminihac, bishop of Cahors, was a vigorous ally, who took upon himself the task of convincing the bishops of his region. But even so, Vincent encountered resistance and this was painful, because it came from men he knew and respected: Étienne Caulet, bishop of Pamiers, and Nicolas Pavillon, bishop of Alet. These prelates believed that in the prevailing climate, this petition would only emphasize the division within the Church rather than calming passions. Vincent wrote them a long letter in June 1651 to tell them that it was vain to wait hopefully for an area of common ground and that heresies should be nipped in the bud.[21]

At the end of 1651, signatures had been obtained from ninety of the 120 bishops of France. But on their side, the Jansenists had not been idle either. They had managed to get twelve bishops to address another petition to the pope, begging him not to make a pronouncement before the Church in France had conducted a detailed examination of the much-contested five propositions. Thenceforth, the battle would unfold in Rome, where the two camps sent delegates to plead their causes.

Apparently this theological dispute did not destroy Vincent's good relations with his former student, Nicolas Pavillon. In 1650, Pavillon sent Vincent two young men, the Chandenier brothers, to be educated. These were the great-nephews of Cardinal de la Rochefoucauld, who doubtless, before his death in 1645, had asked Vincent to watch over them. They were received at Saint-Lazare and participated in the Tuesday Conferencess. The older, Louis de Chandenier, an ordained priest, was abbot of Tournus; the second, Claude, was a deacon and the grand vicar of the abbey of Moutiers-Saint-Jean, of which he would be named abbot in 1655. During the two years that the Chandenier brothers passed with the bishop of Alet, Vincent accepted the vicariate general of this Burgundian abbey. It should be noted that at this time, he was fulfilling the same functions for the abbeys of Saint-Ouen, Marmoutiers, and Saint-Martin-des-Champs, commendatory abbeys in the possession of the Vignerods, nephews of the late Cardinal de Richelieu.

The abbey of Moutiers-Saint-Jean, about twelve kilometers southwest of Montbard, is the oldest abbey in Burgundy. Founded by a hermit, Saint Jean de Réome, in the year 430, it reached the high point of its development in the thirteenth century.[22] Then, like so many other religious foundations, it entered a period of decline as a result of the Hundred Years' War and the War of Religion. Its condition was made even worse by the fact that since the sixteenth century, it had been held by commendatory privilege. In the seventeenth century, the abbey still had a sizable endowment, with a domain consisting of fifteen parishes. Thus, the abbey with its holdings was profitable enough to interest Cardinal de Richelieu, who had himself named abbot in 1629, bringing the total of his benefices to seventeen. Cardinal de la Rochefoucauld accepted the charge of the benefice in 1631 and hoped that his great-nephew, Claude de Chandenier might inherit it when he came of age.

Vincent took over the additional burden of acting as vicar general of this abbey out of friendship for the Chandenier family, but one wonders whether he ever had the time and the opportunity to travel all the way to Moutiers-Saint-Jean. Local tradition states that he visited the abbey and its dependent parishes, but there is no documentary proof that he did so. There is also not a single document nominating a pastor that bears Vincent's signature.[23]

Because of his position in the Church of France and his relations with the great families of the kingdom, Vincent de Paul was obliged to take on responsibilities which he would gladly have passed by, but his thoughts and attention ranged far beyond the regions where his congregation had already established itself. In Italy, after having founded a house in Rome, the missionaries were sought out by Cardinal Durazzo at Genoa. This prelate was an enthusiastic supporter of their work and even placed them in charge of a seminary. Their official establishment in Genoa was ratified by the local senate in 1649 and, by the next year, the house had eight priests who carried out their mission successfully in the surrounding regions.

In contrast, the news from Madagascar was much more troubling. In October 1650, Vincent received a packet of letters from Charles Nacquart.[24] The first of these, dated May 1649, gave an account of their long and difficult crossing, a sea voyage of six months to the port of Fort-Dauphin, where his companion died as soon as they arrived. There followed an account of the difficulties which Nacquart encountered in his relations with the governor and the colonists. Of the latter, he said that they lived a dissolute life and that they treated the native people with harshness and violence. But he also noted that his own work with the native people was effective. By the time his letters arrived in France, Charles Nacquart had already died of an illness, a fact that Vincent only learned much later. But in any case, he was resolved to continue the work of evangelization in Madagascar. He asked for authorization from the Propagation of the Faith to send seven other missionaries to the island. For various reason, the departure of the ship which was to take the priests there was delayed; it did not appear until 1654. This was only the beginning of the trials and the tragedies which were to challenge this mission to Madagascar.

After the failed attempt to implant a mission in Ireland, Vincent did not abandon the idea of laboring in this region. In April 1650, he wrote a letter of encouragement to one of the two missionaries who had survived in hiding, at Limerick.[25] Then the Propagation of the Faith asked him to send missionaries to the Hebrides Islands and to Scotland.[26] Vincent chose two priests of Irish origin and they set out in 1651. Living in Ireland under miserable conditions, among a population bowed low under poverty, at the mercy of a harsh climate, the priests moved from one island to another, constantly the target of official hostility from local authorities.

Vincent was always prompt to give an affirmative answer to requests from far away, and so he was pleased to receive a call from the queen of Poland, Louise-Marie de Gonzague,[27] a French princess who had been one of the first Ladies of Charity. Vincent was aware of the pitiable situation in the kingdom of Poland and knew all of the risks threatening a mission in a country troubled by internal strife and aggression on its borders, but he nevertheless agreed to send a team to Warsaw. As leader, he chose one of his best priests, Lambert aux Couteaux, who set out in September 1651 with four missionaries. Vincent wrote to the queen: "They do not know the language of the country, but since they speak Latin, they can begin by educating young priests."[28] It was his judgment that within one year, the missionaries would be able to educate and form twelve local priests, who could then accompany them on missions. He also announced to the queen that a team of Daughters of Charity was prepared to travel to Warsaw as well. And so began the mission to Poland, which was to gain Vincent much notice.

In addition to concerns directly related to the Congregation of the Mission, Vincent de Paul had to consider other questions as well. Upon his return to Paris in June 1649, Louise de Marillac asked him for help with the Foundling Hospital. The children, at least those who were already weaned, had been moved to the château of Bicêtre, where they would have more space and breathe better air than in the capital. But the move did not have the expected good results.

"Fifty-two children have died at Bicêtre since our arrival, and there are fifteen or sixteen who appear to be near death," wrote Louise de Marillac, soon after their arrival. At the same time, the financial situation was becoming critical. Louise de Marillac had sent a first appeal to Vincent at Fréneville, where he was immobilized by storms. Vincent's response was to implore the Ladies of Charity not to abandon the children to a tragic fate. But in the meantime, the situation had grown worse, armed bands swarmed around the outskirts of Paris, and Bicêtre was not a safe place. It was decided to bring the children back to the city. Louise de Marillac no longer knew how to meet the needs of the Foundling Hospital, and she declared as much to Vincent: "The more I think of what we owe, the more I fear that we will not be able to help ourselves. The wet nurses are beginning to threaten us and to bring the children back, and our debts are growing so fast that soon there will be no hope of repaying them."[29] At this time, she probably had several hundred children in her charge; we do not have exact numbers.

Vincent seems to have remained calm in the face of this crisis. He replied to Louise de Marillac; "The work with the children is in the hands of Our Lord."[30] But he did not throw up his hands. Once more he assembled the Ladies of Charity and confronted them with their moral responsibility. According to notes taken at the time, he is supposed to have addressed them in these terms: "What will these little creatures say! Alas, my dear mothers, you are abandoning us! Our own mothers have failed us, true enough, but they are bad women. But that good women like you should leave us too, that's the same as saying that the Good Lord has abandoned us, and that He is not our God any longer." And when these ladies replied that they had no more money to give, he cried out : "Alas, how many precious little things do you have in your homes, things that serve no purpose whatever! Oh Madame, how far we are from the piety of the Children of Israel, whose women gave their jewels to make a golden calf!"[31]

Once more Monsieur Vincent managed to move his hearers with his eloquence. The Ladies of Charity were persuaded to make one more effort. Gifts poured in and it became possible to repay the debts and meet the needs of every day. Once more, the Foundling Hospital was saved.

For a decade, from 1639 to 1649, Vincent de Paul organized drives for aid to the war victims of Lorraine. Just when a certain quiet was beginning to descend on the province, other regions came to know the horrors and devastation caused by the passage of armies. At the beginning of June 1650, Spanish troops under the leadership of Archduke Leopold, governor of the Low Countries, supported by the troops of Turenne, made their way into the kingdom of France. The fortifications of Hirson and Catelet fell, and Guise was under siege. A French army under the command of marshal du Plessis-Praslin advanced and penetrated the siege of Guise. But in August, a new offensive broke out, the Spanish troops crossed the Aisne and marched on Paris. Their goal was to free the prince of Condé who was being held captive in the château of Vincennes. On July 27, a vanguard led by Turenne was at La Ferté-Milon and at Dammartin, one day's march from the capital. The Spanish were not eager to venture so far forward and decided to stay where they were, obliging their ally of the moment, Turenne, to fall back to the Meuse. The Spanish army was escorted by a corps of mercenaries, recruited after the Peace of Westphalia from Germany, Sweden and Poland. This corps, commanded by the Swiss baron d'Erlach and then by a German roughneck called de Rose, was accustomed to living off the land, devastating everything in its passage.

The comings and goings of these troops, both French and foreign, through the provinces of Picardy and Champagne, all the way to the Île-de-France reduced these unfortunate countrysides to desolation in a period of only a few months. Vincent received information from the missionaries, who had witnessed the siege of Guise and the roads clotted with soldiers, civilians wounded or ill dying in the ditches, and villages empty of all life. He immediately sent two priests to help, with a small store of food and money, but they were soon overcome by the vastness of the need, which they reported to him.

Then, with his organizer's mind and the experience gained from helping in Lorraine, Vincent quickly set up intervention teams which he deployed to the points of gravest suffering. By the end of December 1650, he was able to write: "We have sent seven priests and six brothers to help the poor people of Picardy and Champagne in their extreme physical and spiritual need, just as we did once before in Lorraine."[32] By twos and threes, the missionaries were directed to the dioceses of Laon, Noyon, Soissons, Châlons, and Reims. Their orders were to work with the local authorities; they were to help the parish clergy, not take their place. One brother, Jean Parré,[33] particularly active and effective, provided Vincent with information, just as Brother Mathieu Regnard had done from Lorraine. Sometimes, there were urgent situations to be dealt with. This was the case when Turenne's army, which had been driven from the field near Cambrai, left 1,500 dead behind. The unburied bodies were a likely focus of an epidemic. When Vincent was warned of this, he asked one of his teams to go there at once to bury the dead. Edme Deschamps, priest of the Mission, reported the following: "Today we followed to the letter the precepts of Jesus Christ in the Gospel, to love one's enemies and to treat them with kindness, since we buried those who had ravaged the goods and caused the ruin of our poor countrymen, as well as beating them and treating them with contumely."[34]

At the same time, Vincent was mobilizing women of good will in the capital. At the forefront were the wives of President de Lamoignon and President de Herse, Madame de Miramion, and Madame Fouquet, mother of the Procurator General, Nicolas Fouquet. These women represented the circles of the parlement, the high court, and Port-Royal. The members of the Company of the Blessed Sacrament also took part in this great charitable movement. One of them, Charles Maignart de Bernières, resigned his position as Master of Petitions to devote himself entirely to helping the people of the devastated provinces. He conceived the idea of printing a publication, *Les Relations,*[35] to bring before the public the letters written to Monsieur Vincent by his missionaries, in which they told of their work and described what they found. For example, in January 1651, the following extract appeared: "We have just visited thirty-five villages of the deanery of Guise, where we found almost

600 people in such agonies of starvation that they threw themselves upon the cadavers of dogs and horses after the wolves had had their fill of them. In the village of Guise alone, there are more than 500 sick, huddled in cellars and caverns more suited for animals than people."[36]

Some 4,000 copies of the collection of letters were widely distributed in Paris and other cities. In this new and effective way, a veritable public opinion campaign was launched that yielded 80,000 livres, collected in the capital between September 1650 and March 1651. These subsidies were sent to Picardy and Champagne, where they made it possible to feed 10,000 people—the sick, widows and orphans—and to pass out clothing and blankets to those who had lost everything. There was even enough for seeds and tools so that the healthy could return to work, for Vincent de Paul was convinced that charity should be intelligent and positive. It was not right, he believed, to encourage people to rely on assistance and to be satisfied with idleness: "As soon as a person is strong enough to work, we buy him some tools appropriate for his profession, and that is all one gives him."[37]

Vincent de Paul was not content to organize fund drives and the distribution of aid. He wanted to be on the spot in order to take part in projects and evaluate their usefulness. In the archives of Noyon and Chauny, there are testimonials to his travels through the region. Deeply moved by all the misery he saw, Vincent went to the court to speak to Anne of Austria directly about everything he had seen and experienced himself. His descriptions were so gripping that the regent decided at once to sign an ordinance entrusting him with an official mission to protect and console the people of Picardy and Champagne. "Her Majesty being well aware of the fact that most of the inhabitants of villages in Picardy and Champagne have been reduced to beggary and misery because of the looting and hostilities of the enemies and the billeting and passage of all the armies, and knowing that several churches have been sacked and stripped of their ornaments, and because in the hopes of feeding the poor and repairing the churches, several persons of her stately city of Paris are giving abundant alms which are most effectively applied by the priests of the Mission of Monsieur Vincent. . . . Her Majesty orders all civilian and military authorities to comply with the requests of those same priests of the Mission, so that they may be fully at liberty to practice their charity where it seems appropriate to them."[38]

This remarkable ordinance, signed on February 14, 1651, invested Vincent de Paul with the office of a secretary of state to the war-torn provinces. He was indeed generally thought of in this way, and people turned to him for help. The aldermen of Rethel wrote to him in May 1651 to request his help, describing in pathetic tones the sufferings of their people: "There is no way to tell this story, there is no pen, however richly gifted it might be, which can impart full knowledge of the pitiable state to which the cruelty and ungoverned disorder of the soldiers have reduced this unfortunate land."[39]

Vincent's concern and effective response did not go unseen. One by one, those responsible for large groups of people praised and thanked him. Perhaps the most beautiful epithet came to Vincent from the lieutenant general of Saint-Quentin. Thanking Monsieur Vincent for the help he had sent both to the inhabitants of his city and those who were in exile, he called him "a father of the country."[40]

Face to Face with Misery
1651–1652

After the prince de Condé was freed in January 1651 and Mazarin had gone voluntarily into exile, calm appeared to return to the kingdom, even though intrigue was rife among the different clans circling the throne. The regent, Anne of Austria, managed to preserve a fragile equilibrium until September 7, the day on which the young king officially attained his majority and she symbolically returned to him the power to govern the monarchy. In fact, Anne of Austria continued to preside over the council of government, following the instructions which Mazarin regularly sent her from his exile.

The calm was brief; the civil war soon regained momentum. The prince de Condé left for Guyenne, whose governance he had been given to replace his lost power over Burgundy. The revolution in his favor sparked up at Bordeaux, while his partisans, in alliance with Spain, threatened the frontiers of the kingdom in the regions of Stenay and Champagne.

The young king and his court left the capital at the end of September and journeyed to Poitiers to conduct operations against Condé. The two opposing armies, the king's and Condé's, both pillaged the region around Bordeaux from one end to the other.

During 1651, Vincent de Paul remained prudently quiet in his priory of Saint-Lazare. He certainly had sufficient work, what with organizing aid missions to the devastated provinces. He also had to concern himself with how his houses kept body and soul together as the turmoil of war threatened survival and morale. His work was made more difficult by the fact that he had passed the milestone of his seventieth year in April, and his health was very poor. He had been suffering from pains in his legs for many years, and walking was increasingly difficult. It was not just that his legs no longer obeyed him; they were covered with open sores and infected ulcerations, and there were episodes of fever which sometimes lasted for two weeks at a time. He talked about his poor health contemptuously, dismissing the "feverlets," but these attacks were intense and trying enough to make all activity impossible. At the end of August 1651, he was bedridden at Saint-Lazare, and he admitted in a letter addressed to a Daughter of Charity: "I have been sick for two weeks."[1] Two weeks later, he was still so weak that he could not write to Louise de Marillac in his own hand.

But he had advice for this lady when she was distraught about the state of her son's health. Along with his wishes for the young man's recovery, Vincent encouraged her to follow the doctor's orders, even if she didn't have much confidence in medicine: "I wish the same for you as I wished yesterday . . . namely that you find yourself able to obey the physician. One might say that doctors kill more patients than they cure, since God wishes to be recognized as the sovereign physician of our souls and our bodies as well, particularly for those people who use no remedies. And yet, when one is sick, one must submit to the physician and obey him."[2]

It is hard to say whether Vincent himself was as submissive as he wanted others to be, for the results obtained by his physicians are hardly conclusive. More and more frequently as he grew older, he would write that he was suffering from a bout of fever. The little bit of clinical information we have from his letters makes it difficult to attempt a diagnosis now. However, one hypothesis, which would take into account both his recurrent fever and the pain and weakness in his legs, is that he suffered all his life from severe episodes of malaria. In fact, this disease can attack the arterial system, causing disturbances and pain in the lower extremities.[3] It might be that he was infected with the malaria parasite as a boy when he pastured his flock in the marshes, or he could have contracted the disease on the Barbary Coast or later in the Dombes. In any case, purges and bleedings, the only remedies practiced at the time, could do nothing for malaria and its complications except weaken the patient.

Since he was staying close to home because of his unpredictable health, Vincent had the opportunity to see that life at Saint-Lazare was becoming more and more active. In September 1651, the retreat for ordinands brought in ninety clerks and thirty-five priests. This created problems of provisioning and Vincent admitted that he was in great difficulty because funds were scarce. He spoke of this to his faithful Lambert aux Couteaux, who at that time was stationed in Warsaw: "Our poverty is growing, along with the rise in public misery. At one blow, the troubles have snatched away from us 22,000 or 23,000 livres of income, since we are no longer receiving customs duties and the barges are no longer plying the rivers." Fortunately, this experienced manager had not put all his eggs in one basket, so he was receiving food directly from his farms: "One possible source of bread for next year is the farm at Rougemont, which we are working with our own hands, and the farm at Orsigny, if God will protect them from damage and looting."[4]

In these unfavorable times, it was inadvisable to incur useless expenses, as he firmly reminded the superior of the house at Méen: "Do not spend any extraordinary sums over 6 écus without the orders of the superior general." He reprimanded the superior of Le Mans, who complained that he could not manage all his responsibilities but at the same time took on new projects: "It seems that your workers are almost always complaining, accusing, changing places, prettying things up, spending a great deal of money day by day for wages and supplies. May God give us the grace to use our small means well and to turn holy poverty to our benefit!"[5]

Vincent himself set the tone for this poverty. One of his nephews came to visit him, at the end of a long journey of 600 kilometers, to ask for his advice, but no longer had the money to return home. Vincent consulted with Monsieur Duval to see whether the money could be made available from the funds of the Congregation. The response was that he would have to obtain the consent of the community. Finally, it became necessary for Vincent to ask for alms for his nephew; in this way, he obtained 6 écus with which the young man could get home.[6]

The news which Vincent received from those houses more directly affected by ongoing military operations moved him to write letters of encouragement. For instance, there was the house at Saintes. The town was held by the party of Condé and consequently in danger from the impending arrival of the royal army. The governor of Saintes ordered certain quarters of the town destroyed in order to make the defense of the fortress more efficient. The superior of the house was considering a withdrawal of his people, but Vincent ordered him to remain in place, no matter what: "You must hold firm, Monsieur. It would be very wrong to leave, causing great scandal to the town and to the Congregation. Do not fear. The storm will be followed by tranquility, and perhaps even very soon. In all the time that war has raged in Lorraine, in Flanders, and on our borders, religious houses have remained strong. Our houses at Agen and La Rose are in the same danger as you, and the situation at Cahors is almost as bad."[7]

Early in 1652, the storm Vincent was talking about traveled north from Guyenne toward the Île-de-France. The chaos of the Fronde would reach its climax in the capital city, and this would bring the superior of the Congregation of the Mission out of his retreat.

In the first days of January, Mazarin returned from his exile at the head of an army he had raised in Germany. He joined the royal family at Poitiers and traveled with them up toward Saint-Germain. At the same time, Condé returned to the capital after many ups and downs, having fought the royal forces along the Loire; once in Paris, he struck an alliance with Gaston d'Orléans. To complicate the situation further, the duke de Lorraine arrived with an army of mercenaries and camped on the Marne, near Lagny, waiting to sell his services to the highest bidder.

The countryside of the Île-de-France was sacked by all the armies concerned—the royal army, the troops of Condé, and the troops of Lorraine. As a result, the capital was without food and the suffering of the people became more intense as refugees poured in, fleeing from villages ruined by armed bands. On July 2, a bloody battle pitted the forces of Condé against the king's men led by Turenne. The battle raged right beneath the city walls, near the Porte Saint-Antoine, not far from the enclosure of Saint-Lazare. Vincent de Paul wrote about it in a letter addressed to his house at Genoa: "Only three or four nights ago, we had a whole army around our walls. But since it was being pursued by the king's army, it moved away in the morning at great speed, and the rear guard was attacked behind the Saint-Charles seminary, which was in great danger of being pillaged."[8]

Finally, Condé's army, badly trounced, took refuge behind the walls of the capital, which they were able to enter thanks to the daring intervention of La Grande Mademoiselle.[9] But two days later, a popular uprising outside the Hôtel de Ville, where an assembly of notables was gathered, degenerated into a slaughter for which neither party took responsibility. To all intents and purposes, the city was in a state of insurrection.

In this atmosphere of acute crisis, Monsieur Vincent made a surprising decision. Once more violating his own rule never to interfere in political matters, he took it upon himself to attempt a role as mediator. Was he asked to do this? It is more likely that he acted on his own initiative, for he was moved by the suffering of the people and feared that the situation might worsen until it was beyond control. First he visited Gaston d'Orléans and the prince de Condé, whose troops were occupying the capital. They received him "graciously" and seemed to approve of his intention to approach the court.

Vincent had not seen the queen for six or seven months.[10] He had no idea how he would be received at Saint-Denis, where the court was making a stop on its way to Pontoise. We only know about his interview through a letter he wrote to Mazarin the next day: "I most humbly beg Your Eminence to pardon me for leaving yesterday evening without having had the honor to receive his orders; I was forced to do this because I was not well." Could this have been a diplomatic illness to avoid a contentious meeting with the cardinal? Vincent continues: "Yesterday I spoke to the queen about the separate respectful and gracious meetings I had the honor to have with the two of them [Gaston d'Orléans and Condé]. I told her Royal Highness that if the king were re-established in his authority and a decree of vindication were proclaimed, Your Eminence would give the desired satisfaction."[11]

In other words, Vincent, in agreement with the princes, was suggesting that Cardinal Mazarin should once more distance himself from the court (give the desired satisfaction), which would allow the young king to assert his own authority and re-establish the peace. In return, the parlement of Paris, which had promulgated an edict branding the cardinal a disturber of the public peace and condemned him to be driven out of the kingdom, would rescind its decision (proclaim a decree of vindication).

Further on in the letter, Vincent stated that he was waiting for a message from Gaston d'Orléans approving this first start at negotiations before going to visit the cardinal: "Tomorrow morning, I hope to be able to bring the answer to Your Eminence, with God's help." Did Gaston d'Orléans change his position in the meantime, as was his habit? It seems that Vincent's efforts ended there.

For a better understanding of Monsieur Vincent's apparently remarkable intervention in a matter of politics, one must imagine the situation in the capital and its surroundings. At the beginning of 1652, there were armies camped all around Paris. Villagers abandoned their houses and their goods to find shelter in the city from the extortion of the soldiery. This influx of homeless people was accompanied by the usual epidemic of violence, looting, and sacrilegious despoiling of churches. In May, Vincent wrote to one of his missionaries: "Here, life is more troubled than ever. Paris is swarming with the poor, since the armies have forced the pitiable country folk to come here for refuge. Every day, we try to gather them in and help them; we have rented a few houses in the outlying districts where we take some of them out of harm's way, particularly the poor girls. But we have not given up helping the two frontier regions, Champagne and Picardy, and we still have ten or twelve people there."[12]

Soup kitchens were organized in all the parishes: 900 people were helped in the parish of Saint-Hippolyte, 600 at Saint-Laurent, and 300 at Saint-Martin. Poor parishes like Saint-Médard were hard put to help the many who were assigned to them. At Saint-Lazare, "every day, we give soup to 14,000 or 15,000, who would have died of hunger without this help."[13]

Charitable work like this was done collaboratively by all the religious congregations and the members of the Company of the Blessed Sacrament. The Daughters of Charity were active as well, as Vincent wrote: "The poor Daughters of Charity are doing more than we are as far as the corporal works of mercy are concerned. Every day, at Mademoiselle Le Gras' house, they make and distribute soup for 13,000 of the genteel poor, and in the Faubourg Saint-Denis, for 800 refugees, while in the parish of Saint-Paul alone, four or five of these young women make soup for 5,000 poor people over and above the sixty to eighty sick people for whom they are caring."[14]

In July, the situation grew even worse as the army of Condé, beaten beneath the walls of the capital, entered the city to take refuge. In the meantime Étampes, which had been occupied by the troops of Condé and besieged by the royal forces, found itself in a horrendous state once the siege was lifted. When he was informed of this, Vincent sent priests of the Mission and some Daughters of Charity. They found the population in a state of shock and so weakened that the dead were simply left indoors or in the streets, without burial. Everywhere there were animal carcasses in a state of decomposition, so that the air was filled with the stench, and plague was widespread. The missionaries went to work courageously, burying the dead with the help of any healthy men they could find.

At Palaiseau, the situation was just as bad. The priests of the Mission who were on the scene asked Saint-Lazare for help. Vincent, who was not able to send any, appealed to the duchess d'Aiguillon: "Disease continues at Palaiseau. The first victims who survived now require treatment as convalescents, and those who were healthy are now ill. The soldiers have cut down all the wheat, and there is nothing to harvest. The disease is so virulent that our first four priests have fallen victim to it. Oh! Madame, what a harvest there is to be made here for heaven, in this time when such great misery looms at our gates!"[15]

This is the atmosphere in which Vincent decided that he must go to Anne of Austria, not only to ask her to send away Cardinal Mazarin as a step toward restoring civil peace, but also to beg her to give orders that the villagers must be allowed to harvest their fields without being stopped by the soldiers. In spite of the promises he received, the soldiers continued to confiscate the wheat on the plain of Saint-Denis, as he was able to see for himself, and also between Chapelle and Villette, two villages about a kilometer from Paris. Vincent complained of this in a letter he wrote to the queen soon after his audience with her.[16]

The civil war, aggravated by the consequences of the war against Spain, continued to rage through the provinces of the kingdom, drawing misery and destruction in its wake. In despair, after the failure of his attempt at mediation, Vincent made an astonishing resolve a few months later. On August 16, he wrote to the supreme authority, Pope Innocent X. The man who signs his letter "Most unworthy superior of the Congregation of the Mission" does not hesitate to address the Most Holy Father to beg for his intervention in the interest of peace, when "the royal house is divided by dissent, the people are shattered into factions, cities and persons are tormented by civil war, villages, towns, and cities are toppled, ruined, burned, and the people are almost without sacraments, mass, or any other spiritual comfort."

Vincent added that the apostolic nuncio had attempted to intervene, but that up to that time, the effort had been without result. There was no one left but him, the pastor of the universal church, who could calm the quarrels and bring back peace.[17]

By a curious coincidence, three days after he had signed this letter which could not possibly have arrived at its destination yet, Vincent learned that Mazarin had decided to withdraw from the court. On August 18, the cardinal left for the château of Bouillon, in the diocese of Liège. Now the members of the Fronde had obtained what they demanded, and there was no further impediment to the return of the king to his capital. But he seemed in no hurry to leave Compiègne where he was staying with the court.

Cardinal de Retz, at the head of a delegation of the clergy of Paris, escorted by twenty gentlemen, arrived at Compiègne on September 9 to ask the king to return to his waiting city. But the delegation was given a cool reception. Everyone knew that even though he had withdrawn, Mazarin had not stopped advising the young king and Anne of Austria for a moment, and that no decisions were made without his backing.

Then Vincent took the initiative once more, again stepping out of his habitual pattern. Not only did he decide to break his own rule, never to interfere in public affairs, but he chose to do it for a second time in a few months. On September 1, two days after the deputation of clergy from Paris had failed in its approach to the court, Vincent wrote directly to Mazarin, the man who, officially, had been exiled and removed from power.

One might think that when Monsieur Vincent went to see Anne of Austria to present her with a request to send the cardinal away, he did it as a member of the Council of Conscience and that this step was justified in light of his position and his responsibility as a member of this august body. But in addressing Mazarin, and ascribing to him *de facto* an authority which was no longer vested in him, Vincent was placing himself in an ambiguous position. In his long letter to the cardinal, he gives him, in plain language, some firmly stated advice: "I believe that Your Eminence will be performing an act worthy of his goodness by advising the king and the queen to return and take possession of their city and of the hearts of Paris." After having exhorted him not to stand in the way of the peace process that was already in motion, he even took him to task: "If it is true what people are saying, that Your Eminence has given an order for the king not to listen to milords the princes, and not to give them passports that allow them to present themselves to Their Majesties, and that no deputations or representatives of theirs should be heard, and if to this end Your Eminence has placed strangers close to the king and the queen, attendants who close all avenues of access for anyone who wishes to speak to Their Majesties, it is much to be feared, my lord, that the hatred of the people will turn to rage."[18]

It was in vain that Vincent added that he had spoken to no one of this letter, and that he was acting in his own name alone; he could be certain that his position would produce agitation, for the political situation was complex. The various sectors of the Fronde were still active, and the royal troops and those of Condé faced each other in battle order a few kilometers from the capital. Moreover, the duke de Lorraine had reappeared on the banks of the Marne at the end of August, his army stronger by 3,000 men led by the duke of Württemberg. Discreet negotiations were being conducted between the princes and the court, the princes and Mazarin, the court and the duke de Lorraine, with the latter hoping to be paid well by all sides. In this explosive crisis, an attempt like Vincent's to intervene with the man who continued to hold the reins of power in the hope of convincing him that he should give them up was dangerous, to say the least.

Certainly Mazarin was not pleased to have Monsieur Vincent preach him a sermon. The most immediate result was the decision, made and communicated to Vincent, to remove him from the Council of Conscience. News of this move spread rapidly and on October 20, Alain de Solminihac, bishop of Cahors, wrote to Vincent: "I am sure that it is no great personal loss to you to be delivered from that burdensome position, but the Church is losing a great deal; it would be most desirable to have you still in office."[19]

Barely a month after Vincent sent his letter to Mazarin, the deadlocked situation suddenly began to flow again. The duke de Lorraine, undoubtedly well rewarded for it, folded up his tents and moved away with his mercenaries. The prince de Condé left the capital on October 13, plunging himself and his army into the rebellion. The Fronde fell apart and collapsed like a house of cards. On October 21, the young Louis XIV made a triumphal entry into his stately city of Paris.

Vincent, at peace once more, announced this news to the superior at Genoa, Étienne Blatiron: "I invite you to thank God for bringing the king and the queen back to Paris. Joy is so great on all sides that you cannot imagine it. We now have great hope for a complete end to internal disruptions in the kingdom."[20]

But the end of internal warfare did not repair damage already done and did not suppress, as though with a magic wand, the misery caused by this long period of troubles. A rapid survey initiated by the archbishop of Paris provided a list of the most urgent needs of the poor around the capital. To organize the centralization of the aid effort Christophe du Plessis, baron of Montbard, a director of the Hôtel-Dieu of Paris, set up general storehouses for all gifts of food, clothing, bedding, and tools gathered throughout the capital. One storage facility was located on the Île Saint-Louis, where boats could load these goods and move them to the eastern portion of the city. Another warehouse was opened near the Burgundy gate, where the wagons left for the north of Paris. These supplies were gathered in drives organized in the parishes; money was raised by the Ladies of Charity. The missionaries took part in distributing this aid in the most hard-hit villages as well as organizing centers where the sick could be cared for. All the religious orders contributed to this great impulse of mutual aid and charity. Different areas were allocated to each order: the reformed Franciscans were assigned to Juvisy and Saint-Denis, the Jesuits to Villeneuve-Saint-Georges, the Discalced Carmelites to Tournan, the reformed Dominicans to Gonesse, the Capuchins to Corbeil, and the priests of the Mission devoted themselves to Étampes, Palaiseau, and Lagny.[21]

Vincent de Paul had the experience and the talent to organize and coordinate this great communal impulse of charity. Once more, he functioned as a catalyst for cooperation among all people of good will.

The Desolation
Ravaging the Church
1653–1655

A Sketch Plan for a General Hospital
Success and Failure in Rome
"To End My Days in the Countryside"
Sobering News from Distant Missions
Reforming the Priestly Estate

With the Fronde out of the way and the court once more installed in the capital, the times ahead would be calmer, although the war against Spain continued. The Spanish had received reinforcements of some magnitude in the person of a great captain, the prince de Condé, and the troops of both camps were crisscrossing and devastating the northern provinces of the kingdom, Champagne, Picardy, and the Ardennes. As for the provinces of the Midi, they were slowly recovering from the calamities wrought by the Fronde of Bordeaux.

Although Monsieur Vincent was no longer a member of the council on Church affairs, he was still receiving requests to speak at court in favor of charitable works or in support of petitions. For example, the bishop of Dax, Jacques Desclaux, wrote to him to complain about the harm suffered by the churches of his diocese and to let him know that he was coming to the capital to plead his case and obtain relief from the taxes established by the central power. Vincent tried to dissuade him from this move by reminding him discreetly of his pastoral duty: "Wherever the armies have passed, they have committed sacrilege, theft, and the kind of impiety that your diocese has suffered. And this is true not only in Guyenne and Périgord but also in Saintonge, Poitou, Bourgogne, Champagne, Picardy, and many other places, even close to Paris." He encouraged the prelate to give up his plan and remain among his flock and his clergy, "who will be full of joy at being able to experience your presence there, where it does so much good."[1]

Monsieur Vincent was always the one to be called upon in matters of urgency, when help had to be found. He was on the road at the beginning of January 1653, traveling to give a little conference for the Daughters of Charity, when "the duchess d'Aiguillon and the wife of President de Herse sent someone looking for me there, so that I could consult with them about ways of helping the poor of Champagne that the armies were reducing to a pitiable state." Vincent, who reports this event among many others, asked himself what else he could possibly do to comply with this latest request: "We are already spending large amounts for assistance to this diocese, which requires 6,000 or 7,000 livres a week for its support."[2]

But Providence acts unexpectedly. One day, a rich burgher gave Vincent a considerable sum of money, 100,000 livres, to use for a work of charity of his choice. After long consideration, Vincent decided to create a hospice which would be a house of retirement for poor tradesmen. In this institution, he applied ideas which were dear to his heart: first of all, he wanted to create an establishment on a human scale where the residents would feel free. Next, he did not consider it sufficient to offer shelter and food to these needy people. Rather, he wanted to give them the opportunity to be useful, since idleness is the mother of all vices. He ordered tools so that even in retirement, they could work at their own crafts according to any small energy and desire for work they might have. This hostel, which was called Hospital of the Holy Name of Jesus, was set up in two houses he bought in the faubourg Saint-Laurent. The Sisters of Charity cared for the little community, made up of twenty men and as many women, and a priest of the Mission was in charge of their spiritual welfare.

This foundation was met with enthusiasm by the Ladies of Charity, who immediately wanted to create a general hospital on the same principles where the beggars of the city could be given a place to live. This was, in fact, an idea in wide circulation at the time; some cities had already opened a general hospital, but without much success, so charitable associations and public authorities were planning ways to do this work more effectively. At first, Vincent tried to moderate the enthusiasm of these pious ladies, not wishing to embrace hastily an enterprise whose implications he had not yet studied. What is more, he had no intention of engaging his overburdened Congregation in this additional work. But finally, he was forced to yield to the pressing demands of the Ladies. From Anne of Austria, he obtained the vast enclosure of the Salpêtrière, a former arsenal, near the Seine and facing the new arsenal.

Vincent hoped for a modest start, taking in a maximum of 100 poor beggars before creating an institution on a larger scale. But even so, the project was met with opposition in high places. Once more, Vincent had to ask the duchess d'Aiguillon to try to break the deadlock, so that the work of restoring the Salpêtrière could continue.[3] In spite of the support lent by this powerful lady and the efforts of the Company of the Blessed Sacrament, which showed a lively interest in the project, the work would not be finished until four years later, in 1657. In the meantime, the plans for the institution were modified, and the guidelines for the general hospital which finally emerged did not please Monsieur Vincent at all.

A year earlier, three doctors of the Sorbonne had been sent to the Holy See to defend, against the delegates of the Jansenists, the petition of the bishops of the Church in France, requesting condemnation of the five propositions taken from the *Augustinus* of Jansenius. Vincent kept himself informed of the proceedings, but he was well aware of the dignified pace at which work was done in Rome. It was not until the beginning of January 1653 that a first debate took place in the presence of the pope. After several sessions, the Holy Father pronounced his judgment and published a bull, *Cum occasione,* dated May 31, condemning the indicted propositions of Jansenius. Vincent, who had played an active role in this affair, was delighted. On July 5, he wrote to Alain de Solminihac: "I am sending you news which you will find most agreeable, namely, the condemnation of the Jansenists." Vincent hoped that they would submit to the judgment: "One hopes that they will be able to swallow the pill and that they will not say that even though the opinions of Jansenius have been condemned, their own have not."[4] Contrary to his hopes, however, the papal bull did not bring peace to agitated souls. Indeed, the quarrel of Jansenism degenerated into open warfare. With a heavy heart, Vincent realized that he would yet be involved.

Throughout the ups and downs of his agitated life, and in spite of the many concerns which preoccupied him, Vincent never lost sight of his objectives. What seemed to him of greatest importance in assuring the permanence of his major accomplishment was to give a complete and inviolable Rule to his Congregation. He had already composed draft texts, which had been discussed and revised in assembly, but some matters remained to be clarified. The question that preoccupied him above the rest was the matter of vows, and he gave it a great deal of thought.

Vincent hoped that the missionaries would take the three usual vows—poverty, chastity and obedience—and add to them a special vow of stability. This would avoid the situation where members left the Congregation after completing their studies to join other religious companies. Yet he did not want the Mission to become a religious order. Rather, he insisted that the missionaries remain secular priests instead of becoming order religious.

Was it possible to resolve this paradox, to take vows and still remain secular? There was the additional problem of having this Rule approved both by the archbishop of Paris, who was the authority over the Congregation, and by Rome, the authority over all. The agreement of the archbishop was not difficult to obtain, given the privileged relationship between him and Monsieur Vincent, but the Holy See would be more difficult to convince.

Vincent had already sent several representatives to Rome, and they had had more or less success. After a general assembly of the Congregation held at Saint-Lazare in July 1651, in the course of which the question of vows had been debated, a petition was carried to the pope by a special messenger, Thomas Berthe.[5] It was his assignment to obtain the pope's approval for the Rule of the Congregation of the Mission in the form containing the four vows. Vincent kept close track of Berthe's negotiations. In a letter written to his emissary in April 1653, he set out his thoughts about the vow of stability. "The tasks we do are so varied, so arduous, and spread over such long periods that those who take them on might drift away, become discouraged, or get embroiled in skirmishes; it is difficult to persevere if there is no tie that holds them to the Congregation. And it could go with us as with some other congregations, where the members have no obligation to obedience, and moved around as they pleased." Knowing well that Rome was not at all favorable to the creation of new religious orders, he added: "You can make assurances that ours are simple vows, not the solemn vows of a religious order. We have no intention of separating ourselves from the clergy or of becoming order religious."[6]

Negotiations seemed to be going well, when an unexpected event brought them to an abrupt halt. At the beginning of February 1655, Vincent received a letter from Berthe, announcing that he had just received "a written command in which His Majesty orders us to leave Rome and to return to France at once."[7] What had taken place?

To understand these events, we must look back three years. In February 1652, Jean-François Paul de Gondi, coadjutor of the archbishop of Paris, his uncle, succeeded by a number of intrigues in obtaining the cardinal's hat, which he wore under the name of Cardinal de Retz. But because he was an active member of the Fronde, Cardinal Mazarin had him imprisoned a few months later, on December 19, in the château of Vincennes. Meanwhile, his uncle, the archbishop, died in March 1654. Even from the depths of his prison, Cardinal de Retz was able to take possession, by proxy, of the archbishopric of Paris, thus unleashing the fury of Mazarin and the court. In revenge, he was moved to another prison, the château of Nantes, from which he escaped that August. Hurtling in and out of a thousand adventures, pursued by Mazarin's henchmen, he crossed Spain and arrived in Rome, where he was received in fatherly fashion by Pope Innocent X. This pontiff detested Mazarin and was not sorry to annoy him by showing his friendship for de Retz.

It was at the request of the pope himself that the superior of the Mission at Rome gave hospitality to the illustrious fugitive. In any case, would Vincent not have opened his house freely to receive his former pupil, the son of his benefactor and cofounder of the Congregation? This is why the royal thunder fell upon that unfortunate Thomas Berthe, who had no voice in these events, but was commanded to close his house and leave Rome.

However, it seems that the royal rage and Mazarin's bad temper soon abated. Shortly after this drama, the cardinal summoned Monsieur Vincent, who gave the following account to a friend: "The thing settled itself quite well, thanks be to God. It pleased the goodness of His Majesty to allow us to send back [to Rome] Monsieur Jolly [to replace Berthe]."[8]

The task now was to resume the interrupted negotiation concerning vows for members of the Congregation. Pope Innocent X having died in January 1655, Alexander VII ascended to the throne of Saint

Peter in the month of April. In a brief *ex commissa,* dated September 22, 1655, he confirmed and approved the usage which had already been established in the Congregation of the Mission of making simple vows of poverty, chastity, obedience, and stability. He declared that the missionaries were members of the secular clergy and specified that they were subject to the authority of the bishops for all functions they carried out in the dioceses, such as seminaries, retreats for ordinands, and missions.[9]

Vincent had succeeded in having things the way he wanted them, and he did not hide his satisfaction when he wrote to Edme Jolly, who had served well in conducting the last stages of the negotiations. He gave thanks to God for permitting this happy conclusion: "May His divine goodness be forever glorified through this, may it reward you for the pains you took to bring about these results and reveal to you my gratitude."[10]

Vincent found it intolerable to remain riveted to his work table at Saint-Lazare or restricted to the capital by his numerous responsibilities while all the members of the Congregation traveled hither and yon on missions. He wanted to be out in the field himself. In May 1653, he wrote to the duchess d'Aiguillon to make his excuses for missing the coming assembly of the Ladies of Charity because he was taking part in a mission to be preached at Sevran (sixteen kilometers north of the capital): "It seems to me that I would be offending God if I were not to do everything in my power for the poor people of the fields."[11] The duchess was concerned for Monsieur Vincent's health and sent a word of reproach to Portail: "I cannot get over my astonishment that Monsieur Portail and the other good gentlemen of Saint-Lazare permit Monsieur Vincent to go and work in the country, in this heat, and at his age."[12]

But it was not easy to counsel Vincent to moderation, for he would do nothing but his own will. For him, going to the aid of the rural poor was the one true reason for being alive. He was nostalgic for the days when he was able to devote all his time to preaching missions, as he told a priest of the Congregation in a moving letter that expressed his joy at the success of a recent mission. He wrote: "Indeed, Monsieur, I cannot help but tell you quite simply that your news gives me an intense new desire to go out, in spite of my little weaknesses, and sleep under some bush, as I spend the rest of my days working in a village. I feel that I would be deeply happy if it pleased God to grant me this favor."[13]

Vincent did not receive this blessing. As soon as he returned to Saint-Lazare, he was assailed with many worries, and the problems in need of solution kept him at his desk. "The difficulties are pulling me this way and that," he admitted in a letter to the superior of the house at Warsaw.[14] Much bad news was flowing in from Poland, Madagascar, and the Barbary Coast.

Poland was sorely tried, first by an epidemic of the plague, then by internal unrest and invasions from abroad. The plague appeared in Warsaw at the end of 1652. Lambert aux Couteaux, dear to Vincent's heart, had taken no thought for himself as he nursed the sick, buried the dead, and succored the abandoned. He was stricken with the plague himself and died in January 1653. At the urgent request of the queen, Vincent sent another priest, Charles Ozenne, to take charge of the Mission in Poland. This priest set out from Dieppe with a group of Daughters of the Visitation in August 1653. Their ship was attacked by Corsairs and taken to Dover, where all on board were held in captivity. After fighting for authorization to send sisters to Poland, Vincent now had to struggle to liberate them and to organize resumption of Ozenne's voyage to Warsaw.

The next year, an uprising of Cossacks, who had joined ranks with the Muscovites, threatened the unity of the Polish kingdom, but King Jan-Casimir succeeded in driving them out of Smolensk at the beginning of 1655. Then, in their turn, the Swedes caused a disturbance in Poland. Vincent was concerned about the fate of his missionaries and of the Daughters of Charity, surrounded by Protestant invaders. He approached the French ambassador to Sweden to ask him "to make representations to the king of Sweden requesting protection for the religious of Sainte-Marie, the Daughters of Charity, and even for the priests of the Mission in Warsaw, if necessary."[15] Swedish forces entered Warsaw at the beginning of September, and the king and queen withdrew to Krakow and even further, to Silesia.

At the end of 1655, four priests of the Mission returned to France while two others remained in Warsaw, where they lived in peace, even though the city was controlled by Sweden. Their superior, Charles Ozenne, accompanied the royal family to their retreat. What was to become of the Mission in Poland? "Pray for them," advised Vincent, who was not discouraged, placing his confidence in the unfathomable will of God. "God has His reasons for allowing events to proceed in this way."[16]

The news from Madagascar was even sadder. Vincent had received no mail from the island since the October 1650 letter from Monsieur Nacquart, announcing the death of Monsieur Gondrée and calling for help. He had been trying to obtain authorization to send a team of missionaries to Madagascar as reinforcement. But unfortunate events followed one another and it was not until March 1654 that two priests and a brother were able to embark at Saint-Nazaire. For Vincent, this was the beginning of yet another long wait for news; there would be five months of sailing and as many for letters to return if, in fact, a ship was ready to sail. The first letters arrived at Saint-Lazare in the middle of 1655. They informed Vincent that the missionaries had found a Christian community that had suffered a good deal. Monsieur Nacquart had been dead for four years, and everything had to be started from the ground up. What is more, there was only one survivor of this reinforcement team, Monsieur Bourdaise, the writer the letters. This was the man who had almost been sent home from Saint-Lazare because he was not making decent progress in his studies![17] Vincent immediately began a search for a ship that was sailing and managed to send out three new missionaries from the port of La Rochelle at the end of October 1655.

The fate of the consuls in Algeria and Tunisia also weighed on Monsieur Vincent's mind. He knew the difficulties they were doubtless encountering and the misery of the slaves they were at pains to comfort. The office of consul at Tunis had been held since July 1653 by a young lawyer of the parlement of Paris, Martin Husson, who worked very well with the missionary Jean Le Vacher. As they were setting sail, Vincent had given them sage advice: "They will submit to the laws of the country, and outside of the country's religion, they will never dispute anything, never speak a word of contempt."[18] But in spite of their efforts to avoid confrontations with the local authorities, their life was made impossible by the ill will of the dey of Tunis, who took every opportunity to frustrate them. In the end, the dey demanded that Martin Husson leave the country in April 1657.

The consulship of Algiers had been granted some years earlier to a clerk of the Mission, Jean Barreau, who regularly suffered bad treatment and even imprisonment at the hands of the Turkish authorities. In vain, Vincent commanded Jean Barreau not to incur financial obligations beyond what was reasonable, for it was the man's inclination to give in to his compassion for the miserable slaves and go deep into debt to ransom them. This consul had as second in command a priest of the

Mission, Philippe Le Vacher, to whom Vincent had also made numerous impassioned recommendations. He had exhorted him not to try to convert Turks or renegades.[19] One can only be surprised at this advice, when one remembers that, if we can believe it, Vincent had himself been an important actor in the conversion of a renegade in Tunisia.

The inextricable complications with which the consuls struggled, drawn as they were into cases at law and commercial litigation, all far removed from their apostolic vocation, led Vincent to think that "it would be best to assign these two consulates to persons who could turn them to their profit; this would not prevent the priests from doing what they can to help the poor slaves."[20] In the meanwhile, as though he were connected to the Barbary Coast by an unbreakable tie, Vincent maintained the presence of the Mission there, in spite of the most terrible contempt exhibited by the local authorities.

The question arises whether Vincent was beaten down by the cumulative weight of so much bad news and the apparent failure of his distant projects. Without a doubt, he suffered from this and sometimes, he even allowed a complaint to cross his lips. Yet he was ready to send out his missionaries wherever there was new land to cultivate and evangelize, because he was motivated by a faith that could withstand any test.

Thus, when the marquis Pianezzo, leader of the Council of Savoy, requested that he found a house of the Congregation at Turin, he hastened to write to his representative at Genoa, Étienne Blatiron, asking him to go and negotiate this new implantation.[21] The work was quickly done, and the four first missionaries were sent to Turin in October 1655.

Vincent learned directly from the Jesuit priest Alexandre de Rhodes, just returned from a long stay in Tonkin, that missions in that country and in Cochinchina produced astonishing results but that the men and the means to direct them were lacking. The very thought of all these souls to bring into the fold filled him with enthusiasm and in July 1653, he signed, together with several prelates, petitions addressed to Rome to suggest that "two or three bishops be sent to this nascent Church" so that an indigenous clergy could be raised up.[22]

Shortly thereafter, he received from the Congregation for the Propagation of the Faith a proposal that he did not find troubling: "Rome is demanding from me seven or eight priests to be sent to Sweden and Denmark, where the word is that they would have great success, and that no one would hinder them as long as they did not practice our religion in public." In other words, it was a matter of introducing priests into Protestant countries, after all the disasters suffered in similar undertakings in Scotland and Ireland. But Vincent did not raise a single objection, "I am waiting for the final order to send some priests, either from inside or outside the Congregation of the Mission."[23] But soon Sweden entered into a war against Poland and there would be no more talk of sending missionaries.

Over and above his great need for action, what were the deep motives which pushed Vincent to leap ever forward into adventures in distant lands? He revealed them in a conversation with members of the Congregation in September 1655, when he painted his dark vision of the state of the Church. "This desolation ravishing the Church, this deplorable undermining it has suffered in so many places, so that it has been almost entirely ruined in Asia and Africa, and even in large parts of Europe, such as Sweden, Denmark, England, Scotland, Ireland, Holland and other provinces of the Netherlands, as well as a large part of Germany! And how many heretics we see in France! Or consider Poland, which is already infested with heresy and is now in danger of being totally lost to religion with the invasion of the king of Sweden."

Who was responsible for this wretched situation? Vincent affirmed that it was bad priests: "The Church is ruined in many places by the evil life the priests lead, for it is they who confound and ruin it. It is only too true that the depravity of the priesthood is the principal cause of the ruin of the Church of God." Therefore, in the first place, one must think of reforming the priesthood. In this spirit Vincent wished to send good priests throughout the world to try to change the downhill course on which the Church was engaged, particularly in Europe. Vincent was convinced that it was the vocation of the Congregation of the Mission to re-establish the priesthood in its original purity: "It is on us that God has bestowed the great grace of letting us contribute to restoration of the priestly estate. To do this task, He called on us, not on the doctors or the many communities of religious, full of knowledge and holiness, but on this worthless, poor, and miserable community, the least of all and the most unworthy."

Vincent continued by recalling that Christ had chosen as his first apostles "fishermen, craftsmen, poor people of those days" and that in the same way, the Mission is composed of "weak people, poor workers and peasants." Perhaps he was carried away by his oratorical momentum when he went as far as to exclaim "What did God find in us to suit us for such a great work? By his pure will, He turned to poor miserable idiots to try once more to mend the fissures in His Son's kingdom and the priestly estate."[24]

In this declaration, Vincent gave witness both to his profound humility and his unbelievable ambition to be chosen by God to re-establish His Son's kingdom. This ambition can only be conceived of if it is founded on unshakable faith, which transcends the strength of those who possess it, and makes them able to move mountains.

Kings Promise Easily
1656–1657

Faltering Health
Drama in Distant Missions
Opening of the General Hospital
Condition of the Works of Charity
Vincent's Correspondence
Action against the Jansenists

Toward the end of the year 1655, Vincent was shaken by violent attacks of fever and had no choice but to take to his bed. For three months, he was confined to his room. The ailments that plagued him are described in his letters: painful legs covered with abscesses and fevers that left him without strength. To make things worse, the bloodlettings applied as a treatment left him even weaker.

Louise de Marillac, consumed with worry, was lavish in her advice to Vincent: "Permit me to tell you that it is absolutely necessary never to have your leg hanging down for more than ten minutes, and it should never be exposed to the warmth of the fire. If your leg is cold, it must be warmed up with a hot cloth placed over the stockings."[1]

Vincent himself mentioned his illness in a letter written to one of his missionaries in November: "I am feeling better, thanks be to God, even though I am still in bed and being dosed with medicines for the erysipelas which settled in my leg after the fever left me."[2] But one month later, he was hardly better: "I am still in bed or on a couch, or rather on two couches, because the pain in my legs forces me to put them up, almost as high as my head. Other than that, I am fine."[3] These symptoms seem to correspond to a diagnosis of arteritis, a possible consequence of malaria.

At the end of January, when he began to go out again after this long illness, Vincent was not very firm on his legs. To his great annoyance, he was obliged to use his carriage most of the time, and he showed his dissatisfaction at this turn of events by using every opportunity to speak of his condition as "my ignominy" or "my infamy."[4] Vincent was in his seventy-sixth year now, and in spite of his robust constitution, he was an old man. But even though his physical activity was curtailed, his intellect was in no way diminished and his character remained vigorous and even pugnacious. He held the tiller of the Congregation with a firm hand.

His trials did not shake him, numerous though they were. There was not one packet of mail that did not bring its share of somber news. First there was the plague in Rome and then in Genoa. The superior of the house in Genoa, Étienne Blatiron, put his team at the disposal of the archbishop to help in tending the sick. While Vincent approved this action, he sent these instructions in August 1656: "Let your priests go to tend the victims of the plague in your place. It is right that the members expose themselves to protect the safety of the head; that is how nature does it. For when there is a great catastrophe, where superiors are needed to give the orders, like generals of armies in combat and battles, they should be the last to place themselves in danger."[5]

But the epidemic took on such proportions that the people of Genoa succumbed by the tens of thousands. Of the eight missionaries, seven fell ill, including the superior. By August of the following year, only one missionary was left alive.

News from Madagascar was just as bad. Two missionaries and a young brother sent as reinforcements had embarked at Nantes in October 1656. The ship sank off Saint-Nazaire, but the passengers were saved, thanks to the cool courage of the young brother. Then a few months later, Vincent finally received a letter from "that good Monsieur Bourdaise," announcing the death of three missionaries who had previously been sent as reinforcements.

The mission to Madagascar seemed to be under a relentless curse. No doubt Vincent was pained by this course of events, but his will remained firm and his faith whole. He placed the human drama in a divine perspective: "The blood of Christians has been the seed of Christianity throughout the world." Addressing his missionaries, he spoke in these terms: "Some member of this community might say that we should abandon Madagascar. Flesh and blood will say these things, and declare that we must not send any more of our people there, but I am quite sure that the spirit says something else. What, gentlemen, are we just going to leave our good Monsieur Bourdaise in the lurch?"[6] New volunteers came forward to travel to this far-away island. They too would suffer many trials, but Monsieur Vincent's will was unshakable.

For a long time, there had been no news from Poland where two missionaries were living in Warsaw, a city under Swedish occupation. Finally, a letter came to Vincent from the queen, who had some reassurance to offer about their fate. In September 1657, he wrote: "I hear from Poland that our good Monsieur Desdames has once more lost everything, as Warsaw has again been besieged, taken, and pillaged by the Swedish forces, and then abandoned." As for the other missionary, Monsieur Duperroy, he was seriously ill and the surgeons no longer knew what to do for him. Vincent concluded this letter addressed to the superior of the house at Richelieu with: "So you see, Monsieur, how it pleases God to test the little community in a number of ways."[7]

The information coming from Algeria hardly gave more cause for rejoicing. In spite of the plentiful advice Vincent gave to Brother Jean Barreau, in charge of the consulate, the latter "daily dug himself deeper into an abyss of debt, from which it will be hard indeed, not to say impossible, to pull him out. He does not have the strength to say no when he is asked, and no skill in avoiding snubs. In ruining himself, he is ruining his office as well, and thus any possibility there might be of helping those pitiful slaves."[8]

Vincent was obliged to beg for funds again, moneys which he would then have to transfer by way of his house in Marseilles to Algiers, to wipe out Barreau's debts and ransom a few slaves. No wonder he was again considering the possibility of giving up these consulates, source of so much trouble. But his idea met with the absolute veto of the duchess d'Aiguillon, who had obtained them for him. "For she believes that our priests would have no assurance that they could serve the poor slaves under the rule of consuls who were in office for profit, operating by principles other than those of charity and the public welfare."[9] In the meantime, Jean Barreau was subjected to ill treatment and even torture on account of the bankruptcy of a merchant from Marseilles, whose creditors had lodged a complaint with the pasha of Algiers. This man, believing that the French consul was responsible for all sums owed, had him beaten until he fainted, and then tortured him with thorns inserted under his fingernails. At the end of his strength and only half conscious, Jean Barreau signed a note for 2,500 piastres. Once more, Vincent had to approach the duchess d'Aiguillon to find "the 3,000 or 4,000 piastres the most recent outrage [would] cost him."[10] At the same time, the consul at Tunis, Jean Le Vacher, was expelled by the dey for refusing to allow the importation of a prohibited material.

All these were disappointing events, but when Vincent recounted them to one of his missionaries, he raised the debacles and the deaths in the Congregation to a higher plane: "God be praised for all these losses. Because of them, we should hope for more help before God, both in time and in eternity than if our brothers were still with us."[11]

To show that these many trials did not in any way sap his determination to deploy his missionaries over all the highways of the world, Vincent now envisaged the foundation of a house beyond the Pyrenees. Replying to a letter from the superior of his house in Rome, he spoke of the project this way: "You speak to me of our establishment in Spain and of the offer that this good priest has made, the one who was a Jesuit, to go there under the command of whomever we send. We have not yet designated anyone, and we see no one able to succeed there but Monsieur Martin, but he is needed in Turin."[12]

In fact, it was an inescapable problem for Vincent that he did not have enough men to staff all his houses, seminaries, and the other institutions in his charge. As for those who might be capable of functioning as superiors of a house, especially abroad, they were even rarer. Recruitment had almost ceased during the troubles of the Fronde. Whereas in the past, there had been an average of twenty-three entrants every year, sixteen priests and seven brothers, in 1652 there had been only three admissions to the Congregation. Recruitment increased again in 1653, when internal peace had returned, but some time was required for the formation of the new entrants before they could be sent on missions.[13]

The Ladies of Charity were enthusiastic about the creation of the Name of Jesus Hospital and decided to found a general hospital on the same model, where all the beggars and moneyless people loitering in the streets of the capital could be received. Vincent worked hard to moderate their ardor, for he recognized the chasm between the charitable and generous intentions of these Ladies and the thoughts of the authorities on the same subject. In fact, all those responsible for public order, both in the government and the parlement, wanted nothing more than to rid Paris of all the poor by collecting them in an establishment where they would be locked up and, if possible, disciplined. Such a plan was hardly to Vincent's liking.

In contrast, the duchess d'Aiguillon, president of the Ladies of Charity, was very much in favor of the embryonic project. She wrote to Vincent: "As for the hospital, I respect your ideas, but allow me to tell you mine before you make up your mind," and she emphasized the fact that the Ladies, who had already made a significant financial commitment, feared that if they withdrew, the project would either perish or be altered beyond recognition. Then indeed, their sacrifice would have been in vain.[14]

But a royal edict, signed in April 1656, put an end to the debate. It was decreed that begging was forbidden in the capital, for "it was necessary to cleanse Paris of an insolent and dishonorable band of thieves." It designated places where the beggars would be collected and sheltered; the list included La Pitié, Bicêtre, and the Salpêtrière. The general hospital founded by this document was to be administered by a council including in its ranks the president of the parlement Pompone de Bellièvre and Superintendent Nicolas Fouquet. The care of the souls confined in this institution was entrusted to the Congregation of the Mission.

While work was going on to adapt the Salpêtrière for the reception of the crowd of beggars—it was estimated that there were as many as 40,000 of them in the capital—the Congregation was asked to preach a mission in the other hospitals already in service. Missionaries and members of the Tuesday Conferences, numbering forty, were assigned to do this work. But the ongoing need projected for the chaplaincy of the general hospital once it was in operation—twenty priests working full time—was beyond the resources of the Congregation. Keeping the superiors of his houses informed, as was his custom, Vincent wrote: "In Paris, work is going on toward the establishment of a great hospital where all the poor beggars can be fed, instructed, and kept busy, so that never a one will be seen in the streets or in the churches. It has even been requested that the poor Mission have the duty of providing spiritual direction, but that has been done without consulting us. May God give us the grace we need for this new work, if it is His will that we undertake it, something to which we are not yet quite committed."[15]

Vincent was hesitating for two reasons: first, because no one had asked him before assigning this duty to him and second, because he was in disagreement with the very principle of treating misery by imposing authority and physical constraint. At length, after consultation with members of the Company, he decided to refuse the appointment. He gave official notice of his decision to the superintendent of finances in March 1657, shortly before the opening of the general hospital.[16] However, because he was unwilling to put the administrators in an unpleasant situation by the defection of his congregation, he assembled a corps of chaplains, recruited from outside the Mission, under the direction of Louis Abelly, and he asked the Daughters of Charity to guarantee to serve at the Salpêtrière, while the Ladies of Charity would supervise the personnel in charge of the women and girls confined there.

It is no great surprise that as soon as the police was involved, busily chasing down beggars, beggars were nowhere to be seen. Of the 40,000 people without domicile that had been counted, only 4,000 would agree to being taken to the general hospital. The incarceration model did not solve the problem of begging, and certainly not that of misery. Vincent was quite right not to have wished for any association with this operation.

In the meantime, the war against Spain continued, with engagements taking place chiefly in the northern part of the kingdom of France, adjacent to the Spanish Netherlands. The royal armies were led by the marshals de Turenne and La Ferté. With alternating success and failure, they faced the armies led by the governor of the Netherlands, the count de Fuensaldagna, and then by Don Juan of Austria, supported by the forces of the prince de Condé. The opposing armies besieged fortresses and took or retook objectives in Picardy, Artoise, in the Ardennes, or in coastal Flanders. When there was fighting, there was a great coming and going of troops and in winter, a requisitioning of shelter, much to the detriment of the rural population.

With the help of the Ladies of Charity, Vincent continued tirelessly to collect aid for the ravaged provinces. The industrious Brother Jean Parré worked in the field to distribute alms in the neediest areas. Vincent kept himself informed of the situation and of the developing need. In August 1657, he wrote to Jean Parré that he was waiting for his news about the visit he was currently making to the places where the armies had camped, so that he could plan the work of distributing aid.

He made recommendations to the brother for how to get this aid to the people who needed it most. Thus, for example, he advised that before any distribution of clothing, one should make discreet inquiry about the real needs of the poor, otherwise, "some who already have clothing would hide it and come to the distribution naked."[17] Vincent was inspired by charity, but he was a realist and did not want to be cheated.

In the course of a conference he presented to the Ladies of Charity about this time, Vincent recalled all the work done over the past seven years to help the people of Champagne and Picardy: more than 360,000 livres had been distributed in those regions to feed the poor and the sick; to rescue 800 orphans from the ruined villages and provide for them by clothing them and training them for trades or for service; and to provide for a number of priests in the ruined provinces. He specified the places where the money, clothing, linens, and blankets had been distributed: in and around the cities of Reims, Rethel, Laon, Saint-Quentin, Ham, Marle, Sedan, and Arras. But he also noted that "for the last year or two, since times have been a little better, alms have decreased considerably." The same was true for the Foundling Hospital, with income being lower than expenses for the year just past, whereas "the number of abandoned children does not change from year to year." Vincent pointed out that before the Ladies had involved themselves in the work, "all these children perished in one way or another." Once more, he made a resounding appeal for perseverance: "Your community is not a human institution, but a divine one."[18]

In a tone marked with unaccustomed bitterness, Vincent wrote to one of his missionaries that the gathering of alms was becoming more and more difficult. Even the king himself was becoming less charitable. "Although the king allowed us to hope for some additional alms, we have nothing, because kings promise easily but forget to fulfill their promises unless they have people close to them who can remind them frequently."[19]

And that is where the problem lay. Monsieur Vincent no longer had his connection to the court, since he had been distanced by Cardinal Mazarin. Now he saw the queen only once a year, as he confided to the marquis de Fabert. As for the duchess d'Aiguillon, who often interceded for him to Their Majesties, she no longer seemed to be in favor at court herself: "For several years now, the duchess d'Aiguillon has no longer approached the queen, and we do not know where to turn."[20] In a society where everything flows outward from the royal power, not to be admitted into the circle close to the king means being exiled to oblivion. This was true for the distribution of prebends and privileges as well as for the distribution of alms. Vincent had to learn the bitter truth of this.

Vincent devoted most of his time and attention to directing and managing the Congregation. Every day, he received copious mail from his various houses to which he responded punctually, in his own hand if he was not too tired, but more often by dictation to his two secretaries. Around ten letters went out from Saint-Lazare every day, to his priests on missions, to Louise de Marillac, and to his Daughters of Charity.

Vincent's letters to his missionaries contained both worldly directives and spiritual counsel. They never failed to pass on news of other houses in order to foster cohesion among the members scattered to the four corners of the kingdom and throughout the world. These letters provided encouragement for those who were suffering from momentary loss of energy or from doubt. For example, to a brother who was hoping to be assigned to a new post where he might find work more in accord with his vocation, Vincent sent a long letter, affectionate but firm: "If you only recognized clearly the gift that God has given you, you would not prefer the move to a new house over the joy of serving Our Lord in the state in life to which he has called you."[21] To the superior of the house in Marseilles, who was asking to be relieved of his responsibility on the grounds of his poor health and the advice of the physicians, who judged that the climate of the city was detrimental to him, he wrote: "It is not good to pay so much attention to the advice of physicians, for they are only too obliging, but recognize no other good than the health of the body. Illness strikes wherever you are, when God sends it, and I do not see that the great of this world leave their cities and provinces to avoid sickness, nor do the bishops leave their dioceses or the pastors their parishes."[22]

In other letters, Vincent gives advice on conducting a mission and on preaching: "I told you once that Our Lord blesses sermons delivered in an ordinary and familiar tone because that is how He taught and preached Himself. Moreover, this natural way of speaking is easier than a forced and artificial one, and people enjoy it more and profit from it more fully."[23] Sometimes, Vincent's letters showed him to be fundamentally a man of authority, who could abandon mild tones in order to admonish. To a superior who permitted himself to withhold a letter from Vincent addressed to one of his priests, Vincent wrote: "It is an unheard of fault in the Company, which has displeased me greatly, since it creates significant disorder. I beg of you, Monsieur, to take my advice to heart."[24] To another superior, who had taken the initiative to have a work on the Congregation published without Vincent's authorization, he wrote: "This has caused me such pain that I cannot express it because it was such a breach of humility to publish information about what we are and what we do. I beg of you never to do anything which concerns the Company without telling me about it in advance."[25]

In his correspondence, Vincent occasionally betrayed a joyful mood, an expression of his Gascon nature. About a brother sent to the house at Turin, who was having great trouble acquiring rudimentary Italian, he exclaimed: "I am most relieved that our brother Demortier has already made so much progress in the language that he can now say *Signore, si.*"[26]

A large part of Vincent's correspondence deals with questions of finance. Reading the letters, one discovers the manager who competently preserves and increases the Congregation's means, even going to court if necessary, if he believes that a matter of law is at stake.

At the beginning of 1656, the king, looking for new resources to finance a war which simply would not end, decided to raise some taxes and duties by one quarter. This was the so-called affair of Paris. It was clear to Vincent that this decision would have serious consequences for the Congregation, which counted among its sources of revenue the privilege of levying a certain number of indirect duties on merchandise or foodstuffs. Like an experienced financier, he evaluated different possible outcomes. "If the king revokes this Right of Paris, as he has often done to others in similar situations, we will lose both our privilege and the taxes from Melun, and this is a considerable amount. To say that we will transfer the surplus of the Melun funds and combine them with the taxes from Angers in order to safeguard them, that is a difficult thing."[27] Vincent continued the conversation on this level with his correspondent, Jean-Baptiste Forne, administrator of the Hôtel-Dieu, one of his financial advisers.

Vincent always monitored developments regarding income. The house at La Rose, for instance, depended on the income from barges belonging to the royal domain. But this privilege could be rescinded from one day to the next, simply by the decision of the Superior Council. Vincent called the superior's attention to the fact that his resources were most precarious, and urged him to be prudent: "If you knew how difficult it is for us to safeguard here the money that you take in there, so as to maintain your small resources! Because they are based on one of the king's domains, they rest on a foundation of sand, subject to taxes, retrenchments, and frequent surcharges" or "It takes a number of us to have confiscations reversed or prevent the sale of the barges."[28]

When there was an opportunity to retire part of an annuity agreement made to buy a building at Le Mans, Vincent immediately understood how to go about it. The superior of the Mission in that city had neither the reserves to make the payment nor the ability to borrow the necessary sum. Instead, it was decided that the Congregation would act for him. Vincent dictated to him the terms of the document he was to write.[29]

Although Vincent had always declared that anything was better than going to court, he did not hesitate to advise the superior of the house at Saintes to use legal means to preserve the rights attached to a certain benefice. He justified his inconsistency in the following way: "You should not allow any of the rights of your benefice of Saint-Preuil to be lost. Thus, if your counsel finds that tithes are due to you on the small-holding of Canon d'Albert, you must see that they are protected, and if he refuses to pay after you have spoken to him in all mildness, you must turn the matter over to the court. I find it very difficult to agree to such a trial, but tithes are a privileged case, and it is a matter of conscience to protect them."[30]

Vincent held to his principles firmly, but he was a realist. He admitted that specific cases can arise which call for a dispensation. He had a fine sense of the real and the possible.

Although Monsieur Vincent was no longer a member of the Council of Conscience, taking an active and official part in the fight against Jansenism, he maintained his vigilance with regard to what he called new ideas. It was his intention to keep them away from the Congregation, the Daughters of Charity, and the convents of the Visitation, for which he acted as spiritual director.

After the pope had condemned the five propositions of the *Augustinus* in his bull *Cum occasione* of 1653, the quarrel with the Jansenists should have been at an end. In fact, most of the people who had been tempted by this teaching had bowed before the authority of the Holy See. But at Port-Royal, Arnauld had not laid down the cudgel but had continued to deliver his polemics. Indeed, his writings had caused him to be excluded from the faculty of theology of Paris in June 1656. For this reason, it was still necessary for Vincent to write to Firmin Get, superior of the Mission at Marseilles, to tell him that he was not sending him "the other book you are asking for, from that outfit at Port-Royal, because there is something wrong with everything that comes out of that shop, and since it has pleased God to keep the community completely clean of this doctrine, we should not only try to stay clean, but also avoid, as much as possible, letting anyone else get caught by their beautiful talk or waylaid by their errors."[31]

Vincent was not alone in his resolve. Pope Alexander VII renewed the condemnation pronounced by his predecessor against the five propositions of the *Augustinus*. In the bull *Ad sacrum*, promulgated in October 1656, he repeated the condemnations made earlier and chose as a particular target the subtle distinctions invented by Arnauld in an attempt to hide the fact that the disputed propositions were actually contained in Jansenius's book. As soon as the bull was published, Abelly tells us, Vincent paid a call on the gentlemen at Port-Royal to exhort them to submit, "which did not, however, have the desired effect."[32]

Blaise Pascal was staying at the Granges of Port-Royal at this time. He was working there, at Arnauld's request, on the *Provinciales,* a work which would lend a polemical turn to the debate. Pascal cast his lot with the rigor of the Jansenists against the laxity ascribed to the Jesuits without, however, trying to defend the condemned propositions. We have nothing to indicate that Vincent met him at this time.

On the other hand, we do know about Vincent's attempts to convince the dean of Senlis, Jean Deslions, to submit to the authority of the Church. Vincent had high esteem for this distinguished ecclesiastic, a doctor of the Sorbonne, and bitterly regretted his sympathies for the Jansenist cause. During the years 1656 and 1657, the two men maintained a continuous correspondence. Vincent pressed the other man to declare himself in all frankness, and finally wrote, "What are you waiting for to make up your mind? If you are waiting for God to send you an angel who will bring you more light, God will not do it. He will send you back to the Church, and the Church, assembled at Trent, will send you to the Holy See. If you are waiting for the same St. Augustine to return and explain himself, Our Lord tells us that if one does not believe in Scripture, one will not believe what the resurrected dead tell us. If you are waiting for the judgment of some famous faculty of Theology which is still working on this question, where is it? In all of Christendom, there is not a more famous one than the faculty at the Sorbonne, of which you are a very worthy member."[33] But the eloquence of Vincent was not to convince Jean Deslions.

The Long Awaited Peace
1658–1659

In the first days of January 1658, Monsieur Vincent was returning to Saint-Lazare from a visit to the city. He was seated in his
carriage, jouncing about on the cobblestones, muttering against
the pitiless "ignominy" that made him shiver relentlessly. The
jolts of the carriage were painful to his afflicted legs. Suddenly,
the straps holding the floor of the carriage together gave way.
Vincent was thrown to the ground and his head struck violently against a cobble. After this accident, he was taken by a
high fever; for several days, his health gave cause for grave concern. But gradually he improved, and on January 12, he was able
to write to the duke de la Meilleraye to make his excuses for the
delay in closing some business, "since I took a fall and injured
my head."[1] The shock of this accident was a profound blow to
his already very tired body, but that would not prevent him from
pursuing all his duties with ferocious energy and alert enterprise.

Anne of Austria, on her return from a journey to Metz in
November 1657, had summoned Monsieur Vincent to tell him
of her distress at the spiritual abandonment of the people of
this city, many of whom had been won over to Protestantism.

She had asked him to organize a large mission there. At the time, Vincent had respectfully refused this request, on the grounds that the rules of his community forbade them to preach in cities where there were bishoprics and presidial courts. His vocation, he said, was to preach in rural areas. But he could respond to Her Majesty's wish by organizing some members of the Tuesday Conferences to undertake this mission. Thanks to his talent as an organizer, this was soon done. Preparations were entrusted to Jacques-Bénigne Bossuet, who was at the time canon and arch-deacon of the cathedral of Metz. This man placed himself entirely at the disposal of his former teacher, calling to mind in his response the time spent at Saint-Lazare and "the lessons learned in those days from the Company."[2]

Direction of this mission was given to Louis de Chandenier, abbot of Tournus and a great friend of Vincent; the preaching took place during Lent of the year 1658. Twenty priests, chosen with the greatest care, took turns in the pulpits of the diocese of Metz, and their audience was very large. Bossuet took an active part in this preaching; he was not at all like the canons described by Fléchier as "happily arrived at the stage of honorable inaction." At Saint-Lazare, he had learned the "little method" taught by Vincent, which consisted of preaching without the baggage of rhetorical arguments.[3] Still, when he wrote to his teacher to report on the successful outcome of the mission, he could not resist a slightly lyrical style: "I cannot see these dear missionaries departing without expressing to you the universal regret and the marvelous edification they are leaving behind. I would joyfully expound on that topic if it were not that the effects were so far beyond all of my words."[4]

While the mission was taking place at Metz, Vincent's thoughts turned toward a different kind of project: to bring the Turks to their senses by going to attack Algiers!

At the beginning of February, Vincent wrote to the superior of his house at Marseilles, Firmin Get, to give him a curious charge: "I thank God for the suggestion made by Sir Paul to go to Algiers and demand justice from the Turks. I beg you to see him for me, to congratulate him for his plan, an exploit which only he could carry out." And he added: "I consider myself fortunate to bear his name and to have paid him my respects once at the cardinal's palace."[5]

Who was this knight whose name Vincent felt fortunate to bear and whose warlike nature he approved? A colorful person whose life read like a romance, he was said to have been born in 1597 on a ship, somewhere between the port of Marseilles and the Château d'If. His mother, a laundress, cared for the linens of the governor of this fortified island, and this governor is supposed to have been the father of the child. At the age of thirteen, he shipped out as a cabin boy; he became a sailor on a corsair's ship and then entered the service of the Order of Malta. He established his base of operations on a little island near Mytilene (the ancient Lesbos). From there, he harried Turkish ships, sowing terror among the Barbary merchantmen. His actions earned him a title in the Order of Malta—Commander of the Priory of Saint-Gilles in Provence. Mazarin enrolled him in the royal navy: his participation in battles against the Spanish fleet and his role in aiding the Neapolitan revolution earned him a title of nobility from the king. Sir Paul commanded naval forces with the title of lieutenant general in the expedition on Naples in 1654. Thanks to the many corsairs he seized, he accumulated an immense fortune, and he demonstrated his success by presenting himself at court in a costume decorated with gold embroidery and jewels. At the same time, he presented himself as a defender of religion. When he died at the age of seventy, he left his fortune to the poor and had himself buried with them in the cemetery of Toulon.

This was the man on whom Vincent counted to exact some justice from the Turks. One might be surprised that a man of peace could serenely contemplate having recourse to arms to arrive at his ends, but Vincent belonged to a century in which the defense of Christianity against Islam was a sacred mission. At this time, Catholic sovereigns led by the king of Spain and the pope himself were arming galleys to fight against the Turks. Vincent's position was no more peace-loving than that of all the other churchmen of his time.

But the months passed and the fleet of Sir Paul still did not prepare for departure. Vincent once more advised Firmin Get to go to Toulon to sound out the knight about his intention: "It would have been good if you had seen Monsieur Paul, as I asked you."[6] In fact, Vincent had another possibility, namely to have the expedition against Algiers carried out by the duke de Beaufort, who had inherited leadership of the Admiralty from his father, the duke de Vendôme. At least, that is what the duchess d'Aiguillon seemed to hope for, according to what Vincent wrote to Firmin Get.

Finally, Monsieur Get encountered Sir Paul at Toulon and Vincent was openly delighted: "I was much comforted by your letter, which tells of your trip to Toulon and your negotiation with Commander Paul. I thank God, Monsieur, that he let you find in the heart of this valiant man his willingness to go to Barbary."[7]

What negotiation was Vincent alluding to? Monsieur Get had been charged with promising Sir Paul a sum of 20,000 livres to finance his expedition. In fact, Vincent had succeeded in collecting 30,000 livres, which he had sent to Marseilles, a sum which was intended to clear Barreau completely of his debts in Algiers.[8] However, in reflecting on the situation, Vincent thought it well to be circumspect with such a one as this one-time corsair. Therefore, he sent another message to Firmin Get in July to caution him to be prudent in his dealings and ask for guarantees: "It is true that I told you we would give him 20,000 livres of the money which you have but of course, this means after he delivers the slaves, frees Brother Barreau, and puts another consul in place. Since he cannot do this by means of arms, this money is meant to let him arrange matters in the usual way, which is to free this brother and to return to the poor Christians the sums they have given toward his ransom, so that they can use the funds to ransom themselves. I am waiting to hear what you have to say about this suggestion, namely that he will be paid if he is successful and that there will be no advance."[9]

But the project was to be delayed for a number of reasons. The expedition did not take place in the summer of 1658, nor in the year 1659. In the meantime, Brother Jean Barreau would suffer more insults through the bad behavior of a French merchant. This man, in order to avoid paying local duties, had destroyed his warehouse and set sail with his merchandise and his personnel for the port of Livornia. Vincent could do nothing but send letters of encouragement to his consuls at Algiers and Tunis. He did not know whether he should still hope that Commander Paul would mount his expedition or whether he would do better to keep pursuing him. In the course of the summer of 1659, he wrote to an interim superior at Marseilles and confessed his perplexity: "Supposing that the hope of this sum of 20,000 livres made him undertake this business more willingly, think of whether it would be a good idea to tell him about the sum, or whether we should leave the matter to Providence."[10]

Madagascar was another subject that preoccupied Vincent constantly. A conflict over this territory arose between the India Company, which had received by royal decree the exclusive right to maintain commercial relations with the island and its territories, and the duke de la Meilleraye[11] who, on the strength of his good connections at court, had decided to fit out ships and head for the island. Whereas the India Company had asked Monsieur Vincent to do missionary work in this territory, the duke de la Meilleraye had asked the Capuchins to place twelve priests at his disposal so that he could carry them to the island by ship. Vincent wrote to the duke at the beginning of 1658, to tell him that he was ready either to withdraw or to carry on with his work at Madagascar.[12] After long maneuvering and bargaining, the duke de la Meilleraye declared himself willing to take four priests and two brothers of the Mission on one of his ships. This ship set sail from Nantes in May and was soon caught in a storm so strong that the masts and rudder were snapped. With great difficulty, the captain reached shelter at Lisbon. Once the repairs were made, the ship took to the sea again and was promptly attacked by a Spanish corsair. The missionaries were set on land in Spain. Vincent recounted this adventure in a letter and drew from it the moral that he should submit to the divine will: "Here is a fine opportunity to adore the dispositions of Providence and to submit our puny reasoning to it."[13]

A good year would go by before a new voyage to Madagascar took place, especially because the duke de la Meilleraye was out of patience with Monsieur Vincent who seemed to prefer the undertakings of the India Company to his. Nevertheless, he was willing to take four missionaries on one of his ships in November 1659. Vincent gave these priests a letter for Monsieur Bourdaise, from whom he had not heard for two years. "If you are still among the living, oh! our joy will be great when we are assured of it!" Vincent recalled the death of the first six missionaries who had been sent to the island, and he drew this moral: "It seems, Monsieur, that God is treating you as he treated his Son; He sent Him into the world to establish the Church through His passion. It seems that He wants to introduce the faith to Madagascar by no other means than your suffering."[14]

This letter never reached its addressee. The ship carrying the missionaries was disabled by a storm and the passengers, picked out of the water by a fisherman's rowboat, were taken to Saint-Jean-de-Luz. As for Monsieur Bourdaise, he had already been dead for more than two years.

Another blow struck Vincent in September 1658. He learned that he had just lost a case against the heirs of the benefactors who had deeded the farm at Orsigny to the Congregation of the Mission. The heirs demanded a return of the property. This handsome farm, lying near Saclay, was very useful to the Mission since they derived from it a good part of the food needed at Saint-Lazare. Vincent, who was away from Paris at that moment, wrote to the community: "Everything that God does, He does for the best, and therefore we should hope that this loss will be profitable, since it comes from God." He spoke as a prophet, saying that God "with the wisdom we adore, will turn this event to our advantage in ways we do not know now but that you will see one day."[15] Vincent refused to appeal a judgment that seemed, on the face of it, contestable, and less than five months later, a counselor of the chamber willed to the Congregation a domain as valuable as the one they had lost.

It must be said that in spite of so many reverses, worries, and troubles, Vincent could justly rejoice at the success of the missions and the happy outcome of the many requests that the Congregation accept new responsibilities, addressed to him from all sides. In particular, he was besieged by requests from bishops who asked him to take over the direction of their diocesan seminaries.

Already in 1654, the seminary of Agde had been confided to the Mission by Bishop François Fouquet. When his brother, Louis, succeeded him in the episcopal see in 1659, Vincent took the occasion to have the seminary established on a firmer legal footing. On this occasion, one sees his desire to assure that his works should be lasting: "Monseigneur d'Agde must be willing to draw up a new charter of foundation for his seminary which assigns the direction of it to the Company in perpetuity."[16] The bishop of Meaux, Dominique Séguier, also appealed to the Congregation toward the end of 1658 to correct a situation brought about by the poor management of his diocesan seminary.[17] The bishop of Montpellier, François de Bosquet, begged Vincent to take provisional charge of his seminary. Vincent, contrary to his habit, allowed himself to be influenced without taking the time to study the case in detail. "I see clearly that I was too hasty," he admitted to Monsieur Get, who had been chosen to direct this seminary, and he continued: "It is counter to good order and to our habit, to commit ourselves to a place for a time only, rather than permanently." But what was done was done, and he had to try to make the best of it. So Vincent gave advice to the new director, who would have to do his work in a diocese "to a great extent contaminated by heresy": "In the education of priests, you should have as your principal goal to form them to a life of spirituality, to prayer, to recollection and union with God. This is particularly true where you are, a region where people's minds are naturally vulnerable to being led astray."[18]

Vincent was interested in the project of a new foundation on Corsica, and he discussed it with his superior at the house in Genoa, since at that time, the island was under the authority of the Genoese Republic. It was his advice to send a superior, preferably a Frenchman, and two Italian priests.[19]

François Fouquet, named archbishop of Narbonne, in his turn asked for Vincent's help in September 1659. Vincent sent him three priests to direct the diocesan seminary and to preach missions. With them, he sent three Daughters of Charity.[20] In contrast, he resisted the pressing requests that came to him from all sides for a foundation at Betharram near Lourdes. This was a much-frequented place of pilgrimage, served by priests of the Congregation of Our Lady of Calvary. Vincent did not see how it would be possible to combine his company with this congregation, whose vocation was so different.[21] In any case, the project was abandoned after Vincent's death.

Direction of the twenty-three houses of the Mission in France, in addition to foundations abroad, remained the daily work of Vincent, who was personally acquainted with the approximately 250 members of his congregation. He received copious mail from them, and he answered it without delay. His rule was to write once a week to the superiors of his principal houses. The letters consisted largely of management advice: "Do not commit yourself to any place where you do not find enough to live on," he wrote to the superior of the Mission in Poland.[22] On this point he was always insistent; he did not want his missionaries to be a burden to the parishes where they preached. Therefore, it was necessary that the houses of the Mission be founded on stable and adequate resources. Vincent did not hesitate to engage with details. On the subject of a new farm which had been donated to the Congregation, he was anxious to know its exact value, and so he wrote: "You will have to inquire cleverly to find out how many acres it should include, and if the number is twenty-six, what became of the five they're talking about, and who might have appropriated them. Find out also whether the fields are good and what their value might be in an ordinary year." And he adds in his own hand: "The revenue of this little farm used to be 50 écus per year."[23]

Just as he gave his priests instruction on material things, Vincent used his pen to send them spiritual lessons. First of all, he exhorted them to practice humility: "Always be inclined to lowliness; love your abjection, be eager for contempt and embarrassment, against nature's inclination, which leads us to want to make a good appearance and to succeed."[24]

He recalls the superiors of houses to their duty to be firm with those for whom they are responsible "provided that you do this appropriately, and always in a spirit of mildness." For example, he counsels the superior at Le Mans: "You should not permit anyone to do his work only halfway, and even less should you burden yourself with making up for his negligence and omissions; that would prostrate you."[25]

For a young brother who complained that he had no affection for rules or spiritual exercises, in other words, that he did not feel at home in the Congregation, and who was probably questioning his vocation, Vincent took the time to write a long letter in tones both affectionate and firm: "Before you can cure your trouble, you have to know it. In my opinion, you are suffering from a softening of the will and a laziness of the spirit regarding the things God is asking of you. This does not astonish me; most people are in this state, almost by nature." But, he adds, some people can overcome this laziness, others, not, because "they do not abandon their love of things other than God, and these things are physical comfort, which makes the soul sluggish in practicing virtue. This is what creates and nourishes sloth, which is the vice of people in religion." Vincent concluded: "Heaven suffers violence, one must fight in order to win, fight to the very end the affections of the flesh and the blood."[26]

Vincent did not limit his role as superior general to this monumental flow of correspondence (there were 30,000 letters before they were largely destroyed during the Revolution). He made the effort to convoke the members of the Congregation at Saint-Lazare every week, as he did for the Daughters of Charity, in order to have conversations which he led with simplicity and hominess. In the spring of 1658, on Friday, May 17, Vincent solemnly submitted the text of the Rule of the Congregation to the members of his company.[27] He had waited thirty-three years before giving it final form and having it printed. He asked those who received it to consider it not as the product of a human mind but rather as having been inspired by God.

It was an enormous effort, requiring exceptional energy, for Vincent to leave his room and go to the meetings which he convened. It was increasingly difficult for him to move about and, at the beginning of

December 1658, he confessed to his friend, Abbot Louis de Chandenier: "The increasing pain in my legs is the reason I am no longer allowed to be at the assembly [of the Tuesday Conferences], now that they take place at the Bons-Enfants."[28]

At the beginning of 1659, he felt so poorly that he thought seriously that he was going to die. Therefore, he wrote messages that he thought would be his last to Cardinal de Retz and his former master, Philippe-Emmanuel de Gondi: "The failing state in which I find myself, and a little fever that has come over me, make me suspect what might come next, so I address you, Monseigneur, in order to prostrate myself in spirit at your feet, to ask your pardon for displeasing you with my rustic ways and to take the opportunity to thank you most humbly, as thank you indeed I do, for the charitable support you have shown me."[29]

But once more, his robust constitution took the upper hand and, three months later, he was able to write to Louise de Marillac to calm her fears: "I am doing better, by the grace of God and with your help. I have been suffering from a bout of fever caused by an accidental chill, which brought shivering and terrible sensations of heat, one after the other, in the usual way. It is a kind of fever I am most accustomed to."[30] But this "better" was only relative; his legs no longer carried him, and he was condemned to remain at Saint-Lazare. He only got up to say mass and to take part in the conferences, which he still insisted on leading. In July, he wrote to the superior at Saintes: "I am otherwise not ill, and yet, I have not been out for seven or eight months, because of the pain in my legs, which has grown more intense, and other than that, I have had an inflammation in one eye for the last five or six weeks, of which I cannot seem to be cured, even with the application of several remedies."[31]

At the end of the year, writing to Monsieur Bourdaise, whom he still thought to be alive in Madagascar, he asks for his prayers: "for I shall not make it long, because of my age, which is getting to be eighty, and of my bad legs, which can no longer carry me."[32]

Although he was housebound at Saint-Lazare, Vincent remained informed of the affairs of the kingdom. He knew that after the victories at the fortress of Dunkerque, won by the king's armies under Turenne in June 1658, the famous Battle of the Dunes, the Spanish were determined to obtain a peace treaty. The trump card in the negotiations was to be the marriage of the young king of France to the Infanta of Spain. Discreet talks began, but they were difficult after so many years of war.

Around May 1659, rumors began to fly about this peace so desired by one and all. Vincent, because he was well informed, wrote in early May: "May it please God to have pity on this poor nation! They are speaking of peace as though it were already concluded. This will be a great blessing for the poor borderlands."[33]

A first protocol was signed at Paris on June 4, but there was still a long way to go before a final agreement would be reached. For months, Cardinal Mazarin and the prime minister of Spain Don Louis de Haro sparred with each other on the Île des Faisans, on the frontier between the two kingdoms. The peace was signed on November 7, and this Treaty of the Pyrenees put an end to a conflict which had lasted over a quarter of a century. Vincent gave thanks to God, for this was the end of the suffering of the poor, or at least he hoped so.

Final Afflictions
1660

That Miserable Letter
The Enigma of Vincent's Captivity
Hard at Work to the End

Vincent rejoiced that peace had finally returned to the kingdom, but he knew that he would hardly have time to enjoy it because for him, life on earth was coming to an end. From the room where he was confined, he wrote in January to one of his first and closest collaborators, Jean Dehorgny: "As for me, I can no longer go downstairs because my legs are worse than they have ever been."[1] Two months later, he was no longer able even to stand. "I am well enough, except for my legs, which no longer allow me to say the Holy Mass and which oblige me to remain seated all day long."[2] After much urging, he allowed himself to be moved into a room that had a fireplace, all the while grumbling about this luxury that was being forced upon him.

It was in this miserable state that Vincent, more or less bedridden, suffered two terrible blows, one after the other. At an interval of one month, he lost two beings who were particularly dear to him and who had labored with him, side by side. On February 14, he learned of the death of "our good Monsieur Portail,"[3] and on March 15, of the death of Louise de Marillac, exhausted by thirty years of complete devotion to the poor and the sick with her Daughters of Charity.

Without a doubt, Vincent accepted these separations in a spirit of submission to God's good pleasure, but that did not stop his human heart from aching. And into the bargain, these sorrows came over and above a secret torment that had been gnawing at him for months. When he felt that his end was approaching, one question troubled him to the point of writing this curious letter to Canon de Saint-Martin at Dax: "I implore you, by all the grace that it has pleased God to grant you, to send me that miserable letter that mentions Turkey, the one that Monsieur d'Agès found in his father's papers. I beg of you once more, by the entrails of Jesus Christ Our Lord, to do me the great goodness I ask of you as soon as possible."[4]

What was this miserable letter that caused Vincent so much distress? To answer this, we must go back more than two years. In July 1658, Vincent had received a letter from Canon de Saint-Martin informing him that his nephew, Saint-Martin d'Agès, had found two old letters while going through his father's papers, addressed in 1607 and 1608 to Judge de Comet.[5] These were the letters that Vincent had sent him from Avignon and from Rome after his adventure on the Barbary Coast. The good canon, convinced that the author of these accounts would be happy to be able to read them again, had sent Vincent copies. But Vincent had been quick to destroy them and replied at once that he would very much like to have the originals.

Brother Ducournau had warned Messieurs Portail, Dehorgny, and Alméras, who constituted an advisory council to the superior general. At the command of this council, he had enclosed in the envelope containing Vincent's reply to Canon Saint-Martin a note, asking him to send the originals of the documents in question to Jean Watebled, superior of the Collège des Bons-Enfants. When they arrived in August 1658, Brother Ducournau had thanked the canon in these words: "You have discovered a hidden treasure for us by sending these letters; if they had fallen into his hands, no one would ever have seen them. But so that he does not know we have them, the council has suppressed your letter. If it happens that he asks you once more for his letters, you will be able to write him that you have already addressed them to him, and that you are very sorry that he has not received them." Vincent was waiting for these documents with growing impatience, for he feared that he would die before he could destroy them.

It may seem surprising that in a congregation whose members had made a vow of obedience, some would permit themselves to waylay a letter addressed to their superior general. One remembers Vincent's anger at the superior of Tréguier who thought he had a right to read a letter meant for a member of his house: "This is an unheard of fault," he exclaimed. Now not only were people spiriting away his correspondence, but they were trying to talk the good Canon Saint-Martin into embellishing the truth.

Brother Ducournau justified the action, which had been imposed on him by responsible priests, in the following way: "They would not have wanted to miss obtaining those letters [from Barbary] for anything in the world, because they contain things which one day will give great luster to the holy life of the person who wrote them." Already people were thinking of a time after Vincent and of the creation of his legend! Without a doubt, the intention of these fathers was pure.

However that might be, thanks to this subterfuge, this troubling story of Vincent de Paul's captivity in Barbary came to light again after fifty years. Two questions arise: Why did Vincent always maintain silence about this period of his life, and why did he want to destroy the letters that documented it? In his letter to Canon de Saint-Martin, Brother Ducournau gave an explanation which would be used by almost all of Vincent's biographers: "He often told us that he was the son of a land worker, that he herded his father's swine, and other things to present himself in a humble light, but he never told us anything that could bring him honor, such as having been a slave, not to mention telling us about the good that came of it."[6] In other words, it is out of humility that Vincent hid this part of his life. This explanation does not seem fully convincing.

If we trace the matter back to its beginnings, it is possible to formulate other hypotheses. When Vincent reappeared, after a blank period of two years, he explained his absence in several letters which he addressed in particular to Monsieur de Comet. These missives give a version of the facts which is perhaps neither complete nor entirely truthful as regards the circumstances of his captivity and his escape. Therefore, at the beginning, he might not have wanted to say anything more about this period. As the years went by, it became more and more difficult for him to break his silence about this adventure. Now, he certainly did not lack opportunities to recall his experience, particularly when he insisted on maintaining missionaries in the consulates of Tunis and Algiers in spite of all the catastrophes they encountered.

What he did do, even though he never said a single word to give credence directly to his time in Barbary, was to sprinkle his talks and his conferences with references to the customs and morals of the Turks, as though he had observed them with his own eyes.[7]

But when he discovered, late in life, that this miserable letter that mentions Turkey, and even worse, alchemy, had been rediscovered, his personal position changed entirely. Now he was the founder and the superior general of a congregation, the instigator of various charitable works, the spiritual director of convents of the Visitation, a moral authority in his century. Revelation of such a document could have shattering consequences, not only for him, which he would be willing to suffer gladly in expiation, but for the Mission, for the Daughters of Charity, for all those who had been marked by his example and his radiant spirit.

Thus, to mention only this one point, his first letter to Monsieur de Comet explained clearly that he had carried out alchemical experiments under the direction of his master, the spagiric physician. The pious Brother Ducournau wrote to the canon about it in such a way as to glorify these experiments: "The captivity of this charitable man having provided him with a knowledge of alchemy, he used it more felicitously than those who undertake to change the nature of metals. For he converted evil to good, the sinner into a just man, slavery into liberty and hell into paradise, and this in as many ways as our Community has undertakings." The brother—or the priests who inspired the text of this letter— expresses noble sentiments, but he is masking the reality of the situation. In the middle of the seventeenth century, alchemy was considered to be a practice associated with magic and witchcraft. It was condemned both by the Church and by the government. What a fine scandal it would have been if it had been revealed that Vincent de Paul had engaged in such practices, and that he had even initiated a Roman prelate. What is worse, this same prelate made himself important before the pontifical court and the pope himself by performing the tricks (the word "alchemy" is no longer used in the letters dated at Rome) that Vincent had taught him.

The publication of these documents could have had other harmful consequences. The world would not have hesitated to dissect and analyze the different statements they contained and the facts they recounted. Witnesses who were still alive could perhaps even have shown that young Vincent had masked, manipulated, or concealed certain events. There is a marked difference between the usual stories of young men who sowed their wild oats before they chose the path that leads to holiness and the story of Vincent, who was already an ordained priest at the time he lived out these adventures.

It is easy to understand the emotional turmoil of this weak and bedridden man, who was haunted by the thought that this letter he considered miserable might be made public.

But in spite of his age and his infirmities, Vincent's energy was unconquerable. From his room, which he could no longer leave at all, he continued to inspire the Congregation and to correspond steadily with his missionaries. He thought of the future of his community, directing the superiors of the houses of the Mission to establish archives: "I beg of you to save, from now on, the letters received by you and the members of your house, no matter what the topic, when they contain any remarkable details which could be of some consequence, or which might be instructive in the future."[8]

Always attentive to anything having to do with the material patrimony of the Congregation of the Mission, he advised the superior of the house at Richelieu: "I do not at all agree that you should work the land yourselves, since that is not what we are meant to do. That is why it would be wise for you to find farmers and not to burden yourselves with the equipment and cares of agricultural work."[9] He was interested in the project of a missionary, Guillaume Desdames, who was conducting missions in a village near Warsaw: "I was very satisfied to know of the state of your temporal situation and the measures you have taken to fill the needs of your village, for people's bodies as well as for their souls." He gave the missionary news about France: "Everywhere, they are asking us for men, but we do not have enough. Oh Lord, Monsieur, what a great treasure a good missionary is!" He continued, alluding to missions conducted by Father Eudes and his priest. He rejoiced in their success by emphasizing that the Congregation had been at the origin of this movement of evangelization: "We have the consolation of seeing that our modest activities have seemed so beautiful and so useful that they have made others eager to do the same."[10]

In Rome there was talk of opening a seminary specifically to train priests for the foreign missions, and of entrusting it to the Congregation. Vincent immediately wrote to Edme Jolly, superior of the house in Rome: "I praise God that the plan which has been formed at Rome to establish a seminary for the foreign missions has been turned over to us." Yet Vincent was perfectly aware of the difficulties inherent in these distant missions: "In truth, some men might present themselves for the seminary willingly, but to undertake these foreign missions with the detachment and the zeal the work calls for, not many will be found for that."[11]

He continued his talks with the Daughters of Charity: they came to Saint-Lazare and gathered upstairs in a room next door to his. Wishing to render a final honor to Louise de Marillac, he spoke to them in the course of two meetings in July of the virtues of the woman who had been their superior.[12] He also continued to assemble the members of the Congregation for weekly conferences. On these occasions, he touched on topics connected to recent events, the death of Monsieur Portail, and the death, in May, of his friend Louis de Chandenier, and he spoke of their exemplary lives. He also talked on themes related to the needs of the inner life. From July on, he devoted his last talks to explicating and commenting on the Rule of the Congregation, which, in his eyes, was of capital importance.[13]

What courage, what a will to fight in this sick man, constantly struggling with the pain in his legs, having himself carried into the meeting room, where he displayed a serene and smiling face during these exhausting sessions.

After the success of the great mission preached at Metz, Anne of Austria had entrusted a large sum of money, 60,000 livres, to Vincent, so that he could found a house in that city. He had asked Bossuet to do this work, and to find a house as well as a farm. Bossuet's letters about this business, which Vincent received in August, brought him one last satisfaction.

His health was sinking rapidly. "I am constantly weak, and the good Lord, who is striking me down yet maintains me in the miserable state I live in," he wrote to René Alméras on August 18. Alméras was convalescing himself, and Vincent urges him to recover quickly: "What it takes is rest and the medicines which are available to you, but most particularly, the will of God, who will not deny you the strength of body and soul you need to carry out his designs for you within the Community."[14] Clearly, Vincent was certain that René Alméras would soon be called upon to succeed him at the head of the Congregation of the Mission. He had already inscribed his name in a document which he kept locked in a strong box to be opened after his death.

In one of his last letters to Firmin Get, superior of the house in Marseilles, written on September 17, ten days before he died, Vincent once more dwelt at length on all the questions relating to the Community. In particular, he mentions the most recent news from Algiers. Sir Paul, with a fleet of about fifteen ships, had finally sailed. At the beginning of September he had reached Algiers, but could not land because of the bad weather. He had only been able to gather in about forty slaves who had swum out from shore when they saw the French flags flying from the masts. Vincent noted, "I am suffering from an anxiety which causes me unspeakable pain. There is a rumor here that Commander Paul has laid siege to Algiers, but no one knows the outcome."[15]

For all his life, Barbary would be a secret torment, object of his sorrow and anguish.

The next day, September 18, Vincent fell into a state of extreme weakness. On the 26th, he had himself carried to the oratory on his floor where, half-conscious, he assisted at mass. In the evening, he received the sacrament of Extreme Unction and died the next morning: "He remained seated, as he had been, handsome, more majestic and venerable to see than ever. He died in his chair, completely dressed, near the fire."[16] It was about four o'clock in the morning, an hour when, for so long, he had been accustomed to rise and begin a day filled with prayer and works of charity.

Epilogue

Vincent de Paul carried the secrets of his existence to his grave. When, a half century after his death, the Church undertook the long process of his beatification and canonization, his remains were exhumed and found to be in a perfect state of preservation. His actions, his writings, and his thoughts were examined with the fine-tooth comb of a critical analysis. Would the Promoter of the Faith, the official called the devil's advocate, in this case Prospero Lambertini, the future Pope Benedict XIV, uncover Vincent's secrets?

At first he scrutinized Vincent's relationship with the abbot of Saint-Cyran, who is considered the initiator of Jansenism. Vincent de Paul had made a deposition in an attempt to clear this man who had been his friend. Had the attempt to hide guilty contacts been, at least in part, untruthful? The advocate for Vincent, or postulator of his cause, a priest of the Congregation of the Mission named Couty, succeeded in removing this first obstacle.

The canonization process itself began in December 1717. Many vexed points had to be considered: Vincent's reception of minor orders, the sub-diaconate and diaconate, in the same year without a dispensation from Rome; his participation in alchemical experiments when he was a slave on the Barbary coast; the overly rapid abandonment of his parishioners when he was in charge of the parishes of Clichy and Châtillon-les-Dombes; the scandal arising from the conflict between his missionaries and the Benedictines of Saint-Méen.[1] Even his habit of using snuff was put forward as guilty evidence, but this accusation was fortunately neutralized with the opportune discovery of a medical certificate which recommended this practice to Vincent as a means of treating a chronic cough!

These accusations were considered on the basis of the testimony of some 300 witnesses who had known Vincent in his lifetime, and on his correspondence. Use was also made of a work written by Louis Abelly, bishop of Rodez, which appeared four years after the death of the superior of the Congregation of the Mission. In this hagiography, the date of Vincent's birth was advanced by five years, so as to obscure his premature ordination, when he was, in fact, only in his twentieth year.[2] As for Vincent's participation in alchemical experiments, it was presented blandly in this book, simply by quoting an extract from a letter in which Vincent wrote that his master "liked to lecture me on alchemy." Abelly added immediately that Vincent had exerted every effort to suppress in himself all the knowledge that the spagirist physician had communicated to him concerning various beautiful secrets of Nature and the Art.

The letters sent from Avignon and Rome, shortened and sanitized in this way, could hardly enrich the dossier of the Devil's Advocate. It does indeed seem that the Congregation dispensed itself from providing entire texts of these letters, no doubt because they feared to arouse heated debate. Abelly himself declared that he had worked on copies rather than originals. What is more, all the questions that may have been raised by the story of the capture, detention, and escape of Vincent do not seem to have awakened the slightest suspicion in the mind of the Devil's Advocate. At length, after almost thirty years of investigation, depositions, and debate, including the presentation and analysis of eight cases of miraculous healing, of which half were authenticated, Pope Clement XII promulgated the bull of Vincent's canonization on June 16, 1737.[3]

Whereas the process of beatification and canonization did nothing to lift the veil of obscurity from Vincent's youth, it shed a bright light on the heroic virtue of his subsequent life. The essential point emerges: his example and his message inspired an ever-growing number of disciples. After the Revolution which ravaged the priory of Saint-Lazare on July 13, 1789 and destroyed most of the letters and objects left behind by Vincent,[4] after all the alarms of war which had marked the two preceding centuries, and in spite of the profound changes in mentality both inside and outside the Church, the Vincentian family never stopped developing. Today it has a presence on all five continents, thus fulfilling its founder's wish, expressed in one of his last conferences to his missionaries: "Our vocation is to go not into one parish, nor into only one diocese, but throughout the earth. And to do what? To inflame the hearts of men. It is not enough for me to love God if my neighbor does not love him as well."[5]

Today, the Congregation of the Mission numbers 3,600 members, known under the name of Lazarists, and the community of the Daughters of Charity numbers 27,200 sisters, working in over eighty countries of the world. The charities, directly descended from the first group of Ladies of Charity brought together by Vincent at Châtillon-les-Dombes, are united in an international association with 250,000 members. The Society of Saint Vincent de Paul, founded in 1835 by Frédéric Ozanam, a lay society with obedience to the Church, has 875,000 members in 130 countries. Finally, more than 500 congregations or communities, most of them congregations of women, declare themselves followers of Vincent or under his patronage.

What is the secret of Vincent's remarkable influence? He left us neither a learned treatise nor a body of doctrine, only the little volume of his Rule, a brief synthesis of theological spirituality.[6] He was content to lay out a road, to clear the paths, inviting his disciples to continue the charitable works which he had begun. He opened the doors of the Church, teaching the clergy to work with the laity, the first who dared to value the contribution of women. And the women responded enthusiastically to his call, whether they were country girls or great ladies of the nobility.

Vincent knew how to make his work responsive to all kinds of misery, whether physical or moral, determined to remedy it and finding an appropriate solution for every situation. Thus, he was the initiator of assistance to abandoned children, to prisoners, victims of catastrophe, refugees, and housebound invalids. In all these works, he was a precursor, showing the way which is still followed today by institutions and governmental departments of social services.

Bending himself to the pattern of his model, Jesus Christ, he placed himself at the service of the poor, "who are our lords and our masters."[7] He taught that true charity does not consist only of distributing alms, but of helping the abject to regain their dignity and independence.

He believed in the virtue of action and he loved to use this succinct motto: *Totum opus nostrum in operatione consistit* (Action is our entire task). Then he would add that "Perfection does not come from ecstasy but rather from doing the will of God."[8]

Vincent was first and foremost a man of God, profoundly steeped in the spirit of the Gospel. He recommended long prayer and meditation before action so that one could come to recognize the divine will. One must not hurry, and that is why he counseled people not to leap ahead of Providence. Above all, this man of action was a man of prayer and deep spirituality: "You must have an inner life, everything must tend in that direction. If you lack this, you lack everything."⁹

Appendix 1
Brief Chronology

	VINCENT DE PAUL	FRANCE	THE CHURCH AND EUROPE
1581	Birth of Vincent at Pouy	Birth of Saint-Cyran	
1585		Birth of Arnaud du Plessis, future Cardinal de Richelieu	
1589		Assassination of Henry III, Henry of Navarre becomes Henry IV	
1592			Election of Pope Clement VIII
1593		Henry IV recants Protestantism	
1597	Begins theological studies at the University of Toulouse		
1598	Receives major orders	Promulgation of the Edict of Nantes	
1600	Ordained by the bishop of Périgueux Pilgrimage to Rome		
1601		Birth of Louis XIII	
1604	Bachelor of theology		
1605	Capture by the Barbary pirates Captivity in Tunis		Election of Pope Paul V

	VINCENT DE PAUL	FRANCE	THE CHURCH AND EUROPE
1607	Escape and arrival at Avignon		
1608	Visits Rome		
1609	Settles in Paris		Francis de Sales: *Introduction to the Devout Life*
1610	Chaplain of Queen Marguerite of Valois Acquires the abbey of Saint-Léonard-de-Chaume	Assassination of Henry IV Regency of Maria de Medici	
1611		Foundation of the Oratory by Pierre de Bérulle	
1612	Pastor of Clichy-la-Garenne		
1613	Tutor in the house of Gondi		
1615	Canon of Écouis	The assembly of the clergy calls for reception of the Council of Trent	Francis de Sales: *Traité de l'amour de Dieu*
1616	Renounces the abbey of Saint-Léonard-de-Chaume	Richelieu enters the King's Council	
1617	Pastor of Châtillon-les-Dombes	Assassination of Concini	
	First Confraternity of Charity	Louis XIII takes the throne	
1618	First missions on Gondi lands		Beginning of the Thirty Years' War
	Meeting with Francis de Sales		
1619	Royal chaplain of the galleys	Expedition of Louis XIII against the Protestants of the Béarn	

	VINCENT DE PAUL	FRANCE	THE CHURCH AND EUROPE
1621			Election of Pope Gregory XV
			Foundation of the Congregation for the Propagation of the Faith
1622	Superior of the Visitation's house in Paris	Richelieu receives the cardinal's hat	Death of Francis de Sales
1623			Election of Pope Urban VIII
1624	Installation in the Collège des Bons-Enfants	Richelieu presides over King's Council	
1625	Foundation of the Congregation of the Mission		Marriage of Charles I of England and Henriette of France
	Spiritual director of Louise de Marillac		
1628	First workshops for ordinands	Capitulation of the Protestants at La Rochelle	
1629	Louise de Marillac begins to work with charities	Death of Cardinal Pierre de Bérulle	
1630		Day of the Dupes: Richelieu is confirmed as prime minister	
1632	Installation of the Mission at the Priory of Saint-Lazare	Execution of Marshal de Marillac	Victory of Gustavus Adolphus of Sweden against imperial forces at Lützen
1633	Bull *Salvatoris Nostri* recognizing the Congregation of the Mission	Occupation of Lorraine by Louis XIII	Second condemnation of Galileo
	Beginning of the Tuesday Conferences		
1634	Foundation of the Daughters of Charity	Trial at Loudun	Victory of the imperial forces over the Swedes at Nördlingen
	Foundation of the house at Toul		

	VINCENT DE PAUL	FRANCE	THE CHURCH AND EUROPE
1635			France declares war on Spain and the emperor declares war on France
1636	Missionaries are sent to the army	Fall of Corbie Corneille: *Le Cid*	
1637	Foundation of the house at La Rose	Peasant revolt	
		Descartes: *Discours de la méthode*	
1638	Foundation of the Foundling Hospital	Birth of the dauphin, future Louis XIV	Death of Jansenius
	Foundation of the houses at Richelieu, Troyes, and Luçon	Arrest of Saint-Cyran	
1639	Aid to war-torn Lorraine		
	Foundation of the house at Alet		
1640	Foundation of the house at Annecy		Publication of the *Augustinus*
1641	Foundation of the house at Crécy	Death of Jeanne de Chantal	
		Mazarin receives the cardinal's hat	
1642	Creation of a first seminary at the Collège des Bons-Enfants	Death of Cardinal de Richelieu	Condemnation by Rome of the five propositions of the *Augustinus*
1643	Nomination to the Council of Conscience	Death of Louis XIII and regency of Anne of Austria	
	Foundation of the houses of Marseilles, Cahors and Rome	Victory of Rocroi over the Spanish	
		Antoine Arnauld: *De la fréquente communion*	
1644	Foundation of the houses of Saintes, Montmirail, and Sedan		Election of Pope Innocent X

	VINCENT DE PAUL	FRANCE	THE CHURCH AND EUROPE
1645	Foundation of the houses of Saint-Méen, Le Mans, Genoa, and Turin		
	Acquisition of the consulate at Tunis		
1646	Missions to Ireland and Scotland		
	Acquisition of the consulate at Algiers		
	The community of the Daughters of Charity is raised to the rank of confraternity		
1648	Tour of houses in the provinces	Beginning of the Fronde	Treaty of Westphalia puts an end to Thirty Years' War
	Beginning of the mission in Madagascar		
	Foundation of the houses in Tréguier and Agen		
1650	Foundation of the house of Périgueux	Spanish offensive in Picardy	
1651	Aid to Picardy, Champagne, Île-de-France	Louis XIV reaches majority	
	Beginning of the mission in Poland	First exile of Mazarin	
1652	Foundation of the houses of Montauban and Notre-Dame de Lorm	Fighting around Paris	
		Second exile of Mazarin	
1653	Removed from the Council of Conscience	Return of Mazarin	Condemnation of the propositions of the *Augustinus* by Rome

	VINCENT DE PAUL	FRANCE	THE CHURCH AND EUROPE
1654	Foundation of the house at Agde		
1655	Foundation of the house at Turin		Election of Pope Alexander VII
1656		Pascal: *Provinciales*	
1657		Opening of the general hospital	
1659	Foundation of the houses of Montpellier and Narbonne		Treaty of the Pyrenees between France and Spain
1660	Death of Vincent	Marriage of Louis XIV and the Infanta Maria-Theresa	
		Death of Louise de Marillac	
1661		Death of Mazarin	

Appendix 2
From Saint-Lazare to
the rue de Sèvres

The priory of Saint-Lazare was sacked and pillaged in 1789. The Congregation of the Mission itself was dispersed by the storms of the revolution. A decree of Napoleon reestablished it in 1804, but there was no mother house until 1817, in the Hôtel de Lorges, at 95 rue de Sèvres. This building was given to the Congregation in compensation for the requisitioning of their former house at Saint-Lazare, which was then transformed into a prison. Later acquisitions of land and buildings, both on the rue de Sèvres and the rue du Cherche-Midi, made it possible to create the configuration which exists today. The body of Saint Vincent de Paul has reposed in a shrine there since 1830. The members of the Congregation of the Mission, who were called "these gentlemen of Saint-Lazare" when they were living at the priory, kept this name, which became Lazarists in the nineteenth century.

The Daughters of Charity, also scattered by the revolution, came together again in 1797 in a rented house at the rue des Maçons-Sorbonne, which is now the rue Champollion. From 1801 to 1814, they resided in a house called the House of the Orphans, in the rue du Vieux-Colombier. Then they moved to the Hôtel de Châtillon, at number 140, rue du Bac, which was granted to them by imperial decree. The mother house of the community of Daughters of Charity is still at this address today. They are now also known as Sisters of Vincent de Paul.

Notes

Abbreviations Used in the Notes

S.V. Pierre Coste, C.M., *Saint Vincent de Paul, correspondance, entretiens, documents* (Paris: Librairie Lecoffre J. Gabalda, 1920–1924). English edition: *Saint Vincent de Paul: Correspondence, Conferences, Documents* (Brooklyn, N.Y.: New City Press, 1985).

Abelly Louis Abelly, *Vie de saint Vincent de Paul* (Paris: F. Lambert, 1664; reprint 1986). English edition: *The Life of the Venerable Servant of God Vincent de Paul,* ed. John E. Rybolt, C.M., trans. William Quinn, F.S.C. (New Rochelle, N.Y.: New City Press, 1993).

Coste Pierre Coste, C.M., *Monsieur Vincent, Le grand saint du grand siècle* (Paris: Desclée, 1934). English edition: *The Life and Works of St. Vincent de Paul,* trans. Joseph Leonard, C.M. (Brooklyn, N.Y.: New City Press, 1987).

Collet Pierre Collet, *La Vie de saint Vincent de Paul* (Nancy: A. Lescure, 1748).

Archives CM Archives of the Congregation of the Mission, Paris.

Annales CM *Annales de la congrégation de la Mission et de la compagnie des filles de la Charité* (1833–1963).

Notes to the Prologue

1. This square would be renamed *Place du Trône* in honor of the ceremony. After the Revolution, it became *Place de la Nation.*

2. As Jean-Christian Petitfils tells it in his *Louis XIV* (Paris: Perrin, 1995).

3. S.V. 11:40.

1. Vincent's birth date has been a subject of controversy among his biographers. The first of them, Abelly, has him being born "the Tuesday after Easter" in the year 1576, that is, April 24. This is the date that was chiseled on Vincent's tombstone in the church of Saint-Lazare. On the basis of a detailed study of his letters and conferences, the twentieth-century biographers, particularly Coste, respected the "Tuesday after Easter" but set it in the year 1581. The resulting date March 28, 1581 seems to be more credible.

2. S.V. 13:20.

3. Some writers have tried to find a noble origin for the de Paul family by going back to hypothetical ancestors from Languedoc where there is a de Paul château in the diocese of Lodève. Descendants of these chatelaines, having fallen upon hard times, supposedly left the Languedoc for the Landes. This hypothesis seems shaky. See Oscar de Poli, "Recherches sur la famille de saint Vincent de Paul" (Research on the family of St. Vincent de Paul), *Revue du monde catholique* (1871).

4. The names of brooks in this part of the Landes come from the particular territory they run through; they change their names as they flow along. On the road from Pouy to Buglose, the de Paul bridge crosses the brook which later forms Ice House Pond and then becomes Mill Brook.

5. The sister of Monsieur de Comet, who was a judge at Dax, married a Louis de Saint-Martin, lawyer at the court of Dax. See Charles Blanc, "Parenté de Monsieur Vincent" (Family of Monsieur Vincent), *Revue de la société de Borda* (1960).

6. There is still an oak tree, several hundred years old, near the house called Ranquines, which was reconstructed on the approximate location of the old de Paul cottage.

7. Pouy was the seat of a barony in the Landes which, in the fifteenth and sixteenth centuries, belonged to the Beyrie family. The inhabitants of this village had the privilege of meeting in assembly to name a syndic assisted by three municipal clerks. This assembly also chose council members, tax collectors, officers in charge of calling general meetings, and individuals charged with administering the goods of the church, together with the pastor. See Blanc, "Parenté de Monsieur Vincent."

8. S.V. 9:84.

9. S.V. 4:481.

10. S.V. 9:91.

11. It is not the owner of the horse farm (the cavier) who is noble, but his land, being exempt from feudal rents. The title is transmitted with the land. The special class of these landholders forms a pivotal point between the nobility and the common people. For instance, Jacques de Moras, a relative of Vincent, held the title "cavier of Peyroux."

12. Collet 2:195.

13. Gabriel de Lorges, count of Montgomery (or Montgommeri), 1530–1574. Captain of the Scottish Guard, he accidentally caused the death of King Henry II during a tourney. After spending some time in England, he returned to France to place himself at the service of the Protestant party, and in particular of Jeanne d'Albret, queen of Navarre. He conducted bloody campaigns of repression against the Catholics of the Béarn and in the neighboring provinces of Bigorre, Navarre, the Landes, and all the way to Guyenne. He was imprisoned, tried, and condemned to death for his crimes.

14. When Étienne de Paul took possession of the priory of Poymartet around 1577, he observed that "the chapel was entirely destroyed and the shelter for the poor was uninhabitable. It was impossible to celebrate a divine service there" (Archives of the Hospital of Dax, E.2). However, the revenues of the lands and other privileges attached to the priory were not seriously reduced.

15. S.V. 9:82.

16. Vincent was to repeat this label of "fourth-year pupil" many times. Of course, if one remembers that at this time, the word "pupil" was used to designate university students, it can be interpreted differently. Vincent had completed his studies at the university as a fourth-year student, having passed his first three years of study, the so-called arts curriculum, at Toulouse from 1597 to 1600, and then the four years of theology, from 1600 to 1604. He only failed to state that he had earned the title of bachelor of theology and that he had even taught for one year at Toulouse, as assistant to a master, with the title of sententiary bachelor.

17. The Cordeliers was a name applied to Franciscan friars since the fifteenth century. Internal dissent had caused their separation into Cordeliers, Capuchins, and the Recollects. For a time, the Cordeliers were rivals of the Dominicans, whom they managed to exclude from the University of Paris. After the Revolution, the reformed Franciscans did not resume the name of Cordeliers.

18. S.V. 12:432.

19. Cited in Coste 1:30. This sentiment was supposedly expressed by Vincent before Madame de Lamoignon. It was quoted in the course of his beatification process by the defender, as an argument for sanctity, since Vincent had accused himself publicly as a gesture of humility.

20. Letters of tonsure and the minor orders, December 20, 1596 (S.V. 13:1, 2). The minor orders include the following functions: 1. porter, *ostiariatus;* 2. reader, *lectoratus;* 3. exorcist, *exorcistatus;* 4. acolyte, *acolytatus.*

21. Antoine de Gramont (1604–1678). A marshal of France, he succeeded his father in 1644 as governor and lieutenant-general of Navarre and Béarn. He was made a duke and a peer in 1648.

22. The abbey of Arthous, which belonged to the Premonstratensian Order, had been devastated by passing Huguenot troops in 1569. By the time

Vincent stopped there, it had been only partially restored. However, even in this state, the benefice of the abbey earned large revenues for its commendatory abbot, who came to receive them with great pomp.

23. Louis Abelly (1604–1691). For many years, he lived within Vincent's sphere of influence, participating actively in the Tuesday Conferences. At Bayonne in 1639 he was named vicar general of the episcopal see of François Fouquet, brother of the superintendent and son of Madame Fouquet, a Lady of Charity. He was later named pastor of the parish of Saint-Josse in Paris and bishop of Rodez in 1662. In 1664 he resigned from his bishopric and retired to Saint-Lazare, where he spent the rest of his life in study and reflection. René Alméras, superior of the Mission after the death of Vincent, asked him to write a biography of the founder, a work which was carried out and completed in the period from 1660 to 1664.

Notes to Chapter 2

1. This Catholic St. Bartholomew's Day of 1572 had been preceded in 1569, also on August 24, by an incident of lesser magnitude but equal ferocity. Some Catholic aristocrats and military captains who had surrendered after the siege of the Château de Moncade, in return for a promise that they would be released and allowed to live, were held in captivity at Navarrenx and, on the orders of Montgomery, "stabbed to death in cold blood" (Pierre Tucoo-Chala, *Navarrenx* [Auch, 1981]).

2. Jeanne d'Albret (1528–1572). She was the daughter of Henry II d'Albret, king of Navarre and of Marguerite de Navarre, the daughter of Louise of Savoy, mother of Francis I. In 1548 she took as a second husband Antoine de Bourbon. She was converted to Protestantism in 1560, under the influence of Théodore de Bèze to whom she gave audience at Nérac. In 1562, upon the death of her husband, she became queen of Navarre. She imposed the reformed religion throughout her lands and whipped her troops into such fanaticism that under the command of Montgomery they put the Béarn and surrounding regions to fire and the sword from 1569 to 1572. Her son, Henry of Navarre, would become Henry IV of France.

3. The viscounty of Gabardan, together with the city of Gabarret, midway between Albret and Nérac; the viscounty of Marsan, with the city of Mont-de-Marsan; the viscounty of Tursan, south of the Ardour and east of the viscounty of Dax.

4. Blaise de Monluc (ca. 1500–1577). After fighting in Italy, he was assigned to defend Guyenne against the Protestants, which he did vigorously and harshly. Awarded the rank of king's lieutenant-general in Guyenne in 1565, he received the baton of marshal of France in 1574. His *Commentaries* were published posthumously in 1592.

5. Henri, duke of Joyeuse (1567–1608). He was a member of a great family which included Admiral Anne de Joyeuse, favorite of Henry III, and Cardinal François de Joyeuse, who negotiated the reconciliation of Henry IV at Rome. Henri de Joyeuse, brother of the two aforementioned, became a Capuchin friar upon the death of his wife but returned to the secular life to command a League army in Languedoc. After making an act of submission to Henry IV and receiving the baton of marshal of France, he returned to the Capuchins and remained there to the end of his days.

6. Abelly 1:10.

7. Father José-Maria Roman, in *San Vincente de Paul* (Madrid, 1982), repeats Abelly's statement about the stay at Saragossa and supports it with two arguments. The first is a quotation from Vincent de Paul: "I found myself in a kingdom . . . in that kingdom one does not speak of the king, because he is a sacred personage" (S.V. 10:446). According to Roman, this statement can only apply to Spain. In addition, he supports the statement by citing Vincent de Paul's knowledge of the teaching methods in the Spanish university (S.V. 2:212, 240).

8. Collet (1:9–10) presents this detail: "The division among the professors of this famous university on the topic of *scientia media* and the Decrees on Predestination. . . ." Collet is alluding to the doctrine professed by the Spanish Jesuit Luis Molina (1535–1601) concerning the difficult problem of predestination. In this matter, Molina advocated a *scientia media* retaining both the power of divine grace and human liberty, which he set forth in his treatise on free will, *De liberis arbitri cum gratiae donis concordia* (On the agreement between free will and the gift of faith). On this point, he was violently opposed to the Dominicans. Vincent adopted Molina's doctrine which tends to replace "efficient grace" with "sufficient grace," to which in order to do good, man ought to consent by the power of his free will. Thus he would later oppose the Jansenists who professed anti-molinist ideas. References to Molina can be found in Vincent's letters, which is still not absolute proof that he spent time in Spain.

9. Abelly and Collet had access to this will, but it has disappeared. In the margin of this document, Collet noted "Saturday February 7, 1598.

10. Abelly 1:11; d'Acqs is the old spelling of Dax.

11. The bishopric of Dax was held by François de Noailles from 1556 to 1585. This bishop carried out many ambassadorial missions to London, Venice, and Constantinople. At his death, his brother, Gilles de Noailles, succeeded him. He too received ambassadorial postings. In fact, the bishopric was administered by the vicar general, Guillaume de Massiot (or Demassiot).

12. Jean-Jacques Dusault (or Du Sault) was born in 1570 to a family of Bordeaux. His father was attorney general of Parliament. He himself was dean of Saint-Seurin at Bordeaux. Named bishop of Dax by the king, he was raised to the rank of bishop at Rome in May 1598, but authorized to retain his position at Bordeaux while taking up his functions without residing there. Consecrated at Paris in 1599, he entered Dax at the beginning of 1600.

13. The Council of Trent, one of the most important councils of the Church, was convened in May 1542. It remained in session until 1563, with many interruptions. It dealt with questions of doctrine raised by the Protestant Reformation and matters dealing with the sacraments and the organization of the Church. The decrees of this council were not received by the Church of France until 1615. Of relevance here is the requirement that a man had to be in his twenty-fifth year to be ordained.

14. Dimissorial letters for the sub-diaconate, September 10, 1598 (S.V. 13:3). For the formula *bene intitulato,* see the proceedings of the Council of Trent, session 21 of July 16, 1562, canon 2 ("that no one is to be admitted to Holy Orders without having the means of livelihood"). Cf. *Histoire des conciles* (Paris: Librairie Letouzey, 1938), vol. 10, pp. 420–421.

15. Dimissorial letters for the diaconate, Friday, December 11, 1598 (S.V. 13:4, 5).

16. Dimissorial letters for the priesthood, Monday, September 13, 1599 (S.V. 13:6, 7).

17. François de Bourdeilles (1516–1600). Born to an important family of Périgord, he joined the Benedictines in Paris. He left his monastery in 1575 to take charge of the diocese of Périgueux. Having resigned his office in November 1579, he stayed on as there was no successor to assure his service. He died on October 24, 1600. His cousin, Pierre de Bourdeilles, commendatory abbot of Brantôme, was famous for his gallantry and his writings, in which he presented unvarnished descriptions of the very free mores of his times.

18. Letter from Vincent de Paul to Canon Saint-Martin (ca. 1656) (S.V. 5:567).

19. Abelly does not name Vincent's "competitor" and Collet gives the name S. Soubé. Coste writes Saint-Soubé without noting where he found this name.

20. Letter from Vincent de Paul to François du Coudray, C.M., July 20, 1631 (S.V. 1:114).

21. Camillus de Lellis (1550–1614). After a dissipated life, he was converted under the influence of Philip Neri. He founded the Congregation of the Servants of the Poor Sick (Camillians), also known as the Fathers of the Good Death, raised to the status of a religious order in 1591. Camillus de Lellis was canonized in 1746.

22. S.V. 9:322–323.

23. Peter Lombard (1100–1160). After studies at Bologna, Reims, and Paris, he held a chair in theology in the capital city. He became bishop of Paris in 1159. He was the author of a famous work, *Sententiarum Libri IV* (The four books of Sentences), a theological summa that sought to end disputes by explicating dogma on the basis of scripture, the Church Fathers, and tradition. The *Sentences* was used in the schools as a manual of theology.

24. There is no document supplying categorical proof that he carried out these duties. Perhaps he simply concentrated on the work of directing a small boarding school that had been moved to Toulouse. His letters and lectures do indicate a specialized knowledge of the *Sentences*. Likewise, on more than one occasion, he implied that he had taught and certain of his talks demonstrate that he had mastered the craft of the teacher. See *St. Vincent de Paul, paroles, écrits et autres documents,* presented by Father Bernard Koch, C.M. (Archives CM).

25. Letter from Vincent de Paul to Monsieur de Comet, July 24, 1607 (S.V. 1:3).

26. Jean-Louis Nogaret de la Valette, duke of Épernon (1544–1642). He served Henry III by fighting against the League and the Guise family. He negotiated the reconciliation between Henry III and Henry of Navarre. Governor of Provence, then Angoumois, Saint-Onge, and Aunis, he joined Henry IV in 1596. In 1622, he became governor of Guyenne. He owned the superb château of Cadillac where he often stayed.

Notes to Chapter 3

1. Letter from Vincent de Paul to Monsieur de Comet, July 23, 1607 (S.V. 1:1).

2. See chapter 23 of this book.

3. These bipartisan chambers were composed of equal numbers of Catholic and Protestant magistrates in cities where Huguenots were authorized to govern, according to guidelines set down by the Edict of Nantes.

4. The sum of 300 écus of that time is the equivalent, all other things being equal, of about 150,000 of 1998 francs.

5. At this time, the Ottoman Empire extended to Tunis and Algiers. The term "Turk" was used to apply to all the inhabitants of this vast empire. The treaty signed in 1604 between Henry IV and the sultan of Constantinople, known as the Grand Turk, was a renewal of the capitulations signed in 1535 between Francis I and Sulayman II the Magnificent. These capitulations were privileges conceded by the sultans to certain western countries; they were only valid during the lifetime of the signatory sultan. Thus, they had to be renewed regularly, for they were considered by the Turks as a simple truce in the obligatory battle against the Infidel.

6. The word "spagiri" is composed of two Greek roots—the verb *span*, which means to extract, and the verb *ageirein,* which means to collect. The spagiric science, which is how chemistry used to be designated, sought to analyze substances by separating and then reconstituting them. The spagiric medical system explained changes in the human body in the same way as alchemists explained changes in the mineral kingdom.

7. This document, a copy of an old manuscript, is housed at the Hospice of Marans in Charente-Maritime, an establishment founded in 1684 under the care of the Daughters of Charity.

> St. Vincent de Paul's remedy for stones. Take turpentine of Venice, two ounces; white jalap of India [a purgative], two ounces; iron salts, galanga [*Galanga minor officinalis,* a toner of smooth muscle], clove, cinnamon, all measured at one-half ounce each. powdered aloe wood, one ounce. Make a paste with a half-pound of white honey and a pint of the strongest brandy. Let the mixture rest for some time, and then distill it. Take a fourth of a spoon in the morning, fasting, diluted with borage or bugloss water. Take this as desired, because it can do no harm. On the contrary, it is very good for the health and the principal effect is on the urine. For this reason, it is not necessary to follow any other regimen, except that one must not eat for one hour after taking the medication. But after that, one can go about one's ordinary business. You will see the results. This great servant of God learned this recipe in Barbary, when he was in captivity there. (S.V. 1:7)

To this recipe, Vincent adds fairly bombastic thoughts on predestination and liberty. This tends to show that he has not yet assimilated the theses of Molina completely, but it may also confirm the hypothesis that he heard these theses in Saragossa.

8. François Savary, lord de Brêves, marquis de Maulévrier (1560–1628). After many travels and a stay in the Ottoman Empire, he was named ambassador of France by Henry IV in 1593. He obtained from Sultan Ahmed I the renewal of capitulations and the signing of a commercial treaty in 1604. Recalled to France, he stopped in Tunis in 1606, where he succeeded in having some Christian slaves liberated; in Algiers, he achieved nothing. He was named ambassador to Rome in 1608, then tutor to the young duke of Anjou, the future Gaston d'Orléans.

9. To describe this farm, Vincent uses the correct term "timar," which he misspells as "temat," whereas the French only know the term "macerie." This tends to prove that he heard this word where it is native, in Barbary.

10. Psalm 137, *Super flumina Babylonis:*

> By the waters of Babylon.
> there we sat down and wept,
> when we remembered Zion
> On the willows there
>   we hung up our lyres.
> For there our captors
>   required of us songs,

and our tormentors, mirth, saying,
"Sing us one of the songs of Zion!"
How shall we sing the Lord's song
in a foreign land? . . .

11. Pierre Grandchamp, Chief of Service at the general residence in Tunis, in *La France en Tunisie au XVIIe siècle* (France in Tunisia in the seventeenth century), preface to volume 6 (1928), and "New Observations" in volume 7 (April 1929).

12. André Dodin, *La légende et l'histoire de Monsieur Depaul à saint Vincent de Paul* (Paris: OEIL, 1985), 149.

13. Coste 1:51.

14. See chapter 23 of this book.

15. These letters are inventoried and analyzed in J. Guichard, *St. Vincent de Paul, esclave à Tunis* (St. Vincent de Paul, slave at Tunis) (Paris: Desclée de Brower, 1937), 13–20.

16. The hypothesis advanced by Marcel Émerit to explain the disappearance of Vincent de Paul is founded on the statement that he was supposedly condemned to the galleys for the theft of the livery horse. After having rowed for two years, he is supposed to have escaped and taken refuge in Avignon, a papal territory. Then he is believed to have invented the story of his captivity in Barbary. See Marcel Émerit, "Comment se crée une légende: l'exemple de saint Vincent de Paul" (How a legend is created: the example of St. Vincent de Paul), *Les Cahiers rationalistes* (February 1978).

Notes to Chapter 4

1. Pierre-François Montorio (or Montoro) (1555–1643). From a great Roman family, he was named bishop of Nicastro in Calabria in 1594. He was sent as vice-legate to Avignon, where he stayed from 1604 to 1608. After a time in Rome, he returned to his see before being named nuncio to Cologne from 1621 to 1624. He ended his days in Rome.

2. It was in this way that on June 29, 1608, the successor of Monseigneur Montorio received the recantation of a priest of the Order of Cordeliers, who had become a Calvinist minister, a certain Guillaume Gautier. For some time, historians confused him with the renegade converted by Vincent.

3. At the beginning of the seventeenth century, persons attracted by alchemy or astrology were numerous, even among the princes of the Church. This was no longer the case in the second half of the century, which explains the reaction of Vincent when his letters reappeared and that of Abelly who did not hesitate to censor them.

4. Letter from Vincent de Paul to Monsieur de Comet, Rome, February 28, 1608 (S.V. 1:13–17).

5. "Extract from the fourth register of the Ecclesiastical Insinuations of the Diocese of d'Acqs," May 15, 1608 (S.V. 1:15, 16). "Insinuation" in its old sense means inscription of an act into a register.

6. Nicolas Coeffeteau (1574–1623). Doctor of the Sorbonne, a prolific and serious author, he distinguished himself in controversies with the Protestants. In 1610, he delivered the funeral oration of Henry IV. After receiving the episcopal mitre, he was named archbishop of Marseilles in 1621, shortly before his death.

7. Paul V, Camillo Borghese (1552–1621). In 1605, he succeeded Clement VIII on the throne of St. Peter. His signature is found on two documents concerning Vincent: the attributions of the abbey of Saint-Léonard-de-Chaume and of the parish of Clichy-la-Garenne.

8. Writing in October 1657 to Monsieur Jolly, superior of the Mission at Rome, Vincent mentioned Monsieur Gueffier to him, calling him "such a good, sweet-natured, wise man" (S.V. 6:509).

Notes to Chapter 5

1. Bertrand Dulou (or du Lou) belonged to an important Gascon family. He had been a king's judge for more than a decade in the little city of Sore, halfway between Dax and Bordeaux, in the heart of the Landes. We do not know where he stayed in Paris—in rooms belonging to his family or in a rented room

2. Marguerite de Valois (1553–1615). Daughter of Henry II and Catherine de Medici, she married Henry of Navarre just before the tragedy of St. Bartholomew's Night in an unhappy union that ended in a separation. Expelled from the court of France, she held court brilliantly at Nérac before being imprisoned in the château of Usson. After Henry IV took the throne, her marriage was annulled in Rome. She obtained permission to live in Paris in 1605, where she had a palace built on the left bank of the Seine, opposite the Louvre.

3. Four brothers of the Order of St. John of God had arrived from Italy in 1601. They had obtained letters patent from Henry IV to found the hospital of St. John the Baptist of Charity.

4. *Monitoire,* a term of ecclesiastical law, is a notice from ecclesiastical lawyers read out during the announcements at mass to obligate parishioners to make their deposition about facts under investigation.

5. Abelly 1: chapter 5, 21. This anecdote was told by Vincent himself at the end of his life, in 1656. He attributed it to "a member of the Company" (S.V. 11:337).

6. Jean Duvergier de Hauranne, canon of Saint-Cyran (see note 3 in chapter 13). His nephew, Martin de Barcos, states that Vincent shared a dwelling and finances with his uncle, without giving a date (*Dépense de feu Monsieur Vincent contre les faux discours des livres de sa vie publiés par Abelly* [Paris, 1668], 11, 12).

7. Charles du Fresne, lord de Villeneuve, secretary of Queen Marguerite of Valois, entered the service of Emmanuel de Gondi when the queen died. He was secretary and then manager of his household. He became an intimate friend of Vincent de Paul.

8. Dispatch of letters of ordination, extracted from the fourth register of Ecclesiastical Insinuations of the Diocese of Dax, Thursday, May 15 and Saturday, May 17, 1608 (Archives CM).

9. National archives, KK 180. The document specifies that for the year 1608, the queen's good works reached a sum of 1,900 écus.

10. S.V. 13:8, 12, 14.

11. The university diploma attesting to the fact that Vincent was licensed *in utroque jure* (in both laws), civil as well as canon law, was presented by Brother Chollier at the beatification process. In the meantime, the document has disappeared and its date is no longer known. The title appears for the first time in a document dated March 2, 1624, but it is possible that he had obtained this university degree much earlier (S.V. 13:60, n. 1).

12. Letter from Vincent de Paul to his mother at Pouy, February 17, 1610 (S.V. 1:18).

13. The abbey of Saint-Léonard, about twenty kilometers east of La Rochelle, was founded in 1036 by Benedictines, who were replaced by Cistercians in the sixteenth century. Destroyed by Huguenots and then partially restored, it was suppressed in 1791. Paul Hurault de l'Hôpital was archbishop of Aix from 1599 to 1624 and a member of the Council of State.

14. "St. Vincent, guarantor for Arnault Dozier, lessee of the abbey of Saint-Léonard-de-Chaume," Friday, May 14, 1610 (*Annales CM,* vol. 106–107 [1941–1942]: 260–262; text reviewed and annotated by Bernard Koch, C.M., in 1996 [Archives CM]). "Resignation of the Abbey of Saint-Léonard-de-Chaume in favor of St. Vincent," Monday, May 17, 1610 (S.V. 13:8–13).

15. "Assumption of the abbey of Saint-Léonard-de-Chaume by St. Vincent," Saturday, October 16, 1610 (Archives CM).

16. "Granting of power of attorney by St. Vincent to Pierre Gaigneur for the affairs of the abbey of Saint-Léonard-de-Chaume," Thursday, October 18, 1610 (Archives CM).

17. Pierre de Bérulle (1575–1629). He was son of a counselor in the parlement of Paris and of Louise Séguier, of the family of the chancellor. After serious studies in law and theology, he was ordained in 1599. He played an important role in the Church as founder of the Congregation of the Oratory and in politics through the missions entrusted to him by the king. He opposed Richelieu in foreign policy. He was created cardinal in 1627.

18. Jacques Davy du Perron (1556–1618). Son of a Protestant minister, he became an ordained priest after recantation and was named bishop of Évreux in 1591. In Rome, in 1594, he obtained absolution for Henry IV. Created cardinal and archbishop of Sens in 1606, he was an eloquent orator and a brilliant poet.

19. Madame Acarie (1566–1618). Daughter of a master of the accounts, Nicolas Avrilot, she married Pierre Acarie under family pressure, and had six children. Early on, she chose the spiritual path under the direction of Benoît de Canfield. The "beautiful Acarie," simultaneously a mystic and full of practical good sense, was at the center of a circle of clergy and laity. Her influence in church reform was well known. When she was widowed, she entered the Carmelite convent she had helped to establish in Paris and where three of her daughters had already taken the veil.

20. Conversation in October 1643 (S.V. 11:128).

21. André Duval (1564–1638). Doctor of theology of the Sorbonne, he was a counselor to Vincent de Paul after the death of Bérulle.

22. Pierre Coton (1564–1626). Educated by the Jesuits, he entered that order and became the confessor of Henry IV, who held him in high esteem. He obtained from the king permission for the Society of Jesus to return to France. Conciliatory in spirit, he entered into dialogue with the Protestants. He was also the spiritual adviser of the young Louis XIII.

23. "Account of a temptation against faith" (Abelly 3:116–118 and S.V. 11:32–34).

24. Cf. S.V. 12:256 and 13:29.

25. All items concerning trials and sentences handed down by the court of La Rochelle from February to December 1611 come from the archives of the Department of Charente-Maritime. They were graciously made available to Bernard Koch, C.M., in February 1997 by Mr. Pascal Even, director of the departmental archives. They now have a place in the Archives of the Congregation of the Mission. The Cistercian Order, which grew considerably since its foundation in the eleventh century, consisted of four families, the "four daughters of Cîteaux," whose principal abbeys were La Ferté, Clairvaux, Pontigny, and Morimond. In the trial of March 17, 1611, it was a question of whether Saint-Léonard-de-Chaume was a dependency of Pontigny or Morimond.

26. When an abbey was commendatory, its revenues were normally divided as follows: one third to the commendatory abbot, one third for the prior and his community, and one third for the general expenses of the domain. In the case of Saint-Léonard, it is known that Vincent agreed to pay the former abbot, Hurault de l'Hôpital, 1,200 livres a year, that he would be obliged to give the same amount to the prior, André de la Serre, from an overall income of 3,600 livres (total of the lease agreement signed by Doziet and deeded to Vincent). Other aspects of the case are not known nor do we know whether Vincent had made other commitments with regard to this abbey. One witness remains to the financial difficulties with which Vincent was struggling: an admission of debt, con-

tracted on December 7, 1612 with Jacques Gasteaud, doctor of theology, living at La Rochelle, for a sum of 320 tournois livres (S.V. 13:19).

27. "St. Vincent pursued by Monseigneur Paul Hurault de l'Hôpital," Saturday, May 28, 1611 (*Annals CM,* vol. 106–107 [1941–1942]: 262–263).

28. This sum was due to be paid by the king to pay a ship-owner for the loss of a ship of 8,400 cubic meters, home port Biarritz, which was scuttled in a battle against Spain. After complicated proceedings, this sum came into the hands of Jean de la Tanne, who because of his official functions could not appear to be the donor (S.V. 13:14).

29. H. de Brémond, *Histoire littéraire du sentiment religieux en France* (Literary History of Religious Sentiment in France)(Paris: Bloud et Gay, 1929), vol. 3, 159.

30. Deed of possession of the parish of Clichy, May 1612 (S.V. 13:17).

31. This territory corresponds approximately to the seventeenth and eighteenth arrondissements and half of the eighth in today's Paris.

32. Conference presented to missionaries, September 26, 1659 (S.V. 12:339).

33. Alexandre Hennequin, lord of Clichy-la-Garenne, was born in 1583. His father was killed in the attempt on the life of Henry III in 1589 and he was raised by his uncle and tutor, Michel de Marillac, counselor in the parlement of Paris. The title of lord of Clichy originates with an Olivier Allegret, advocate general to the parlement of Paris, one of whose daughters married Louis Hennequin, grandfather of Alexandre. Another daughter married Guillaume de Marillac, father of Michel de Marillac. The sister of the latter, Marie de Marillac, married a Nicolas Hennequin, one of whose sons, Monsieur de Vincy, and one of whose daughters, Mademoiselle du Fay, would play a role in the life of Vincent de Paul.

34. Conference presented to the Daughters of Charity, July 27, 1653 (S.V. 9:646).

Notes to Chapter 6

1. Abelly 1: chapter 7, 27. No document gives the exact date of Vincent's appointment by the Gondis. In the official documents dating from this period, he did not use the title of tutor; he simply gave his address, corresponding to that of the Hôtel Gondi (rue des Petits Champs and then rue Pavée).

2. There is no document marking the end of his responsibility as chaplain and counselor to Queen Marguerite of Valois. From 1612 onward, he no longer used this title in documents, replacing it with abbot of Saint-Léonard-de-Chaume. It is probable that when he entered the Gondi household he was no longer attached to the household of Queen Marguerite of Valois.

3. Cardinal Pierre de Gondi acquired the county of Joigny in 1603, upon the death of the countess Gabrielle de Laval. He offered it to his nephew Philippe-Emmanuel de Gondi as a wedding gift on June 11, 1604, while retaining

the usufruct for himself. He lived at Joigny until his death in 1616, and this is where Vincent must have met him when Philippe-Emmanuel's family stayed at Joigny. The cardinal probably told him tales of his missions to Pope Clement VIII to negotiate the reconciliation of Henry IV and the scruples which the pope suffered on this account. Vincent often used these scruples, and the manner in which Clement was delivered from them, as an example (S.V. 5:318; 12:347; 13:336).

4. Cardinal de Retz, *Mémoires* (Paris: Bibliothèque de la Pléiade, 1984), 129.

5. Ibid., 159.

6. Abelly 3:177–178.

7. S.V. 11:25–28.

8. Gamaches is a village of the region of Vexin in Normandy, about four kilometers from the castle of Étrepagny and twelve kilometers from Écouis. Philippe-Emmanuel de Gondi was baron of Écouis. Vincent probably did not take possession of the parish, but was satisfied to keep the title and the revenue for a while. The document concerning "the appointment of Monsieur Vincent as dean of Gamaches" on Friday, February 28, 1614, has been translated and analyzed by Bernard Koch (Archives CM). It was published in *Mission et Charité* no. 8 (October 1962): 495.

9. In the historical notarial archives there is found under the date of February 1, 1614, a declaration made by "Messire Vincent Depaul, priest, abbot of Saint-Léonard, living in the house of the General of the Galleys . . . that of the sum of 1,800 livres, taken and borrowed from demoiselle Anne le Prestre, wife of the nobleman François Lhuillier, lord of Interville, by Philippe-Emmanuel de Gondi . . . the sum of 1,500 livres was given to him in the form of a loan to settle his urgent business, by the aforementioned lords and lady." No details are given of what the urgent business was that Vincent had to settle. It might have been related to his legal claims on the abbey of Saint-Léonard. This loan was transformed into a gift on April 1, 1620. It should be noted that the lenders, Anne le Prestre and François Lhuillier, had a daughter, Hélène-Angélique, who in 1620 was received into the Convent of the Visitation and became its superior, and a second daughter, Marie, wife of Claude-Marcel de Villeneuve, who was closely connected to Louise de Marillac and Madame de Lamoignon. When she was widowed, Marie founded the Daughters of the Cross, around 1640. In this way was woven the network of relations which supported Vincent's work, both spiritual and financial. (Document translated and analyzed by Bernard Koch, Archives CM).

10. Sermon of St. Vincent on the catechism (S.V. 13:25). Judging from the context of this sermon, it must have been preached in 1616, after the death of Cardinal Pierre de Gondi, when Philippe-Emmanuel took on responsibility for the county of Joigny.

11. The collator is the individual who has the right to confer the benefice. Philippe-Emmanuel de Gondi enjoyed this privilege by right of being the baron de Plessis-Écouis. In this way, he was able to transfer these responsibilities to "Monsieur Vincent, tutor to Messieurs his children" (S.V. 13:19–24).

12. Abbé Jacques Leviste, "Le château du Fay et la seigneurie de Villecien depuis le XVIᵉ siècle" (The Château du Fay and the Domain of Villecien since the sixteenth century), *Etudes Villeneuviennes*, nos. 6 and 7.

13. Letter from Vincent de Paul to Edme Meaujean, vicar general of Sens, June 21, 1616 (S.V. 1:20).

14. Letter from Vincent de Paul to Jacques Tholard, C.M., August 22, 1640 (S.V. 2:107). The monastery of Valprofonde was located near the village of Béon, a scant eight kilometers southwest of Joigny. Nothing is left of it today but a farm building.

15. "Resignation by St. Vincent of the abbey of Saint-Léonard-de-Chaume," October 29, 1616 (S.V. 13:37–39).

Notes to Chapter 7

1. Henri de Bourbon, prince de Condé (1588–1646). In 1609, he married Charlotte de Montmorency, beloved of Henry IV. He is the father of Louis de Bourbon, the Grand Condé.

2. Charles d'Albert, duke of Luynes (1578–1621). This modest gentleman, who gained the confidence and friendship of the king, was showered with favors. After he received a portion of Concini's estate, he married Marie de Rohan and received the title of duke de Luynes. In 1621, he was raised to the rank of constable. Shortly thereafter, during the siege of Saint-Jean-d'Angély, he was carried off by a fever.

3. Folleville is sixteen kilometers west of Montdidier and four kilometers north of Breteuil. Gannes is twelve kilometers south of Folleville.

4. "Talk on the Mission given at Folleville in 1617" (S.V. 11:4–5). Recalling this sermon at Folleville, Vincent emphasized the fact that January 25 is the feast day of the Conversion of Saint Paul, and he compared this celebration and the first sermon of the Mission, adding that this was something that God had not brought about on this very day without a plan.

5. S.V. 13:25–37.

6. The archbishop of Lyon wrote to Monsieur de Bérulle that after having installed a house of Carmelite nuns at Châtillon, he wanted to implant the Congregation of the Oratory in the same town, hoping to transform it into a center from which Catholic ideas would radiate throughout the region. Father de Bourgoing had just preached a very successful mission there and asked whether he could take on responsibility for the parish of Châtillon, whose

titular pastor was about to withdraw (letter from Monseigneur Denis de Marquemont to Monsieur de Bérulle, October 18, 1616, Archives of the Department of the Rhône, copy in Archives CM). "Instrument of Accession to the Cure of Châtillon-les-Dombes" (S.V. 1:354).

7. Letter from Vincent de Paul to Robert de Sergis, C.M., September, 29 1636 (S.V. 1:354).

8. After a long and bloody conflict, Charles-Emmanuel of Savoy was obliged to cede to the king of France, Henry IV, a large portion of his territory (Gex, Valroney, le Bugey, and the Bresse) in the treaty of Lyon in 1602.

9. François de Bonne, duke of Lesdiguières (1543–1626). He was chief of the Huguenot resistance in the Dauphiné, then allied himself with Henry IV, who named him marshal of France in 1609. He abjured Protestantism in 1622 and Louis XIII named him constable.

10. "Instrument of Relinquishment of the Cure of Châtillon by Jean Lourdelot," April 19, 1617 (S.V. 13:40).

11. "Instrument of Nomination of Vincent Depaul to the Cure of Châtillon," July 29, 1617 (S.V. 13:41–43).

12. "Instrument of Accession to the Cure of Châtillon-les-Dombes," August 1, 1617 (S.V. 13:43, 44).

13. At the beatification process of Vincent de Paul, a report was made in 1665 by a priest, Charles Demia, doctor of the University of Paris. With an obviously hagiographic purpose, he painted the condition of the parish when Vincent arrived at Châtillon as black as possible. The testimony that he gathered locally, from what he called the oldest inhabitants of the town, should also be taken with caution. Most biographies of Vincent were based on Father Demia's report. The scenario of the film in which Pierre Fresnay embodied Monsieur Vincent in masterful fashion is also inspired by this document. The recent discovery of the letter of Monseigneur de Marquemont makes it possible to topple this legend. See the report of Charles Demia on the time Saint Vincent spent as pastor of Châtillon-les-Dombes (S.V. 13:45–54).

14. "Minutes of the Pastoral Visit of Monseigneur Denis de Marquemont, bishop of Lyon to the parish of Châtillon-les-Dombes," 1614. The original of this document is held in the Archives of the Department of the Rhône. The same is true of the document concerning construction of two new chapels in the church of Saint-Martin (documents transcribed by Bernard Koch, C.M., Archives CM).

15. The authenticating signature of Louis Girard is to be seen on the first certificate of a baptism performed by Vincent de Paul, August 16, 1617 (Archives CM).

16. Of the forty or more baptisms celebrated at the church at Châtillon during the five months of Vincent's stay there, only four or five are signed by him. The others were performed by his curates. Most were signed by his first curate, Louis Girard, who was to succeed Vincent as pastor. (The entries of

baptisms in the register were transcribed and evaluated by Bernard Koch, C.M., Archives CM).

17. Conference given by Vincent de Paul, May 16, 1659 (S.V. 12:231–233).

18. Conference given by Vincent de Paul, February 13, 1646 (S.V. 9:243).

19. "Women's Confraternity of Charity at Châtillon-les-Dombes," November and December 1617 (S.V. 13:423–429). The original document is in the hand of Louis Girard, and the handwriting of Vincent only appears at the end, just before the signature. In the same way, the opening of the notebook of accounts, December 15, is in the hand of Louis Girard, as Vincent was at that time on the verge of leaving.

20. Letter from Vincent de Paul to Philippe-Emmanuel de Gondi, August 1617 (S.V. 1:21).

21. Letter from Madame de Gondi to Vincent de Paul, September 1617 (S.V. 1:21).

22. Letter from Vincent de Paul to Madame de Gondi, September or October 1617 (S.V. 1:23).

23. Letter from Philippe-Emmanuel de Gondi to Vincent de Paul, October 15, 1617 (S.V. 1:23).

Notes to Chapter 8

1. "Women's Charité of Châtillon-les-Dombes," November and December 1617 (S.V. 13:423–439).

2. Villecien is in the valley of the Yon, downstream from Joigny; Paroy-sur-Tholon is four kilometers south of Joigny.

3. "Women's Charité of Joigny," September 1618 (S.V. 13:439–446).

4. "Women's Charité of Montmirail," October 1, 1618 (S.V. 13:461–475). Madame de Gondi was both countess of Joigny and baroness of Montmirail.

5. Vincent was following the practice of his times in not confiding the control of finances directly to the Ladies of Charity, but as he would often state later, his personal conviction was not in agreement. In his opinion, women were perfectly capable of managing and administering finances (S.V. 1:78, 79; S.V. 4:71).

6. Pierre de Bérulle spoke of himself as a man of action, leading the Oratory with a firm hand and organizing, before Vincent, numerous missions throughout the kingdom. Many delicate diplomatic missions were entrusted to him, but in politics he opposed Richelieu when the latter allied himself with Protestant states to fight against Spain. At the same time, he developed a doctrine inspired by Augustinian thought and the school of Theresa of Avila, Flemish, and Italian mystics. He expounded this doctrine in a work published in 1622: *Discours sur l'état et les grandeurs de Jésus* (Discourse on the nature and the greatness of Jesus).

7. Francis de Sales (1567–1622). Ordained priest in 1593, he was made bishop of Geneva in 1602, the year of his first stay in Paris, where he had come to negotiate the religious status of Bugey, a town ceded by Savoy to France. He preached that Lent at the Louvre. In 1610, at Annecy, he founded the Order of the Visitation with Jeanne de Chantal. He died in 1622, was canonized in 1665, and was proclaimed a doctor of the Church in 1877.

8. "Deposition of Vincent de Paul at the beatification process of Francis de Sales," April 17, 1628 (S.V. 13:66–84).

9. Letter from Vincent de Paul to Jean Martin, C.M., November 26, 1655 (S.V. 5:471).

10. Jeanne-Françoise Frémyot (1572–1641). Daughter of the president of the parlement of Burgundy, in 1592 she married the baron de Chantal, who left her a widow with six children in 1601. In 1610, under the direction of Francis de Sales, she founded the first house of the Visitation at Annecy. By the time of her death, on December 13, 1641, the congregation had eighty-seven convents. She was canonized in 1787.

11. Concerning the original intentions of Francis de Sales, see his letters written on May 24, 1610, to Father Nicolas Polliens, S.J.: "As for the sisters, they will go out to serve the sick after the year of their novitiate" and on April 3, 1611, to the abbot of l'Abondance: "After their profession, they will go to serve the sick, with great humility, so God will" (*Oeuvres de St. François de Sales* [Works of St. Francis de Sales], Book 14 *Letters,* vol. 4 [Librairie catholique Emmanuel Vitte, 1906]). See also the 1641 study by J. P. Camus, reporting a conversation with Francis de Sales: "I only intended to establish one house at Annecy, where there was a simple congregation of widows and girls, without vows or enclosure, whose work it was to keep themselves free to visit and comfort the poor sick" (*Oeuvres complètes de St. François de Sales,* ed. J. P. Migne [1861], vol. 2, pp. 360–362).

12. Charles de la Saussaye (1525–1621). From an old noble family, doctor of theology, canon of Orléans, he became pastor of Saint-Jacques in 1617. He made the acquaintance of Francis de Sales at the Confraternity of St. Charles Borromeo.

13. "Letter of accreditation of the royal chaplain," February 8, 1619 (S.V. 13:55).

14. Later, in 1632, Vincent would receive from the king and the aldermen an order that galley slaves who were ill would be transported to a square tower, part of the ancient wall of the capital city between the gate of Saint-Bernard and the Seine, where they would be cared for under more humane conditions.

15. The hospital for the galley slaves at Marseilles was not completed until 1646, when it came into being thanks to the persistent work of Gaspard de Simiane, friend of the bishop of that city. Vincent would support this work at court and obtain its funding by the duchess d'Aiguillon. The king made a donation of the land, located within the walls of the arsenal of the

galleys. By letters patent of July 1646, the king undertook to support the up-keep of the hospital to the amount of 9,000 livres (cf. AN A2 II f 277–286 and B6 77f 231–253).

16. S.V. 13:475–490.

17. Abelly 1:54–57, and S.V. 11:34–37.

18. "Monsieur Vincent is attached to the Order of Friars Minim," Friday, February 26, 1621 (document in Archives CM and in Collet 1:100). An order founded by the hermit Francesco, born around 1416 near Paola in Calabria, and died in 1507 in the hermitage of Plessis-les-Tours. This order had a very rigorous rule which added to the usual three vows a fourth one of perpetual fasting. King Louis XI, when he was ill, called the hermit Francesco to come to him because he had a reputation for saintliness. The king hoped that the hermit would bring him healing. He was canonized in 1519 under the name Francesco di Paola. We do not know what services Vincent rendered to the Minims, but probably he obtained support which made their foundation of houses in France easier.

19. "Mixed Charité of Joigny," May 1621 (S.V. 13:446–461).

20. Letter from Vincent de Paul to Louise de Marillac, July 21, 1635 (S.V. 13:833).

21. Record of the Charité of Mâcon, twelve documents, twenty-three pages (Archives CM). Record containing extracts of the registers of the city hall of Mâcon for the sessions of September 16 and 17 and of the register of chapter deliberations of September 17, 1621. See also Abelly 1:61–63; Collet 1:107–108; and S.V. 13:504–510.

22. The viscounty of Béarn was not returned to the Crown until 1594, in the statute of autonomous principality by Henry IV. According to the chroniclers, Henry sought to satisfy the spirit of independence of the Béarnais people by proclaiming to them that he was re-uniting France to the Béarn! But the edict was not published until 1620, in the reign of Louis XIII.

23. The date of this mission to Bordeaux is disputed. Some date it to the year 1622, others to March 1624. This is the position of Joseph Guichard (study in Archives CM), but according to this hypothesis, it is difficult to place Vincent's journey to Pouy. Coste has chosen an intermediate date, 1623. Some biographers indicate this date for Vincent's edifying story. Moved by the fate of a galley slave, he asked to take his place on the rowers' bench. This rather unlikely story has been the theme of many paintings.

24. S.V. 12:219. Tradition has it that during this stay, Vincent went with his family to make a pilgrimage to Buglose, four kilometers from Pouy, where a statue of the Virgin had recently been found. A chapel had been built on the spot and consecrated in 1622 by Bishop J. J. Dusault.

25. The help given to his family was revealed later (cf. S.V. 13:61–63).

26. "Mandate for Accession to the Priory of Saint-Nicolas-de-Grosse-Sauve," February 7, 1624 (S.V. 13:56) The priory was located about sixteen kilometers southeast of Langres, in the commune of Loges. Parties to the

suit were the chapter of Saint-Mamès and the Oratory. Vincent was not directly involved.

Notes to Chapter 9

1. Letter from Vincent de Paul to Bernard Codoing, C.M., April 1, 1642 (S.V. 2:247).

2. The Collège des Bons-Enfants was not a teaching establishment but an institution which provided room and board for an annual fee of 350 livres. In 1624, it housed only seven or eight students, two of whom held scholarships from a foundation created by a former rector of the University of Paris, Jean Pluyette.

3. His university diplomas were found in Vincent's room after his death. They disappeared during the sack of Saint-Lazare on July 13, 1789 (S.V. 13:60, n. 1). The document naming Vincent de Paul "principal of the Collège des Bons-Enfants" Friday, March 1, 1624, was also lost under the same circumstances (Collet 1:113).

4. "Charter of Foundation of the Congregation of the Mission," April 17, 1625 (S.V. 13:197–202).

5. Certain details of the charter were dictated by the ideas of Madame de Gondi. They limited the freedom of action of the congregation's superior. After the death of his wife, Philippe-Emmanuel de Gondi established a "modification of the charter of foundation of the Mission" (Saturday, April 17, 1627), as he was entering the Congregation of the Oratory. By this document, he freed "Master Vincent de Paul . . . in whom he has complete and entire confidence" from all the relevant articles (document found in the National Archives, central records by Monsieur Jean-Charles Niclas, Chartist, director of the National Library at Sablé).

6. At the death of Pierre de Bérulle in 1629, Father de Gondi was proposed as the new superior of the Oratory, but this was opposed by Cardinal de Richelieu. Later, at the time of the Fronde, Mazarin exiled Father de Gondi to his estate at Villepreux because of the actions of his son, Cardinal de Retz. Father de Gondi ended his days at Joigny, where he died in 1662.

7. Abelly 1:73

8. Letter from Vincent de Paul to Nicolas de Bailleuil, July 25, 1625 (S.V. 1:24).

9. Conference of May 17, 1658 (S.V. 12:8).

10. "Letters of Association of the First Missionaries," September 4, 1626 (S.V. 13:203). The four first missionaries, who were signatories to this document, were: Vincent de Paul, priest and principal of the Collège des Bons-Enfants; François de Coudray, priest of the diocese of Amiens; Antoine Portail, priest of the diocese of Arles; Jean de la Salle, priest of the diocese of Amiens.

11. "Donation of Vincent de Paul to his relatives," September 4, 1626 (S.V. 13:61).

12. A receipt for 400 livres, corresponding to the arrears of four years of room and board payments which were to be paid by "Monsieur Jean Souillard, presently pastor of Clichy-la-Garenne," to Vincent de Paul, is dated July 1630 (S.V. 13:85).

13. Letters patent by which the king approved the Congregation of the Mission, May 1627 (S.V. 13:206–208).

14. Letter from King Louis XIII to Pope Urban VIII, June 24, 1628 (S.V. 13:219) and letter from King Louis XIII to Monsieur de Béthune, June 24, 1628 (S.V. 13:220).

15. "Petition addressed to Pope Urban VIII," June 1628 (S.V. 1:42–51). The document was signed by Vincent de Paul and his first eight companions in the Mission. Among them was Louis Callon, doctor of the Sorbonne, who soon returned to his parish of Aumale in Normandy. In 1629 he made a donation of 4,000 livres so that two priests of the Mission could come to "preach, catechize, and hear the general confessions of the poor people of the diocese of Rouen, and especially in the deanery of Aumale, place of his birth" (V.E. Veuclin, *Saint Vincent de Paul en Normandie* [Vincent de Paul in Normandy] [1890]).

16. "Report presented to the Congregation for the Propagation of the Faith on the petition of Saint Vincent, June 1628," August 22, 1628 (S.V. 13:222–224). "Decision on the petition . . . of St. Vincent in June 1628" (S.V. 13:225).

17. Letter from Cardinal de Bérulle, November 1628 (Dagens, *Correspondance du cardinal de Bérulle,* vol. III, 434–345, cited in Coste 1:185). This seems to have been the only intervention by Bérulle against Vincent's project. From the beginning of 1629 on, the cardinal turned against the ambassador of France, who had not supported the candidacy of an Oratorian to be pastor of Saint Louis des Français at Rome.

18. "Opposition of the Priests of Paris to Approval of the Congregation of the Mission," December 4, 1630 (S.V. 13:227–232).

19. Letter from Vincent de Paul to François de Coudray, C.M., 1631 (S.V. 1:115).

20. See Luigi Mezzadri and José-Maria Roman, *Histoire de la Congregation de la Mission* (Paris: Desclée de Brouwer, 1994), 1:40, 61.

21. Adrien Bourdoise (1584–1655). Ordained priest in 1613 after coming under the influence of Pierre de Bérulle, he became pastor of Saint-Nicolas-du-Chardonnet. There he organized a community of priests and then a seminary which was officially recognized in 1644, financed by the members of the Company of the Blessed Sacrament. Vincent de Paul adopted some of his methods when he began creating his own seminaries.

22. Augustin Potier (?–1650). He was son of Nicolas Potier, lord of Blancmesnil, who was named chancellor by Maria de Medici. Bishop of Beauvais in

1616, he dedicated himself to evangelizing his diocese. He was Grand Almoner to Anne of Austria and aspired to political influence during her regency. He was pushed aside by Mazarin and returned to govern his diocese.

23. Letter from Vincent de Paul to François du Coudray, C.M., September 15, 1628 (S.V. 1:66, 67).

24. Letter from Vincent de Paul to François du Coudray, C.M., September 12, 1631 (S.V. 1:122).

25. Louise de Marillac (1591–1660). Daughter of Louis de Marillac, she married in 1631 Antoine Le Gras, secretary attaché in the household of Maria de Medici. As wife of a simple esquire, she was called Mademoiselle Le Gras. Widowed in 1625, she raised her only son with difficulty. Later, she hoped that he would become a priest but he preferred to marry. She was second in command to Vincent de Paul in all his works and particularly the Daughters of Charity. She died a few months before Vincent, and was canonized in March 1934.

26. Jean-Pierre Camus, bishop of Belley, was the nephew of the second wife of Louis de Marillac, father of Louise.

27. In the *Ecrits spirituels* (Spiritual Writings) of Louise de Marillac, we find this passage: "I was once more assured that I was to remain tranquil and rest upon my spiritual director, the one whom God had chosen for me. I felt dislike for him but nevertheless I obeyed and it did not seem right to change yet" (Archives, mother house of the Daughters of Charity).

28. Letter from Vincent de Paul to Louise de Marillac, May 6, 1629 (S.V. 1:73).

29. Letter from Vincent de Paul to Louise de Marillac, September 15, 1631 (S.V. 1:126).

30. Armand-Jean du Plessis, cardinal de Richelieu (1585–1642). After his years of study at the Collège de Navarre and the Académie Pluvinel, he studied theology. Consecrated bishop in Rome in 1606, he occupied the see of Luçon. He received the cardinal's hat in 1622. From 1626 until his death, he was the right hand of King Louis XIII. Having consolidated his power on the Day of the Dupes in 1630, he determined to build a new city near his family chateau of Richelieu, since his domain had been raised to the status of a peerage duchy by the king. At his request, a house of the Mission was founded in the city of Richelieu in 1638.

31. The Marillacs, an old family originating in the Auvergne, occupied important positions from the fifteenth century on. A Guillaume de Marillac, Comptroller General, married twice. With his first wife, Renée Allégret, he had eight children. One of them, Louis, lord de Ferrières, was the father of Louise de Marillac and another, Michel, became Keeper of the Seals. With his second wife, Geneviève de Bois-Levêque, he had four children. One of them, another Louis, became a marshal of France.

Michel de Marillac (1563–1632). Counselor in the parlement of Paris, superintendent of finances in 1624 and Keeper of the Seals, he was considered the head of the Party of the Devout. He opposed Richelieu, who managed to have him disgraced and exiled.

Louis de Marillac, count of Beaumont (1573–1632). At the end of a brilliant career, he received, in 1629, the baton of a marshal and command of the Army of Italy. Implicated in the plots against Richelieu, he was condemned and executed on May 10, 1632.

32. The duchy of Mantua belonged to the Gonzague family. When Duke Vincent de Gonzague died without an heir in December 1627, the duchy was to revert to his closest relative, Charles de Gonzague, duke of Nevers. But the Spanish did not want a Frenchman governing a strategically placed territory near the duchy of Milan, a Spanish possession. They supported the candidacy of Duke Guastella, an Italian, distant cousin of the Gonzagues. Charles de Gonzague went to take possession of his duchy, which also included Montferrat. He was attacked by the Spanish, which brought about the intervention wished for by Richelieu.

33. Letter from Vincent de Paul to Louise de Marillac, May 1632 (S.V. 1:155).

Notes to Chapter 10

1. Letter from Vincent de Paul to Nicolas Étienne, C.M., July 30, 1650 (S.V. 5:533).

2. Adrien Le Bon (1577–1651). Canon regular of Saint Augustine, after ceding his priory of Saint-Lazare to the Congregation of the Mission in return for support of himself and his canons, he made the Congregation heir to all his possessions. Vincent de Paul always remained deeply grateful to him for this, assisted him in his last moments, and wrote his funeral eulogy.

3. The seigniorial rights attached to this included the levying of duties and the collection of certain taxes such as the tax on the Fair of Saint-Laurent which was held near Saint-Lazare, and the exercise of high, middle, and low justice. This explains the presence of a prison within the walls of the priory.

4. The enclosure of Saint-Lazare extended over an area which today is bounded by the rue Faubourg-Poissonière, rue Faubourg-Saint-Denis, Boulevard de la Chapelle, and the rue de Paradis. This land is largely occupied today by the Gare du Nord and the Hôpital de Lariboisière. After the Revolution, old buildings had been converted into a women's prison which was torn down between 1935 and 1940. Some apartment houses, built in the eighteenth century by the Lazarists as income properties, survive along the rue Faubourg-Saint-Denis, bearing a large monogram S.V. on their facades.

5. Charles Faure (1594–1644). He was charged with applying the reform to the monastery of Sainte-Geneviève in Paris. He was so successful that Cardinal de la Rochefoucauld named him to head the Congregation of France, in

which all the houses of canons regular of all the provinces in the kingdom were united. Vincent de Paul later noted that he had little credit with Father Faure (S.V. 1:137).

6. Letter from Vincent de Paul to Guillaume de Lestocq, 1631(S.V. 1:137).

7. "Act of Union between the Priory of Saint-Lazare and the Congregation of the Mission," January 8, 1632. "Approval by the archbishop of Paris of the unification of Saint-Lazare and the Mission," January 8, 1632 (S.V. 13:234–257).

8. Letter from Vincent de Paul to N., 1632 (S.V. 1:151).

9. Jean Orcibal, "Jean Duvergier de Hauranne, abbé de Saint-Cyran, et son temps" (Jean Duvergier de Hauranne, abbot of Saint-Cyran, and his times), Bibliothèque de la revue d'histoire ecclésiastique, no. 26, *Les Origines du Jansénisme,* vol. 2 (1947).

10. Letter from Vincent de Paul to Étienne Blatiron, C.M., September 1650 (S.V. 4:70).

11. S.V. 13:331, n. 2.

12. Letter from Vincent de Paul to N., 1633 (S.V. 1:180).

13. Wife of President de Herse, née Charlotte de Ligny, was since 1634, widow of Michel de Vialard, lord de Herse, Master of Petitions at the palace. Their son, Félix de Vialard de Herse was consecrated bishop of Châlons in 1642.

14. Nicolas Pavillon (1597–1677). Ordained priest in 1626, he took part in the missions before being named bishop of Alet in 1637. He was a zealous, reform-minded bishop who refused to sign the formulary condemning the Jansenist theses.

François-Étienne de Caulet (1610–1680). Son of a hooded magistrate in the parlement of Toulouse, educated by Jesuits, he was named bishop of Pamiers in 1644. Very strict in the area of morality, he, like Pavillon, refused to sign the formulary against the Jansenists.

15. The title "Tuesday Conferences" was purposely chosen because of the etymology of "conference": *cum ferre,* to bring together. The conference is the bringing together of reflections on a given subject. These meetings were not the occasion of a passive audience listening to a prepared talk.

16. "Rule for Priests Participating in the Tuesday Conferences" (S.V. 13:128–132). The first article of the Rule defines the spirit of the conference: "to honor the life of Jesus Christ, his eternal priesthood, his Holy Family, and his love for the poor . . . to try to make one's life conform to His."

17. Letter from Vincent de Paul to Jean de Fonteneil, January 8, 1637 (S.V. 1:373). The letter refers to Antoine Godeau, named bishop of Grasse, François Fouquet, bishop of Bayonne, and Nicolas Pavillon, bishop of Alet.

18. Letter from Vincent de Paul to Louise de Marillac, around 1632 (S.V. 1:155).

19. Letter from Vincent de Paul to Louise de Marillac, June 1632 (S.V. 1:157, 159). Madame Goussault, née Geneviève Fayet, widow of Antoine Goussault,

lord de Souvigny, president of the Chamber of Accounts of Paris, devoted herself until her death in 1639 to all the programs founded by Vincent de Paul.

Mademoiselle Poulaillon, née Marie de Lumagne (1599–1657), widow of François Poulaillon (or Polallion), gentleman of the king's household, had chosen Vincent de Paul as her spiritual director, and she assisted Louise de Marillac. With the help of Vincent, she founded an order to care for delinquent girls, the Daughters of Providence.

20. "Conference on the virtues of Marguerite Naseau" (S.V. 9:77–79).

21. Letter from Vincent de Paul to Louise de Marillac, May 1, 1633 (S.V. 1:197). On the question of medicine and Vincent de Paul, see the long study of Bernard Koch, C.M., *Saint Vincent and the Sick,* December 1994 (Archives CM).

22. Letter from Vincent de Paul to Antoine Portail, C.M., November 28, 1632 (S.V. 1:175–178). We should note that for this important mission, the members of the Tuesday Conferences were more numerous than the members of the Congregation.

Notes to Chapter 11

1. François de la Rochefoucauld (1558–1645). Bishop of Clermont, ardent member of the League, he cast his lot with Henry IV who named him to the bishopric of Senlis. Raised to the cardinalate in 1607, he played a prominent role in the assembly of the clergy in 1614, which decided how the decrees of the Council of Trent would be applied. Grand Almoner of France in 1618, he presided over the king's council in 1622. At this time, he resigned the bishopric of Senlis to dedicate himself to the reform of the abbeys belonging to the orders of Saint Benedict, Saint Augustine, and Saint Bernard. When he was abbot of Sainte-Geneviève, he confided its reform to Father Charles Faure, and then extended this reform movement to houses of canons regular throughout the kingdom. Vincent de Paul was with him in his last hours, on February 14, 1645.

2. The guérinets, named after Father Guérin, were a group of mystics in Picardy who were considered to be dangerous illuminati. The king, following the advice of Richelieu and of his powerful confidential adviser, Father Joseph, asked Cardinal de la Rochefoucauld to have Monsieur Vincent defend their case in September 1630. Vincent, with the advice of the learned theologian, Duval, absolved the guérinets of all suspicion of heresy. He even became a protector of the Daughters of the Cross, founded by Father Guérin and Marie Lhuillier, sister of Hélène-Angélique, who became superior of the first monastery of the Visitation in Paris. The two women were daughters of the financier who had helped Vincent de Paul in 1614 (see chapter 6, note 10).

3. Jean-Louis de Rochechouart, count de Chandenier, was brought up in the household of Cardinal de la Rochefoucauld, his maternal uncle. Two of his sons, Claude and Louis, became disciples of Vincent de Paul.

Claude de Chandenier, pastor of Moutiers-Saint-Jean, of which he would make Vincent vicar general from 1650 to 1652, while he himself went for instruction to Nicolas Pavillon, bishop of Alet. He lived until 1670.

Louis de Chandenier, abbot of Tournus, faithful member of the Tuesday Conferences. As such, he took part in many missions. In 1658, he directed the mission at Metz, which was noteworthy. He died in 1660, as he was returning from a pilgrimage to Rome. Both brothers refused to be named bishop.

4. Marie-Madeleine de Vignerod, duchess d'Aiguillon (1604–1675). Married to the marquis de Combalet, she became a widow at the age of eighteen. At that time, she entered the Carmelite Order as a novice, but her uncle, Cardinal Richelieu, removed her from the convent with the authorization of Rome and placed her in the queen's household as a lady in waiting. In 1638, he raised the lands of the duchy of Aiguillon to the status of peerage and had them attributed to her. At the death of her uncle, she inherited a most significant fortune which she largely devoted to charitable works, all the while proving to be very severe with her creditors. She conducted long lawsuits with the princes de Condé who were contesting Richelieu's will.

5. Henri de Lévis, duke of Ventadour (1596–1680). His wife, Marie-Liesse de Luxembourg, being childless, entered the Carmel house at Avignon in 1629. After fighting against the Huguenots in Languedoc, he worked for the triumph of the Catholic cause by other means. Together with the help of a Capuchin friar, Philippe d'Angoumois, and a Jesuit, Father Suffren, he founded the Company of the Blessed Sacrament in 1630. In 1641, he received the order of sub-deacon and accepted the office of canon at Notre-Dame of Paris in 1650. At that moment, he resigned his title of duke and peer in favor of his younger brother. The Company of the Blessed Sacrament was dissolved in 1660 by Mazarin.

6. Cf. *Bulletin de littérature ecclésiastique,* no. 8 (October 1917), "Saint Vincent de Paul et la compagnie du Saint-Sacrement" (Saint Vincent de Paul and the Company of the Blessed Sacrament) edited by the Institut catholique de Toulouse.

7. On the territory of Gonesse, there were three different sources of revenue: farming on the lands belonging to the Mission, taxes levied on lands of the king at Gonesse and reserved for the use of the Mission, and the operation of four mills, whose rents were also allocated to the Mission. These two last resources, taxes and mills, were attributed to the priory of Saint-Lazare in accordance with royal patents dating from the twelfth century. They were both dedicated by Vincent de Paul to the work of the Daughters of Charity.

8. Charités publiques et financiers privés, Monsieur Vincent gestionnaire et saint" (Public charities and private financiers: Monsieur Vincent administrator and saint), doctoral dissertation of Monsieur René Wulfmann, defended March 8, 1950 (Archives CM).

9. Cf. "Une suppliqe inédite de Monsieur Vincent en faveur des domaines de Saint-Lazare: celui du domaine de Gonesse et celui de la prévôté de Paris" (An unpublished petition of Monsieur concerning lands of Saint-Lazare: the estate of Gonesse and lands of the provostship of Paris), study by Bernard Koch, C.M., August 1996 (Archives CM).

10. The priory of Saint-Lazare had disciplinary areas for prisoners of seigniorial justice. They were used to incarcerate unruly young people at the request of their families. They also came to be used for the incarceration of clerics who had broken the laws of the Church. In addition, Saint-Lazare received mentally disturbed individuals who were kept in spaces which had earlier been used for lepers. Vincent was very concerned with treating these people well. Their number was always limited.

11. Geneviève Bouquet (1590–1665). Daughter of a goldsmith of Paris, she had been placed early in life in the household of Queen Marguerite of Valois but left in 1613 to enter the convent of the Augustinians of the Hôtel-Dieu. She worked there for fifteen years before making her profession in 1629. She soon became novice mistress and then superior, playing an important role in the reform of her order. Cf. Alexis Chevalier, *L'Hôtel-Dieu de Paris et les soeurs augustines* (The Hôtel Dieu of Paris and the Augustinian Sisters) (Paris: H. Champion, 1901).

12. Letter from Vincent de Paul to François du Coudray, C.M., July 25, 1634 (S.V. 1:253).

13. At the death of Mademoiselle Poulaillon in 1657, Vincent arranged to allow the Daughters of Providence, numbering about eighty girls at that time, to continue their work.

14. S.V. 1:186, n. 4.

15. Letter from Vincent de Paul to François du Coudray, C.M., January 17, 1634 (S.V. 1:223, 224). The congregation of Christophe d'Authier de Sisgau (1609–1657) was approved by the pope in 1647. He was named bishop of Bethlehem in 1651.

16. Cf. draft for a talk to the Sisters of the Visitation (S.V. 13:144).

17. Talk given on November 13, 1654 (S.V. 12:167).

18. Letter of Vincent de Paul to Jeanne de Chantal, July 14, 1639 (S.V. 1:566). Their correspondence has largely been lost. We have only a few letters, fewer than a dozen from each of them. They met four times, when Jeanne de Chantal was visiting Paris (April 1619, January 1628, July 1635, October 1641).

19. Letter from Jeanne de Chantal to Vincent de Paul, December 1636 (S.V. 1:370).

20. Letter from Vincent de Paul to Jeanne de Chantal, August 26, 1640 (S.V. 2:99). It seems that Jeanne de Chantal reconsidered her intransigent position and that in her spiritual testament, she supported the idea of a visitor (or inspector) who would not be designated by the bishops but elected by the

monasteries. But this document, dated December 12, 1641, was supposedly partially censored after the death of Jeanne de Chantal by the sister charged with publishing it (*Revue d'histoire de la spiritualité* 48 [1972]: 453–475).

21. Letters from Vincent de Paul to Louise de Marillac, July 13, 1635 (S.V. 1:302) and in 1636 (S.V. 1:321).

22. This charitable foundation was endowed with 1,400 livres by André Le Bon, former superior of Saint-Lazare, who came from this area. Cf. Veuclin, *St. Vincent de Paul en Normandie.*

23. Noël Brulart de Sillery (1577–1640). Knight of Malta and commander of Troyes, he was the brother of Nicolas Brulart, chancellor of France. After having occupied important diplomatic posts, he entered the religious life under the direction of Vincent de Paul. Ordained in 1634, he settled near the first monastery of the Visitation. Very active within the Company of the Blessed Sacrament, he dedicated his enormous fortune to financing religious congregations, particularly the congregation of the Visitation, the priests of the Mission, and the monastery of the Madeleine.

24. Letter from Vincent de Paul to Antoine Portail, May 1, 1635 (S.V. 1:295).

25. Letter from Vincent de Paul to Antoine Portail, October 16, 1635 (S.V. 1:311).

26. Letter from Jean-Jacques Olier to Vincent de Paul, June 24, 1636 (S.V. 1:332). Jean-Jacques Olier (1608–1657.) Disciple of Vincent de Paul and Charles Condren of the Oratory, in 1641 at Vaugirard he formed a group of priests to conduct the seminary which he had founded. Named pastor of Saint-Sulpice, he transferred the seminary there, and it attracted an elite group of young men. His disciples spread throughout the provinces and even to Canada. Olier was a mystic in the stream of spirituality of Bérulle.

27. Even so, these missions sometimes aroused certain criticisms. Thus, at the end of the mission at Bordeaux, in October 1634, one read in a local newspaper: "The archbishop had the so-called Fathers of the Mission come from Paris and go around preaching, which was very fruitful. But this was only a straw fire, burning brightly but not lasting very long" (*Chronique Bordelaise,* cited in *Mission et Charité* no. 26–27, 282).

Notes to Chapter 12

1. Letter from Vincent de Paul to Antoine Portail, C.M., August 15, 1636, (S.V. 1:340).

2. Abelly 1:154.

3. Letter from Vincent de Paul to Robert de Sergis, C.M., September 1636 (S.V. 1:351).

4. Letter from Vincent de Paul to Louise de Marillac, around November 1636 (S.V. 1:367).

5. According to Abelly, Vincent de Paul used the discipline every day upon arising.

6. Letter from Vincent de Paul to Louise de Marillac, May 2, 1637 (S.V. 1:387).

7. This schedule was set on solar time, which is to say, two hours earlier than the time in use today.

8. "Talk given to the Ladies of Charity on the Foundling Hospital" (S.V. 13:798).

9. Letter from Vincent de Paul to Louise de Marillac, end of 1637 (S.V. 1:410). The procurator general at the time was Mathieu Molé, who was named Keeper of the Seals in 1651.

10. Letter from Vincent de Paul to Louise de Marillac, end of 1638 (S.V. 1:433).

11. The three bishoprics, Metz, Toul, and Verdun, had been annexed in 1552 by the king of France, Henry II. Their situation was only regularized officially in 1648 by the Treaty of Westphalia, when they were attached to the kingdom. As far as Rome was concerned, Toul remained a bishopric of Lorraine, connected to the archbishopric of Trèves. For this reason, resolution of the questions was complex, and the decisions of the Holy See were slow in coming.

12. Letter from Vincent de Paul to Lambert aux Couteaux, C.M., January 30, 1638 (S.V. 1:426).

13. Cf. *Histoire de la congrégation de la Mission,* 1:64. Vincent used the term "internal seminary" instead of novitiate so that the missionaries would be kept distinct from monks. The brothers coadjutor were laymen who took part in the missions. "Their duty is to help the priests in all their ministries" (Common Rules I, 2).

14. Letter from Vincent de Paul to Bernard Codoing, C.M., December 27, 1637 (S.V. 1:412).

15. When the company of the Daughters of Charity was officially recognized in 1645, it was able to buy these houses back from the Mission for a sum of 17,650 livres, thanks to gifts from various sources and a legacy of 9,000 livres from Madame Goussault, who died in 1639.

16. Letter from Vincent de Paul to Guillaume Delville, C.M., February 18, 1657 (S.V. 6:189).

17. Letter from Vincent de Paul to Louise de Marillac, not dated (S.V. 2:190).

18. Letter from Vincent de Paul to Lambert aux Couteaux, C.M., February 20, 1638 (S.V. 1:48). Vincent came back to this point twice (S.V. 1:457 and 463), fearing that some of his missionaries might enter into too much detail on the subject of the sixth commandment, Thou shalt not commit adultery (Exodus 20:14; Deuteronomy 20:5–17).

19. Letter from Vincent de Paul to Louise de Marillac, November 30, 1639 (S.V. 1:603). Vincent always took care to be precise and did not hesitate to

go into detail. He prescribed a somewhat tortuous itinerary for the sisters, which may be explained by the lower fares they could expect to pay on coach lines in which the Mission was a shareholder. The term "gray serge," at that time, designated anything which was neither black nor of a bright color; the fabric may well have been brown or a dull blue.

20. Letter from Vincent de Paul to Louise de Marillac, December 12, 1639 (S.V. 1:605).

21. Letter from Vincent de Paul to Louise de Marillac, December 31, 1639 (S.V. 1:611).

Notes to Chapter 13

1. Jean Martin, baron de Laubardemont, magistrate and counselor in the parlement of Bordeaux, was on many occasions the agent of Richelieu's orders. In 1633, he played a sad part in the affair of the Ursulines known as the Possessed of Loudon, by having their chaplain, Urbain Grandier, burned alive, and again in 1642, in the condemnation of Cinq-Mars.

2. Testimony of Martin de Barcos (1600–1678), nephew and collaborator of Saint-Cyran, whom he succeeded in 1643 as commendatory abbot. Living at Port-Royal, he was the spiritual director of Mother Angélique. He was actively engaged in all the quarrels involving Port-Royal and in the debate of the Jansenist theses.

3. Jean Duvergier de Hauranne, abbot of Saint-Cyran (1581–1643). After his ordination in 1618, he was named by the bishop of Poitiers, Chasteigner de la Roche-Posay, grand vicar and canon of the cathedral. He was awarded the benefice of the abbey of Saint-Cyran in Brenne. Installed in Paris in 1622, he joined with Pierre de Bérulle and Arnauld d'Andilly. He directed the formation of Antoine Arnauld (called the Grand Arnauld) and became the spiritual director of the nuns of Port-Royal. After the death of Pierre de Bérulle, he placed himself at the head of the Party of the Devout and opposed the politics of Richelieu.

4. Cornelius Jansen (Cornelius Jansenius) (1585–1638). Named bishop of Ypres in 1637, he died there the next year in an epidemic of the plague which struck the city.

5. Interrogation of the Abbot de Saint-Cyran, May 14–31, 1639 (S.V. 13:105).

6. See Brémond, *Histoire littéraire du sentiment religieux en France,* 4:38. Father Rapin (1621–1687) was a Jesuit, author of numerous literary works and devotional writings. In his day, he was the historian of Jansenism.

7. Ibid., 72.

8. Relations between Saint-Cyran and Richelieu became progressively cooler for reasons of both religious doctrine and political position. The ap-

pearance in Flanders in 1636 of a virulent pamphlet against French policy, *Mars Gallicus,* signed by Jansenius, a friend of Saint-Cyran, roused the cardinal's rage to the extent that he decided to break definitively with the head of the Party of the Devout.

9. Jacques Lescot (1593–1656). Professor of theology at the Sorbonne, canon of Notre-Dame, he was confessor of Richelieu before receiving the bishopric of Chartres in 1643, upon the death of the cardinal.

10. "Testimony of Saint Vincent regarding the Abbot de Saint-Cyran" (S.V. 13:86–93). Henri Brémond calls this document "a little masterpiece of charitable exegesis."

11. Letter from Vincent de Paul to Nicolas Marceille, C.M., June 10, 1638 (S.V. 1:482).

12. Letter from Vincent de Paul to Jean Dehorgny, C.M., June 1638 (S.V. 1:486).

13. Letter from Vincent de Paul to Denis de Cordes, 1638 (S.V. 1:490).

14. Letter from Vincent de Paul to Robert de Sergis, C.M., December 17, 1638 (S.V. 1:529).

15. Letter from Vincent de Paul to Bernard Codoing, C.M., August 29, 1638 (S.V. 1:501).

16. Letter from Vincent de Paul to Lambert aux Couteaux, C.M., November 1, 1638 (S.V. 1:519).

17. Letter from Vincent de Paul to Robert de Sergis, C.M., August 14, 1638 (S.V. 1:496).

18. Letter from Vincent de Paul to Robert de Sergis, C.M., December 17, 1638 (S.V. 1:528).

19. Letter from Vincent de Paul to Nicolas Durot, C.M., December 1638 (S.V. 1:608).

20. Letter from Vincent de Paul to Louis Lebreton, C.M., May 14, 1639 (S.V. 1:551).

21. Estimate made in Abelly 2: chapter 11, 388.

22. Letter from Vincent de Paul to Bernard Codoing, C.M., July 20, 1640 (S.V. 2:80).

23. Brother Mathieu Regnard wrote an account of his adventures, but the manuscript disappeared in the pillage of Saint-Lazare in 1789. But Abelly alludes to certain of his adventures: "Sometimes, passing through forests filled with thieves or demobilized soldiers, as soon as he heard them or saw them, he threw his purse, which he usually carried in a torn pilgrim's pouch in the manner of beggars, into a bush or into the mud, and then walked right up to them, like a man without fear. Sometimes they searched him and when they found nothing, they would let him go unharmed. When they were gone, he would return to recover the purse" (Abelly 2:390).

24. Letter from Vincent de Paul to Louis Lebreton, C.M., October 12, 1693 (S.V. 1:590–591).

25. Collet 1:290.

26. Letter from Vincent de Paul to François de Coudray, C.M., July 10, 1640 (S.V. 2:60). Anne-Mangot, lord de Villarceaux, was the administrator of the Three Bishoprics.

27. Letter from Vincent de Paul to Louis Lebreton, C.M., October 12, 1693 (S.V. 1:590–591).

28. Letter from Julien Guérin, C.M., to Vincent de Paul, early 1640 (S.V. 2:24).

29. Letter from Vincent de Paul to the duchess d'Aiguillon, April–May 1640 (S.V. 2:42)

30. Gaston de Renty (1611–1649). After serving in the army, he devoted himself entirely to the spiritual life under the direction of Father de Condren of the Oratory and to charitable works with the Company of the Blessed Sacrament.

31. See the letters of the magistrates of Metz (S.V. 2:131), of Pont-à-Mousson (S.V. 2:145), and of Lunéville (S.V. 2:257).

Notes to Chapter 14

1. Abelly 3:11 and S.V. 4:116.

2. The Rule was being composed during retreats; in 1632 and 1635, Vincent gives extracts from it in the form of advice (S.V. 11:100–104).

3. Letter from Vincent de Paul to N., around 1635 (S.V. 1:291).

4. Letter from Vincent de Paul to Louis Lebreton, C.M., February 28, 1640 (S.V. 2:28).

5. This was the case for the Carthusians at the time, who only made a vow of stability although they were a great religious order. They did not make the other three vows explicitly.

6. Cardinal de Richelieu had hoped to receive the titles of Perpetual Legate of the Holy See and Patriarch of the Gauls or of the West. Urban VIII had not been willing to satisfy this wish, and this resulted in their quarrel. (See Leopold Willaert, *Histoire de l'Eglise* (History of the Church), vol. 18, *La restauration catholique (1563–1648)* (the Catholic restoration) (Paris: Bloud et Gay, 1960).

7. Letter from Vincent de Paul to Louis Lebreton, C.M., November 14, 1640 (S.V. 2:137).

8. Minutes of the assembly held in October 1642 (S.V. 13:292).

9. Letter from Vincent de Paul to Bernard Codoing, C.M., December 7, 1641 (S.V. 2:207).

10. Letter from a bishop to Vincent de Paul, no date (S.V. 2:428).

11. When prelates requested seminaries for young men, they were asking for something different from the practice arising from the Council of Trent and applied in France at the end of the sixteenth century of seminaries which

received children from the age of twelve, keeping them until the age of twenty-four. This system was unsuccessful.

12. Adrien Bourdoise (1584–1655). An orphan, he first earned his living as a domestic servant. He became a disciple of Bérulle and was ordained in 1613. He formed a group of priests who took charge of the parish of Saint-Nicolas-du-Chardonnet, which became a showcase for Catholic reform.

Jean-Jacques Olier (1608–1657). Disciple of Condren and Vincent de Paul, he was installed at Vaugirard in 1641 and dedicated himself to working with a team of priests engaged in the direction of seminaries. Named pastor of Saint-Sulpice, he founded a seminary there and undertook the foundation of numerous centers in France and Canada.

François Bourgoing (1585–1662) yielded the parish of Clichy-la-Garenne to Vincent de Paul in 1612 in order to join the first team sent out by the Oratory. He succeeded Condren in 1641 as head of the Congregation of the Oratory.

Jean Eudes (1601–1680) entered the Oratory in 1623 and left it in 1643 to found the Congregation of Jesus and Mary, devoted to the direction of seminaries and the work of the missions.

13. Letter from Vincent de Paul to Bernard Codoing, C.M., September 15, 1641 (S.V. 2:188).

14. In 1645, Le Mans and Saint-Méen; in 1648, Marseilles, Tréguier, and Agen; in 1650, Périgueux; in 1651, Montauban; in 1653, Agde and Troyes; in 1658, Meaux; in 1659, Montpellier and Narbonne.

15. Letter from Vincent de Paul to a superior of a seminary, no date (S.V. 4:597).

16. A conversation about study, October 1643 (S.V. 11:128).

17. Marguerite de Gondi was the widow of the marquis de Maignelay. Very much devoted to the service of the poor, she counted neither her time nor her money. She supported various works, including the Convent of the Madeleine and the Daughters of Providence.

18. Letter from Vincent de Paul to Louise de Marillac, August 30, 1640 (S.V. 2:110). Anne de Neubourg, marquise de Vigean, was closely connected to the duchess d'Aiguillon. One of her sons, twenty years old, had just been killed at the siege of Arras. Her oldest daughter, Anne, married a grand-nephew of the cardinal and became duchess de Richelieu. Her youngest daughter, Marthe, entered the Carmelites in the rue Saint-Jacques in 1647, taking the name of Sister Marthe de Jésus.

19. This anecdote was confirmed by Sister Marthe de Jésus in a declaration signed in her own hand before her death in 1665. See Victor Cousin, *Madame de Longueville* (Paris, 1853), 465.

20. Jules Mazarin (Mazarini) (1602–1661). Of Italian origin, he was in Rome in the service of Cardinal Antonio Barberini, nephew of His Holiness. After having fulfilled the duties of vice-legate in Avignon (1634) and of nuncio

in France (1634–1636), he arrived in Paris in 1640, where he became the closest collaborator of Richelieu. He received the cardinal's hat in 1641.

Léon Bouthiller, count de Chavigny (1608–1652). Secretary of State and loyal collaborator of Richelieu, he was opposed to Mazarin. He fell into disgrace after the death of Richelieu.

The duke de Liancourt was one of the aristocrats who belonged to the Company of the Blessed Sacrament and who was active in numerous works. His wife, closely connected to Louise de Marillac, was a benefactress of charities.

21. Letter from Vincent de Paul to Bernard Codoing, C.M., February 9, 1639 (S.V. 2:223).

22. Letter from Vincent de Paul to Jeanne de Chantal, August 15, 1639 (S.V. 1:575).

23. Letter from Vincent de Paul to Lambert aux Couteaux, C.M., October 1, 1638 (S.V. 1:520).

24. Letter from Vincent de Paul to M. Perriquet, vicar general at Bayonne, March 31, 1641 (S.V. 2:171).

Notes to Chapter 15

1. Henri Coëffier d'Effiat, marquis of Cinq-Mars (1620–1642). Son of Marshal d'Effiat, he was brought to court by Richelieu as a captain of the guard and attached to the person of the king in an attempt to counteract the influence of a favorite, Mademoiselle de Hautefort. He rapidly became a favorite of the king, who named him grand equerry with the title Monsieur le Grand. Ambitious and giddy with the royal favor, he became entangled in a plot against his former protector, Richelieu, and signed a secret treaty in favor of Spain, aimed at eliminating the cardinal and replacing him with Gaston d'Orléans. He was unmasked, tried, and executed in September 1642.

2. Letter from Vincent de Paul to Bernard Codoing, C.M., April 17, 1643 (S.V. 2:387).

3. Conference for the Daughters of Charity, November 11, 1657 (S.V. 10:342).

4. Letter from Vincent de Paul to Bernard Codoing, C.M., May 15, 1643 (S.V. 2:393).

5. Letter from Vincent de Paul to Bernard Codoing, C.M., June 18, 1640 (S.V. 2:406).

6. See *Dictionnaire du Grand Siècle* (Paris: Fayard, 1990), especially the entry on the Council of Conscience by Raymond Darricau, p. 390.

7. The concordat signed at Bologna in 1516 by Pope Leo X and the king of France, Francis I, regularized the relations between the Church and the French state. All ongoing matters were to be ruled upon by judges in France, with recourse to the Holy See being reserved for exceptional cases. In particu-

lar, the king was authorized to designate the leaders of the Church in France and to award ecclesiastical benefices.

8. Letter from Vincent de Paul to Louise de Marillac, May 1643 (S.V. 2:384).

9. Conversation with the Daughters of Charity, June 14, 1643 (S.V. 9:120).

10. Letter from Vincent de Paul to Antoine Portail, C.M., October 14, 1644 (S.V. 2:483).

11. Letter from Michel Le Tellier to the count d'Harcourt, viceroy of Catalonia, July 8, 1645 (see *Annales CM,* no. 469 [1953]: 508).

12. Letter from Cardinal Mazarin to the count d'Harcourt, viceroy of Catalonia, July 19, 1645 (see *Annales CM,* no. 473 [1954]: 184).

13. Extracts from the journals of Mazarin (S.V. 13:136–138). No doubt this refers to Philippe-Emmanuel de Gondi who had entered the Oratory after he was widowed. It was intended to raise him to the cardinalate and to allow him to succeed Pierre de Bérulle in 1629, but the hostility of Richelieu doomed this plan to failure. Father de Gondi had even been exiled to Lyon in 1641. It is possible that Vincent intervened on behalf of his former master in order to put an end to his exile.

14. Coste 3:110. Mademoiselle Danse (Dans) was one of the young ladies of the queen's court. Later, she was connected to the plot against Mazarin and the queen (the Fronde), for which reason she was sent away by the queen.

15. "Father Vincent is not so powerless that he could not prevent the donation made to the son of Monsieur de la Rochefoucauld at the recommendation of His Eminence Cardinal Mazarin and request that it be given instead to Abbot Olier, pastor of Saint-Sulpice," letter from Gaudin to Servien, March 12, 1644 (Archives des Affaires Etrangères, Mémoires et Documents France, vol. 849, folio 116).

16. Letter from Vincent de Paul to Bernard Codoing, C.M., January 10, 1645 (S.V. 2:499).

17. Letter from Vincent de Paul to Guillaume Gallais, C.M., February 13, 1644 (S.V. 2:448).

18. Letter from Vincent de Paul to Charles de Montchal, archbishop of Toulouse, February 24, 1645 (S.V. 2:503).

19. Letter from Vincent de Paul to the count de Brienne, June 2, 1645 (S.V. 2:527). The Corpus Christi procession was becoming an unedifying carnival.

20. Letter from Vincent de Paul to Jean Dehorgny, C.M., July 5, 1645 (S.V. 2:531). If Vincent permitted himself to confide in this way, it is because he held Dehorgny in particular esteem and affection. Vincent assigned him to important positions such as director of the Collège des Bons-Enfants, assistant to the superior general, superior of the Mission's house in Rome, visitor of several houses of the Congregation of the Mission. Later he had to struggle with Dehorgny's Jansenist tendencies, but succeeded in bringing him back to the mainstream.

21. Bertrand Ducournau (1614–1677). Originally from the region of Chalosse, he was secretary to the deputy bailiff of Bayonne. He was received into the Congregation in July 1644 and after the death of Vincent, became the archivist of the Mission. From 1647, his assistant in the secretariat was Brother Louis Robineau.

22. Jean-Baptiste Amador de Vignerod (1632–1662) was the grandson of Françoise du Plessis, sister of Cardinal de Richelieu. She had married René de Vignerod and had two children: a daughter, widow of the lord de Combalet, who became the duchess d'Aiguillon, and a son, François de Vignerod, who had five children from an unhappy marriage. The duchess d'Aiguillon took charge of their education after requiring that their parents resign their parental rights. When Amador was twenty years old, in 1652, he resigned his abbeys in favor of his younger brother Emmanuel, who was then thirteen years old. Vincent de Paul was vicar general of these abbeys until his death. The abbey of Saint-Ouen alone had a dependency of eighty parishes and chapels, whose staffing was one of the chief responsibilities of the vicar general. The Archives of the Mission contains the nomination documents for many of these positions; see Alex Feron, *Saint Vincent de Paul, vicaire général des Richelieu Vignerod, abbés de Saint-Ouen de Rouen* (St. Vincent de Paul, vicar general for the Richelieu Vignerod family, abbots of Saint-Ouen de Rouen) (Archives CM).

23. Louis XIII had provided in his testament for a legacy of 64,000 livres for the Mission, of which 24,000 were meant for Sedan "to be used there for missions and for work to strengthen the Catholics and to try to return to the Catholic community many souls whom heresy has turned from the right way." Anne of Austria and Mazarin modified the terms of the royal testament, allocating the entire legacy for perpetual support of the Mission's responsibility for the parish of Sedan with a complement of six priests and two brothers. Vincent used the entire legacy to build thirteen houses at the Champ-Saint-Laurent at the end of the Faubourg Saint-Denis and allocated the income from renting these houses to the use of the Mission at Sedan. See Pierre Congar, "Saint Vincent de Paul, curé de Sedan" (St. Vincent de Paul, pastor of Sedan), *Mission et charité,* no. 28 (Oct.–Dec. 1967): 326–339.

24. For the testament of Richelieu, see Michel Carmona, *Richelieu* (Paris: Fayard, 1983), 699 ff. Armand de Vignerod was the older brother of Amador (see note 22 above). Armand de Maillé was the son of Nicole du Plessis, sister of the cardinal and wife of marshal Urbain de Maillé-Brézé.

25. Letter from Vincent de Paul to Bernard Codoing, C.M., December 25, 1642 (S.V. 2:321). Ponts-de-Cé is on the Loire, near Tours.

26. Letter from Vincent de Paul to Bernard Codoing, C.M., May 15, 1643 (S.V. 2:390). The charter of foundation of the house at Rome specified that in exchange for a donation of 50,000 livres, assuring a revenue of 5,000 livres, a mass be celebrated daily for the repose of the soul of Cardinal Richelieu and that after the death of the duchess d'Aiguillon, a mass would

also be said daily for the repose of her soul. The house at Rome was meant to provide missions for the neighboring countryside. It was also to receive ordinands for retreats.

27. Letter from Vincent de Paul to Bernard Codoing, C.M., August 24, 1643 (S.V. 2:413).

28. Letter from Vincent de Paul to Bernard Codoing, C.M., August 12, 1644 (S.V. 2:474).

29. "Unpublished request of Monsieur Vincent in favor of the domain of Saint-Lazare, the mills of Gonesse and the provostship of Paris," June 1645 (private archives and copy in the Archives CM. The text of the petition was transcribed with a commentary by Bernard Koch, C.M., August 1995.)

30. Letter from Vincent de Paul to Bernard Codoing, C.M., January 31, 1643 (S.V. 2:360).

31. "Foundation of the house of Marseilles by the duchess d'Aiguillon," July 25, 1643 (S.V. 13:298).

32. Letter from Vincent de Paul to Bernard Codoing, C.M., August 24, 1643 (S.V. 2:414).

33. Letter from Vincent de Paul to Bernard Codoing, C.M., August 12, 1644 (S.V. 2:474).

34. Letters from Vincent de Paul to Bernard Codoing, C.M., March 10, 1644 (S.V. 2:452) and August 14, 1644 (S.V. 2:456).

35. Letter from Cardinal Durazzo to Vincent de Paul, August 1645 (S.V. 2:544).

36. Letter from Cardinal Barberini to Vincent de Paul, February 25, 1645 (S.V. 2:506).

37. Letter from Vincent de Paul to Bernard Codoing, C.M., July 9, 1644 (S.V. 2:466).

38. Letter from Vincent de Paul to Jean Dehorgny, C.M., August 31, 1645 (S.V. 3:35).

Notes to Chapter 16

1. Arthur Loth, *Saint Vincent de Paul et sa mission sociale* (St. Vincent de Paul and his social mission) (Paris: Dumoulin, 1881).

2. Until that time, Vincent considered the Daughters of Charity as an adjunct to the Ladies of Charity. They were attached to parish Confraternities of Charity or the Confraternity of Charity of the Hôtel-Dieu for the Founding Children. It is from this time onward that he began to recognize their autonomy and to call them not "my daughters" but "my sisters."

3. Letter from Vincent de Paul to J. F. de Gondi, archbishop of Paris, August–September 1645 (S.V. 2:549), and the text promoting the Daughters of Charity to the rank of confraternity, November 20, 1646 (S.V. 13:557).

4. Conversations with the Daughters of Charity (S.V. 9).

5. See S.V. 9:138.

6. By letters patent, Louis XIII conferred an annual income of 4,000 livres on the estate of Gonesse, and Anne of Austria conferred an income of 8,000 livres, derived from the revenues of several large farms, for the work of the Foundling Hospital (S.V. 2:472). But by the end of 1658, the royal donations had been only very partially honored; they fell 30,000 livres short!

7. The little houses were meant to recreate family units, with each dwelling welcoming ten to twelve children.

8. See S.V. 13:801.

9. Letter from Louise de Marillac to Vincent de Paul, April 19, 1645 (S.V. 2:545).

10. Letter from Vincent de Paul to Jean Bourdet, C.M., September 1, 1646 (S.V. 3:37).

11. Letter from Vincent de Paul to Guillaume Galais, C.M., February 13, 1644 (S.V. 2:447). The governor of Sedan at this time was a Huguenot, Abraham de Fabert, future marshal of France, to whom Vincent de Paul gave due credit: "The governor sees his duty more clearly than you or I do."

12. Letter from Vincent de Paul to Antoine Portail, C.M., October 6, 1646 (S.V. 3:70). Pituitous: This has to do with the mucosa of the nose. Since the nose is close to the brain, it was thought that a runny nose was related to intense mental activity. The term "pituitous" once signified a nature that was serious and disposed to study. (See Alain rey, ed., *Dictionnaire historique de la langue française* [Paris: Dictionnaires Le Robert, 1998]). Atrabiliary (from the Latin *ater, atra* = black and *bilis* = bile) refers to a personality which produces black bile and is therefore subject to fits of rage.

13. Letter from Vincent de Paul to a superior, April 9, 1647 (S.V. 3:167).

14. Letter from Vincent de Paul to Antoine Portail, C.M., December 20, 1647 (S.V. 3:258). Gilbert Cuissot (1607–1666), entered the Congregation in 1637 and directed the Collège des Bons-Enfants. He was at the seminary of Saint-Lazare in 1647; later he became the superior of the seminary of Cahors and finally of the house at Richelieu.

Jean Chrétien, born in 1606, entered the Congregation in 1640. He directed the house at Marseilles from 1645 and remained there until 1653, before being named sub-assistant at the mother house and then superior at La Rose.

15. Letter from Vincent de Paul to Mathurin Gentil, C.M., September 17, 1647 (S.V. 3:234).

16. Letter to the aldermen of the city of Paris, July 14, 1648 (S.V. 3:339).

17. Abelly 2:146.

18. Letter from Julien Guérin to Vincent de Paul, toward 1646 (S.V. 3:138).

19. Letter from Julien Guérin to Vincent de Paul, June 1647 (S.V. 3:203). Julien Guérin was particularly sensitive to the fate of young captives who, whether voluntarily or under duress, were at risk of becoming renegades. On

this subject, see the book by Bartolomé and Lucile Bennassar, *Les Chrétiens d'Allah, l'histoire extraordinaire des renégats, 16ᵉ et 17ᵉ siècle* (Allah's Christians: the extraordinary story of the renegades in the sixteenth and seventeenth centuries) (Paris: Perrin, 1989).

20. Letter from Vincent de Paul to Antoine Portail, C.M., October 20, 1646, (S.V. 3:83). The Order of Mercy had been founded in the thirteenth century to ransom prisoners from the Moors.

21. Letter from Vincent de Paul to Monseigneur Ingoli, March 15, 1647 (S.V. 3:158).

22. Letter from Vincent de Paul to Jean Dehorgny, C.M., May 2, 1647 (S.V. 3:182).

23. Petition to the Congregation for the Propagation of the Faith, 1648 (S.V. 3:336).

24. Letter from Vincent de Paul to René Alméras, C.M., October 23, 1648 (S.V. 3:380).

25. Letter from Vincent de Paul to Charles Nacquart, C.M., March 22, 1648 (S.V. 3:278). The first attempts at evangelizing the island of Madagascar, then called the Island of Saint-Laurent, were carried out by Portuguese Jesuits at the beginning of the seventeenth century. They were not at all successful. When the East India Company had obtained from Richelieu the monopoly of commerce with this island, a governor was sent there with about 100 colonists who settled in the region of Fort Dauphin. This company was not satisfied with the actions of the first governor and decided to replace him with Monsieur de Flacourt, asking the nuncio to send some religious men and women with him.

26. Antoine Arnauld, called the Grand Arnauld (1612–1694). His father, a celebrated lawyer, was an unrelenting enemy of the Jesuits. His mother, after giving birth to twenty-two children, withdrew to Port-Royal. Ordained priest in 1635 and pronounced a doctor of theology in 1641, Antoine Arnauld had the abbot of Saint-Cyran as spiritual director. He withdrew to Port-Royal-des-Champs, where he spent most of his life, writing many books, including both anti-Jesuit and anti-Protestant polemics as well as learned treatises on the philosophy of language. In 1679, he was forced to go into exile in the Netherlands during the persecution of the Jansenists. His older sister, Angélique Arnauld (1591–1661), called Mother Angélique, was abbess of Port-Royal at the age of fourteen. She reformed the abbey in 1609, imposing a very austere rule. It was she who introduced Jansenist ideas to Port-Royal.

27. Letter from Vincent de Paul to Bernard Codoing, C.M., March 16, 1644 (S.V. 2:454).

28. Letter from Cardinal Mazarin to Vincent de Paul, September 1646 (S.V. 3:45). The topic was a nomination to a chair at the Sorbonnne. The Jansenists wanted to seat one of their number, but Vincent de Paul was opposed.

29. "A Study on Grace" (S.V. 13:147–156). According to the critical analysis carried out by Bernard Koch, C.M., this study on grace was written toward

1648. The original autograph has disappeared, but there is a copy in the Archives of the Congregation.

30. Letter from Vincent de Paul to Jean Dehorgny, C.M., June 25, 1648 (S.V. 3:329).

31. Letter from Vincent de Paul to Jean Dehorgny, C.M., September 10, 1648 (S.V. 3:371).

Notes to Chapter 17

1. Pierre Goubert, *Mazarin* (Paris: Fayard, 1990), 186.

2. Michel Pernot, *La Fronde* (Paris: Éditions de Fallois, 1994), 39.

3. Ibid., 21.

4. Annual fee paid by the holders of a royal office to assure that it can be inherited.

5. Olivier Lefebvre d'Ormesson, *Journal*, 2 vols. (Paris: Édition de Cheruel, 1860), 1:583.

6. The Treaty of Westphalia, signed in 1648, ended the Thirty Years' War with the German Empire. It was signed at Münster by the Catholic states and at Osnabrück by the Protestant states. France and Sweden were the principal beneficiaries and Germany was the great loser.

7. Cardinal de Retz, *Oeuvres* (Works) (Paris: Gallimard "La Pléiade," 1983), 159, 173.

8. Letter from Vincent de Paul to Louise de Marillac, September 5, 1648 (S.V. 3:360 and n. 2).

9. Coste 3:674.

10. Mathieu Molé (1584–1656). Named first president of the parlement in 1641, he would play the role of a moderator during the Fronde, remaining loyal to the crown. In 1651, he was made Keeper of the Seals and remained in this office until his death.

11. Collet 1:469–470. Michel Le Tellier (1603–1685). Secretary of State from 1643, he remained loyal to the king throughout the Fronde, playing a primary role during Mazarin's exile. In 1661, he began to share his office with his son, Louvois. He was named Chancellor and Keeper of the Seals in 1677.

12. Letter from Vincent de Paul to Antoine Portail, C.M., January 22, 1649 (S.V. 3:402).

13. Letter from Vincent de Paul to Jacques Norais, February 5, 1649 (S.V. 3:408).

14. Letter from Vincent de Paul to the Ladies of Charity, February 11, 1649 (S.V. III, 409).

15. Letter from Vincent de Paul to Denis Gautier, C.M., February 25, 1649 (S.V. 3:412, 413).

16. Letter from Vincent de Paul to Antoine Portail, C.M., March 4, 1649 (S.V. 3:416).

17. Letter from Vincent de Paul to Louise de Marillac, April 5, 1649 (S.V. 3:424, n. 3).

18. Clothilde Duvauferrier, *Saint-Méen-le-Grand* (1983) (Archives CM).

19. Letter from Vincent de Paul to Louise de Marillac, April 9–15, 1649 (S.V. 3:428, 429).

20. Letter from Vincent de Paul to Antoine Portail, C.M., May 11, 1649 (S.V. 3:434).

21. Letter from Vincent de Paul to Louise de Marillac, May 14, 1649 (S.V. 3:436).

Notes to Chapter 18

1. Claire-Clémence de Maillé-Brézé was the wife of the prince de Condé (Le Grand Condé) and the niece of Cardinal de Richelieu.

2. Letter from Cardinal Mazarin to Vincent de Paul, October 13, 1649 (S.V. 3:497).

3. Letter from Vincent de Paul to Jean Midot, vicar general at Toul, June 8, 1650 (S.V. 4:28).

4. Letter from Alain de Solminihac to Vincent de Paul, May 25, 1650 (S.V. 4:24). The letter has reference to the bishop of Saint-Flour, Jacques de Montrouge.

5. Claude-Emmanuel Luillier, called Chapelle (1626–1680). A writer of playful, delicate verse, he lived an Epicurean life, keeping company with libertines. Sainte-Beuve judged him severely: "A lazy man, drunk much too often." The poem on "The Charms of Saint-Lazare" was published in the *Bulletin des lazaristes de France* (December 1996).

6. Letter from Vincent de Paul to Guillaume Delattre, C.M., October 23, 1649 (S.V. 3:502).

7. Letter from Vincent de Paul to Jacques Chiroye, C.M., January 9, 1650 (S.V. 3:531).

8. Letter from Vincent de Paul to Mathurin Gentil, C.M., November 9, 1649 (S.V. 3:504).

9. *Documents du minutier central des notaires, concernant l'histoire littéraire (1650–1670)* (Documents of the central notarial archive, concerning literary history (1650–1670) (Paris: Presses Universitaires Françaises, 1960).

10. Letter from Vincent de Paul to Bernard Codoing, C.M., February 23, 1650 (S.V. 3:618).

11. Letter from Vincent de Paul to Antoine Lucas, C.M., March 23, 1650 (S.V. 3:625).

12. Letter from Vincent de Paul to Jean Gicquel, C.M., December 5, 1649 (S.V. 3:513).

13. Circular to superiors of houses of the Congregation, January 15, 1649 (S.V. 3:536).

14. Letter from Vincent de Paul to Marc Coglée, C.M., August 13, 1650 (S.V. 4:51).

15. Letter from Vincent de Paul to a priest of the Mission, no date (S.V. 4:53).

16. Letter from Vincent de Paul to a priest of the Mission, March 27, 1650 (S.V. 3:628).

17. Letter from Vincent de Paul to a priest of the Mission, December 28, 1650 (S.V. 4:125).

18. Letter from Vincent de Paul to Jean Dehorgny, June 25, 1648 (S.V. 3:323).

19. Text of the petition addressed to Pope Innocent X, calling for condemnation of the five propositions contained in the *Augustinus* (Coste 3:177, 178). These propositions can be summarized as follows: 1. There are commandments of God that are impossible to practice without a gift of divine grace; 2. When this grace is vouchsafed, one cannot resist it; 3. In order to merit or lose eternal salvation, it is sufficient not to undergo external pressure. It is not necessary to be free of all interior impulses; 4. To believe that in his present state man can choose to resist an interior grace or to acquiesce to it is a heresy; 5. To believe that Jesus died and poured out his blood for all men is a heresy. It is against this last proposition, to believe that Christ did not die for all men, but only for the elect, that Vincent protested most energetically. (See S.V. 13:147–156).

20. To some bishops of France, February 1651 (S.V. 4:148).

21. Letter from Vincent de Paul to Nicolas Pavillon and Étienne Caulet, June 1651 (S.V. 4:204–210).

22. It was a monk from this abbey, Aurelian, who around 850 codified the theory of the song of the Church, according to the musical practice of the Greeks and Romans (Max Manitius, *Histoire de la littérature latine du Moyen Âge,* vol. 1, part 1, no. 63, 444–446).

23. Abbot Claude de Chandenier founded a confraternity of Charity and had two Daughters of Charity assigned to the market town of Moutiers-Saint-Jean. He also founded a hospice whose pharmacy, still in operation, contains a pot, an egg cup, and a salt cellar which Vincent supposedly used when he was staying at the abbey. In the chapel of this hospice there is a painting of Vincent in a surplice painted by Simon François de Tours around 1660 when the painter stayed at Saint-Lazare.

24. Letters from Charles Nacquart, C.M., to Vincent de Paul, May 27, 1649 (S.V. 3:438) and February 9 and 16, 1650 (S.V. 3:580 and 590).

25. Letter from Vincent de Paul to Gérard Brin, C.M., April 1650 (S.V. 4:16).

26. Letter from Vincent de Paul to Cardinal Barberini, October 7, 1650 (S.V. 4:92).

27. Louise-Marie de Gonzague (1612–1667). Daughter of Charles de Gonzague, duke of Nevers and Mantua, in 1644 she married the king of Poland, Ladislas IV, and at his death, his brother Ian-Casimir, who succeeded him on the throne of Warsaw. Being without heirs, she would have liked to raise a Condé to the throne; the Grand Condé himself was briefly taken with this prospect, but the opposition of the great Polish lords persuaded him to give it up.

28. Letter from Vincent de Paul to Louise-Marie de Gonzague, September 6, 1651 (S.V. 4:246).

29. Letter from Louise de Marillac to Vincent de Paul, December 1649 (S.V. 3:523).

30. Letter from Vincent de Paul to Louise de Marillac, December 1649 (S.V. 3:524).

31. On the institution of the Foundling Hospital (S.V. 13:799–800).

32. Letter from Vincent de Paul to Jean Dehorgny, C.M., December 29, 1650 (S.V. 4:127).

33. Jean Parré entered the Congregation in 1638, at the age of twenty-seven. This brother coadjutor was to play a most important role in bringing aid to the people of Picardy and Champagne, provinces through which he would travel endlessly, beginning in 1649. He wrote regularly to Vincent and the Ladies of Charity to keep them informed of his work and the needs of the unfortunate. Vincent also sent him numerous letters, filled with encouragement and advice.

34. Letter from Edme Duchamps, C.M., to Vincent de Paul, December 1650 (S.V. 4:143).

35. The first issue of *Relations*, which appeared in September 1650, was entitled "State of the unfortunate on the Picardy front. Extracts of several letters written by priests and other persons of piety, worthy to hold the faith, who have fled from Paris for their safety." These accounts appeared every month in the form of a sheet of 20 by 28 centimeters, folded in two. This represented four little pages, written in a direct and striking style and ending with a call to send donations, with the addresses of the organizers. For information about the activities of Charles Maignart de Bernières, founder of this publication and mainspring of most of the aid to the devastated provinces, who lived under the influence of Port-Royal, see the study by Alex Féron, *Un Rouennais méconnu, Charles. Maignart de Bernières, 1616–1662* (A little-known man from Rouen, Charles Maignart de Bernières, 1616–1662) (Rouen: Imprimerie Lecerf Fils, 1922) (Archives CM).

36. Letter from a priest of the Mission to Vincent de Paul, January 1651 (S.V. 4:136).

37. Letter from Vincent de Paul to Marc Coglée, C.M., April 26, 1651 (S.V. 4:183).

38. A. Feillet, *La Misère au temps de la Fronde* (Misery at the time of the Fronde) (Perrin, 1886), 246. "Ordinance of the king, granting protection to all the villages of the frontiers of Picardy and Champagne where the priests of the Mission go to comfort the poor" (and S.V. 13:324).

39. Letter from the aldermen of Rethel to Vincent de Paul, May 8, 1651 (S.V. 4:195).

41. Feillet, *La Misère,* 249.

Notes to Chapter 19

1. Letter from Vincent de Paul to Sister Marie-Madeleine, September 4, 1651 (S.V. 4:245).

2. Letter from Vincent de Paul to Louise de Marillac, September 20, 1651 (S.V. 4:256).

3. See Gaston Parturier, *La vocation médicale de saint Vincent de Paul* (The Medical Vocation of Saint Vincent de Paul) (Lyon: Éditions Cartier, 1943) and Dr. Peyresblanque, *"Monsieur Vincent malade"* (Monsieur Vincent in Illness), *Bulletin de la société de Borda,* Dax (1982).

4. Letter from Vincent de Paul to Lambert aux Couteaux, C.M., March 1, 1652 (S.V. 4:327). Adrien Le Bon had reserved the farm of Rougemont in the forest of Bondy for himself, and left it to the Congregation in his will. But in February 1645, he turned it over, "for the sake of the good friendship and affection" which he felt for the gentlemen of Saint-Lazare (S.V. 1:257, n. 4). The Congregation owned two farms at Orsigny, one of which was the farm presented by the Norais family.

5. Letter from Vincent de Paul to Mathurin Gentil, C.M., November 23, 1651 (S.V. 4:273).

6. Letter from Vincent de Paul to Étienne Blatiron, C.M., February 15, 1652 (S.V. 4:321). According to Abelly, this charitable gift came from the de Maignelay, who had learned of the difficulty in which Vincent's nephew found himself (Abelly 3:292).

7. Letter from Vincent de Paul to Pierre Watebled, C.M., November 26, 1651 (S.V. 4:276).

8. Letter from Vincent de Paul to Étienne Blatiron, C.M., July 5, 1652 (S.V. 4:418).

9. Anne-Marie Louise d'Orléans, duchess de Montpensier (1627–1693). Daughter of Gaston d'Orléans, known as La Grande Mademoiselle, she was the first cousin of Louis XIV. At the battle of the faubourg Saint-Antoine, she

saved Condé's army by having the canons of the Bastille fire on the royal forces and by giving the order to open the gates of Paris so that the prince's army could find refuge within.

10. Letter from Vincent de Paul to the wife of President du Sault, May 15, 1652 (S.V. 4:384).

11. Letter from Vincent de Paul to Cardinal Mazarin, around July 10, 1652 (S.V. 4:423).

12. Letter from Vincent de Paul to Philippe Vageot, C.M., May 22, 1652 (S.V. 4:392).

13. Letter from Vincent de Paul to some priests at Rome, June 21, 1652 (S.V. 4:402).

14. Letter from Vincent de Paul to Lambert aux Couteaux, C.M., June 21, 1652 (S.V. 4:407).

15. Letter from Vincent de Paul to the duchess d'Aiguillon, July 1652 (S.V. 4:424).

16. Letter from Vincent de Paul to Anne of Austria, July–August 1652 (S.V. 4:430).

17. Letter from Vincent de Paul to Pope Innocent X, August 16, 1652 (S.V. 4:458).

18. Letter from Vincent de Paul to Cardinal Mazarin, September 11, 1652 (S.V. 4:473).

19. Letter from Alain de Solminihac to Vincent de Paul, October 20, 1652 (S.V. 4:491).

20. Letter from Vincent de Paul to Étienne Blatiron, C.M., October 25, 1652 (S.V. 4:513).

21. A. Feillet, *La Misère*, 447–450 (and S.V. 4:539, nn. 8–10).

Notes to Chapter 20

1. Letter from Vincent de Paul to Jacques Desclaux, around 1653 (S.V. 5:90).

2. Letter from Vincent de Paul to Lambert aux Couteaux, C.M., January 3, 1653 (S.V. 4:518).

3. Letter from Vincent de Paul to the duchess d'Aiguillon, July 3, 1653 (S.V. 5:47).

4. Letter from Vincent de Paul to Alain de Solminihac, July 5, 1653 (S.V. 4:620).

5. Thomas Berthe (1623–1697). Ordained in 1645, he held important positions in the Congregation. Superior of the Collège des Bons-Enfants, then superior at Rome (1653–1655), assistant to the superior general (1662–1667). Monsieur Vincent had proposed his name together with that of René Alméras as possible replacements for himself at the head of the Mission.

6. Letter from Vincent de Paul to Thomas Berthe, C.M., April 25, 1653 (S.V. 4:578).

7. Letter from Thomas Berthe to Vincent de Paul, February 5, 1655 (S.V. 5:270).

8. Letter from Vincent de Paul to Louis de Chandenier, April 27, 1655 (S.V. 5:366).

9. Letter from Vincent de Paul to Étienne Blatiron, C.M., October 22, 1655 (S.V. 5:452).

10. Letter from Vincent de Paul to Edme Jolly, C.M., October 22, 1655 (S.V. 5:453). Edme Jolly (1622–1695), received into the Congregation in 1646, ordained in 1649, had studied in Rome. In charge of the seminary of Saint-Lazare in 1654, he replaced Thomas Berthe at Rome in 1655. Assistant head of the Congregation after the death of Vincent, he succeeded René Alméras at the head of the Congregation in 1672.

11. Letter from Vincent de Paul to the duchess d'Aiguillon, May 1, 1653 (S.V. 4:586).

12. Letter from the duchess d'Aiguillon to Antoine Portail, C.M., May 20, 1653 (S.V. 4:587).

13. Letter from Vincent de Paul to a priest of the Mission, October 17, 1654 (S.V. 5:204). It is this same thought and the same desire, that his missionaries be transfixed by charity, that he expressed in one of his talks: "If, nevertheless, God permitted them to be reduced to begging for their bread or to sleeping under a hedge, all torn and pierced by cold, and if in that state one of them were asked: 'Poor priest of the Mission, who has brought you to this state?' what joy it would be to be able to reply, 'It was Charity'" (Abelly 3: chapter 11, 108; S.V. 11:76).

14. Letter from Vincent de Paul to Charles Ozenne, C.M., October 9, 1654 (S.V. 5:195).

15. Letter from Vincent de Paul to Charles Ozenne, C.M., August 27, 1655 (S.V. 5:411).

16. Letter from Vincent de Paul to Marc Coglée, C.M., November 20, 1655 (S.V. 5:468), and response of the prayer for September 12, 1655 (S.V. 11:305).

17. See S.V. 11:445.

18. "Rule of life for Jean Le Vacher and Martin Husson," 1653 (S.V. 13:364).

19. Letter from Vincent de Paul to Philippe Le Vacher, C.M., 1651 (S.V. 4:122).

20. Letter from Vincent de Paul to Firmin Get, C.M., April 16, 1655 (S.V. 5:364).

21. Letter from Vincent de Paul to Étienne Blatiron, C.M., December 31, 1654 (S.V. 5:250)

22. Letter to Pope Innocent X, July 1653 (S.V. 4:643), and letter to the Congregation for the Propagation of the Faith, September 1653 (S.V. 5:14).

This notion of an indigenous clergy had already been introduced by Charles Nacquart, envoy to Madagascar, who asked Vincent whether he could recruit "companions from this country to be priests" (letter dated April 1, 1648, S.V. 3:289).

23. Letter from Vincent de Paul to Nicolas Guillot, January 30, 1654 (S.V. 5:64).

24. "Talk on Priests," September 1655 (S.V. 11:308).

Notes to Chapter 21

1. Letter from Louise de Marillac to Vincent de Paul, November 14, 1655 (S.V. 5:464).

2. Letter from Vincent de Paul to Marc Coglée, C.M., November 20, 1655 (S.V. 5:468).

3. Letter from Vincent de Paul to Étienne Blatiron, C.M., December 17, 1655 (S.V. 5:487).

4. See S.V. 5:344 and S.V. 13:21 and 251).

5. Letter from Vincent de Paul to Étienne Blatiron, C.M., August 11, 1656 (S.V. 6:58).

6. Repeated in a speech August 30, 1657 (S.V. 11:415 and 420).

7. Letter from Vincent de Paul to Pierre de Beaumont, C.M., September 9, 1657 (S.V. 6:451).

8. Letter from Vincent de Paul to Firmin Get, C.M., February 9, 1657 (S.V. 6:178).

9. Letter from Vincent de Paul to Firmin Get, C.M., June 8, 1657 (S.V. 6:316).

10. Letter from Vincent de Paul to Firmin Get, C.M., September 7, 1657 (S.V. 6:447).

11. Letter from Vincent de Paul to Louis Rivet, C.M., September 16, 1657 (S.V. 6:474).

12. Letter from Vincent de Paul to Edme Jolly, C.M., July 6, 1657 (S.V. 6:342). This Spanish project would not come to fruition in Vincent's lifetime. It was not revived until a peace was signed between France and Spain. The first house of the Congregation was founded at Barcelona in 1704.

13. See *Histoire de la congrégation de la Mission,* 64.

14. Letter from the duchesse d'Aiguillon to Vincent de Paul, October 17, 1656 (S.V. 6:110). According to Coste (2:501) the Ladies of Charity had already spent 50,000 livres to renovate the buildings of the Salpêtrière and they had signed a contract for 100,000 livres for the subsistence of the residents of the general hospital.

15. Letter from Vincent de Paul to Jean Martin, C.M., February 23, 1657 (S.V. 6:239).

16. Letter from Vincent de Paul to Monsieur de Mauroy, March 23, 1657 (S.V. 6:256).

17. Letter from Vincent de Paul to Brother Jean Parré, August 11, 1657 (S.V. 6:394).

18. Report on the state of charitable works, July 11, 1657 (S.V. 13:802).

19. Letter from Vincent de Paul to Guillaume Delville, C.M., November 10, 1657 (S.V. 6:597).

20. Letter from Vincent de Paul to the marquise de Fabert, November 15, 1656, (S.V. 6:130).

21. Letter from Vincent de Paul to Brother Pierre Leclerc, November 12, 1656 (S.V. 6:125).

22. Letter from Vincent de Paul to Firmin Get, C.M., November 23, 1657 (S.V. 6:618).

23. Letter from Vincent de Paul to a priest of the Mission, July 1657 (S.V. 6:378).

24. Letter from Vincent de Paul to Louis Dupont, C.M., February 7, 1657 (S.V. 6:175).

25. Letter from Vincent de Paul to Guillaume Delville, C.M., February 7, 1657 (S.V. 6:177).

26. Letter from Vincent de Paul to Jean Martin, C.M., June 22, 1657 (S.V. 6:330).

27. Letter from Vincent de Paul to Monsieur Forne, January 1656 (S.V. 5:497).

28. Letter from Vincent de Paul to Jean Chrétien, C.M., January 17, 1657 (S.V. 6:161).

29. Letter from Vincent de Paul to Donat Crouly, C.M., July 16, 1657 (S.V. 6:357).

30. Letter from Vincent de Paul to Louis Rivet, C.M., July 29, 1657 (S.V. 6:377).

31. Letter from Vincent de Paul to Firmin Get, C.M., September 22, 1657 (S.V. 6:88).

32. Abelly 1:209.

33. Letter from Vincent de Paul to Jean Deslions, April 6, 1657 (*Mission et Charité*, no. 19–20 [January–June 1970]: 116).

Notes to Chapter 22

1. Letter from Vincent de Paul to the duke de la Meilleraye, January 12, 1658 (S.V. 7:45).

2. Letter from J. B. Bossuet to Vincent de Paul, January 12, 1658 (S.V. 7:48). Jacques-Bénigne Bossuet (1627–1704), son of a magistrate of the parlement of Dijon and ordained priest in 1652 after studying at the Collège de Navarre, had

spent seven years at Metz as canon and archdeacon. There he learned to conduct a dialogue with the Protestants, with whom he wanted to attempt a rapprochement. At Paris, from 1659 onward, he became a much admired preacher, pronouncing the funeral orations of the great and the princes. He was named bishop of Meaux in 1681. He was both a great orator and a great writer, and most of all, an ardent fighter for the faith. His struggle against quietism brought him into violent opposition to Fénelon in the last years of the seventeenth century.

3. For a discussion of the "little method," see the conference given by Monsieur Vincent on August 20, 1655 (S.V. 11:257–287).

4. Letter from J.B. Bossuet to Vincent de Paul, May 23, 1658 (S.V. 7:155). On the course of the mission at Metz, see Joseph Girard, C.M., *Saint Vincent de Paul, son oeuvre et son influence en Lorraine* (St. Vincent de Paul, his work and his influence in Lorraine) (Metz, 1955), 46–50.

5. Letter from Vincent de Paul to Firmin Get, C.M., February 8, 1658 (S.V. 7:78).

6. Letter from Vincent de Paul to Firmin Get, C.M., May 3, 1658 (S.V. 7:139).

7. Letter from Vincent de Paul to Firmin Get, C.M., June 7, 1658 (S.V. 7:171).

8. To gather the sum that Brother Barreau committed to paying under torture, Vincent had once more called on the Ladies of Charity. They organized a special fundraising drive, in which they distributed, in the form of a prospectus, the "Tale of the Misfortunes of Brother Barreau." Vincent speaks of this in one of his letters: "a little tale we published, telling of what happened to the consul of Algiers" (S.V. 7:627).

9. Letter from Vincent de Paul to Firmin Get, C.M., July 5, 1658 (S.V. 7:197).

10. Letter from Vincent de Paul to Philippe Le Vacher, C.M., summer 1659 (S.V. 8:25).

11. Charles de la Porte, duke de la Meilleraye (1602–1604). Cousin of Cardinal de Richelieu, who would be helpful at the beginning of his career; marshal of France in 1637, Superintendent of Finance in 1648, duke and peer in 1663, he was the governor of Brittany, achieving this title at the moment when the Congregation was installed at the abbey of Saint-Méen.

12. Letter from Vincent de Paul to the duke de la Meilleraye, January 12, 1658 (S.V. 7:45).

13. Letter from Vincent de Paul to Jean Martin, C.M., July 5, 1658 (S.V. 7:196).

14. Letter from Vincent de Paul to Toussaint Bourdaise, C.M., November 1659 (S.V. 8:157).

15. Letter from Vincent de Paul to the community of Saint-Lazare, September 1658 (S.V. 7:251). The farm at Orsigny had been given as a gift to the

Mission by Monsieur Norais in December 1644. The Congregation in return paid a pension to the donor, but at his death in 1658, his heirs went to court over the validity of this donation. Certain judges, Jansenists by conviction, are said to have been warned against Monsieur Vincent, on the grounds of his very marked opposition to Jansenism. As the Congregation owned another farm at Orsigny, and land as well, the loss of the farm of the Norais family was certainly a setback, but not a catastrophe.

16. Letter from Vincent de Paul to Antoine Durand, C.M., August 29, 1659 (S.V. 8:101). François Fouquet, and then his brother Louis, who succeeded him, bore the titles bishop and count of Agde.

17. Letter from Vincent de Paul to Gérard Brin, C.M., November 6, 1658 (S.V. 7:338).

18. Letter from Vincent de Paul to Firmin Get, C.M., June 13, 1659 (S.V. 7:593).

19. Letter from Vincent de Paul to Jacques Pesnelle, C.M., May 30, 1659 (S.V. 7:578). This foundation on Corsica did not take place until 1678, after the death of Vincent.

20. Letter from Vincent de Paul to François Fouquet, archbishop of Narbonne, September 12, 1659 (S.V. 8:123). Vincent could refuse nothing to the archbishop of Narbonne, whose mother was a very pious and very active Lady of Charity and whose six sisters were Visitandine nuns.

21. Letter from Vincent de Paul to Canon Truchette at Tarbes, January 29, 1659 (S.V. 7:442), and letter from Vincent de Paul to Jean du Haut de Saliès, bishop of Lescar, August 11, 1660 (S.V. 8:358). The contract concerned assumption of the parish of Lestelle, adjoining the pilgrimage site. Except in extraordinary cases, Vincent did not wish to accept the responsibility for a parish.

22. Letter from Vincent de Paul to Charles Ozenne, C.M., April 30, 1658 (S.V. 7:249).

23. Letter from Vincent de Paul to Jean Monvoisin, C.M., May 5, 1659 (S.V. 7:533). At issue was a farm bequeathed by the late Monsieur François Vincent at Neuilly-Saint-Front in the Aisne.

24. Letter from Vincent de Paul to Jacques Pesnelle, C.M., October 15, 1658 (S.V. 7:289

25. Letter from Vincent de Paul to Denis Laudin, C.M., April 26, 1659 (S.V. 7:518).

26. Letter from Vincent de Paul to Brother Jean de Fricourt, September 7, 1659 (S.V. 8:111

27. Conference of May 17, 1658 (S.V. 12:1–14).

28. Letter from Vincent de Paul to Louis de Chandenier, December 6, 1658 (S.V. 7:390).

29. Letter from Vincent de Paul to Father Philippe-Emmanuel de Gondi, January 9, 1659 (S.V. 7:435).

30. Letter from Vincent de Paul to Louise de Marillac, March 1659 (S.V. 7:461).

31. Letter from Vincent de Paul to Louis Rivet, C.M., July 13, 1659 (S.V. 8:23).

32. Letter from Vincent de Paul to Toussaint Bourdaise, November 1659 (S.V. 8:160).

33. Letter from Vincent de Paul to Brother Jean Parré, May 3, 1659 (S.V. 7:528).

Notes to Chapter 23

1. Letter from Vincent de Paul to Jean Dehorgny, C.M., January 11, 1660 (S.V. 8:222).

2. Letter from Vincent de Paul to Guillaume Desdames, C.M., March 5, 1660 (S.V. 8:259).

3. Portail, Vincent's first companion, had been ill and depressed for many months. He had withdrawn to a cabin in a far corner of the enclosure of Saint-Lazare. Louise de Marillac wrote to a sister, Mathurine Guérin, in January 1600: "As for Monsieur Portail, only a great lord can see him. He has some kind of hermitage at the edge of their enclosure, from which he does not move" (*Écrits de sainte Louise* [Writings of Saint Louise], Letter 650, p. 666).

4. Letter from Vincent de Paul to Canon de Saint-Martin, March 18, 1660 (S.V. 8:271).

5. The daughter of Monsieur de Comet, judge at Dax and first patron of Vincent, married Jean de Saint-Martin, one of whose sons held the title of Saint-Martin d'Agès. Canon de Saint-Martin, uncle of Monsieur d'Agès, had a friendly correspondence with Vincent.

6. Letter from Brother B. Ducournau to Canon de Saint-Martin, August 1658 (S.V. 8:271).

7. Curiously enough, in a conference on the theme of observance of the Rule given to the sisters by Vincent on July 14, 1658, he evoked the city of Carthage, about which he said: "There is nothing left but dilapidated huts," as though he had seen the site with his own eyes. This was the first and only time that he spoke of it, as though this name had escaped him at the very moment when he received "those miserable letters." Could they have awakened memories of his captivity? In similar conferences, speaking of the dangers of not following the Rule, he was more likely to use images of shipwreck. This rather troubling coincidence raises some questions (S.V. 10:534).

8. Letter from Vincent de Paul to superiors, 1660 (S.V. 8:388).

9. Letter from Vincent de Paul to Pierre de Beaumont, C.M., May 19, 1660 (S.V. 8:293).

10. Letter from Vincent de Paul to Guillaume Desdames, C.M., June 18, 1660 (S.V. 8:319). Jean Eudes (1601–1680) was educated and trained at the Oratory. In 1643, he founded the Congregation of Jesus and Mary, devoted to directing seminaries and the work of the missions. He also established a congregation for women, the Daughters of Our Lady. Vincent supported his work, although it was so similar to the work of the Mission. Jean Eudes was canonized in 1925.

11. Letter from Vincent de Paul to Edme Jolly, C.M., August 13, 1660 (S.V. 8:368).

12. On the virtues of Louise de Marillac, July 3 and July 24, 1660 (S.V. 10:709, 725).

13. See S.V. 12:484–485.

14. Letter from Vincent de Paul to René Alméras, C.M., August 18, 1660 (S.V. 8:376) and August 22, 1660 (S.V. 8:385).

15. Letter from Vincent de Paul to Firmin Get, C.M., September 17, 1660 (S.V. 8:446).

16. Journal of the last days of Vincent de Paul (S.V. 13:191).

Notes to the Epilogue

1. "The Beatification of Saint Vincent de Paul," *Annales CM,* vol. 94 (1929).

2. "He who enters canonical orders without dimissory letters or before the canonical age, is *ipso facto* suspended from the order received" (canon 2, 374 in the *Codex Juris Canonici,* 1917). In 1600, when Vincent was ordained, the Council of Trent being not yet officially received in France, this violation of the canonical age does not seem too serious, but in 1660, it would have been very poorly regarded. It is understandable that the Congregation was eager to keep Vincent's real birth date a secret.

3. Pope Benedict XIII inscribed Vincent de Paul in the list of the Blessed on August 21, 1729.

4. Abbé Lamourette, "Désastre de la maison de Saint-Lazare" (Catastrophe of the house of Saint-Lazare), August 3, 1789 (Paris, Mérigot le jeune).

5. Conference of May 30, 1659 (S.V. 12:262).

6. See Pierre Defrennes, S.J., "La vocation de saint Vincent de Paul, étude de psychologie surnaturelle" (The Vocation of Saint Vincent de Paul, a study of supernatural psychology), *Revue d'ascétique et de mystique,* vol. 13 (1932): 60–86, 165–183, 294–321, 389–411.

7. S.V. 9:119.

8. S.V. 11:41, 317.

9. S.V. 12:131.

Index

Abelly, Louis (bishop of Rodez), 45, 117,
139, 229, 289n.5, 291n.23, 304n.6
on the Gondis, 49
relationship with Vincent, 107,
224, 264n.23
on Tilh, 16–17
on Vincent's birth date, 262n.1
on Vincent's captivity in Tunis, 29,
250, 269n.3
on Vincent's character, 21, 53
on Vincent's childhood, 11
on Vincent's education, 15, 265n.7
on Vincent's mission to Henry IV, 37
on Vincent's physical appearance,
86–87
Acarie, Mme, 44, 272n.19
Agen, 187, 201
Ahmed I, 26, 27, 268n.8
Aiguillon, Marie de Vignerod, duchess
d,' 154, 169, 176, 233, 286n.4,
293n.18, 296nn.22, 26
relationship with Vincent, 107, 121,
133, 141, 153, 155–56, 158, 163, 184,
204, 209, 210, 213, 221–22, 223,
225, 278n.15
Aix-en-Provence, 152
Albert, Charles d'. *See* Luynes, Charles
d'Albert, duke de

Albret, Jeanne d,' 13–14, 263n.13, 264n.2
alchemy, 26–27, 29, 33, 34–35, 215–16,
244, 249, 250, 267n.6, 269n.3
Alexander VII, 212–13, 229
Allegret, Olivier, 273n.33
Alméras, René, 242, 246, 264n.23,
305n.5, 306n.10
Amiens, 185
Andilly, Arnauld d,' 290n.3
Angers, 123, 124, 162
Angoumois, Philippe d,' 286n.5
Annecy, 122, 131, 137, 140, 142,
167, 278n.11
Anne of Austria, x, 123, 172, 298n.6
during the Fronde, 175–76, 178, 179,
184, 185, 186, 196–97, 198, 202, 204,
205, 295n.14
relationship with Mazarin, 148–49,
175, 176, 178, 179, 185, 186, 198, 205,
282n.22, 296n.23
relationship with Vincent, 150, 152,
156, 161, 163, 164, 178–79, 183–84,
186, 196–97, 202, 204, 205, 210,
225, 231–32, 246
Arabia, 170–71
Ardennes, the, 208, 224
Argenson, count d,' 107
Arnaudin (notary in Dax), 24

Comet, M. de, 5, 8, 9, 10, 14, 16, 18, 23, 24,
25, 30, 34, 35, 105, 106, 242, 243, 244
Company of the Blessed Sacrament, 94,
155, 174, 195, 203, 210, 281n.21,
286n.5, 288n.23, 292n.30, 294n.20
and Vincent, 107–8, 128, 130, 131, 133
Concini, Concino, 58, 59, 62
Condé, Henry de Bourbon, prince de,
43, 58, 59, 275n.1
Condé, Louis de Bourbon, duke
d'Enghien, prince de, x, 141, 142,
154, 161, 176, 208, 224, 275n.1,
286n.4, 301n.1, 303n.27
during the Fronde, 176–77, 184, 185,
186, 194, 198–99, 201–2, 203–4,
206, 304n.9
Condren, Charles de, 107, 288n.26,
292n.30, 293n.12
Confraternities of Charity, 77, 79–80,
106, 129, 162, 183
finances of, 80
founding of, 65–66, 71–72, 73–74, 180
Hôtel-Dieu of Paris, 109–10, 120, 162,
181, 207, 297n.2
and Louise de Marillac, 92–93, 101
Rule for, 65–66, 72
See also Ladies of Charity
Congregation for the Propagation of the
Faith, 88, 90, 158, 159, 168, 170–71,
192, 216–17
Congregation of France, 283n.5
Congregation of Jesus and Mary,
293n.12, 312n.10
Congregation of Missionary Priests of
the Most Blessed Sacrament, 111
Congregation of Our Lady of
Calvary, 237
Congregation of the Blessed
Sacrament, 170
Congregation of the Mission, 250–51,
280n.5, 306n.10
expansion of, 120–22, 164–71

finances of, 86, 96, 108–9, 114, 131–32,
133–34, 141, 153–55, 156–57,
200–201, 227–28, 237, 245, 286n.7,
296n.23
founding of, 83, 84–93, 281n.17
Rule for, 103–4, 132, 135–37, 188–89,
211–12, 238, 246, 251
seminaries established by, 138–40, 167
See also Saint-Lazare, priory of;
Vincent de Paul, Saint
Congregation of the Oratory, 83, 85, 155,
280n.6, 281n.17, 293n.12
and Bérulle, 47, 62, 89, 90, 271n.17,
275n.6, 277n.6, 280n.6, 295n.13
Congregation of the Servants of the
Poor Sick, 37, 266n.21
Conti, Armand de Bourbon, prince de,
177, 185
Convent of the Madeleine, 293n.17
Coqueret, Jean, 72–73
Corbie, fortress of, 115, 116
Cordeliers, 9, 40, 263n.17
Cornuel, Claude, 138
Corsica, 237
Cospéan, Philippe (bishop of Aire),
40, 149
Coste, Pierre, 29–30, 178, 179, 262n.1,
279n.23
Coton, Pierre, 44, 272n.22
Coudray, François du, 90, 91, 110, 111,
132, 280n.10
Council of Conscience, 149, 151, 152, 161,
178, 179, 186, 205, 206, 228
Council of Trent, 17, 18, 90, 128,
266nn.13, 14, 285n.1, 292n.11,
312n.2
Couty (advocate for Vincent), 249
Crécy, 154
Crécy-en-Brie, 141
Cromwell, Oliver, 168
Croquants revolt, 19
Cuissot, Gilbert, 298n.14

Fouquet, Marie de Maupeou, Mme, 195, 264n.23

Fouquet, Nicolas, 195, 223

Fouquet family, 107

Fourché, Fr. (Jesuit at Amiens), 60

Francesco di Paola, Saint, 279n.18

Franciscans, 207
    Capuchins, 207, 235, 263n.17, 265n.5, 286n.5
    Cordeliers, 9, 40, 263n.17
    Recollects, 263n.17

Francis I, 267n.5, 294n.7

Fréneville, farm of, 114, 118, 128−29, 180−81

Fresnay, Pierre, 276n.13

Fresne, Charles du, 40, 66, 271n.7

Fronde, the, 52, 174−80, 185−86, 198−207, 212, 222, 280n.6, 295n.14, 300nn.10, 11

Fuensaldagna, count de, 224

Gabardan, 14, 264n.3

Gaigneur, Pierre, 44

Gallais, Guillaume, 166

galley slaves, 78−79, 138, 153, 155−56, 158, 167, 168−69, 278nn.14, 15, 279n.23

Gamaches, parish of, 54, 56, 82, 274n.8

Gasteaud, Jacques, 273n.26

Gault, Jean-Baptiste (bishop of Marseille), 155

Gautier, Guillaume, 269n.2

Genoa, 159, 191−92, 207, 216, 220, 237

Get, Firmin, 229, 232, 233−34, 236, 246−47

Girard, Louis, 64, 67, 276n.16, 277n.19

Godeau, Antoine (bishop of Grasse), 107, 284n.17

Gondi, Albert de, 51

Gondi, Antoine de, 50−51

Gondi, Charles de, 51

Gondi, Françoise-Marguerite de Silly, Mme de, 52, 87, 277n.4
    relationship with Vincent, 53, 54−55, 56, 59−62, 66−67, 71, 73, 74, 85, 86, 91−92, 99, 105, 180, 280n.5

Gondi, Henri de, 52

Gondi, Henri de (bishop of Paris, Cardinal de Retz), 51, 54, 66, 78, 152−53

Gondi, Jean-François de (archbishop of Paris), 51, 110, 177, 207, 212
    relationship with Vincent, 85, 87, 88, 91, 98, 99, 141, 162, 211

Gondi, Jean-François Paul de (Cardinal de Retz), 86, 186, 205, 280n.6
    relationship with Vincent, 52−53, 141, 177−78, 212, 239

Gondi, Marie-Christine de Pierre-Vive, Mme de, 50−51

Gondi, Philippe-Emmanuel de, 51−55, 56−57, 61, 82, 87, 271n.7, 273n.3, 274n.10, 275n.11, 280n.6
    relationship with Vincent, 49, 51−52, 53−55, 56, 60, 62, 66, 78, 86, 106, 151, 155, 180, 212, 239, 273n.1, 274n.8, 280n.5, 295n.13

Gondi, Pierre de (bishop of Paris, Cardinal), 51, 52, 54, 56, 61, 86, 273n.3

Gondi family, 85−86, 106, 107, 141

Gondrée, Nicolas, 215

Gonesse, 157, 207, 286n.7, 298n.6

Gontière (counselor-clerk), 72−73

Gonzague, Charles de, 283n.32, 303n.27

Gonzague, Louise-Marie de, 192−93, 303n.27

Gournay, Charles de (bishop of Toul), 120

Goussault, Geneviève Fayet, 102, 110, 284n.19, 289n.15

Gramont, Antoine de, 10, 263n.21

Gramont, count de, 10

Molé, Mathieu, 111, 138, 179, 289n.9, 300n.10

Molina, Luis, 265n.8, 268n.7

Monluc, Blaise de, 14, 264n.4

Montbard, Christophe du Plessis, baron of, 207

Montgaillard, Castle of, 7

Montgaillard, Persin de (bishop of Saint-Pons), 7

Montgomery, Gabriel de Lorges, count of, 8, 13–14, 17, 263n.13, 264nn.1, 2

Montmirail, 71, 73–74, 79, 92–93, 103, 153

Montmorency, Charlotte de, 43, 275n.1

Montorio, Pierre-François, 32–35, 36, 37, 40, 90, 105, 106, 244, 269n.1

Montpensier, Anne-Marie-Louise d'Orléans, duchess of, 202, 304n.9

Montry, Robert de, 110–11

Moras, Bertrande de, 3, 4, 7, 11, 16, 24, 41

Moras, Jacques de, 7, 262n.11

Moras, Jean de, 4–5

Mother Angélique. *See* Arnauld, Angélique

Moutiers-Saint-Jean, 191, 302n.23

Nacquart, Charles, 171, 192, 215, 307n.22

Nancy, 130, 131

Nantes, 183

Napoleon I, 259

Naseau, Marguerite, 102

Navarre, 13–14, 263n.13

Neri, Philip, Saint, 266n.21

Neufchâtel-en-Braye, 113

Noailles, François de (bishop of Dax), 265n.11

Noailles, Gilles de (bishop of Dax), 16, 265n.11

Norais, Jacques, 181, 310n.15

Normandy, 113, 157

Notre-Dame-de-la-Rose, 121

Nouelly, Boniface, 169, 170

Noyon, 195

Office of Records, 154

Olier, Jean-Jacques, 107, 114, 139, 151, 288n.26, 293n.12, 295n.15

Oratorians. *See* Congregation of the Oratory

Order of Mercy, 158, 299n.20

Order of St. John of God, 270n.3

Order of the Friars Minim, 79, 279n.18

Order of the Mathurins, 158

Order of the Redemption, 158

Order of the Visitandines/Visitation, 274n.9, 285n.2, 288n.23, 310n.20
founding of, 77, 106–7, 278nn.7, 10, 11
and Vincent, 93, 105, 106, 111–12, 228, 244

Orléans, Gaston d,' 116, 130, 147, 176–77, 184, 186, 201, 202, 203, 268n.8, 294n.1

Orsigny, farms at, 180, 235–36, 304n.4, 309n.15

Orthevielle, 7

Orthez, 14

Ossat, Armand, Cardinal d,' 37

Ottoman Empire, 267n.6, 268n.8
See also Barbary coast

Ozanam, Frédéric, 251

Ozenne, Charles, 214

Paillart, 71, 79

Paillole, Jean de, 6

Palaiseau, 204, 207

Paris, ix–xi, 37, 38–41, 108, 116–17, 138, 142, 222–24, 227, 273n.31
during the Fronde, 175–80, 184, 185, 201–4, 205–6, 304n.9
See also Saint-Lazare, priory of

Paroy-sur-Tholon, 73, 277n.2

Parré, Jean, 195, 224–25, 303n.33

Party of the Devout, 94–95, 127, 128, 151, 174, 283n.31, 290n.3, 291n.8

Pascal, Blaise, 229

Paul, Bernard de, 6

Paul, Dominique de "Gayon," 6

Paul, Étienne de, 7, 8, 263n.14

Paul, Jean de (brother of Vincent), 6

Paul, Jean de (father of Vincent), 4, 5, 10, 15, 16

Paul, Marie de (spouse of Lartigue), 6

Paul, Marie de (spouse of Paillole), 6

Paul, Sir, 232–34, 246–47

Paul V, 37, 43, 270n.7

Pavillon, Nicolas (bishop of Alet), 100, 123, 140, 190–91, 284nn.14, 17, 286n.3

Peace of the Pyrenees, ix

Périgord, 157

Perrochel, François (bishop of Boulogne), 107

Perron, Jacques Davy du, Cardinal, 44, 272n.18

Peyrehorade, 7

Peyroux, 7

Pianezzo, Philippe de Simiane, marquis de, 216

Picardy, 67, 71, 79, 130, 186, 194–95, 196, 203, 208, 224, 225, 303nn.33, 35

Plessis-Praslin, César du, 194

Pluvinel, Antoine de, 52

Pluyette, Jean, 280n.2

Poitiers, 121

Poland, 192–93, 200, 214, 217, 221, 237, 245, 303n.27

Portail, Antoine de, 280n.10
    relationship with Vincent, 48, 78, 85, 103–4, 113, 116, 150, 167, 180, 183–84, 213, 241–42, 246, 311n.3

Potier, Augustin (bishop of Beauvais), 91, 107, 128, 149, 281n.22

Potier, Nicolas, 281n.22

Poulaillon, Marie de Lumagne, Mademoiselle, 102, 110, 285n.19, 287n.13

Pouy, 4, 5, 82, 262n.7, 279n.23

Poymartet, priory of, 7–8, 14, 263n.14

Provence, 99

Ranquines, 4, 5–7, 8, 262n.6

Raoul, Jacques (bishop of Saintes), 140, 153

Rapin, Fr., 126–27, 290n.6

Ravaillac, François, 42

Recollects, 263n.17

Redier, Antoine, 29

Regnard, Mathieu, 132, 195, 291n.23

Reims, 195, 225

Les Relations, 195

Renty, Gaston, baron de, 133–34, 292n.30

Rethel, 197, 225

Rey, Hugues, 63

Rhodes, Alexandre de, 216

Richelieu, Armand du Plessis, Cardinal de, 52, 58, 81, 93–94, 121, 191, 280n.6, 286n.4, 291n.9, 294n.1, 296n.22, 301n.1, 309n.11
    death of, 153–54, 174, 176, 286n.4, 294n.20, 296n.26
    policies of, 94, 95, 115, 116, 127, 128, 136, 147, 149, 153–54, 271n.17, 277n.6, 282n.30, 283nn.31, 32, 285n.2, 290n.3, 295n.13, 299n.25
    relationship with Mazarin, 147, 294n.20
    relationship with Saint-Cyran, 125, 126, 290n.8
    relationship with Urban VIII, 142, 292n.6
    relationship with Vincent, 107, 121, 125, 127, 128, 131, 136, 139–40, 141, 142, 150, 154, 178

Richelieu, village of, 121, 123–24, 137, 154, 162, 171, 181, 184, 188, 245, 282n.30

Robineau, Louis, 178, 296n.21

Rohan, Henri, duke of, 94

Rohan, Marie de, 275n.2

Roman, Fr. José-Maria, 265n.7

Rome, 20–21, 34–37, 50, 154–55, 156, 159, 173, 191, 242, 245–46, 250, 296n.26, 305n.5, 306n.10

Roucherolles, Pierre de, 55

Rouen, 139
Rougemont, count of, 64–65

Saint-André, Church of, 63
Saint-Charles, 167
Saint-Cyran, Jean Duvergier de
    Hauranne, abbot of, 39, 98–99,
    125–28, 173, 249, 271n.6, 290nn.2,
    3, 8, 299n.26
Saint-Denis, 207
Saint-Denis, abbey of, 97
Sainte-Marie-Madeleine, Monastery
    of, 111
Saintes, 153, 201, 228
Saint-Germain-en-Laye, 123
Saint-Ilpize, 114
Saint-Lazare, priory of, x, 96–101, 111,
    116–19, 127, 133, 140, 142, 157,
    181–82, 187, 238, 250, 259,
    283nn.2, 4, 286n.7, 287n.10
    and Fair of Saint-Laurent, 97,
        108, 283n.3
    Tuesday Conferences at, 101, 107, 123,
        223, 232, 239, 264n.23, 284nn.15, 16,
        285n.22, 286n.3
Saint-Léonard-de-Chaume, abbey of, 42,
    43, 45–46, 56, 57, 82, 109, 270n.7,
    271n.13, 272n.26, 273n.2
Saint-Magloire, parish of, 139
Saint-Martin, Jean de, 242, 243, 311n.5
Saint-Martin, Jeanne de, 5
Saint-Martin, Louis de, 262n.5
Saint-Martin d'Agès, M. de, 242, 311n.5
Saint-Martin-des-Champs, abbey of,
    153, 191
Saint-Martin family, 106
Saint-Méen, abbey of, 153, 164–66, 167,
    182–83, 249, 309n.11
Saint-Nicholas-de-Grosse-Sauve, priory
    of, 83, 109, 140, 279n.26
Saint-Nicolas-du-Chardonnet, parish of,
    102, 138, 139, 293n.12

Saint-Ouen, abbey of, 153, 191, 296n.22
Saint-Quentin, 225
Sales, Francis de (bishop of Geneva),
    75–77, 79, 92, 105, 106–7, 112,
    278nn.7, 10, 11, 12
Salpêtrière, 210, 223–24, 307n.14
Sancy, Achille Harlay de (bishop of
    Saint-Malo), 153, 164–66
Schomberg, duke of, 107
Sedan, 151–52, 153, 162, 166, 225,
    296n.23, 298n.11
Séguier, Dominique (bishop of
    Meaux), 236
Séguier, Pierre, 117, 149
Senlis, 117
Sérévilliers, 71, 79
Sergis, Robert de, 117–18
Sillery, Noël Brulart, Commander de,
    113, 122, 288n.23
Simiane, Gaspard de, 155–56, 278n.15
Society of Saint Vincent de Paul, 251
Soissons, 84, 85, 195
Solminihac, Alain de (bishop of Cahors),
    107, 140, 153, 186–87, 190, 206, 210
Soubé, S., 20, 266n.19
Souvageon (curate at Châtillon),
    63, 64
spagiric medical system, 26–27,
    129, 267n.6
Spain, 222, 307n.12
    Barcelona, 307n.14
    Philip III of, 44
    relations with France, 115–16, 130, 147,
        156, 186, 204, 208, 224, 239–40,
        277n.6, 294n.1
    University of Saragossa, 15, 265nn.7,
        8, 268n.7
St. Bartholomew massacre, 12, 264n.1
Stenay, 198
Suarez (bishop of Séez), 40
Suffren, Fr., 286n.5
Sulayman II, 267n.5

BERNARD PUJO is a historian and the author of several biographies, including *Juin, Maréchal de France, Vauban,* and *Le Grand Condé.*